BUSINESS AND
GENERAL
REFERENCE
BOOK SERIES
FROM IDG

Wine For Dummies, 2nd Edition

W9-BKA-007

Quick Pronunciation Guide to Common Wine Names

The stressed syllable in each word is capitalized; if no syllable is capitalized, all syllables carry equal weight.

Auslese	*OUSE lay seh*
Beaujolais	*boh jhoe lay*
Beaulieu Vineyards	*bol yuh*
Bourgogne	*bor guh nyeh*
Brut	*brute*
Cabernet Sauvignon	*cab er nay saw vee nyon*
Chablis	*shah blee*
Chardonnay	*shar dohn nay*
Châteauneuf-du-Pape	*shah toe nuf-doo-pahp*
Côte Rotie	*coat roe tee*
Gewürztraminer	*geh VAIRTZ trah mee ner*
Haut-Brion	*oh bree ohn*
Hermitage	*er mee tahj*
Loire	*lwahr*
Mâcon	*mah cawn*
Meritage	*MER eh tej*
Merlot	*mer loh*
Meursault	*muhr so*
Moët	*moh ett*
Montepulciano d'Abruzzo	*mon tay pul CHA noh dah BREWTZ zoh*
Montrachet	*mon rah shay*
Mosel-Saar-Ruwer	*MOH zel-zar-ROO ver*
Muscadet	*moos cah day*
Pauillac	*poy yac*
Perrier-Jouët	*per ree yay-joo ett*
Pinot Grigio	*pee noh GREE joe*
Pinot Noir	*pee noh nwahr*
Pouilly-Fuissé	*pwee fwee say*
Riesling	*REESE ling*
Rioja	*ree OH hah*
Sancerre	*sahn sehr*
Spätlese	*SHPATE lay seh*
Viognier	*vee oh nyay*
Vosne Romanée	*vone roh mah nay*
Willamette Valley	*wil LAM ette*

Ten Most Useful Wine Descriptors

1. **Aroma or bouquet:** The smell of the wine. Aroma generally applies to younger wines, and bouquet applies to older wines.

2. **Body:** The apparent weight of a wine in your mouth (light, medium, or full)

3. **Crisp:** A wine with refreshing acidity

4. **Dry:** Not sweet

5. **Finish:** The impression a wine leaves as you swallow it

6. **Flavor intensity:** How strong or weak the flavors of a wine are

7. **Fruity:** A wine that has aromas and flavors of fruit; does *not* imply sweetness

8. **Oaky:** A wine that has oak flavors

9. **Soft:** A wine that is smooth and not crisp

10. **Tannic:** A red wine that is firm and leaves the mouth feeling dry

...For Dummies: Bestselling Book Series for Beginners

Guide to Wine Vintages

Like any vintage wine chart, this must be considered only a rough guide. Many wines will be exceptions to the vintage's rating.

Wine Region	1988	1989	1990	1991	1992	1993	1994	1995	1996
Bordeaux: Médoc, Graves	85a	90b	95a	75b	75b	80a	85a	90a	90a
Bordeaux: Pomerol, St Emilion	85a	90b	95a	65c	75b	80a	85a	90a	85a
Côte de Nuits-Red Burgundy	85b	85b	95b	85b	75b	85a	80b	90a	90a
Côte Beaune-Red Burgundy	85b	85c	90b	70c	80b	85a	80b	90a	90a
Burgundy, White	80c	90b	85c	70d	85b	75c	85c	90a	90a

Cut out this card and carry it in your wallet as a handy guide to picking out the best wines!

Wine For Dummies, 2nd Edition

Cheat Sheet

Instant Wine Identifier

Wine Name	Grape or Place	Wine Color
Barbera	Grape	Red
Bardolino	Place/Italy	Red
Barolo	Place/Italy	Red
Beaujolais	Place/France	Red
Bordeaux	Place/France	Red or white
Burgundy (Bourgogne)	Place/France	Red or white
Cabernet Sauvignon	Grape	Red
Chablis	Place/France	White
Champagne	Place/France	White or rosé
Chardonnay	Grape	White
Chianti	Place/Italy	Red
Côtes du Rhône	Place/France	Red or white
Dolcetto	Grape	Red
Merlot	Grape	Red
Mosel	Place/Germany	White
Pinot Grigio/Pinot Gris	Grape	White
Pinot Noir	Grape	Red
Port (Porto)	Place/Portugal	Red (fortified)
Pouilly-Fuissé	Place/France	White
Rhine (Rheingau, Rheinhessen)	Place/Germany	White
Riesling	Grape	White
Rioja	Place/Spain	Red or white
Sancerre	Place/France	White
Sauternes	Place/France	White (dessert)
Sauvignon Blanc	Grape	White
Sherry	Place/Spain	White (fortified)
Soave	Place/Italy	White
Syrah/Shiraz	Grape	Red
Valpolicella	Place/Italy	Red
Zinfandel	Grape	Red or pink

Positive Thinking for Wine Shoppers

No one in the world knows everything about wine.

Smart people aren't afraid to ask "dumb" questions.

The purpose of wine is to be enjoyed.

Expensive doesn't necessarily mean better.

I am my own best judge of wine quality.

Most wines *are* good wines.

Experimentation is fun.

Advice is free for the asking.

Every bottle of wine is a live performance.

I'll never know . . . until I try it!

Wine Region	1988	1989	1990	1991	1992	1993	1994	1995	1996
Northern Rhône	90c	95b	90a	90b	75c	65c	85a	90a	85a
Southern Rhône	85c	95a	95b	70c	75c	80b	85a	90a	80b
Germany	85c	90b	95b	80c	85c	85c	90b	85b	95a
Rioja (Spain)	85b	90b	85b	75c	85b	85b	90b	90b	85a
Piedmont	90a	95a	95b	80c	70c	85b	80b	85a	95a
Tuscany	90a	70c	90b	75c	70c	75c	85b	90a	75b
Calif. N. Coast Cab. Sauvignon	75c	80b	95b	95a	90b	85b	95a	90a	90a
Calif. N. Coast Chardonnay	85c	75d	90c	85c	90c	90c	85c	90b	85b

Vintage Key:
100 = Outstanding   85 = Good   70 = Below Average
95 = Excellent   80 = Fairly Good   65 = Poor
90 = Very Good   75 = Average   50 – 60 = Very Poor

a = Too young to drink   b = Can be consumed now, but will improve with time
c = Ready to drink   d = May be too old

IDG BOOKS WORLDWIDE

...For Dummies: Bestselling Book Series for Beginners

Praise for Wine For Dummies . . .

"A delightfully formatted compendium of everything you need to know about wine . . . This book will appeal to all wine drinkers, from the occasional drinker to the seasoned pro."

— Piero Antinori, Proprietor
Marchesi Antinori Winery
Florence, Italy

"[*Wine For Dummies*] is the least intimidating book of its scope and caliber I've ever seen . . . If you are just getting interested in wine, or wouldn't mind a brush-up course, this is a book with a genuine difference."

— Copley News Service

"[*Wine For Dummies*] manages to be smart and totally readable, with something to say to total novices, occasional imbibers and those who have caught the bug. . . ."

— *Newsday*

"[McCarthy and Ewing-Mulligan] have accomplished the almost impossible feat of writing a book about wine that both novices and connoisseurs will love because it's fun to read and crammed with authoritative information."

— *Wine & Spirits* magazine

"Although this lively book is crammed with useful, accurate information for tyros, even experienced hands could probably learn a thing or two from it."

— *Wine Spectator*

"BUY THE BOOK . . . [*Wine For Dummies*] is well organized, packed with information and filled with reader-friendly graphics. . . ."

— *Food & Wine* magazine

"Mulligan and McCarthy will make you smarter with every page. At the next dinner party, you will impress your friends."

— *Wine Enthusiast Magazine*

"[*Wine For Dummies*] is complete and done in an agreeably relaxed style."
— *New York Times*

Praise for Wine Buying Companion For Dummies

"A thirst-inspiring guide to the pleasures of wine."
— Kermit Lynch, *Kermit Lynch Wine Merchant*

"Ed and Mary have done it again! *Wine Buying Companion For Dummies* is the perfect source for wine lovers — novices and connoisseurs alike. The authors share their expertise in a clear, fun, and easy-to-follow format. A toast of J Sparkling Wine to the authors and readers of this fabulous book!"
— Judy Jordan, *J Wine Company*

"*Wine Buying Companion For Dummies* solves many of the mysteries of finding and buying good wine values. You are sure to enjoy trying the numerous wine-and-food combinations that Ed and Mary recommend. I can't wait to try some of them myself."
— Philip H. Tenenbaum, *President, The Chicago Wine Company*

"In Italy, wine is part of our lives, and we have enjoyed it with food for years. I applaud Ed and Mary's information and their straightforward approach — everyone should enjoy wine with a meal!"
— Francesco Bolla, *Bolla Wine Company*

"Communicating the characteristics of wines is an art in itself, and Mary and Ed have been able to do this in a clear and concise style. Their rating-system format emphasizes the subjectivity of wine evaluation and serves as a practical aid for the buyer."
— Dick Ponzi, *Ponzi Vineyards*

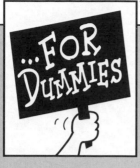

TM

References for the Rest of Us!™

BESTSELLING BOOK SERIES FROM IDG

Do you find that traditional reference books are overloaded with technical details and advice you'll never use? Do you postpone important life decisions because you just don't want to deal with them? Then our *...For Dummies®* business and general reference book series is for you.

...For Dummies business and general reference books are written for those frustrated and hard-working souls who know they aren't dumb, but find that the myriad of personal and business issues and the accompanying horror stories make them feel helpless. *...For Dummies* books use a lighthearted approach, a down-to-earth style, and even cartoons and humorous icons to diffuse fears and build confidence. Lighthearted but not lightweight, these books are perfect survival guides to solve your everyday personal and business problems.

> *"More than a publishing phenomenon, 'Dummies' is a sign of the times."*
>
> — The New York Times

> *"A world of detailed and authoritative information is packed into them..."*
>
> — U.S. News and World Report

> *"...you won't go wrong buying them."*
>
> — Walter Mossberg, Wall Street Journal, on IDG Books' ...For Dummies books

Already, millions of satisfied readers agree. They have made *...For Dummies* the #1 introductory level computer book series and a best-selling business book series. They have written asking for more. So, if you're looking for the best and easiest way to learn about business and other general reference topics, look to *...For Dummies* to give you a helping hand.

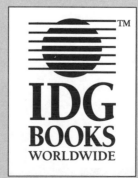

TM

IDG BOOKS
WORLDWIDE

8/98i

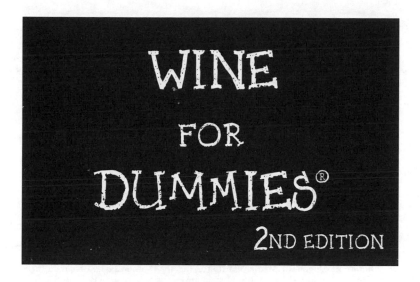

WINE FOR DUMMIES®

2ND EDITION

by Ed McCarthy and
Mary Ewing-Mulligan, MW

Foreword by Piero Antinori, Proprietor,
Marchesi Antinori Winery, Florence, Italy

IDG Books Worldwide, Inc.
An International Data Group Company

Foster City, CA ♦ Chicago, IL ♦ Indianapolis, IN ♦ New York, NY

Wine For Dummies®, 2nd Edition

Published by
IDG Books Worldwide, Inc.
An International Data Group Company
919 E. Hillsdale Blvd.
Suite 400
Foster City, CA 94404
www.idgbooks.com (IDG Books Worldwide Web site)
www.dummies.com (Dummies Press Web site)

Library of Congress Catalog Card No.: 98-87099

ISBN: 0-7645-5114-0

Printed in the United States of America

10 9 8 7 6 5 4 3 2

2B/QR/RS/ZY/IN

Distributed in the United States by IDG Books Worldwide, Inc.

Distributed by Macmillan Canada for Canada; by Transworld Publishers Limited in the United Kingdom; by IDG Norge Books for Norway; by IDG Sweden Books for Sweden; by Woodslane Pty. Ltd. for Australia; by Woodslane (NZ) Ltd. for New Zealand; by Addison Wesley Longman Singapore Pte Ltd. for Singapore, Malaysia, Thailand, and Indonesia; by Norma Comunicaciones S.A. for Colombia; by Intersoft for South Africa; by International Thomson Publishing for Germany, Austria and Switzerland; by Distribuidora Cuspide for Argentina; by Livraria Cultura for Brazil; by Ediciencia S.A. for Ecuador; by Ediciones ZETA S.C.R. Ltda. for Peru; by WS Computer Publishing Corporation, Inc., for the Philippines; by Contemporanea de Ediciones for Venezuela; by Express Computer Distributors for the Caribbean and West Indies; by Micronesia Media Distributor, Inc. for Micronesia; by Grupo Editorial Norma S.A. for Guatemala; by Chips Computadoras S.A. de C.V. for Mexico; by Editorial Norma de Panama S.A. for Panama; by Wouters Import for Belgium; by American Bookshops for Finland. Authorized Sales Agent: Anthony Rudkin Associates for the Middle East and North Africa.

For general information on IDG Books Worldwide's books in the U.S., please call our Consumer Customer Service department at 800-762-2974. For reseller information, including discounts and premium sales, please call our Reseller Customer Service department at 800-434-3422.

For information on where to purchase IDG Books Worldwide's books outside the U.S., please contact our International Sales department at 317-596-5530 or fax 317-596-5692.

For information on foreign language translations, please contact our Foreign & Subsidiary Rights department at 650-655-3021 or fax 650-655-3281.

For sales inquiries and special prices for bulk quantities, please contact our Sales department at 650-655-3200 or write to the address above.

For information on using IDG Books Worldwide's books in the classroom or for ordering examination copies, please contact our Educational Sales department at 800-434-2086 or fax 317-596-5499.

For press review copies, author interviews, or other publicity information, please contact our Public Relations department at 650-655-3000 or fax 650-655-3299.

For authorization to photocopy items for corporate, personal, or educational use, please contact Copyright Clearance Center, 222 Rosewood Drive, Danvers, MA 01923, or fax 978-750-4470.

is a trademark under exclusive license to IDG Books Worldwide, Inc., from International Data Group, Inc.

About the Authors

Ed McCarthy and **Mary Ewing-Mulligan** are two wine lovers who met at an Italian wine tasting in New York City's Chinatown in 1981. Two years later, they formally merged their wine cellars and wine libraries when they married. They have since coauthored four wine books (all for IDG Books Worldwide, Inc.), taught hundreds of wine classes together, run five marathons, and raised nine cats. Along the way, they have amassed more than half a century of professional wine experience between them.

Mary grew up in Pennsylvania and attended the University of Pennsylvania, where she majored in English literature. She got started in the wine business right out of college, by complete chance, when she accepted a position with the Italian Trade Commission. Today, her true love in wine is still Italian.

Ed, a New Yorker, graduated from City University of New York with a master's degree in psychology. He taught high school English in another life, while working part-time in wine shops to satisfy his passion for wine and to subsidize his growing wine cellar. That cellar is especially heavy in his favorite wines — Bordeaux, Barolo, and Champagne.

Mary has spent half her professional career as owner and director of the International Wine Center in New York. She teaches classes at the Center, mainly for professionals in the wine business. She is the wine columnist for the New York *Daily News* and contributes to various other publications. In 1993, Mary became America's first — and only — woman Master of Wine (MW) after five years of independent study. There are only a few more than 200 Masters of Wine in the world, including 18 in America.

Ed teaches at the International Wine Center and writes for *Wine Enthusiast Magazine* as well as the *Underground Wine Journal.* He and Mary are both accredited as Certified Wine Educators (CWE).

When they are not writing or teaching, Mary and Ed maintain a busy schedule of continuing education by visiting the wine regions of the world, judging at professional wine competitions, and tasting as many new wines as possible. They admit to leading thoroughly unbalanced lives in which their only non-wine pursuits are jogging and picnicking in the Italian Alps. At home, they wind down to the tunes of Bob Dylan and Neil Young, in the company of their feline roommates, La Tache, Léoville, Pinot Grigio, Brunello, Dolcetto, Clicquot, and Black & Whitey.

ABOUT IDG BOOKS WORLDWIDE

Welcome to the world of IDG Books Worldwide.

IDG Books Worldwide, Inc., is a subsidiary of International Data Group, the world's largest publisher of computer-related information and the leading global provider of information services on information technology. IDG was founded more than 30 years ago by Patrick J. McGovern and now employs more than 9,000 people worldwide. IDG publishes more than 290 computer publications in over 75 countries. More than 90 million people read one or more IDG publications each month.

Launched in 1990, IDG Books Worldwide is today the #1 publisher of best-selling computer books in the United States. We are proud to have received eight awards from the Computer Press Association in recognition of editorial excellence and three from Computer Currents' First Annual Readers' Choice Awards. Our best-selling ...For Dummies® series has more than 50 million copies in print with translations in 31 languages. IDG Books Worldwide, through a joint venture with IDG's Hi-Tech Beijing, became the first U.S. publisher to publish a computer book in the People's Republic of China. In record time, IDG Books Worldwide has become the first choice for millions of readers around the world who want to learn how to better manage their businesses.

Our mission is simple: Every one of our books is designed to bring extra value and skill-building instructions to the reader. Our books are written by experts who understand and care about our readers. The knowledge base of our editorial staff comes from years of experience in publishing, education, and journalism — experience we use to produce books to carry us into the new millennium. In short, we care about books, so we attract the best people. We devote special attention to details such as audience, interior design, use of icons, and illustrations. And because we use an efficient process of authoring, editing, and desktop publishing our books electronically, we can spend more time ensuring superior content and less time on the technicalities of making books.

You can count on our commitment to deliver high-quality books at competitive prices on topics you want to read about. At IDG Books Worldwide, we continue in the IDG tradition of delivering quality for more than 30 years. You'll find no better book on a subject than one from IDG Books Worldwide.

John Kilcullen
Chairman and CEO
IDG Books Worldwide, Inc.

Steven Berkowitz
President and Publisher
IDG Books Worldwide, Inc.

Eighth Annual Computer Press Awards ≥1992

Ninth Annual Computer Press Awards ≥1993

Tenth Annual Computer Press Awards ≥1994

Eleventh Annual Computer Press Awards ≥1995

Dedication

We dedicate this book to all of you readers who made our first edition of *Wine For Dummies* such a success; you are the reason that this book exists.

Authors' Acknowledgments

Our challenge in writing *Wine For Dummies,* 2nd Edition, was to improve upon the first edition. Since we thought that the first edition was darn near perfect, this wasn't easy. But with the assistance of an excellent team of editors at IDG Books Worldwide, we think that we did achieve our goal.

First, we thank CEO John Kilcullen and President Steven Berkowitz for making the *...For Dummies* books the phenomenal success that they are; we are honored to be part of your team. We sincerely thank Vice President and Publisher Kathleen Welton, who first engaged us to write *Wine For Dummies,* and Acquisitions Editor Holly McGuire. Really special thanks go to our Senior Project Editor Mary Goodwin, who, miraculously, is always in a good mood despite our persistent phone calls, and to our excellent Copy Editors, Stacey Mickelbart and Paula Lowell.

We thank our technical reviewers, colleagues Patrick Fegan and Joel Butler MW, for their expertise and patience while wading through our manuscript with a fine-toothed comb. It's a better, more accurate book because of both of you.

Special thanks to Steve Ettlinger, our agent and friend, who brought us to IDG Books in the first place, and who is always there for us.

We thank all of our friends in the wine business for your information and kind suggestions for our book; the book reviewers, whose criticism has been so kind and generous; and our readers, who have encouraged us with their enthusiasm for our previous four books in this series.

Thanks also to Elise McCarthy and Cindy and David Tomarchio for their encouragement, and special thanks to E.J. McCarthy for his generous support of our books.

Publisher's Acknowledgments

We're proud of this book; please register your comments through our IDG Books Worldwide Online Registration Form located at http://my2cents.dummies.com.

Some of the people who helped bring this book to market include the following:

Acquisitions, Development, and Editorial

Senior Project Editor: Mary Goodwin

Acquisitions Editor: Holly McGuire

Copy Editors: Paula Lowell, Stacey Mickelbart

Technical Editors: Joel Butler, MW, Patrick Fegan

Editorial Manager: Kelly Ewing

Editorial Assistant: Paul Kuzmic

Acquisitions Coordinator: Jon Malysiak

Editorial Coordinator: Maureen F. Kelly

Production

Project Coordinator: Karen York

Layout and Graphics: Lou Boudreau, Maridee V. Ennis, Angela F. Hunckler, Jane E. Martin, Anna Rohrer, Brent Savage, Michael A. Sullivan

Proofreaders: Kelli Botta, Michelle Croninger, Rachel Garvey, Betty Kish, Janet M. Withers

Indexer: Rachel Rice

Special Help

Robert Garber

General and Administrative

IDG Books Worldwide, Inc.: John Kilcullen, CEO; Steven Berkowitz, President and Publisher

IDG Books Technology Publishing: Brenda McLaughlin, Senior Vice President and Group Publisher

Dummies Technology Press and Dummies Editorial: Diane Graves Steele, Vice President and Associate Publisher; Mary Bednarek, Director of Acquisitions and Product Development; Kristin A. Cocks, Editorial Director

Dummies Trade Press: Kathleen A. Welton, Vice President and Publisher; Kevin Thornton, Acquisitions Manager

IDG Books Production for Dummies Press: Michael R. Britton, Vice President of Production and Creative Services; Cindy L. Phipps, Manager of Project Coordination, Production Proofreading, and Indexing; Kathie S. Schutte, Supervisor of Page Layout; Shelley Lea, Supervisor of Graphics and Design; Debbie J. Gates, Production Systems Specialist; Robert Springer, Supervisor of Proofreading; Debbie Stailey, Special Projects Coordinator; Tony Augsburger, Supervisor of Reprints and Bluelines

Dummies Packaging and Book Design: Robin Seaman, Creative Director; Kavish + Kavish, Cover Design

◆

The publisher would like to give special thanks to Patrick J. McGovern, without whom this book would not have been possible.

◆

Contents at a Glance

Cartoons at a Glance

By Rich Tennant

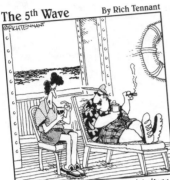

"Well, I'm enough of a wine expert to know that if the boat were sinking, there'd be several cases of this Bordeaux that would go into a lifeboat before you would."

page 131

"We're not what you'd call a 'prestige vineyard.' This year most of our grapes will be used to make a very nice 'Windex.'"

page 359

Worse than "Wine Snobs" are "Wine Toughs"

Hey! You call this a varietal?!

page 69

"Wine reminds me of opera. I enjoy it even though I don't always understand what's being said."

page 5

"No wonder the salesman said this was a dessert wine. I can hear the 'snickers' from my guests."

page 295

"I want something that will go well with a retired admiral and his wife, a best-selling author from the Hamptons, and a media wonk."

page 373

Fax: 978-546-7747 • E-mail: the5wave@tiac.net

Table of Contents

Foreword

. . . .

*I*t is my privilege to have been asked to write the foreword to Ed McCarthy and Mary Ewing-Mulligan's book. I've known them for 25 years and can wholeheartedly vouch for their knowledge, their enthusiasm, and their pure pleasure in the joy of wine. I honestly can't think of anyone whose talents are better suited to *Wine For Dummies*.

I consider it particularly appropriate that wine was among the first ...*For Dummies* books written for a subject other than computers, since many people consider winespeak as foreign and intimidating as computerese. Ed and his wife Mary prove in this down-to-earth, humorous yet thorough book that nothing could be further from the truth.

In everyday language (something missing from most wine literature), they explain all that you ever wanted to know about wine: where and how to buy it, how to read wine labels and speak the language of wine; how to taste wine, how to recognize a bad one, how to navigate restaurant wine lists, and even how to open a bottle. They cover every topic from the most basic to the more advanced. Truly a delightfully formatted compendium of everything you need to know about wine. And its timing is perfect.

These days, wine production is at an all-time high, as is wine quality. More varieties of wine are coming from more regions than ever before, creating more confusion in consumers' minds (though I hope that my wines, from Italy's regions of Tuscany and Umbria, do not add to that confusion!) Anyway, we now have the spirited and personal assistance of *Wine For Dummies*.

Wine is for everyone, after all, and we should not treat it as if it were something reserved for a mystical elite. Producers such as myself must support the effort to help the uninitiated and the intimidated.

This book will appeal to all wine drinkers, from the occasional drinker to the seasoned pro. Whether you read this book from cover to cover, dip into it for an occasional bit of knowledge, or turn to it in a moment of crisis, you will be rewarded with the wit and wisdom of two expert teachers. To your health!

Piero Antinori, Proprietor
Marchesi Antinori Winery
Florence, Italy

Piero Antinori's family has been making wine since 1385; his wines are prized by connoisseurs the world over. He also owns Atlas Peak winery in Napa, California and an interest in a Hungarian winery. He has been honored by many of the leading international wine organizations and has often acted as a spokesman for the Italian wine industry.

Introduction

. . . .

*I*n some parts of the world, people have a very interesting attitude toward wine. They just drink it.

The servers in neighborhood restaurants just ask, "Will you be having white or red?" Then they bring a bottle or a carafe of wine, and everyone drinks it. Sometimes guests even drink it out of squat little glasses that we would use only for orange juice. If the guests talk about the wine at all, they use fancy words like *good* to describe it.

Somehow, all that has gotten lost in the translation. Sophisticates, information addicts, and seekers of status have made wine so complicated that many people are too confused to drink it. The jumble of wine types, brands, vintages, and scores is dizzying to anyone who presumes to buy a bottle of wine without first seeking the counsel of a personal trainer.

Of course, if there weren't some incredibly fabulous wines that are as much art as beverage, the intellectualization and complication of wine would never have happened. The fact is that some wines inspire passion and enthusiasm; that's why some people spend all their leisure time collecting wine, comparing vintages, visiting winemakers, and reading the latest reviews. *But not all wine has to be taken so seriously.*

Wine can be complicated, sure, but the good news is that you really don't have to know very much in order to enjoy it. And if you learn just a little and decide that wine is fascinating, it can become a wonderful hobby.

Welcome to Wine For Dummies, 2nd Edition

If you already own or have read the original *Wine For Dummies*, you might be wondering whether you need this book. The answer to your question is an emphatic "Yes," for the following reasons:

- ✔ The world of wine, like so many other things in life, is constantly changing. In this edition, for example, we include among our recommendations lots of new wineries that we have discovered or rediscovered, and drop some that we feel have slipped, or that have gone out of business.

> ✔ Remember those prices that we listed for your favorite wines three years ago? Well, as they say in Brooklyn, *forgeddabout it!* Unfortunately, the prices of most wines have increased quite a bit in three short years. But we point out some bargains, especially in Part III (Around the World of Wine).

> ✔ New vintages have come and gone; we give you the lowdown on them, throughout the book, and especially in our updated vintage chart in Appendix C.

> ✔ Talking about Appendixes, we've added two new ones: a much-needed Pronunciation Guide to major wine terms and a wine glossary.

> ✔ We've restructured the book into what we think is a more orderly, organized fashion. And we've given Italy and the U.S. entire chapters of their own in Part III (joining France, which already had its own chapter in the 1st edition).

How to Use This Book

We consider this book a wine textbook of sorts, a user's manual, and a reference book, all in one.

We have included very basic information about wine for readers who know nothing (or next to nothing) about wine, but we have also included tips, suggestions, and more sophisticated information for seasoned wine drinkers who want to take their interest to a more advanced level. Depending on where you fall on the wine-knowledge gradient, different chapters will be relevant to you.

Part I: Getting Started with Wine

The five chapters that comprise Part I get you up and sipping even if you have never tasted a wine before in your life. We tell you how to taste wine, what types of grapes are used in winemaking, how wine is made, and how it is named.

Part II: Close Encounters of the Wine Kind

This part deals with practical wine matters: in the wine shop, in the restaurant, and in your home. Find out how to handle snooty wine clerks, restaurant wine lists, and those stubborn corks. In addition, we show you how to decipher cryptic wine labels.

Part III: Around the World of Wine

Visit this part, the heart of the book, for a tour of the major wine regions of the world and the wine produced in them. We give the wines of France, Italy, and the U.S. their own chapters, and we do the same for sparkling wines and dessert wines.

Part IV: When You've Caught the Bug

You find a wealth of practical advice and recommendations in this part, including where and how you can buy wine beyond the outlets already available where you live. We also tell you how you can pursue your love and knowledge of wine beyond this book, how to describe and rate wines you taste, how to pair food with wine, and how to store wine properly.

Part V: The Part of Tens

What ...*For Dummies* book would be complete without this final part? It's a synopsis of interesting tips and recommendations about wine to reinforce our suggestions earlier in the book. We're particularly happy to debunk ten prevalent myths about wine so that you can become a more savvy consumer and a more contented wine drinker.

Part VI: Appendixes

In Part VI, you can look up those hard-to-pronounce wine words in our pronunciation guide, and you can improve your wine vocabulary by checking out our glossary. Finally, you can consult our vintage chart to aid you in your search for a wine to enjoy.

Icons Used in This Book

This odd little guy is a bit like the two-year-old who constantly insists on knowing "Why, Mommy, why?" But he knows that you might not have the same level of curiosity that he has. Where you see him, feel free to skip over the technical information that follows. Wine will still taste just as delicious.

Advice and information that will make you a wiser wine drinker is marked by this bull's-eye so that you won't miss it.

There's very little you can do in the course of moderate wine consumption that can land you in jail — but you could spoil an expensive bottle and sink into a deep depression over your loss. This symbol will warn you about common pitfalls.

 Some issues in wine are so fundamental that they bear repeating. Just so you don't think we repeated ourselves without realizing it, we'll mark the repetitions with this symbol.

 Wine snobs practice all sorts of affectations designed to make other wine drinkers feel inferior. But you won't be intimidated by their snobbery if you see it for what it is. (And you can learn how to impersonate a wine snob!)

 A bargain's not a bargain unless you really like the dress (or suit), as they say. To our tastes, the wines we mark with this icon are bargains because we like them, we believe them to be of good quality, and their price is low compared to other wines of similar type, style, or quality. You can also interpret this logo as a badge of genuineness, as in "This Chablis is the real deal."

 Unfortunately, some of the finest, most intriguing, most delicious wines are made in very small quantities. Usually, such wines cost more than wines made in large quantities — but that's not the only problem; the real frustration is that such wines have very limited distribution, and you can't always get your hands on a bottle even if you're willing to pay the price. We mark such wines with this icon, and hope that your search proves fruitful.

Wine Is for Everyone

Because we hate to think that wine, which has brought so much pleasure into our lives, could be the source of anxiety for anyone, we want to help you feel more comfortable around wine. Some knowledge of wine, gleaned from the pages of this book and from our shared experiences, will go a long way toward increasing your comfort level.

But ironically, what will *really* make you feel comfortable about wine is accepting the fact that you'll never know it all — and that you've got *plenty* of company.

You see, after you really get a handle on wine, you discover that *no one* knows everything there is to know about wine. There is just too much information, and it's always changing. And when you know that, you can just relax and enjoy the stuff.

Part I
Getting Started with Wine

The 5th Wave   By Rich Tennant

"Wine reminds me of opera. I enjoy it even though I don't always understand what's being said."

In this part . . .

To grasp the material in this part of the book, it helps to have some preliminary knowledge: what a grape is, and where your tongue and nose are located.

If you've got those bases covered, you're ready to begin understanding and enjoying wine — even if you've never tasted wine before in your life. We'll start slowly so that you can enjoy the scenery along the way.

Chapter 1
Wine 101

• •

• •

*W*e visit wineries all the time, and when we do, we usually end up talking with the winemaker about how he makes his wine. One of us is thrilled by these conversations because they're opportunities to learn more about why wines taste the way they do. But the other one gets bored very quickly, because who cares how wine is made, as long as it's delicious?

It seems that there are two types of wine lovers in the world: the *hedonists,* who just want to enjoy wine and find more and more wines they can enjoy; and the *thinkers,* who are fascinated by how wine happens. (The hedonists call the thinkers *wine nerds.*) Our family has one of each.

If you're a thinker, you'll enjoy discovering what's behind the differences in wines. And even if you're a hedonist, a little knowledge can help you discover more wines that you'll enjoy. Of course, this is the thinker speaking.

How Wine Happens

The recipe for turning fruit into wine goes something like this:

1. **Pick a large quantity of ripe grapes from grapevines.**

   You could substitute raspberries or any other fruit, but 99.9 percent of all the wine in the world is made from grapes.

2. **Put the grapes into a clean container that doesn't leak.**

3. **Crush the grapes somehow to release their juice.**

   Once upon a time, feet performed this step.

4. **Wait.**

In its most basic form, winemaking is that simple. After the grapes are crushed, *yeasts* (tiny one-celled organisms that exist naturally in the vineyard and, therefore, on the grapes) come into contact with the sugar in the grapes' juice and gradually convert that sugar into alcohol. Yeasts also produce carbon dioxide, which evaporates into the air. When the yeasts are done working, your grape juice is wine. The sugar that was in the juice is no longer there — alcohol is present instead. (The riper and sweeter the grapes, the more alcohol the wine will have.) This process is called *fermentation*.

What could be more natural?

Fermentation is a totally natural process that doesn't require man's participation at all, except to put the grapes into a container and release the juice from the grapes. (And the grapes could even do that second step themselves, by crushing themselves with their own weight.) Fermentation occurs in fresh apple cider left too long in your refrigerator, too, without any help from you. In fact we read that milk, which contains another sort of sugar, develops small amounts of alcohol if left on the kitchen table all day long.

Speaking of milk, Louis Pasteur is the man credited with discovering fermentation in the 19th century. That's discovering, not inventing. Some of those apples in the Garden of Eden probably fermented long before Pasteur came along. (Well, we don't think it could have been much of an Eden without wine!)

Modern wrinkles in winemaking

Now if every winemaker actually made wine as crudely as we just described, we'd be drinking some pretty rough stuff that would hardly inspire us to write a book about wine.

But today's winemakers have a bag of tricks as big as George Foreman's appetite. That's one reason why no two wines will ever taste exactly the same.

The men and women who make wine can control the type of container they use for the fermentation process (stainless steel and oak are the two main materials), as well as the size of the container and the temperature of the juice during fermentation — and every one of these choices can make a big difference in the taste of the wine. After the fermentation, they can choose how long to let the wine *mature* (a stage when the wine sort of gets its act together) and in what kind of container. Fermentation can last three days or three months, and the wine can then mature for a couple of months or a couple of years or anything in between. If you have trouble making decisions, don't ever become a winemaker.

The main ingredient

Obviously, one of the biggest factors in making one wine different from the next is the nature of the raw material, the grape juice. Besides the fact that riper, sweeter grapes make a more alcoholic wine, different *varieties* of grapes (Chardonnay, Cabernet Sauvignon, or Merlot, for example) make different wines. Grapes are the main ingredient in wine, and everything the winemaker does, he docs to the particular grape juice he has. Chapter 4 covers specific grapes and the kinds of wine they make.

What Color Is Your Appetite?

Your inner child will be happy to know that when it comes to wine, it's okay to like some colors more than others. You can't get away with saying, "I don't like green food!" beyond your sixth birthday, but you can express a general preference for white wine, red wine, or pink wine for all your adult years.

What white wine is

Whoever coined the term "white wine" must have been color blind. All you have to do is look at it to see that it's not white, it's yellow. But we've all gotten used to the expression by now, and so *white wine* it is. (Let's hope that person didn't live in a snowy city.)

White wine is wine without any red color (or pink color, which is in the red family). This means that *White Zinfandel,* a popular pink wine, isn't white wine. But yellow wine, golden wine, and wine that's pale as water are all white wines.

Contains sulfites

Sulfur dioxide, a compound formed from sulfur and oxygen, occurs naturally during fermentation, in very small quantities. Winemakers add it, too. Sulfur dioxide is to wine what aspirin and vitamin E combined are to humans — the wonder drug that cures all sorts of afflictions and prevents others. Sulfur dioxide is an antibacterial, preventing the wine from turning to vinegar. It inhibits yeasts, preventing sweet wines from refermenting in the bottle. It's an antioxidant, keeping the wine fresh and untainted by the demon oxygen. Despite these magical properties, winemakers try to use as little sulfur dioxide as possible because most of them share a belief that the less you add to wine, the better — just as many people prefer to ingest as little medication as possible.

Now here's a bit of irony for you:

Today — when winemaking is so advanced that winemakers need to rely on sulfur dioxide's help less than ever before — wine labels in America say "Contains Sulfites" (meaning sulfur dioxide). That's because in 1988, Congress passed a law requiring that the phrase appear on the label. So now you might think that there's *more* sulfur in the wine than there used to be; but, in reality, sulfur dioxide use is probably at an all-time low.

Approximately 5 percent of asthmatics are extremely sensitive to sulfites. To protect them, Congress mandated that any wine containing more than 10 parts per million of sulfites carry the "Contains Sulfites" phrase on its label. Considering that 10 to 20 parts per million occur naturally in wine, that covers just about every wine.

Actual sulfite levels in wine range from about 100 to 150 parts per million (about the same as in dried apricots), and the legal max in the U.S. is 350. White dessert wines have the most sulfur — followed by medium-sweet white wines and blush wines — because those types of wine need the protection more. Dry white wines generally have less, and dry red wines have the least.

Wine becomes white wine in one of two ways. First, white wine can be made from white grapes — which, by the way, are not white. (Did you see that one coming?) *White* grapes are greenish, greenish yellow, golden yellow, or sometimes even pinkish yellow. Basically, white grapes include all the grape types which are not dark red or bluish. If you make a wine from white grapes, it's a white wine.

The second way a wine can become white is a little more complicated. The process involves using red grapes — but only the *juice* of red grapes, not the grape skins. The juice of most red grapes has no red pigmentation — only the skins do — so a wine made with only the juice of a red grape can be a white wine. In practice, though, very few white wines are made from red grapes. (Champagne is one exception; Chapter 15 addresses the use of red grapes to make Champagne.)

In case you're wondering, the skins are removed from the grapes by either *pressing* large quantities of grapes so that the juice flows out and the skins stay behind — sort of like squeezing the pulp out of grapes, the way kids do in the cafeteria — or by *crushing* the grapes by putting them through a machine with a huge screw that breaks the skins and lets the juice drain away from the skins.

Is white always right?

You can drink white wine anytime you like — which for most people means as a drink without food or with lighter foods.

White wines are often considered *apéritif* wines, meaning a wine to have before dinner, in place of a cocktail, or at parties. If you ask U.S. or Canadian officials who busy themselves defining such things, an apéritif wine is a wine that has flavors added to it, as vermouth does. But unless you're in the business of writing wine labels for a living, don't worry about that. In common parlance, an apéritif wine is just what we said.

Lots of people like to drink white wines when the weather is hot because they are more refreshing than red wines, and they are usually drunk chilled (the wines, not the people).

We serve white wines cool, but not ice-cold. Sometimes restaurants serve white wines too cold, and we actually have to wait a while for the wine to warm up before we drink it. If you like your wine cold, fine; but try drinking your favorite white wine a little less cold sometime, and we bet you'll discover it has more flavor that way.

For suggestions of foods to eat with white wine, turn to Chapter 20; for really detailed information about white wine and food (and white wine itself, for that matter), refer to our book, *White Wine For Dummies* (published by IDG Books Worldwide, Inc.).

Red, red wine

In this case, the name is correct. Red wines really are red. They can be purple red, or pale brick red, or ruby red, but they're red.

Red wines are made from grapes that are red or bluish in color. So guess what wine people call these grapes? Black grapes! We suppose that's because black is the opposite of white.

White wine styles: There's no such thing as just plain white wine

White wines fall into three general taste categories, not counting sparkling wine or the really sweet white wine you drink with dessert (see Chapter 16 for more on those). If the words we use to describe these taste categories sound weird, take heart — they're all explained in Chapter 2. Here are the three categories:

- Some white wines are *dry and crisp, with no sweetness and no oaky character.* (Turn to Chapter 3 for the lowdown on oak.) Most Italian white wines, like Soave and Pinot Grigio, and some French whites, like Sancerre and Chablis, fall into this category.

- Some white wines are *dry and full-bodied, with oaky character.* The more expensive Californian and French wines — like California Chardonnays selling for $18 a bottle on up in the U.S. or most white wines in the same price category from the Burgundy region of France — fall into this group.

- Finally, some white wines are *off-dry* (that is, not bone-dry). Examples include many of the less expensive American wines (under $10 a bottle in the U.S.) as well as a lot of German wines, especially the least expensive ones like Liebfraumilch (described in Chapter 12).

The most obvious difference between red wine and white wine is the color. The red color occurs when colorless juice sits in contact with the red grape skins during fermentation and absorbs the skins' color. Along with color, the grape skins give the wine *tannin,* a substance that's an important part of the way a red wine tastes. (See Chapter 2 for more about the taste of tannin.) The presence of tannin in red wines is actually the most important difference between red wines and white wines.

Red wines tend to be more *complex* than white wines, meaning that they have more going on when you taste them (which is logical when you consider that red wines have at least one more component than white wines do: tannin).

Red wines also vary in style more than white wines do. This is partly because winemakers have more leverage in *styling* a red wine (that is, more ways of adjusting their winemaking to achieve the kind of wine they want). For example, if winemakers leave the juice in contact with the skins for a long time, the wine becomes more *tannic* (firmer in the mouth, like strong tea; tannic wines can make you pucker). If winemakers drain the juice off the skins sooner, the wine is softer and less tannic.

Red wine tends to be consumed more often as part of a meal than as a drink on its own.

Red wine styles: There's no such thing as just plain red wine, either

Here are just three of the many red wine styles:

- *Light-bodied red wines* with not much tannin (like many Beaujolais wines from France, Valpolicella from Italy, and many U.S. and South American wines selling for less than $10 a bottle)

- *Medium-bodied, moderately tannic red wines* (like less expensive wines from Bordeaux, in France; Italian Chianti; many Australian red wines; and some American Merlots)

- *Full-bodied, tannic reds* (such as the best Bordeaux wines; the most expensive California Cabernets; Barolo, from Italy; and lots of other expensive reds)

Thanks to the wide range of red wine styles, you can find red wines to go with just about every type of food and every occasion when you want to drink wine (except the times when you want to drink a wine with bubbles, because most bubbly wines are white or pink). In Chapter 20, we give you some tips on matching red wine with food. You can also consult Chapter 5 of our book about red wine, *Red Wine For Dummies,* published by IDG Books.

One sure way to spoil the fun in drinking most red wines is to drink them cold. Those tannins can taste really bitter when the wine is cold — just like in a cold cup of very strong tea. On the other hand, many restaurants serve red wines too warm. (Where do they store them? Next to the boiler?) If the bottle feels cool to your hand, that's a good temperature.

A rose is a rose, but a rosé is "white"

Rosé wines are pink wines. Although rosé wines are made from red grapes, the wines aren't red because the grape juice is left in contact with the red skins for a very short time — only a few hours, compared to days or weeks for red wines. Because this *skin contact* (the period when the juice and the skins intermingle) is brief, very little tannin is absorbed from the skins in rosé wines. Therefore, you can chill rosé wines and drink them as you would white wines.

Back in the late '60s and early '70s, rosé wines were very popular. Now, lots of people are drinking rosé again — only they're not calling them rosés.

Red wine sensitivities

Lots of people complain that they can't drink red wines without getting a headache or feeling ill. Usually, they blame the sulfites in the wine. We're not doctors or scientists, but we can tell you that red wines contain far less sulfur than white wines. That's because the tannin in red wines acts as a preservative, making sulfur dioxide less necessary. Red wines do contain histamine-like compounds and other substances derived from the grape skins that could be the culprits. Whatever the source of the discomfort, it's probably not sulfites.

You see, the people who market wine in America have figured out that wines called *rosé* don't sell, so they invented the term *blush* wines. Lest someone figures out that *blush* is a synonym for *rosé,* the labels call the wine *white.* But even a child can see that White Zinfandel is really pink.

The blush wines that call themselves *white* are fairly sweet. Wines labeled rosé can be sweetish, but some wonderful rosés from Europe (and a few from America, too) are *dry* (not sweet). Although hard-core wine lovers hardly ever drink rosé wine, we love to drink dry rosés in the summer. For the names of our personal faves among dry rosés, see "Recommended dry rosé wines" at the end of Chapter 8 in *Wine Buying Companion For Dummies* (IDG Books Worldwide).

Even if a rosé wine is dry, most people will assume that it's sweet, because the common perception among Americans is that rosés are sweet. Yet lots of people who drink White Zinfandel believe that they're drinking a *dry* wine, because it's not called rosé. Go figure.

Ten occasions to drink rosé (and defy the snobs)

1. When she's having fish and he's having meat (or vice versa)

2. When a red wine just seems too heavy

3. With lunch — hamburger, grilled cheese sandwiches, and so on

4. On picnics on warm, sunny days

5. To wean your son/daughter, mate, friend (yourself?) off cola

6. With Sunday brunches and egg dishes

7. To celebrate the arrival of spring or summer

8. With ham (hot or cold) or other pork dishes

9. When you feel like putting ice cubes in your wine

10. On Valentine's Day (or any other pink occasion)

Other Ways of Categorizing Wine

There's a game we sometimes play with our friends. "Which wine," we ask them, "would you want to have with you if you were stranded on a desert island?" In other words, which wine could you drink for the rest of your life without getting tired of it? Our own answer is always Champagne, with a capital *C* (more on the capitalization later in this section).

In a way, it's an odd choice because, as much as we love Champagne, we don't drink it *every day* under normal circumstances. We welcome guests with it, we celebrate with it after Sunday football games, and we toast our cats with it on their birthdays. We don't need much of an excuse to drink Champagne, but it's not the type of wine we drink every night.

What we drink every night is regular wine — red, white, or pink — without bubbles. There are various names for these wines. In America, they are called *table* wines, and in Europe they're called *light* wines. Sometimes we refer to them as *still* wines, because they don't have bubbles moving around in them.

Table wine

Table wine, or light wine, is fermented grape juice whose alcohol content falls within a certain legal range. Furthermore, table wine is not bubbly. (Some table wines have a very slight carbonation, but the amount is not enough to disqualify them as table wines.) According to U.S. standards of identification, table wine may have an alcohol content that is no higher than 14 percent; in Europe, light wine must contain from 8.5 percent to 14 percent alcohol by volume, generally speaking (with a few exceptions). So unless a wine has more than 14 percent alcohol or has bubbles, it's a table wine or a light wine, in the eyes of the law.

The regulations-makers didn't get the number 14 by drawing it from a hat. Historically, the juice of ripe grapes usually attained not more than 14 percent alcohol when it was fermented. That number therefore became the legal borderline between wines that have no alcohol added to them (table wines) and wines that do have alcohol added to them (see "Dessert wine," in the next section).

Today, however, the issue isn't as clear-cut as it was when the laws were written. Many grapes are now grown in warm climates where they become so ripe, and have so much natural sugar, that their juice attains more than 14 percent alcohol when it's fermented. These wines include many red Zinfandels, Cabernets, and Chardonnays from California. Wine drinkers still consider them table wines, but legally they don't qualify. Which is just to say that laws and reality don't always keep pace.

How to learn the alcohol content of a wine (but not really)

Wineries are required by law to show the alcohol percentage on the label (again, with some minor exceptions). It can be expressed in *degrees*, like 12.5 degrees, or as a percentage, like 12.5 percent. If a wine carries the words "Table Wine" on its label in the U.S., but not the alcohol percentage, it should have less than 14 percent alcohol by law.

For wines sold within the U.S. — whether the wine is American or imported — there's a big catch, however. The labels are allowed to lie. U.S. regulations give wineries a 1.5 percent leeway in the accuracy of the alcohol level. If the alcohol level is actually 12.5 percent, the label can indicate a level as high as 14 percent or as low as 11 percent. The leeway does not entitle the wineries to exceed the 14 percent maximum, however.

If the alcohol percentage is stated as a number that's neither a full number nor a half-number — not 12 or 12.5, for example, but 12.8 or 13.2 — odds are it's precise. If the label states "Alcohol by volume 11 to 14 percent," the alcohol level is anybody's guess.

Here's our own, real-world definition of table wines: They are the normal, non-bubbly wines that most people drink most of the time.

Dessert wine

If a wine has more than 14 percent alcohol, odds are that alcohol was added during or after the fermentation. That's an unusual way of making wine, but some parts of the world, like the Sherry region in Spain and the Port region in Portugal, have made quite a specialty of it.

Dessert wines is the legal U.S. terminology for these wines, probably because they're usually sweet and often enjoyed after dinner. We find that term misleading, because dessert wines are not *always* sweet and not *always* consumed after dinner. (Dry Sherry is categorized as a dessert wine, for example, but it's dry, and we drink it before dinner.)

In Europe, this category of wines is called *liqueur wines,* which carries the same connotation of sweetness. We prefer the term *fortified,* which suggests that the wine has been strengthened with additional alcohol. But until we get elected to run things, the term will have to be *dessert wine* or *liqueur wine.*

Sparkling wine (and a highly personal spelling lesson)

Sparkling wines are wines that contain carbon dioxide bubbles. The bubbles are a natural by-product of fermentation that winemakers sometimes decide to trap in the wine.

In the U.S., Canada, and Europe, *sparkling wine* is the official name for the category of wines with bubbles. Isn't it nice when everyone agrees?

Champagne (with a capital C) is the most famous sparkling wine — and probably the most famous *wine,* for that matter. Champagne is a specific sparkling wine (made from certain grape varieties and produced in a certain way) that comes from a region in France called Champagne. It is the undisputed Grand Champion of Bubblies.

Unfortunately, for the people of Champagne, France, their wine is so famous that the name *champagne* has been borrowed again and again by producers elsewhere, until the word has become synonymous with practically the whole category of sparkling wines. In the U.S., for example, you can legally call a sparkling wine *champagne* — even with a capital C, if you want — as long as the carbonation was not added artificially. Winemakers in Canada and Australia are also permitted by local law to use the name *champagne* for their sparkling wine. (They do have to add a qualifying geographic term such as *American* or *Californian* before the word Champagne, however.)

For the French, limiting the use of the name *champagne* to the wines of the Champagne region has become a *cause célèbre.* European Union regulations not only prevent any other member country from calling its sparkling wines *champagne* but also prohibit the use of terms that even *suggest* the word *champagne,* such as fine print on the label saying that a wine was made using the "champagne method." What's more, bottles of sparkling wine from countries outside the European Union — such as the U.S. and Australia — that use the word champagne on the label are banned from sale in Europe. The French are that serious.

To us, this seems perfectly fair. You'll never catch us using the word *champagne* as a generic term for wine with bubbles. We have too much respect for the people and the traditions of Champagne, France, where the best sparkling wines in the world are made. That's why we stress the capital "C" when we say Champagne. *Those* are the wines we want on our desert island, not just any sparkling wine from anywhere that calls itself champagne.

Popular white wines

These types of white wine are available almost everywhere in the U.S. We describe these wines in Part III of this book.

- ✔ **Chardonnay:** Can come from California, Australia, France, and other places

- ✔ **Sauvignon Blanc:** Can come from California, France, New Zealand, South Africa, and other places

- ✔ **Riesling:** Can come from Germany, California, New York, Washington, France, and other places

- ✔ **Pinot Grigio** or **Pinot Gris:** Can come from Italy, Oregon, France, and other places

- ✔ **Soave:** Comes from Italy

When someone tries to impress you by serving a pseudo-Champagne, don't be impressed. In places where it is legal to call sparkling wines champagne, usually just the least expensive, low quality wines actually use that name. Most of the top sparkling wine companies in America, for example, won't call their wines champagne — even though it's legal — out of respect for their French counterparts. (Of course many of California's top sparkling wine companies are actually owned by the French — so it's no surprise that *they* won't call their wines champagne — but many other companies won't use the term, either.)

Popular red wines

You'll find descriptions and explanations of these popular and widely available red wines all through this book.

- ✔ **Cabernet Sauvignon:** Can come from California, Australia, France, and other places

- ✔ **Merlot:** Can come from California, France, Washington, New York, Chile, and other places

- ✔ **Pinot Noir:** Can come from California, France, Oregon, and other places

- ✔ **Beaujolais:** Comes from France

- ✔ **Lambrusco:** Usually comes from Italy

- ✔ **Chianti:** Comes from Italy

- ✔ **Zinfandel:** Usually comes from California

- ✔ **Bordeaux:** Comes from France

Chapter 2
These Taste Buds Are for You

*O*ur friends who are normal people (as opposed to our friends who are wine people) like to mock us when we do things like bring our own wine to a party or drive all the way from New York to Boston to go wine shopping. Most of the time, we don't even try to defend ourselves. We realize how ridiculous our behavior must seem.

In our early days as wine drinkers, we, too, used to think that all wines taste more or less the same. Wine was wine. All that changed when we started to taste wine the way the pros do.

The Special Technique for Tasting Wine

We know you're out there — the cynics who are saying, right about now, "Hey, I already know how to taste. I do it every day, three to five times a day. All that wine-tasting humbug is just another way of making wine seem fancy."

And you know, in a way, those cynics are right. Anyone who can taste coffee or a hamburger can taste wine. All you need are a nose, taste buds, and a brain. Unless you're like our friend who lost his sense of smell from the permanent-wave solution he used every day as a cosmetology teacher back in the '60s, you, too, have all that it takes to taste wine properly.

You also have all that it takes to speak Mandarin. Having the ability to do something is different from knowing how to do it and applying that know-how in everyday life, however.

Two very complicated rules of wine tasting

You drink beverages every day, tasting them as they pass through your mouth. In the case of wine, however, drinking and tasting are not synonymous. Wine is much more complex than other beverages, meaning that there's more going on in a mouthful of wine. Most wines have lots of different (and subtle) flavors, all at the same time, and they give you multiple sensations when they're in your mouth, such as softness and sharpness together.

If you just drink wine, gulping it down the way you do soda pop, you miss a lot of what you paid for. But if you *taste* wine, you can discover its nuances. In fact, the more slowly and attentively you taste wine, the more interesting it tastes.

And with that, we have two of the fundamental rules of wine tasting:

1. Slow down.

2. Pay attention.

The appearance of the wine

We enjoy looking at the wine in our glass, noticing how brilliant it is and the way it reflects the light, trying to decide precisely which shade of red it is and whether it will stain the tablecloth permanently if we tilt the glass too far.

Most books tell you that you look at the wine to determine whether it is clear (cloudiness generally indicates a flawed wine). That advice dates itself, though. Ever since high technology infiltrated the wine industry, visual flaws in wine are as rare as a winning lottery ticket. You could probably drink wine every night for a year without encountering a cloudy wine.

But look at the wine for a moment, anyway. Tilt your (half-full) glass away from you and look at the color of the wine against a white background (using a colored background distorts the color of the wine). Once at a black-tie dinner we even saw a distinguished fellow, who must have been a *very* serious wine lover, pull up his tuxedo sleeve and hold his glass against his white shirt to judge the color!

Look at the wine in your tilted glass and just notice how dark or how pale it is and what color it is, for the record. Eventually, you'll begin to notice differences from one wine to the next; but for now, just observe.

If you have time to kill, at this point you can also swirl the wine around in your glass (see "The nose knows" section later) and observe the way the wine runs back down the side of the glass. Some wines form *legs* or *tears* that flow slowly down. Once upon a time, these legs were interpreted as the sure sign of a rich, high-quality wine. Today, we know that a wine's legs are a complicated phenomenon having to do with the surface tension of the wine, and the evaporation rate of the wine's alcohol. If you're a physicist, this is a good time to show off your expertise and enlighten your fellow wine tasters — but if you're not, don't bother drawing much conclusion from the legs.

The nose knows

Now we get to the really fun part of tasting wine: swirling and sniffing. This is when you can let your imagination run wild, and no one will ever dare to contradict you. If you say that a wine smells like wild strawberries to you, how can anyone prove that it doesn't?

Before we explain the smelling ritual, and the tasting technique that goes along with it (described in the next section), we want to assure you that: a) you don't have to apply this procedure to every single wine you drink; b) you won't look foolish doing it, at least in the eyes of other wine lovers (we can't speak for the other 90 percent of the human population); and c) it's a great trick at parties to avoid talking with someone you don't like.

To get the most out of your sniffing, swirl the wine in the glass first. But don't even *think* about swirling your wine if your glass is more than half full.

Keep your glass on the table and rotate it so that the wine swirls around inside the glass and air mixes with the wine. Then bring the glass to your nose quickly. Stick your nose as far as it will go into the airspace of the glass without actually touching the wine and smell the wine. Free-associate. Is the aroma fruity, woodsy, fresh, cooked, intense, light? Your nose tires quickly, but it recovers quickly, too. Wait just a moment and try again. Listen to your friends' comments and try to find the same things they find in the smell.

You can revitalize your nose more quickly by smelling something else, like your water, a piece of bread, or your shirt sleeve — but be prepared for the odd looks you'll get from everyone around you.

As you swirl, the aromas in the wine vaporize, and you can smell them. Wine has so many *aromatic compounds* that whatever you find in the smell of a wine is probably not merely a figment of your imagination.

The point behind this whole ritual of swirling and sniffing is that what you smell should be pleasurable to you, maybe even fascinating, and that you should have fun in the process. But what if you notice a smell that you don't like?

Tips for smelling wine

1. Be bold. Stick your nose right into the glass where all the aromas are captured in the air space.

2. Don't wear strong scent; it will compete with the smell of the wine.

3. Don't wear yourself out smelling a wine when there are strong food aromas around. The tomatoes you smell in the wine could really be the tomato in someone's pasta sauce.

4. Become a smeller. Smell every ingredient when you cook, everything you eat, the fresh fruits and vegetables you buy at the supermarket, even the smells of your environment — like leather, wet earth, fresh road tar, grass, flowers, your wet dog, shoe polish, and your medicine cabinet. Stuff your mental database with smells so that you'll have aroma memories at your disposal when you need to draw on them.

5. Try different techniques of sniffing. Some people like to take short, quick sniffs, while others like to inhale a deep whiff of the wine's smell. Keeping your mouth open a bit while you inhale can help you perceive aromas. (Some people even hold one nostril closed and smell with the other, but we think that's a bit too kinky, especially in family restaurants.)

Hang around wine geeks for a while, and you'll start to hear words like *petrol, manure, sweaty saddle, burnt match,* and *asparagus* used to describe the aromas of some wines. "Yuck!" you say? Of course you do! Fortunately, the wines which exhibit such smells are not the wines you'll be drinking for the most part — at least not unless you really catch the wine bug. And when you do catch the wine bug, you might discover that those aromas, in the right wine, can really be a kick. Even if you don't learn to enjoy those smells (some of us do, honest!), you'll appreciate them as typical characteristics of certain regions or grapes.

Then there are the bad smells that nobody will try to defend. It doesn't happen often, but it does happen, because wine is a natural, agricultural product with a will of its own. Often when a wine is seriously flawed, it shows immediately in the nose of the wine. Wine judges have a term for such wines. They call them *DNPIM* — Do Not Put In Mouth. Not that you'll get ill, but why subject your taste buds to the same abuse that your nose just took? Sometimes it's a bad cork that is to blame, and sometimes it's some other sort of problem in the winemaking or even the storage of the wine. Just rack it up to experience and open a different bottle.

Wines have noses

With poetic license typical of wine tasters, someone once dubbed the smell of a wine its *nose* — and the expression took hold. If someone says that a wine has a huge nose, he means that the wine has a very strong smell. If he says that he detects lemon *in the nose* or *on the nose*, he means that the wine smells like lemons.

In fact, most wine tasters rarely use the word *smell* to describe how a wine smells because the word *smell* (like the word *odor*) seems pejorative. Wine tasters talk about the wine's nose or aroma. Sometimes they use the word *bouquet,* although that word seems to be falling out of fashion.

While you're choosing the next bottle, make up your own acronyms. *SOTYWE* (Serve Only To Your Worst Enemies) for example, or *ETMYG* (Enough To Make You Gag) or our own favorite, *SLADDR* (Smells Like A Dirty Dish Rag).

When it comes to smelling wine, many people are concerned that they aren't able to detect as many aromas as they think they should. Smelling wine is really just a matter of practice and attention. If you start to pay more attention to smells in your normal activities, you'll get better at smelling wine.

Tasting the wine

After you've looked at the wine and smelled it, you're finally allowed to taste it. This is when grown men and women sit around and make strange faces, gurgling the wine, and sloshing it around in their mouths with looks of intense concentration in their eyes. You can make an enemy for life if you distract a wine taster just at the moment when he is focusing all his energy on the last few drops of a special wine.

Here's how the procedure goes. Take a medium-sized sip of wine. Hold it in your mouth, purse your lips, and draw in some air across your tongue, over the wine. (Be utterly careful not to choke or dribble, or everyone will strongly suspect that you're not a wine expert.) Then swish the wine around in your mouth as if you are chewing it. Then swallow it. The whole process should take several seconds, depending on how much you are concentrating on the wine. (Wondering what to concentrate on? The next two sections tell you, along with the section "Describing Taste" later in this chapter.)

Wines have palates, too

Just as a wine taster might use the term *nose* for the smell of a wine, he might use the word *palate* in referring to the taste of a wine. A wine's palate is the overall impression the wine gives in your mouth, or any isolated aspect of the wine's taste — as in "This wine has a harmonious palate," or "The palate of this wine is a bit acidic." When a wine taster says that he finds raspberries *on the palate*, he means that the wine tastes like raspberries to him.

What's really happening

Different parts of the tongue specialize in registering different sensations; sweetness is perceived most keenly on the front of the tongue, sourness is triggered principally on the sides, and bitterness is detected across the rear of the tongue. (The tongue can also detect saltiness, but that taste is uncommon in wine.) By moving the wine around in your mouth, you give it a chance to hit all of these places so that you don't miss anything in the wine (even if sourness and bitterness sound like things you wouldn't mind missing).

As you swish the wine around in your mouth, you are also buying time. Your brain needs a few seconds to figure out what the tongue is tasting and make some sense of it. Any sweetness in the wine registers in your brain first because the sensation of sweetness corresponds to the first place the wine hits in your mouth; the *acidity* registers next (acidity, by the way, is what normal people call sourness), and then the bitterness. While your brain is working out the relative impressions of sweetness, bitterness, and acidity, you can be thinking about how the wine feels in your mouth — whether it's heavy, light, smooth, rough, and so on.

Tasting the smells

Until you cut your nose in on the action, that's all you can taste in the wine — those three sensations of sweetness, acidity, and bitterness and a general impression of weight and texture. Where have all the wild strawberries gone?

They're still there in the wine, right next to the chocolate and plums. But — to be perfectly correct about it — these flavors are actually *aromas* that you taste, not through tongue contact, but by inhaling them up an interior nasal passage in the back of your mouth called the *retronasal passage* (see Figure 2-1). When you draw in air across the wine in your mouth, you are vaporizing the aromas just as you did when you swirled the wine in your glass. (There's a method to this madness.)

Ten aromas (or flavors) associated with wine

1. Fruits
2. Herbs
3. Vegetables
4. Earth
5. Flowers

6. Grass
7. Tobacco
8. Toast
9. Smoke
10. Coffee, mocha, or chocolate

Figure 2-1:
Most wine flavors are actually aromas that are vaporized in the mouth and perceived through the rear nasal passage.

Nasal cavities
The nasal passage
The retronasal passage

After you go through all this rigamarole, it's time to reach a conclusion: Do you like what you tasted? The possible answers are yes, no, an indifferent shrug of the shoulders, or "I'm not sure, let me take another taste," which means that you have serious wine-nerd potential.

Ten odors not associated with wine

1. Paint
2. New car
3. Fax paper
4. Glue
5. Gorgonzola

6. Cannabis
7. Magic Marker
8. Elephant dung
9. Chanel No. 5
10. Fabric softener

The Pleasure Principle: Discovering What You Like

All this wine tasting stuff is so automatic to us by now that we probably practice it on every sip of every wine we drink, without even realizing it. Sometimes we catch ourselves doing it with beer or orange juice — much to our embarrassment if we're out in public.

We've discovered that there are drawbacks to tasting like this — besides the risk of looking foolish. When you taste wine the fancy way, you bring out all the characteristics of the wine, good *or* bad. Most wines are up to the challenge, but some wines are better left unscrutinized.

This brings us to the fundamental issue behind wine tasting: pleasure. If you're drinking mediocre wine, ignorance can be bliss. But when you can pick and choose the wine you drink, the exercise of tasting wine thoughtfully can help you find the wines that give you the most pleasure. And unless you discover what you like, how can you ask for it?

You get what you ask for

Now we have to confess that there is one more step between knowing how to taste wine and always drinking wine that you like. And it's a doozy. That step is putting taste into words.

We wouldn't have to bother with this detail if only we could choose our wines the way that customers choose cheese in a gourmet shop. (Can I try that one? No, I don't like it; let me taste the one next to it. Good. I'll take half a pound.)

"Like/Don't Like" is a no-brainer once you have the wine in your mouth. But most of the time you have to buy the stuff without tasting it first. So unless you want to drink the same wine for the rest of your life, you're going to have to decide what it is that you like or don't like in a wine and communicate that to another person who can steer you in the right direction.

Parlez-vous Winespeak?

There are two hurdles here: Finding the words to describe what you like or don't like, and then getting the other person to understand what you mean. Naturally, it helps if we all speak the same language.

Unfortunately, Winespeak is a dialect with an undisciplined and sometimes poetic vocabulary whose definitions change all the time, depending on who is speaking. In case you really want to get into this wine thing, we'll treat you to some sophisticated wine language in Chapters 3 and 19. For now, a few basic words and concepts should do the trick.

Describing Taste

Appearance and aroma are not critical in getting a wine you like. If you prefer white, red, or pink, it's because of the way the wine tastes, not because of the color itself (unless you're seriously into color-coordinating your food). And the aromas of the wine are more or less similar to its flavors.

Describing the *taste* of a wine in your mouth is the whole trick. When we first began to taste wine, we noticed that we usually faced one of two opposite dilemmas:

- ✔ The wine was so simple that we really couldn't find anything to say about it.
- ✔ The flavors of the wine came so fast and furious that we couldn't sort them out.

We eventually learned to taste wine one step at a time.

The tastes of a wine actually reveal themselves sequentially according to where they are detected on the tongue. We recommend that you follow this natural sequence when you try to put words to what you're tasting.

Sweetness

Right there, on the tip of your tongue, as soon as you put the wine into your mouth, you can notice sweetness or the lack of it. In Winespeak, *dry* is the opposite of *sweet*. Classify the wine you're tasting as either *dry, off-dry* (in other words, slightly sweet), or *sweet*.

Is it sweetness or fruitiness?

Beginning wine tasters sometimes describe dry wines as *sweet* because they confuse fruitiness with sweetness. A wine is *fruity* when it has distinct aromas and flavors of fruit. You smell the fruitiness with your nose; in your mouth, you "smell" it through your retronasal passage.

Sweetness, on the other hand, is perceived on the surface of your tongue. When in doubt, try holding your nose when you taste the wine; if the wine really is sweet, you'll be able to taste the sweetness despite the fact that you can't smell the fruitiness.

Touchy-feely

Softness and firmness are actually *textural impressions* a wine gives you as you taste it. Just as your mouth feels temperature in a liquid, it feels texture. Some wines literally *feel* soft and smooth in your mouth, while others feel hard, rough or coarse. In white wines, acid is usually responsible for impressions of hardness or firmness (or crispness); in red wines, tannin is usually responsible. Low levels of either substance can make a wine feel pleasantly soft — or too soft, depending on the wine and your taste preferences. Alcohol and unfermented sugar also contribute to an impression of softness.

Acidity

All wine contains acid (mainly *tartaric acid,* which exists in grapes), but some wines are more acidic than others. Acidity is more of a taste factor in white wines than in reds. For white wines, acidity is the backbone of the wine's taste (it gives the wine firmness in your mouth). White wines with a good amount of acidity taste *crisp,* and those without enough acidity taste *fat* and *flabby.* The sides of the tongue trigger your perception of acidity. You can also sense the consequences of acidity (or the lack of it) in the overall style of the wine — whether it's a tart little number or a soft and generous sort, for example. Classify the wine you're tasting as *tart, crisp, soft,* or "couch potato."

Tannin

Tannin is a substance that exists naturally in grapeskins and elsewhere in the grape (see Chapter 1). Because red wines are fermented with their grapeskins, tannin levels are far higher in red wines than in white wines. Have you ever taken a sip of a dark red wine and rapidly experienced a drying-out feeling in your mouth, as if someone had shoved a blotter in there? That's tannin.

To generalize a bit, tannin is to a red wine what acidity is to a white: a backbone. Because tannin sometimes tastes bitter, you sense tannin near the back of your tongue, but you can detect it elsewhere, too — on the inside of your cheeks and between your cheeks and gums — if the amount of tannin in a wine is high. Depending on the amount of tannin, a red wine can be called *astringent, firm,* or *soft.*

Is it acid or tannin?

Red wines have acid as well as tannin, and distinguishing between the two as you taste a wine can be a real challenge. When you're not sure whether it's mainly tannin or acid you're perceiving, pay attention to how your mouth feels *after* you've swallowed the wine. Both tannin and acid will make your mouth feel dry, but acid makes you salivate in response to the dry feeling (saliva is alkaline, so it neutralizes the acid). Tannin just leaves your mouth dry.

Body

A wine's body is an impression you get from the whole of the wine — not at any one place on your tongue. It's the impression of the weight and size of the wine in your mouth, which is usually attributable principally to a wine's alcohol. We say "impression" because, obviously, one ounce of any wine will occupy exactly the same space in your mouth and weigh the same as one ounce of any other wine. But some wines *seem* fuller, bigger, or heavier in the mouth than others. Think about the wine's fullness and weight as you taste it. Don't tell your friends that you're doing this, but imagine that your tongue is a tiny postal scale and judge how much the wine is weighing it down. Classify the wine as *light-bodied, medium-bodied,* or *full-bodied*.

Flavors

Wines have flavors (er, we mean *mouth aromas*), but wines don't come in a specific flavor. While you might enjoy the suggestion of chocolate in a red wine that you're tasting, you wouldn't want to go to a wine store and ask for a chocolatey wine, unless you don't mind the idea of people holding their hands over their mouths and trying not to laugh aloud at you.

Instead, you should refer to *families of flavors* in wine. There are your *fruity wines* (the ones that make you think of all sorts of fruit when you hold the wine in your mouth), your *earthy wines* (these make you think of mushrooms, walks in the forest, turning the earth in your garden, dry leaves, and so on), your *spicy wines* (cinnamon, cloves, black pepper, or Indian spices, for example), your *herbal wines* (mint, grass, hay, rosemary, and so on), and so on, and so on. There are so many flavors in wine that we could go on and on (and we often do!), but you get the picture, don't you?

If you like a wine and want to try another wine that's similar but different (and it will always be different, we guarantee you), try to decide what flavors in the wine you like and mention that to the person selling you your next bottle. In Part III, you'll find wines that fit these specific flavors.

Now you have 13 words — and a whole community of families — that allow you to explain what kind of wine you like. (If you're superstitious, consider *couch* and *potato* as separate words, and you have 14.) In Chapter 19, we'll elaborate on Winespeak and show you how to describe a wine as *round and supple, regal yet without pretension, gutsy yet not overbearing.*

The Quality Issue: What's a Good Wine?

Did you notice, by any chance, that nowhere on the list of terms we use to describe wines were the words *great, very good,* or *good?* Instead of worrying about crisp wines, earthy wines, and medium-bodied wines, wouldn't it just be easier to walk into a wine shop and say, "Give me a very good wine for dinner tonight"? Isn't *quality* the ultimate issue — or at least, quality within your price range, also known as *value?*

Well, quality is so important that, our cats will tell you with some embarrassment, we sometimes argue at the dinner table about the quality of the wine we're drinking. It's not that we don't know a great wine when we find one; in fact, we usually agree on whether the wine we are drinking is good. What we debate is *how* good the wine is or isn't — because it's a matter of personal taste.

One man's meat . . .

The instrument that measures the quality of a wine is a human being's *palate,* and because we're all different, we all have different opinions on how good a wine is. The combined opinion of a group of trained, experienced palates (also known as wine experts) is usually considered a definitive judgment of a wine's quality. (Turn to "Rating Wine Quality" in Chapter 19 for more about expert opinion.) But there's no guarantee that you will *like* the wine that the experts agree is very good. We've purchased highly rated wines and ended up pouring them down the sink because we didn't think they were very good at all.

We know it sounds like we're describing some kind of anarchy here, with everyone deciding for himself what's good and what isn't. But that's the way it is. When the primary purpose of a wine is to taste good, the person tasting the wine is the only one who can decide whether a particular wine works.

Of course, there are degrees of good and bad. Our old clunker works if it gets us where we're going, but it's probably not considered a good car because we feel every bump in the road. Somewhere along the way, someone established quality standards for cars that say that the best cars are quiet, ride smoothly, and are easy to steer — and ours isn't.

Quality standards exist for wine, too. What's frustrating is that there's no Detroit testing ground where scientific instruments can measure each wine against these quality standards. The measurement rests with your own palate.

So, what's a good wine? It is, above all, a wine that you like enough to drink. After that, how good a wine is depends on how it measures up to a set of (more or less) agreed-upon standards of performance established by experienced, trained experts. These standards involve mysterious concepts like *balance, length, depth, complexity,* and *trueness to type* (*typicity* in Winespeak, *typicité* in Snobwinespeak). None of these concepts are objectively measurable, by the way.

Balance

Those words we talk about in "Describing Taste" — sweetness, acidity, tannin — represent three of the major *components* (parts) of wine. The fourth is alcohol. Besides being one of the reasons we usually want to drink a glass of wine in the first place, alcohol is an important element of wine quality.

Balance is the relationship of these four components to one another. A wine is balanced when nothing sticks out as you taste it, like harsh tannin or too much sweetness. Most wines are balanced to most people. But if you have any pet peeves about food — if you really hate anything tart, for example, or if you never eat sweets — you might perceive some wines to be unbalanced. If you perceive them to be unbalanced, then they are unbalanced for *you*. (Professional tasters know their own idiosyncrasies and adjust for them when they judge wine.)

Tannin and acidity are *hardening elements* in a wine (they make a wine taste firmer in the mouth), while alcohol and sugar (if any) are *softening elements*. The balance of a wine is therefore the interrelationship of the hard and the soft aspects of a wine, and a key indicator of quality.

Length

When we call wines *long* or *short,* we're not referring to the size of the bottle or how quickly we empty it. *Length* is a word used to describe a wine that goes all the way on the palate — you can taste it across the full length of your tongue — and doesn't stop short halfway through your tasting of it.

A wine with good length hits all the taste centers on your tongue and lingers after you swallow it, too. Many wines today are very up-front on the palate — they make a big impression as soon as you taste them — but they are short. Length is a sure sign of quality.

Depth

This is another subjective, unmeasurable attribute of a high-quality wine. We say a wine has *depth* when it does not taste flat and one-dimensional on the palate but instead seems to have underlying layers of taste. A flat wine can never be great.

Complexity

There's nothing wrong with a simple, straightforward wine any more than there's something wrong with Homer Simpson — they are what they are. But a wine that keeps revealing different things about itself, always showing you a new flavor or impression — a wine that has *complexity* — is usually considered better quality.

Typicity

In order to judge whether a wine is true to its type, you have to know how that type is supposed to be. So you have to know of the textbook characteristics of wines made from the major grape varieties and of the classic wine regions of the world. (For example, the Cabernet Sauvignon grape typically has an aroma and flavor of blackcurrants, and the French white wine called Pouilly-Fumé typically has a slight gunflint aroma.) Turn to Chapters 10 through 16 for all those details.

Balance in action

For firsthand experience of how the principle of taste balance works, try this. Make a very strong cup of tea. When you sip it, the tea will taste bitter, because it's very tannic. Now add lemon juice; the tea will taste astringent (constricting and drying out your mouth), because the acid of the lemon and the tannin of the tea are accentuating each other. Now add lots of sugar to the tea. The sweetness should counter-balance the acid-tannin impact, and the tea will taste softer than it did before.

What's a Bad Wine?

Strangely enough, the right to declare a wine "good" just because you like it does not carry with it the right to call a wine a "bad" just because you don't. In this game, you get to make your own rules, but you don't get to force other people to live by them.

The fact is, there are very few bad wines in the world today compared to even 20 years ago. And many of the wines we could call bad are actually just bad *bottles* of wine — bottles that were handled badly, so that the good wine inside them got ruined. (Poor boy; he had everything going for him until he fell in with those wild kids. . . .)

Here are some characteristics that everyone agrees indicate a bad wine. Let's hope you never meet one. You might not.

- **Moldy fruit:** Have you ever eaten a raspberry from the bottom of the container that had a dusty, cardboardy taste to it? That same taste of rot can be in a wine if the wine was made from grapes that were not completely fresh and healthy when they were harvested. Bad wine.

- **Vinegar:** In the natural evolution of things, wine is just a pit stop between grape juice and vinegar. Most wines today remain forever in the wine stage because of technology or careful winemaking. If you find a wine that has crossed the line toward vinegar, it's bad wine.

- **Chemical or bacterial smells:** The most common are acetone (nail polish remover) and sulfur flaws (rotten eggs, burnt rubber, bad garlic). Bad wines.

- **Oxidized wine:** Smells flat, weak, or maybe cooked, and tastes the same. It might have been a good wine once, but air — oxygen — got in somehow and killed the wine. Bad bottle.

- **Cooked aromas and taste:** When a wine has been stored or shipped in heat, it can actually taste cooked or baked as a result. Often there's telltale leakage from the cork, or the cork is pushed up a little. Bad bottle. (Unfortunately, every other bottle of that wine that experienced the same shipping or storage will also be bad.)

- **Corky wine:** The most common flaw, a smell of damp cardboard that gets worse with air. It's caused by a bad cork, and even the best wines in the world are not immune to it. Bad bottle.

The Final Analysis: Do You Like It?

Let's not dwell too long on what can go wrong with a wine. If you find a bad wine or a bad bottle — or even a wine that is considered a good wine, but you don't like it — just move on to something you like better. Drinking a so-called great wine that you don't enjoy is as stupid as watching foreign films that bore you. Change the channel. Explore.

Chapter 3

Behind the Scenes of Winemaking

· ·

In This Chapter

▶ Separating the meaningful wine terms from the mumbo jumbo

▶ The difference between *barrel-fermented* and *barrel-aged*

▶ *ML, pH,* and *stirred lees*

▶ Reasons for blending

▶ Technical terms to wow your friends

· ·

The most frustrating thing about wine has got to be the technical lingo. All you want is a crisp, fruity white wine to serve with tonight's fried chicken. But to find it, you have to fight your way through a jungle of jargon on the back labels of the wine bottles, in the words the sales clerk uses to explain his recommendations, and on the signs all around the wine shop. Why on earth is everyone making wine so complicated?

Here's the problem: Wine is two products. On the one hand, it's a beverage, and it should taste good — period. On the other hand, it's an art form — something lots of people like to talk about, study, and collect. Some people who enjoy wine as an art form (a *delicious* art form) are so engaged by the subject that they sometimes forget that other people aren't. They end up reciting technical information about winemaking that you never asked for.

How much of this information (if any) is pivotal in helping you get the kind of wine you want, and how much is pretentious babble? Read on.

A Reality Check for Wine Jargon

Winemakers use numerous procedures to make wine. These procedures vary according to the grapes they have and the type of wine being made. (If a winemaker is producing huge quantities of a wine that sells for $5.99 retail, for example, he or she probably won't ferment the wine in new barrels of French oak because the cost of the barrels alone could add $2 to the price of every bottle.)

No winemaking procedure is inherently good or inherently bad; it all depends on the grapes and the type of wine being made. How the wine tastes is the ultimate justification of the method: The procedures themselves are meaningless if they don't create a wine that is appealing to wine drinkers.

The *taste* of the wine involves the wine's aroma, body, texture, length, and so on (see Chapter 2) and not just its flavors. And the taste of a wine is a subjective experience.

Every winemaking technique affects the taste of the wine — in one way or another. Most of the technical words that are bandied about in wine circles therefore represent procedures that *are* relevant to the taste of a wine. (Of course, if you dig deep enough, figuratively speaking, even dinosaur droppings can be relevant to the taste of a wine.) But — here's the key point — these technical words each represent isolated elements in the making of the wine, and they are only *parts* of the total picture.

Operation: Delicious

Everything that a winemaker does in producing his wine has just one purpose: to make the best-tasting wine possible under the circumstances. Some winemakers make wines that are intended to taste good right away, while others make wines that are intended to taste good down the road, after the wine has matured (see Chapter 21).

Producing wine actually involves two separate steps: the growing of the grapes, called *viticulture,* and the making of the wine, called *vinification.*

Sometimes both steps are performed by the same company, as with *estate-bottled* wines (see Chapter 9), and sometimes the two steps are completely separate. Some large wineries, for example, contract with hundreds of private grape growers. These growers don't make wine; they just grow grapes and sell their grapes to whatever wine company offers them the highest price per ton.

Vine-growing vernacular

Much more jargon is associated with the making of a wine than with the growing of its grapes. But a few technical terms relating to grape growing do crop up on wine labels or in wine descriptions. Here are the expressions that you're likely to encounter:

 ✔ **Low yields.** Example: "Our fruit comes from low-yielding vineyards." The operative concept is that the more grapes a grapevine produces (the higher its *yield* of grapes), the less intense the flavors of those grapes will be, and the lower in quality they — and their wine — will be.

In most European vineyards, maximum yields are set by law (although these maximums are usually quite generous), but in American vineyards there are no limits. In the end, just about any wine producer anywhere can *claim* that his yields are low, because it's too complicated to prove otherwise. If the wine tastes thin or watery, we'd be suspicious.

✔ **Ripeness.** Example: "Our grapes were perfectly ripe at harvest." Harvesting the grapes when they are perfectly ripe — a brief stage between under-ripe and over-ripe — is one of the crucial points in wine production. But ripeness is a subjective issue.

In cooler climates, full ripeness is an extraordinary thing that doesn't happen every year, and the wine should be unusually good as a result. In warmer climates, ripeness is almost automatic; the trick becomes not letting the grapes get too ripe too fast, which causes them to be physiologically mature but undeveloped in their flavors (like a physically precocious but immature teenager). And in some places, winemakers purposely pick their grapes a little early because they want higher acids in their wine. (See Chapter 4 for a discussion of how grapes ripen.) There's no fixed definition of perfect ripeness.

✔ **Canopy.** Example: "We use an open canopy to get perfect ripeness in our grapes." Left untended, grapevines would grow along the ground, up trees, wherever they could take hold (they're *vines,* after all!). But commercial viticulture involves attaching the shoots of vines to wires or trellises in a systematic pattern. The purpose of *training* the vine — as this activity is called — is to position the grape bunches so that they'll get enough sun and ripen well and so that the fruit will be easy for the harvesters to reach.

An *open canopy* is a trellising method that maximizes the sunlight exposure of the grapes. *Canopy management,* the practice of maneuvering the grape leaves and fruit into the best position for a given vineyard, is a popular buzzword. Winemakers who offer you this information want you to know that they are doing everything possible to get their grapes ripe.

✔ **Microclimate.** Example: "Our vineyards benefit from a microclimate that assures perfect ripeness every year." Every wine region has climatic conditions (the amount and timing of sun, rain, wind, humidity, and so on) that are considered the norm for that area. But individual locations within a region — the south-facing side of a particular hill, for example — can have a climatic reality that is different from neighboring vineyards. The unique climatic reality of a specific location is called its *microclimate.* Naturally, every wine producer thinks his microclimate is ideal — or wants to convince you that it is.

Winemaking wonder words

The vinification end of wine producing falls into two parts: *fermentation,* the period when the grape juice turns into wine, and *maturation* (or *finishing*), the period following fermentation when the wine settles down, loses its rough edges, goes to prep school, and gets ready to meet the world. Depending on the type of wine being made, the whole process could take three months or five years — or even longer if the bank isn't breathing down the winery's neck.

Winemakers don't have as many options in making wine as chefs do in preparing food — but almost! Maybe that's why wine talk abounds with details of the winemaking process. Of all the jargon you're likely to hear, information about oak is probably the most common.

When wood becomes magic

Oak barrels, 60 gallons in size (about twice as big as a garbage can), are often used as containers for wine either during fermentation or for maturation. The barrels lend oaky flavor and aroma to the wine, which many people find very appealing. The barrels are expensive — about $600 per barrel if they're made from French oak. (Most people consider French oak to be the finest.) We suppose the expense is one good reason to boast about using the barrels.

But not all oak is the same. Oak barrels vary in the origin of their oak, the amount of *toast* (a charring of the inside of the barrels) each barrel has, the age of the barrels (they lose their oakiness with time), and even the size of the barrels. Even if all oak *were* the same, a wine could turn out differently depending on whether unfermented juice or actual wine went into the barrels, and how long it stayed there.

In fact, the whole issue of oak is so complicated that anyone who suggests that a wine is better simply because it has been oaked is guilty of gross oversimplification. *There is no automatic correlation between the use of oak and wine quality.*

Barrel-fermented versus barrel-aged

You don't have to venture very far into wine before you find someone explaining to you that a particular wine was barrel-fermented or barrel-aged — not that you asked. What in the world does he mean, and should you care?

The term *barrel-fermented* means that unfermented juice went into barrels (almost always oak) and changed into wine there. The term *barrel-aged* usually means that wine (already fermented) went into barrels and stayed there for a maturation period of a few months or a couple of years.

Because most wines that are fermented in barrels remain there for several months after the fermentation is finished, *barrel-fermented* and *barrel-aged* are sometimes used together. The term *barrel-aged* alone suggests that the fermentation happened somewhere other than the barrel — usually in stainless steel.

Barrel-fermentation applies mainly to white wines, and the reason is very practical. As we mention in Chapter 2, the juice of red wines ferments together with the grape skins in order to become red, and that's a mighty

---

Is oaky okay?

So many wines are oaked these days that wine lovers use the word *oaky* as a descriptor all the time. But the magazine editor reviewing a wine column written by a friend of ours had never heard the term applied to wine, and thought it was a typo. The editor changed the text to read: "Lovely okay nuances on the nose of this wine are followed by a strong okay flavor on the palate...."

---

messy mixture to have to clean out of a small barrel! Red wines are usually fermented in larger containers — stainless steel or even large wooden vats — and then *aged* in small oak barrels after the wine has been drained off the grape skins. (Some light, fruity styles of red wine might not be oaked at all.)

Here's why you might care whether a white wine is barrel-fermented or just barrel-aged. Wines that are fermented in barrels actually end up tasting *less* oaky than wines that were simply aged in barrels, even though they might have spent more time in oak. (A barrel-fermented and barrel-aged Chardonnay might have spent 11 months in oak, for example, and a barrel-aged Chardonnay may have spent only five months in oak.)

Lots of people who are supposed to know more about wine than you do — for example, the salesperson at your wine shop — get the effects of the two processes backward and tell you that the barrel-fermented wine tastes oakier. If you have a strong opinion about the flavor of oak in your wine, you'll end up buying the wrong wine on their advice.

Other winemaking terms

Become a wine expert overnight and dazzle your friends with this amazing array of wine jargon. (Just don't fool yourself into believing that any one of the procedures described necessarily creates a high quality wine. The merit of each procedure depends on the particular wine being made.)

- **Lees.** Example: "Our Chardonnay had 11 months of lees contact." *Lees* is the name for various solids that precipitate to the bottom of a wine after fermentation. These solids can interact with elements of the wine and create more complex flavor in the wine. (Sometimes the winemaker stirs the lees in the wine periodically to accelerate this process.) A white wine with extended lees contact is usually richer in texture and tastes less overtly fruity than it would otherwise.

- **ML** or **malolactic.** Example: "We put our wine through a full malolactic." *Malolactic,* nicknamed *ML* or *malo,* is a secondary fermentation that changes the nature of the acids in the wine. The net result is that the wine is softer and less acidic. ML usually happens naturally, but a winemaker can also incite it or can prevent it.

Red wines almost always undergo malolactic fermentation, but for white wines, ML is a stylistic judgment call on the winemaker's part. Sometimes, ML can contribute a buttery flavor to a white wine. Malolactic fermentation can be a key process in creating delicious white wines — if you like the style of wine it creates.

✔ **pH.** Example: "The pH of this wine is 3.4." The chemical term, pH, means exactly the same thing for wine as it does in other scientific fields. ("Our facial cream is pH-balanced for sensitive skin.") If you want a technical explanation, look up your former chemistry teacher. If you'll settle for the general concept, pH is a measurement of acidity; wines with low pH (approximately 3.4 or less) have higher acidity and wines with high pH have lower acidity.

✔ **Fining** and **filtering.** Example: "*Our* wine is unfined and unfiltered." The processes of *fining* and *filtering* are carried out on most wines near the end of the maturation period when they are almost ready for bottling. The purpose of these procedures is to *clarify* the wine — that is, to remove any cloudiness or solid matter in the wine — and to *stabilize* it — to remove any yeast, bacteria, or other microscopic critters that might change the wine for the worse after it is bottled.

There's a popular belief among anti-tech wine lovers that fining and filtration strip a wine of its character — and that unfined, unfiltered wines are inherently better, even if they're not always brilliant in appearance. But it's a complex issue. (For one thing, there are *degrees* of fining and filtration, like *light* fining and *gentle* filtration.)

✔ **Blending.** Example: "We blend the wines of five different grapes to create layers of complexity in our wine." In winemaking, different grape varieties are fermented separately and then brought together afterward. But *blending* also applies to the mixing of various barrels (or lots) of wine from the same grape variety to create one homogeneous lot of wine before bottling. Blending is also the term for mixing liquid oak extract in a wine. Hold the confectioner's sugar, please.

The reasons for blending wines of different grapes together are either to reduce costs by diluting an expensive wine like Chardonnay with something else far less expensive, or to improve the quality of the wine by using complementary grapes whose characteristics enhance each other. Many of Europe's traditional wines — such as red Rioja, red Bordeaux, Châteauneuf-du-Pape and Champagne — are blended wines that owe their personalities to several grapes.

Chapter 4

Pinot Envy and Other Secrets about Grape Varieties

. . . .

. . . .

*W*ouldn't it be a pity if some mad scientist were to invent a way to make wine without using actual grapes? We'd hate to see grapes eliminated from the process because grapes are one of the most fascinating things about wine.

Land covered with row upon row of grapevines is a stirring sight to wine drinkers. The tending of the vines and the harvesting of the grapes hold ritualistic meaning for farmers all over the world who grow grapes and for the winemakers who transform those grapes into wine. Grapes are the link — literally and emotionally — between the land and the wine.

Grapes also give us one of the easiest ways of classifying wine and making sense of the hundreds of different types of wine that exist.

It's the Grape Whodunit

If anyone were to invent a mystery game about wine, it would probably be a big flop because there's no real mystery in knowing what makes most wines taste the way they do. The grapes done it. With Mother Nature and a winemaker as accomplices, the grapes are responsible for the style and personality and, sometimes, the quality of every wine, because they are the starting point of the wine. (Sure, a winemaker can do things to make the grapes unrecognizable in the final wine — like over-oaking the wine or letting it oxidize — but the grapes dictate the genetic structure of the wine and how it will respond to everything that is done to it.)

Think back to the last wine you drank. What color was it? If it was white, the odds are that's because it came from white grapes; if it was pink or red, that's because the wine came from red grapes.

Did it smell herbal or earthy or fruity? Whichever, those aromas came from the grapes. Was it firm and tannic or soft and voluptuous? Thank the grapes (with a nod to their two co-conspirators, Mother Nature and the winemaker).

The specific grape variety (or varieties) that makes any given wine is largely responsible for the sensory characteristics the wine offers — from its appearance to its aromas, its flavors, and its alcohol-tannin-acid profile.

Of genus and species

By *grape variety,* we mean the fruit of a specific type of grapevine: the fruit of the Cabernet Sauvignon vine, for example, or the fruit of the Chardonnay vine.

The term *variety* actually has specific meaning in scientific circles. A variety is a subdivision of a species. Most of the world's wines are made from grape varieties that belong to the species *vinifera* — a subdivision of the genus *Vitis.* This species originated in Europe and western Asia; other distinct species of *Vitis* are native to North America.

Some wine *is* made from grapes of other species; for example, the Concord grape, which makes Concord wine as well as grape juice and jelly, belongs to the native American species *Vitis labrusca.* But the grapes of this species have a markedly different flavor from vinifera grapes — *foxy* is the word used to describe that taste. The number of non-vinifera wines is small because their flavor is unpopular in wine. In juice or jelly, though, the grapes do fine; just ask Welch's!

A variety of varieties

Snowflakes and fingerprints aren't the only examples of Nature's infinite variety. Within the genus *Vitis* and the species vinifera, there are as many as 10,000 varieties of wine grapes. If wine from every one of these varieties were commercially available and you drank the wine of a different variety every single day, it would take you more than 27 years to experience them all!

Not that you would want to. Within those 10,000 varieties there are grapes that have the ability to make extraordinary wine, grapes that tend to make very ordinary wine, and grapes that only a parent could love. Most of the 10,000 varieties are obscure grapes whose wines rarely enter into international commerce.

The phylloxera threat

If endangered species lists had existed at the end of the 19th century, *Vitis vinifera* certainly would have been on them. The entire species was nearly eradicated by a tiny louse called *phylloxera* that emigrated to Europe from America and proceeded to feast on the roots of vinifera grapevines, wiping out vineyards across the continent.

To this day, no remedy has been found to protect vinifera roots from phylloxera. What saved the species was grafting vinifera vines onto rootstocks of native American species that are resistant to the bug. The practice of grafting the fruit-bearing part of *Vitis vinifera* onto the rooting part of other, phylloxera-resistant species continues today everywhere in the world where phylloxera is present and fine wine is made. (The fruit-bearing part is called a *scion*, and the rooting plant is called a *rootstock*.) Somehow, each grape variety maintains its own character despite the fact that its roots are alien.

An extremely adventuresome wine nut who has plenty of free time to explore the back roads of Spain, Portugal, Italy, and Greece might be able to encounter 1,500 different grape varieties (only four years' worth of drinking) in his lifetime. The grape varieties you might encounter in the course of your normal wine enjoyment probably number fewer than 50.

How the Grape Done It

All sorts of attributes distinguish each of those 50 grape varieties from the next. These attributes fall into two categories: personality traits and performance factors. *Personality traits* are the characteristics of the fruit itself — its flavor, for example. *Performance factors* refer to how the grapevine grows, how its fruit ripens, and how quickly it can get from 0 to 60 miles per hour.

Both the personality traits of a specific grape variety and its performance factors affect the ultimate taste and style of the wines that are made from that grape.

Personality traits of grape varieties

Skin color is the most fundamental distinction among grape varieties. Every grape variety is considered either a white variety or a red (black) one, according to the color of its skins when the grapes are ripe. (A handful of red-skinned varieties are further distinguished by having red pulp rather than white pulp.)

Individual grape varieties can also be distinguished from one another in other ways.

- **Aromatic compounds:** Some grapes (like Muscat) contribute floral aromas and flavors to their wine, for example, while other grapes contribute herbaceous aromas and flavors (like Sauvignon Blanc). Some grapes have very neutral aromas and flavors and, therefore, make fairly neutral wines. (The Trebbiano grape that's used for lots of Italian white wines is an example.)

- **Acidity levels:** Some grapes are naturally disposed to higher acid levels at harvest time than others, which naturally influences the wine made from those grapes.

- **Thickness of skin and size of the individual grapes (called berries):** Grapes with thick skins naturally have more tannin than grapes with thin skins; ditto for small-berried varieties compared to large-berried varieties.

The skins of the grapes, the grape *pips* (or seeds), and the stems all contain tannin, that somewhat-bitter-tasting substance that is important to the style of red wines. Generally, the stems are discarded before fermentation, so their tannin doesn't count. White wines are usually made only from the juice, without the skins or seeds, so tannin is less of an issue for those wines. But during red wine fermentation, the skins and the seeds both soak in the grape juice and contribute their tannins to the wine. Tannins are a mixed bag: Some of them are beneficial to the wine, giving the wine firmness and character, and some of them are not, loading the wine with pungent and overly bitter flavors. It's up to the winemaker to figure out how to get the good tannins into the wine without the bad ones. Assuming that the wine-making doesn't vary, grape varieties that have thick skins or small berries (and therefore a greater skin-to-juice ratio) will make a more tannic wine.

The composite personality traits of each grape variety are fairly evident in the wines that are made from that grape. A Cabernet Sauvignon wine is almost always more tannic and slightly lower in alcohol than a Merlot wine, for example, because that's the nature of those two grapes.

Performance factors of grape varieties

The performance factors that distinguish grape varieties are vitally important to the grape grower because those factors determine how easy — or how challenging — it will be for him to cultivate a specific grape variety in his vineyard. But performance factors also affect the flavor and style of the wines made from each grape variety, according to the specific location where the grape variety grows.

Every grape variety has a predictable length-of-ripening period, for example. If a grape variety with a long ripening period is grown in a region where summers are short and cool, the grapes won't ripen sufficiently, and the wine made from them could taste tart and *vegetal* (like green vegetables). If a grape variety that ripens quickly is grown in a very warm climate, it could ripen so fast that the wine made from it tastes overly ripe (like mushy fruit) and is very high in alcohol.

Other grape performance factors that can affect the taste of a wine include

- **Density of the cluster:** Some grape varieties have very dense, compact bunches (or clusters) of fruit. Grow a variety like that in a warm, damp climate, and you'd better be prepared to spend the whole summer fighting off the mildew that wants to grow within the grape clusters. If the grapes manage to get slightly moldy despite your best efforts, they'll give a dusty, moldy taste to the wine.

- **Amount of vegetation:** Some grape varieties have a natural tendency to grow more leaves and shoots than others. This vegetation can shade the fruit and prevent the grapes from ripening completely, giving under-ripe flavors to the wine. If that grape variety is naturally high in acid, the wine will taste doubly tart.

The reasons some grape varieties perform brilliantly in certain places (and make excellent wine as a result) are so complex that grape growers haven't figured them all out yet. The amount of heat and cold, the amount of wind and rain (or lack of it), and the slant of the sun's rays on the hillside of vines are among the factors affecting the vine's performance. But remember that no two vineyards in the world have precisely the same combination of these factors — precisely the same *terroir* (see Chapter 5). The issue simply defies simple generalizations.

Like grape, like wine

There are things a winemaker can do to correct deficiencies or excesses in his grapes — to an extent.

In places where it's legal, he can add acid to the juice if the grapes are too ripe, for example, or add sugar to the juice to simulate a level of ripeness that Mother Nature denied that year. (That added sugar will be fermented into alcohol.) If he decides to put the juice or wine into oak barrels, he could create oaky aromas and flavors in the wine that are beyond what the grapes brought to the wine.

But for the most part, what the grapes give is what the wine is. The person-ality traits of each grape variety, tempered by its performance wherever it's grown, more or less define the nature of each wine.

Chardonnay, do you take this limestone soil?

One important factor in how a grape variety performs is the soil in the vineyard. Over the centuries, some classic compatibilities between grape varieties and types of soil have become evident: Chardonnay in limestone or chalk, Cabernet Sauvignon in gravelly soil, Pinot Noir in limestone, and Riesling in slatey soil. At any rate, these are the soils of the regions where these grape varieties perform at their legendary best.

Soil affects a grapevine in several ways (besides simply anchoring the vine): It is a nutritional medium for the grapevine; it can influence the temperature of the vineyard to the extent that the soil may or may not retain heat; and it provides a water-management system for the plant. Of these three tasks, providing a water-management system is considered the most important, and influencing the temperature of the vineyard is considered the least important.

A safe generalization is that the best soils are those that have good drainage and are not particularly fertile. (An extreme example is the soil — if we can call it that — of the Châteauneuf-du-Pape district in France's Rhône Valley: It's just stones.) The wisdom of the ages decrees that the grapevine must struggle to produce the best grapes — and well-drained, less fertile soils challenge the vine to struggle, regardless of what specific variety the grapevine is.

Royalty and Commoners in the Kingdom of Grapes

Bees have their queens, wolves have their alpha males, gorillas have their silverbacks, and humans have their royal families. In the grape kingdom, there are nobles, too — at least as interpreted by the human beings who drink the wine made from those grapes.

Noble grape varieties (as they are referred to colloquially by wine people) have the potential to make great — not just good — wine. Every noble grape variety can claim at least one wine region where it is the undisputed king. The wines made from noble grapes on their home turf can be so great that winemakers in far-flung regions are inspired to grow the same grape in their own vineyards. The noble grape might prove itself noble there, too — but frequently the grape does not. Adaptability is not necessarily a prerequisite of nobility.

Cloning the perfect grapevine

If you hang around wine people long enough, you're sure to hear them talk about *clones* or *clonal selection* of grape varieties. Has the Brave New World of grape growing arrived?

In botanical terms, a *clone* is a subdivision of a variety. Remember all those things we said about how every grape variety is different from the next? Well, the individuality doesn't end with the grape variety. Even within a single variety, such as Chardonnay, there can be differences from one plant to the next. Some vines ripen their fruit slightly more quickly, for example, or produce grapes with slightly different aromas and flavors than the next vine.

Grapevines are usually propagated asexually by taking cuttings from a *mother plant* and allowing those cuttings to root (until the plant is mature enough to be grafted onto a phylloxera-resistant rootstock). The new plants are genetically identical to the mother plant. Naturally, grape growers usually choose the most ideal plants (in terms of ripening, fruit flavor, disease resistance, heartiness — or whatever it is they're looking for) to use as the mother plants. Voilá! They have made a clonal selection.

Actually, much of the clonal selection these days takes place in universities and other research institutions where the mother vines are checked for viruses before they are propagated. Commercial nurseries obtain mother plants from these institutions, and grape growers purchase their grapevines from the nurseries, specifying which particular clones they want.

Fortunately for most of us, human parents don't have the same options!

Classic examples of noble grape varieties at their best are

- The Chardonnay grape and the Pinot Noir grape in Burgundy, France
- The Cabernet Sauvignon grape in Bordeaux, France
- The Syrah grape in France's Northern Rhône Valley
- The Chenin Blanc grape in France's Loire Valley
- The Nebbiolo grape in Piedmont, Italy
- The Sangiovese grape in Tuscany, Italy
- The Riesling grape in the Mosel and Rheingau regions of Germany

A Primer on the Major White Grape Varieties

Here are descriptions of the 12 most important white *vinifera* varieties today. In describing the grapes, naturally we describe the type(s) of wine that are made from each grape. You'll encounter these wines in various guises: as varietal wines, or as place-name wines that don't mention the grape variety anywhere on the label (a common practice for European wines). You'll also encounter these grapes as blending partners for other grapes — sometimes public partners, sometimes secret cohorts.

The differences among white grape varieties are mainly in their acidity levels and aromas, or flavors. (Turn to Chapter 2 for a quick review of some of the descriptors we use in this section.)

Chardonnay

Today's darling white grape, Chardonnay, is a shoo-in for Miss Congeniality. But despite its populist appeal, Chardonnay is actually quite a regal grape, producing the greatest dry white wines in the world — white Burgundies. Chardonnay is also one of the main grapes of Champagne.

The Chardonnay grape is planted in practically every wine-producing country of the world. This grape is universal for two reasons: The variety is relatively adaptable to a wide range of climates, and the name Chardonnay on a wine label is, these days, a sure-fire sales tool.

Because the flavors of Chardonnay are very compatible with those of oak — and because white Burgundy (the great prototype) is generally an oaked wine, and because wine drinkers generally love the flavor of oak — most Chardonnay wine receives some oak treatment either during or after fermentation. (For the best Chardonnays, oak treatment means expensive barrels of French oak; but for lower-priced Chardonnays it could mean soaking oak chips in the wine or even adding liquid essence of oak. See Chapter 3 for more on oak.) Outside of northern Italy and France's Chablis and Mâconnais districts, where oak is usually not used for Chardonnay, oaky Chardonnay wine is the norm and unoaked Chardonnay is the exception.

Oaked Chardonnay is so common that some wine drinkers confuse the flavor of oak with the flavor of Chardonnay. If your glass of Chardonnay smells or tastes toasty, smoky, spicy, vanilla-like, or butterscotch-like, that's the oak you're perceiving, not the Chardonnay!

Chardonnay itself has fruity aromas and flavors that range from apple — in cooler wine regions — to tropical fruits, especially pineapple, in warmer regions. Chardonnay also can display earthy aromas, such as mushroom or minerals. Chardonnay wine has medium to high acidity. It is generally rich and full-bodied.

Classically, Chardonnay wines are dry. But a lot of Chardonnays coming out of California these days are off-dry — especially, but not exclusively, at the lower-price end.

Chardonnay is a grape that can stand on its own in a wine, and the top Chardonnay-based wines (except for Champagne and similar bubblies) are 100 percent Chardonnay. But less expensive wines that are labeled *Chardonnay* — those selling for less than $6 a bottle in the U.S., for example — are likely to have some other, far less distinguished grape blended in. That's because blending in wine from an ordinary grape like Colombard helps reduce the cost of making the wine. Anyway, it's perfectly legal. And who can even tell if it's all Chardonnay or not, behind all that oak?

Riesling

The great Riesling wines of Germany have put the Riesling grape on the map as an undisputedly noble variety. Riesling shows its real class only in a few places outside of Germany, however. The Alsace region of France, Austria, and the Finger Lakes district of New York are among the few.

Riesling wines are as unpopular today as Chardonnay is popular. Maybe that's because Riesling is the antithesis of Chardonnay. While Chardonnay is usually gussied up with oak, Riesling never is; while Chardonnay can be full-bodied and rich, Riesling is more often light-bodied and refreshing. Riesling's fresh, vivid personality can make many Chardonnays taste clumsy in comparison.

The common perception of Riesling wines is that they are sweet, and many of them are — but plenty of them aren't. Alsace Rieslings are normally dry, many German Rieslings are dry, and there are a few dry Rieslings from America. (Riesling can be vinified either way, according to the style of wine a producer wants to make.) Look for the word *trocken* (meaning dry) on German Riesling labels and the word *dry* on American labels if you prefer the dry style of Riesling.

High acidity, low to medium alcohol levels, and aromas/flavors that range from ebulliently fruity to flowery to minerally are the trademarks of Riesling wines.

Riesling wines are sometimes labeled as *White Riesling* or *Johannisberg Riesling* — both synonyms for the noble Riesling grape. With wines from Eastern European countries, though, read the fine print: Olazrizling, Laskirizling, and Welschriesling are from another grape altogether.

If you consider yourself a maverick who hates to follow trends, check out the Riesling section of your wine shop instead of the Chardonnay aisle.

Sauvignon Blanc

While just about everybody likes Chardonnay, Sauvignon Blanc is controversial with wine drinkers. That's because it has such distinctive character.

For one thing, Sauvignon Blanc is high in acidity — great if you like crisp wines, but not so great otherwise. For another thing, its aromas and flavors can be herbaceous (suggestive of herbs or grass) — delicious and intriguing to some wine lovers, but too pronounced for others.

Sauvignon Blanc wines are light-bodied to medium-bodied and usually dry. European examples are unoaked more often than oaked, but in California they are often oaky and not fully dry — in the Chardonnay-wanna-be style. Besides herbaceous character (sometimes referred to as *grassy*), Sauvignon Blanc wines display mineral aromas and flavors, vegetal character, or — in warmer climates — fruity character, such as ripe melon.

France has two classic wine regions for the Sauvignon Blanc grape: Bordeaux and the Loire Valley. The Bordeaux wine is called Bordeaux Blanc (white Bordeaux), and the two best-known of the Loire wines are called Sancerre or Pouilly-Fumé (both described in Chapter 10). In Bordeaux, Sauvignon Blanc is sometimes blended with a grape called Sémillon (described in Table 4-1); some of the wines that are blended about 50-50 from the two grapes are among the great white wines of the world. Sauvignon Blanc is also important in regions like California, northeastern Italy, New Zealand, and South Africa.

Pinot Gris/Pinot Grigio

The Pinot Gris grape is one of several grape varieties called *Pinot:* there's Pinot Blanc (white Pinot), Pinot Noir (black Pinot), Pinot Meunier (we don't know how that one translates), and Pinot Gris (gray Pinot). Until about 15 years ago, some people included Chardonnay in this group, calling it Pinot Chardonnay, but we now know that Chardonnay is no relation to the others.

Pinot Gris is believed to have mutated from the black Pinot Noir grape. Although it's considered a white grape, its skin color is unusually dark for a white variety.

Wines made from Pinot Gris can be deeper in color than most white wines — although Italy's Pinot Grigio wines are quite pale. Pinot Gris wines are medium- to full-bodied, with rather low acidity and fairly neutral aromas. Sometimes the flavor and aroma can suggest the skins of fruit, such as peach skins or orange rind.

Going organic

Although just about everyone wants to support the health of the planet, buying organic is easier said than done when it comes to wine. Wine can be considered organic in various ways: It could be made from organically grown grapes, for example, or the winemaking itself could be organic in the sense that chemicals are not used. But is sulfur dioxide — a derivative of elemental sulfur and oxygen — a chemical? Some organizations that accredit organic products permit the use of SO_2 in winemaking (see Chapter 1 for more on sulfur dioxide), while others do not. Until everyone agrees on a definition, organic wine is a moving target.

Pinot Gris is an important grape throughout northeastern Italy and is also present in Germany, where it is called Ruländer. The only region in France where Pinot Gris is important is in Alsace, where it really shows its stuff. Oregon has had good success with Pinot Gris, and some winemakers in California are taking a shot at it.

Gewürztraminer

That's *geh-VAIRTZ-trah-mee-ner*. It's German for "spicy grape from Tramin," a town that's actually located in the German-speaking part of northern Italy. The Italians call their town Termeno, but all the world calls the grape Gewürztraminer.

Gewürztraminer is a wonderfully exotic grape. It makes fairly deep-colored, aromatic white wines. Roses and lychee fruit are the classic descriptors for the aroma of Gewürztraminer wines. To experience Gewürztraminer, try a bottle from Alsace, France. Although the wine smells floral and fruity and has pronounced, exotic fruit and floral flavors, it is actually dry — fascinating and delicious.

The grape Gewürztraminer tends to be high in sugar but low in acid. Its wines are therefore high in alcohol and soft. (Because their acidity is low, these wines age quickly.) Gewürztraminer wines also have high extract, which counterbalances all that softness on the palate. (*Extract* is a particularly difficult wine term to translate; it's the solid matter of the wine left if you were to boil off all the water and anything else that evaporates. On the palate, high extract comes across as an impression of substance and character.)

A best-selling style of Gewürztraminer in the U.S. is light and sweetish, with the grape's flowery aroma and flavor toned down several decibels from the Alsace versions. Dry Gewürztraminer is also made in California and Oregon.

Aliases and a.k.a.'s

The same grape variety will often go by different names in different countries or even in different districts within the same country. Often it's just a case of traditional local synonyms. But sometimes grape growers call one variety by the name of another because they think that's what they're growing (until a specialized botanist called an *ampelographer* examines their vines and tells them otherwise). In California, for example, some of the so-called Pinot Blanc is really another grape entirely: the Melon de Bourgogne. In Chile, much of what grapegrowers call Merlot is really the Carmenère grape — while in the Friuli region of Italy, some of what is called Cabernet Franc is actually Carmenère.

For more tales of viticultural intrigue, read Jancis Robinson's classic book on grape varieties, *Vines, Grapes and Wines* (Alfred A. Knopf), an indispensable and fascinating reference.

Other white grapes

Unfortunately, we don't have room to describe more than a few grapes in any sort of detail. Table 4-1 describes some other grapes whose names you will see on wine labels, or whose wine you could drink in place-name wines without realizing it.

Table 4-1	Other White Grapes and Their Characteristics
Grape Type	*Characteristics*
Chenin Blanc	A noble grape in the Loire Valley of France, for Vouvray and other wines. The best wines have high acidity and a fascinating oily texture (they feel slightly viscous in your mouth). Some good dry Chenin Blanc comes from California, but so does a ton of very ordinary off-dry wine. In South Africa, Chenin Blanc is called *Steen*.
Müller-Thurgau *(MULE-lair TOOR-gow)*	Germany's most-planted grape variety, reportedly a crossing between Riesling and Silvaner. Because its fruit ripens very early, this grape is useful in cool climate regions such as England, New Zealand, northern Italy, and Austria, but its wines can lack character.
Muscat	An aromatic grape that makes Italy's sparkling Asti (which, incidentally, tastes *exactly* like ripe Muscat grapes). Extremely pretty floral aromas. In Alsace, makes a dry wine, and in lots of places (southern France, southern Italy, Australia) makes a delicious sweet dessert wine through the addition of alcohol.

Grape Type	Characteristics
Pinot Blanc	Fairly neutral in aroma and flavors, but with far more character than, say, Trebbiano. High acidity and low sugar levels translate into dry, crisp, medium-bodied wines. Alsace, Austria, northern Italy, and Germany (where it is called Weissburgunder) are the main production zones, with California in the wings.
Sémillon (seh-mee-yohn)	Sauvignon Blanc's blending partner and a good grape in its own right. Sémillon is relatively low in acid (compared to Sauvignon Blanc, anyway) and has attractive but subtle aromas — lanolin sometimes, although it can be slightly herbaceous when it is young. A major grape in Australia, South Africa, and southwestern France, including Bordeaux (where it is the major player in Sauternes).
Trebbiano	Called Ugni Blanc in France. A thoroughly unremarkable grape except that so much Italian white wine is based on it. High acid, light body, neutral aromas, low sugar. Makes wines that provide a useful, neutral background for all sorts of foods.
Viognier (vee-ohn-yay)	A grape from France's Rhône Valley that is becoming popular in California, although quantities are still minuscule. Floral aroma, delicately apricot-like, medium- to full-bodied with low acidity.

A Primer on the Major Red Grape Varieties

Descriptions of 12 important red *vinifera* grape varieties follow. These red grapes differ from one another in their tannin levels, as well as their aromas/flavors and the amount of alcohol they tend to deliver to wines made from them.

The grape varieties described in the following paragraphs are used in wines that carry the grape name, as well as in place-name wines that do not carry a designation of their grape varieties. See Chapter 5 for a chart listing the grape varieties of major place-name wines.

Cabernet Sauvignon

Cabernet Sauvignon is not only a noble grape variety but also an adaptable one, growing well in just about any climate that isn't very cool. It became famous through the age-worthy red wines of the Médoc district of Bordeaux (that usually also contain Merlot and Cabernet Franc, a related grape, in varying proportions; see Chapter 10). But today California is an equally important region for Cabernet Sauvignon — not to mention the rest of the U.S. and vineyards in southern France, Italy, Australia, South Africa, Chile, and so on.

The Cabernet Sauvignon grape makes wines that are high in tannin and are medium- to full-bodied. The textbook descriptor for Cabernet Sauvignon's aroma and flavor is *blackcurrants* or *cassis;* the grape can also contribute vegetal tones to a wine when or where the grapes are less than ideally ripe.

Cabernet Sauvignon is like Chardonnay in that the name alone is a powerful sales device. As a result, there are Cabernet Sauvignon wines at all price and quality levels. The least-expensive versions are usually quite soft — belying the grape's characterization as tannic — and nondescriptly fruity (not specifically blackcurrants), with medium body at best. The best wines are rich and firm with great depth and classic Cabernet flavor. *Serious* Cabernet Sauvignons can age for 15 years or more.

Because Cabernet Sauvignon is fairly tannic (and because of the blending precedent in Bordeaux), the wine is often blended with other grapes; usually Merlot — being less tannic — is considered an ideal partner. In Australia, there is an unusual practice of blending Cabernet Sauvignon with Syrah. (More on that in "Odd couples" in Chapter 13.)

Cabernet Sauvignon often goes by just its first name, Cabernet (although there are other Cabernets) or even by its nickname, *Cab.*

Merlot

Deep color, full body, high alcohol, and low tannin are the characteristics of wines made from the Merlot grape. The aromas and flavors can be plummy or sometimes chocolatey.

Merlot — not Cabernet Sauvignon — is actually the most-planted grape variety in Bordeaux. But Merlot's history in that region is shorter. The legendary Bordeaux wines of the 19th century were Cabernet-dominant blends. Not until after World War II did the Merlot-dominant wines of Bordeaux's Right Bank (the eastern part of Bordeaux) gain prominence — and Merlot with them (more on Bordeaux in Chapter 10).

Merlot is much easier to like than Cabernet Sauvignon because it is less tannic. (But some winemakers feel that Merlot is not satisfactory in its own right, and it is thus often blended with Cabernet Sauvignon, Cabernet Franc, or both.)

Besides Bordeaux, Merlot is important in Washington state, California, the Long Island district of New York, northeastern Italy, and, increasingly, Chile.

Pinot Noir

The late Andre Tchelitscheff, the legendary winemaker of some of California's finest Cabernets, once told us that if he could do it all over again, he'd make Pinot Noir instead of Cab. He's probably not alone. While Cabernet is the sensible wine to make — a good, steady, reliable wine that doesn't give the winemaker too much trouble and can achieve excellent quality — Pinot Noir is finicky, troublesome, enigmatic, and challenging. But a great Pinot Noir can be one of the greatest wines ever.

The prototype for Pinot Noir wine is red Burgundy, from France, where tiny vineyard plots yield rare treasures of wine from 100 percent Pinot Noir. Oregon and California also produce good Pinot Noir. But Pinot Noir's production is rather limited, because this variety is very particular about climate and soil.

Pinot Noir wine is lighter in color than Cabernet or Merlot wine. It has relatively high alcohol, medium-to-high acidity, and medium-to-low tannin (although oak barrels can contribute additional tannin to the wine). Its flavors and aromas can be very fruity — often like a melange of red berries — or earthy and woodsy depending on how it is grown and/or vinified.

Syrah/Shiraz

The northern part of France's Rhône Valley is the classic site of greatness for the Syrah grape, and Rhône wines like Hermitage and Côte-Rôtie are the inspiration for its dissemination to Australia, California, South Africa, and Italy.

Syrah produces deeply colored wines with full body, firm tannin, and aromas/flavors that can suggest smoked meat, roasted peppers, tar, or even burnt rubber (believe it or not). In Australia, though, Syrah (called Shiraz) is made in a broad range of styles — some of them soft, medium-bodied wines with strawberry-like flavor that are quite the opposite of the northern Rhône's majestic Syrahs. Turn to "Winemaking, grapes, and terroir," in Chapter 13 for more on Shiraz.

Syrah doesn't require any other grape to complement its flavors, although in Australia it is commonly blended with Cabernet.

Zinfandel

White Zinfandel is such a popular wine — and so much better known than the red version of Zinfandel — that its fans might argue that Zinfandel is not a red grape. But — it is so!

Zinfandel is one of the oldest grapes in California; therefore, Zinfandel has a certain stature there. Its aura is enhanced by its mysterious history: Although Zinfandel is clearly a vinifera grape and not a native American variety, authorities are uncertain where it really came from. The current theory suggests that Zinfandel came from the Dalmatian region of Croatia.

Zin — as devotees of red Zinfandel call it — is a rich, deeply colored wine that is high in alcohol and medium to high in tannin. It can have a blackberry or raspberry aroma and flavor, a spicy character, or even a jammy flavor. There are Zins that are meant to be enjoyed young, and serious Zins that are built for aging. (You can tell which is which by the price.)

Nebbiolo

This noble grape is short on adaptability. Outside of scattered sites in northwestern Italy — mainly the Piedmont region — Nebbiolo just doesn't make remarkable wine. But the extraordinary quality of Barolo and Barbaresco, two Piedmont wines, prove what greatness it can achieve under the right conditions.

The Nebbiolo grape is high in both tannin and acid, which can make a wine tough. Fortunately, it also gives enough alcohol to soften the package. Its color can be deep when the wine is young, but can develop orangey tinges within a few years. Its aroma is fruity (strawberry and jam), earthy and woodsy (tar, truffles), and herbal (mint, eucalyptus).

Lighter versions of Nebbiolo are meant to be drunk when young (the wine, not you) — wines labeled Nebbiolo d'Alba, Roero, or Nebbiolo delle Langhe, for example — while Barolo and Barbaresco are wines that really deserve a *minimum* of six years' age before drinking.

Sangiovese

This Italian grape has proven itself in the Tuscany region of Italy, especially in the Brunello di Montalcino and Chianti districts, and is increasingly popular in California. Sangiovese makes wines that are medium to high in acidity and medium in tannin; the wines can be light-bodied to full-bodied, depending on exactly where the grapes grew and how the wine was made. The aromas and flavors of the wines are fruity — especially cherry, often tart cherry — with floral nuances of violets and sometimes a slightly nutty character.

Tempranillo

Tempranillo is Spain's candidate for greatness. It gives wines deep color, low acidity, and only moderate alcohol. However, much of the color can be lost to extended wood aging and blending with varieties that lack color, such as Grenache, as is the practice in Spain's Rioja district.

Other red grapes

Table 4-2 describes additional red grape varieties that you could encounter, either as varietal wines or as the basis of wines that are named for their place of production.

Table 4-2	Other Red Grapes and Their Characteristics
Grape Type	*Characteristics*
Aglianico	Little known outside of southern Italy, where it makes Taurasi and other age-worthy, powerful red wines.
Barbera	Italian grape that, oddly for a red grape, has little tannin but very high acidity. When fully ripe it can give big, fruity wines with refreshing crispness. Lately, producers are aging the wine in new oak to increase the tannin level of their wine.
Gamay	Excels in the Beaujolais district of France. It makes grapey wines that are deep in color and relatively low in tannin. Neither the grape called *Gamay Beaujolais* in California nor the grape called *Napa Gamay* is true Gamay.
Grenache	A Spanish grape by origin, called Garnacha there. (Most wine drinkers associate Grenache with France's southern Rhône Valley more than with Spain, however.) Sometimes Grenache makes light-colored wines that are high in alcohol but not much else. Under the right circumstances, Grenache can make deeply colored wines with velvety texture and fruity aromas and flavors suggestive of raspberries.

Chapter 5

Is It a Grape? Is It a Place?

- -

In This Chapter

▶ Hidden information behind wine names

▶ The myth of varietal wines

▶ The secret cult of *terroir*

▶ Branded wines, generics, and proprietary names

- -

We remember a cartoon in *The New Yorker* in 1980 that depicted the students of a private New York City nursery school lined up for their class picture. The caption identified the children only by their first names. Every girl was Jennifer, and every boy was Scott.

When you walk into a wine shop these days, you'd think that the people who name wines have the same fixation as the parents of those nursery school children. More than half the white wines are named *Chardonnay,* and the majority of the red wines are named either *Cabernet Sauvignon* or *Merlot.*

Actually, one Chardonnay is no more identical to the next than one little Jennifer is identical to the next Jennifer. But to distinguish one Chardonnay from the other (without opening the bottles, that is), you need more information. You need to read the rest of the label.

What's in a Name

All sorts of names can appear on wine labels. These names often include

- The name of the *grape* from which the wine was made
- A *brand name,* which is often the name of the company or person that made the wine (who is called the *producer*)
- Sometimes a special, invented name for that particular wine (called a *proprietary name*)
- The name of the *place,* or *places,* where the grapes were grown (such as the wine region and/or the name of the specific vineyard property)

Then there's the *vintage* year (the year the grapes were harvested), which is part of the wine's identity; and sometimes you see a descriptor like *reserve,* which either has specific legal meaning or means nothing at all, depending on where the wine came from.

In this age of full disclosure, the more enlightened the producer, the more information he will give you on the wine label. Good winemakers want you to know that they have nothing to hide. Think twice when you encounter a wine label that tells you next to nothing about the wine. Chances are, the producer is trying to fool you into thinking that the wine is something it's not.

Veteran wine lovers appreciate the detailed information on wine labels because they know how to interpret it. But to anyone who is just discovering wine, the information embodied in wine names is more confusing than enlightening. We'd all agree that little Jennifer needs more than just the name *Jennifer* to identify herself in the world (unless she plans to become a rock star or comedienne), but does she really need the equivalent of: Jennifer Smith, "Jenny," Caucasian female, upper middle-class, produced by Don and Louise Smith, New York City, Upper West Side, 1980?

Of course she doesn't. But — we know you don't want to hear this — for bottles of wine the answer, frankly, is yes.

The Wine Name Game

Most of the wines that you find in your wine shop or on restaurant wine lists are named in one of two basic ways: either for their *grape variety* or for the *place where the grapes grew.* That information, plus the name of the producer, becomes the shorthand name we use in talking about the wine.

Robert Mondavi Winery Cabernet Sauvignon, for example, is a wine made by Robert Mondavi Winery and named after the Cabernet Sauvignon grape. Ruffino Chianti Classico is a wine made by the Ruffino winery and named after the place called Chianti Classico.

You might recognize some names as grape names (see Chapter 4) and other names as place-names right off the bat; but if you don't, don't panic. That information is the kind of thing you can look up. (Chapters 10 through 16 will help.)

Hello, my name is Chardonnay

A *varietal* wine is a wine that is named after either the *principal* or the *sole* grape variety that makes up the wine.

Each country (and in the U.S., some individual states) has laws that dictate the minimum percentage of the named grape that a wine must contain if that wine wants to call itself by a grape name. The issue is truth in advertising.

For California wines, the legal minimum percentage of the named grape is 75 percent (which means that your favorite California Chardonnay could have as much as 25 percent of some *other* grape in it). In Washington — and most of the rest of the U.S., for that matter — it's 75 percent. In Oregon, the minimum is 90 percent (except for Cabernet, which can be 75 percent). In Australia, it's 85 percent. And in the countries that form the European Union (EU), the minimum is 85 percent.

Some varietal wines are made *entirely* from the grape variety for which the wine is named. There's no law against that anywhere. The minimum percentage is what the laws concern themselves with.

Why name a wine after a grape variety

Grapes are the raw material of a wine. Except for whatever a wine absorbs from oak barrels (certain aromas and flavors, as well as tannin) and from certain winemaking processes described in Chapter 3, the juice of the grapes is what any wine *is*. So to name a wine after the grape it came from is very logical.

Naming a wine after its grape variety is also very satisfying to exacting consumers. Knowing what grape a wine is made from is akin to knowing what type of oil is in the salad dressing, how many grams of fat are in the soup, and whether the egg roll contains any MSG. Just the facts, ma'am.

On some unconscious level, naming a wine after its grape variety also appeals to our sense of fairness. Chardonnay is Chardonnay, and one nation's Chardonnay is as good as the next nation's Chardonnay. In the hierarchical world of wine, where some countries are accorded more prestige than others by virtue of their history, varietal wines are inherently egalitarian and class-less (as in "classless society," not "this wine has no class").

Varietal wines are not an American invention — but they might as well be, considering how prevalent such names are in the U.S. and how well varietal wines do at the cash register. Most California (and New York and Washington and Oregon) wines carry varietal names. Likewise, most Australian, South American, and South African wines are named using the *principal* principle. Even some countries that don't normally name their wines after grapes, like France, are jumping on the varietal-name bandwagon for certain wines that they especially want to sell to Americans.

A common perception among most wine lovers is that a varietal wine is somehow *better* than a non-varietal. Although we understand how that perception came to be, we believe it has gotten entirely out of hand. The fact that a wine is named after its principal grape variety is absolutely *no indication of quality*.

The varietal name game

For several decades after Prohibition was repealed in 1933, most American wines were named after types of European wines, such as Chianti, Burgundy, Champagne, and Chablis. (Some still are, but their numbers are fading fast.) The wines didn't necessarily resemble *real* Chianti, Burgundy, Champagne or Chablis — that is, the wines that really come from those places — but the names were familiar and understandable to the people who bought the wine. There were — and still are — no prohibitions over derivative names like these. Today, we call such names *generic.* (To read more about generic wines, turn to the "Generic wines" section at the end of this chapter.)

Rumor has it that some wineries used to bottle the same wine under a couple of different labels. A customer would buy either Chianti or Burgundy according to personal preference, but they were both the same wine! We're too young to have any personal knowledge of all this, but we wouldn't be surprised if it were true.

When California wineries began naming their wines after grape varieties several decades ago, intelligent wine drinkers all over America began to feel more comfortable with the wines. Even if, in those days, the law said the wine had to contain only 51 percent of the named grape, we felt that we were drinking Known Entities rather than some labeling gimmick.

The wineries that used varietal names in those days were the most avant-garde wineries around, which usually meant that they produced the best wines. Varietal wines were, almost by definition, better, more genuine, and more interesting than generic wines.

Now, varietal wines are commonplace. When you buy a wine named after a grape variety today, you are *not* necessarily getting a wine on the cutting edge of the quality wine movement. You definitely *are* getting a wine made by someone who knows the selling power of a varietal name. And you are still getting the same cozy feeling from knowing exactly what you are drinking.

Hello, my name is Bordeaux

Unlike American wines, most European wines are named for the *region* (place) where they are made rather than for their grape variety. Many of the European wines are made from precisely the same grape varieties as American wines (like Chardonnay, Cabernet Sauvignon, Sauvignon Blanc, and so on), but they don't say so on the label. Instead, the labels say Burgundy, Bordeaux, Sancerre, and so on: the *place* where those grapes grow.

Is this some nefarious plot to make wine incomprehensible to English-only wine lovers who have never visited Europe and flunked geography in grade school?

The most common place-names

Bardolino	Chianti	Rioja
Beaujolais	Côtes du Rhône	Sancerre
Bordeaux	Mosel	Sauternes
Burgundy (Bourgogne)	Port (Porto)	Sherry
Chablis	Pouilly-Fuissé	Soave
Champagne	Rhine (Rheingau, Rheinhessen)	Valpolicella

Au contraire! The European system of naming wines is actually intended to provide more information about each wine and more understanding of what's in the bottle than varietal naming provides. The only catch is that you have to learn something about the different regions from which the wines come. (Turn to Chapters 10 through 14 for some of that information.)

Why name a wine after a place?

Grapes, the raw material of wine, have to grow somewhere. Depending on the type of soil, the amount of sunshine, the amount of rain, the slope of the hill, and the many other characteristics that each *somewhere* has, the grapes can be different. If the grapes are different, the wine is different. Each wine, therefore, reflects the place where the grapes are grown.

When we say *the grapes can be different* according to where they're grown, we mean two things. First, the same grape variety, such as Chardonnay, can turn out differently when it is planted in two different places. The same variety can get riper in one place than the other, for example (the riper grapes make a wine higher in alcohol with riper fruit flavors), or the grapes (and wine) can have some subtle, unusual flavors — such as mineral flavors — attributable to a particular place. In one way or another, the place will *always* affect the character of the grapes.

Second, in two different places you very well might grow different grape varieties. Even if business sense dictates that you always plant Chardonnay because Chardonnay wines are so popular, that variety might not be the grape best suited to a particular piece of land with the climate and soil that land has (and had and always will have). So you'd have to plant a different grape, which, naturally, makes a different wine.

In Europe, where grape growers/winemakers have had centuries to figure out which grape grows best where, they have systematized most of their grape/location match-ups and codified them into law. Therefore, the name of a *place* where they grow grapes and make wine in Europe automatically connotes the grape (or grapes) used to make the wine of that place. The label on the bottle usually doesn't tell you the grape (or grapes), though. Which brings us back to our original question: Is this some kind of nefarious plot to make wine incomprehensible to non-Europeans?

Decoding common European place-names

Wine Name	Country	Grape Varieties
Bardolino	Italy	Corvina, Molinara, Rondinella*
Beaujolais	France	Gamay
Bordeaux (red)	France	Cabernet Sauvignon, Merlot, Cabernet Franc, and others*
Bordeaux (white)	France	Sauvignon Blanc, Sémillon, Muscadelle*
Burgundy (red)	France	Pinot Noir
Burgundy (white)	France	Chardonnay
Chablis	France	Chardonnay
Champagne	France	Chardonnay, Pinot Noir, Pinot Meunier*
Châteauneuf-du-Pape	France	Grenache, Mourvèdre, Syrah, and others*
Chianti	Italy	Sangiovese, Canaiolo, and others*
Côtes du Rhône	France	Grenache, Mourvèdre, Carignan, and others*
Mosel	Germany	Riesling or others (named on label)
Port (Porto)	Portugal	Touriga Nacional, Tinta Barroca, Touriga Francesa, Tinta Roriz, Tinto Cão, and others*
Pouilly-Fuissé	France	Chardonnay
Rhine (Rheingau, Rheinhessen)	Germany	Riesling or others (named on label)
Rioja (red)	Spain	Tempranillo, Grenache, and others*
Sancerre	France	Sauvignon Blanc
Sauternes	France	Sémillon, Sauvignon Blanc*
Sherry	Spain	Palomino
Soave	Italy	Garganega and others*
Valpolicella	Italy	Corvina, Molinara, Rondinella*

*Indicates that a blend of grapes is used to make these wines.

The terroir name game

Terroir (pronounced *ter wahr*) is a French word that has no direct translation in English, so wine people just use the French word, for expediency (not for snobbery).

There's no fixed definition of *terroir;* it's a concept, and, like most concepts, people tend to define it more broadly or more narrowly to suit their own needs. The word itself is based on the French word *terre,* which means soil; so some people define *terroir* as, simply, dirt (as in "Our American dirt is every bit as good as their French dirt").

But *terroir* is really much more complex (or complicated) than just dirt. *Terroir* is the combination of immutable natural factors — such as topsoil, subsoil, climate (sun, rain, wind, and so on), the slope of the hill, and altitude — that a particular vineyard site has. Chances are, no two vineyards in the entire world have precisely the same combination of these factors. So we consider *terroir* to be the *unique* combination of natural factors that a particular vineyard site has.

Terroir is the guiding principle behind the European concept that wines should be named after the place they come from (thought we'd gotten off the track, didn't you?). The name of the place connotes which grapes were used to make the wine of that place (because the grapes are dictated by law) — the thinking goes — and the place influences the character of those grapes in its own unique way. Therefore, the most accurate name that a wine can have is the name of the place where its grapes were grown, not the name of its grapes.

It's not some nefarious plot; it's just a whole different way of looking at things.

Place-names on American wine labels

France might have invented the concept that wines should be named after their place of origin, but neither France nor even greater Europe has a monopoly on the idea. Wine labels from countries outside of Europe can also tell you where a wine is made — usually by featuring a place-name (called an *appellation of origin* in Winespeak) somewhere on the label. But there are a few differences.

First of all, on an American wine label (or an Australian or Chilean or South African label, for that matter) you have to go to some effort to find the place-name on the label. The place of origin is not the fundamental name of the wine (as it is for most European wines); the grape usually is.

Second, place-names in the U.S. mean far less than they do in Europe. Okay, if the label says Napa Valley, and you've visited that area — and you loved eating at Mustards, and you'd like to spend the rest of your life in one of those houses atop a hill off the Silverado Trail — Napa Valley will mean something to you. But *legally,* the name Napa Valley only means that at least 85 percent of the grapes came from an area defined by law as the Napa Valley wine zone. The name Napa Valley does not define the type of wine that can be made, nor does it imply specific grape varieties, the way a European place-name does. (Good thing the grape name is there, as big as day, on the label.)

Place names on labels of non-European wines, for the most part, merely pay lip service to the concept of *terroir.* For example, some non-European appellations are ridiculously broad. We have to laugh when we think how the typical European winemaker must react to all those wine labels that announce a wine's place of origin simply as *California.*

Great. This label says that this wine comes from a specific area that is 30 percent larger than the entire country of Italy! Some specific area! (Italy has almost 300 specific wine areas.)

When the place on the label is merely *California,* in fact, that information tells you next to nothing about the wine. California's a big place, and those grapes could come from just about anywhere. Same thing for all those Australian wines labeled *South Eastern Australia* — an area only slightly smaller than France and Spain *combined.*

Wines named in other ways

Now and then, you might come across a wine that is named for neither its grape variety nor its region of origin. Such wines usually fall into three categories: *branded wines, wines with proprietary names,* or *generic wines.*

Bigger than a bread basket

When we travel to other countries, we realize that people in different places have different ways of perceiving space and distance. If someone tells us that we'll find a certain restaurant "just up ahead," for example, we figure it's the equivalent of about three blocks away — but they might mean three miles.

Discussing place names for European wines can be just as problematic. Some of the *places*

are as small as several acres, some are 100-square miles big, and others are the size of New Jersey. Certain words used to describe wine zones suggest the relative size of the place. In descending order of size and ascending order of specificity: country, region, district, subdistrict, commune, vineyard.

Grape names on European wines

Although most European wines are named after their place of production, grape names do sometimes appear on labels of European wines.

In Italy, for example, several place-names routinely have grape-names appended to them — the name Trentino (place) Pinot Grigio (grape) is an example. Or the official name of a wine could be a combination of place and grape — like the name Barbera d'Alba, which translates as Barbera (grape) of Alba (place).

In France, some producers have deliberately added the grape name to their labels even though the grape is already implicit in the wine

name. For example, a white Bourgogne (place-name) might also have the word Chardonnay (grape) on the label, for those wine drinkers who don't know that white Bourgogne is 100 percent Chardonnay. (This practice is likely to be prohibited by French authorities in the future, however, probably because it goes against the grain of tradition.)

And German wines often carry grape names along with their official place-names.

But even if a European wine does carry a grape name, the most important part of the wine's name, in the eyes of the people who make the wine, is the place.

Branded wines

Most wines have brand names, including those wines that are named after their grape variety — like Simi (brand name) Sauvignon Blanc (grape) — and those that are named after their region of origin — like Bolla (brand name) Soave (place). These brand names are usually the name of the company that made the wine, called a *winery*. Because most wineries make several different wines, the brand name itself is not specific enough to be the actual name of the wine.

But sometimes a wine has *only* a brand name. For example, the label says *Salamandre* and *red French wine* but provides little other identification.

Wines that have *only* a brand name on them, with no indication of grape or of place — other than the country of production — are generally the most inexpensive, ordinary wines you can get. If they're from a European Union country, they won't even be *vintage dated* (that is, there won't be any indication of what year the grapes were harvested) because EU law does not allow such wines the privilege of carrying a vintage date.

Wines with proprietary names

You can find some pretty creative names on wine bottles these days: Tapestry, Conundrum, Insignia, Cardinale, Isosceles, Mythology, Trilogy. Is this stuff to drink, to drive, or to dab behind your ears?

Names like these are *proprietary names* (often trademarked) that producers create for special wines. In the case of American wines, the bottles with proprietary names usually contain wines made from a *blend* of grapes; therefore, no one grape name can be used as the name of the wine. (Remember California's 75 percent policy?) In the case of European wines, the grapes used to make the wine were probably not the approved grapes for that region, and the regional name could, therefore, not be used on the label.

Although a brand name can apply to several different wines, a proprietary name usually applies to one specific wine. You can find Zinfandel, Cabernet Sauvignon, Chardonnay, and numerous other wines under the Fetzer brand from California, for example, and you can find Beaujolais, Pouilly-Fuissé, Mâcon-Villages and numerous other wines under the Louis Jadot brand from France. But the proprietary name Luce applies to a single wine.

A producer who creates a wine with a proprietary name has high-minded motives. He is driven by artistic impulse, intellectual curiosity, or sheer ego to form a wine that surpasses the norm for his part of the world. He develops the wine personally, nurses it to maturity, and then dresses it up in the best possible package so that all the world can see how fine the expression of his art, intellect, or ego is. The price tag on the bottle confirms the magnitude of his endeavor.

Wines with proprietary names are usually made in small quantities, are quite expensive ($20 to $75 a bottle), and are, in fact, at a high level of quality. They particularly satisfy wine lovers who must be the first in their crowd to taste the newest, most unusual wines. Sometimes they draw rave reviews from the critics and end up as established successes that endure in the marketplace. Sometimes they take the route of old soldiers.

Generic wines

A generic name is a wine name that has been used inappropriately for so long that it has lost its original meaning in the eyes of the government (exactly what Xerox, Kleenex, and Band-Aid are afraid of becoming).

Burgundy, Chianti, Chablis, Champagne, Rhine wine, Sherry, Port, and Sauterne are all names that rightfully should apply only to wines made in the specific places that those names imply. But these names have been usurped by very large and powerful wine companies. So now both the U.S. and Canadian governments recognize these names as broad *types* of wine rather than as wines from specific regions.

Most California wines carried generic names until the late '60s or early '70s when varietals came into vogue. Generics are still around, but they are less popular in the marketplace with every passing year.

When you buy a generic wine, you have absolutely no idea what you are getting except that it is a piece of history.

Part II
Close Encounters of the Wine Kind

The 5th Wave   By Rich Tennant

In this part . . .

Now that you know such basics as grape varieties, wine types, and wine names, you're ready to apply your knowledge at the practical level. Corkscrews, wine glasses, restaurant wine lists, and wine shops won't be any challenge at all, once you get the hang of them — by browsing through the pages of the chapters that follow. Even all those technical terms on wine labels will become as clear as day.

Chapter 6
Navigating a Wine Shop

· ·

· ·

*U*nless you enjoy a permanent, dependent relationship with an indulgent and knowledgeable wine lover, the day will come when you have to purchase a bottle of wine yourself. If you're lucky, the shop owner will just happen to be some enlightened fellow whose life purpose is to make good wine easy and accessible to others. If you're lucky, you'll also be awarded an honorary doctorate from Harvard and receive a tax-free inheritance from a great aunt you've never met. The odds are about equal.

Buying Wine Can Intimidate Anyone

Common sense suggests that buying a few bottles of wine should be less stressful than, say, applying for a bank loan or interviewing for a new job. What's the big deal? It's only grape juice.

But memories tell us otherwise. There was the time the wine shop wouldn't take back one of the two bottles of inexpensive German wine that we bought the week before, even when we explained how awful the first bottle had been. (Were *we* wrong about the wine or were *they* arrogant? We wasted days wondering.) And the time we pretended we knew what we were doing and bought a full case — 12 bottles — of a French wine based on the brand's general reputation, not realizing that the particular vintage we purchased was a miserable aberration from the brand's usual quality. (Why didn't we just *ask* someone in the store?) Then there was all that time we spent staring at shelves lined with bottles whose labels might as well have been written in Greek, for all that we could understand from them.

Fortunately, our enthusiasm for wine caused us to persevere. We eventually discovered that wine shopping can be fun. We also discovered a strange thing about bottles of fermented grape juice: The prospect of buying or selling them can turn normally kind and sensitive individuals into victimizers or victims, depending on whether they are trying to show off what they know or are trying to hide what they don't know. But it doesn't have to be that way.

Too much information about wine is constantly changing — new vintages each year, hundreds of new wineries, new wines, advances in wine technology, and so on — for *anyone* to presume that he knows it all or for anyone to feel insecure about what he doesn't know.

Our experience has taught us that the single most effective way to assure yourself of more good experiences than bad ones in buying wine is to come to terms with your knowledge — or lack thereof — of the subject. If we'd all quit pretending that we know more than we do and give up our defensiveness about what we don't know, buying wine would become the simple exchange that it should be.

Where Wine Is Sold

There are four really great things about buying wine in a store to drink later at home. Stores usually have a much bigger selection of wines than restaurants. The wine is less expensive than in restaurants. You can touch the bottles and compare the labels. And the guy who sells the wine to you can't watch you or listen to what you say when you're drinking it.

On the other hand, you have to provide your own wine glasses, and you have to open the bottle yourself (see Chapter 8 for the lowdown on all that). And that big selection can be downright daunting.

You can buy wine at all sorts of stores: supermarkets, wine superstores, discount warehouses, or small specialty wine shops. Each type of store has its own advantages and disadvantages in terms of selection, price, or service.

Because wine is a regulated beverage in many countries, governments often get involved in deciding where and how wine may be sold (and sometimes even when). So you will have more or fewer choices of where to buy your wine depending on where you live.

Some states within the U.S. and some provinces in Canada have raised government control of alcoholic beverage sales to a fine art. Some states and provinces not only decide *where* you can buy wine, but they also decide *which wines* will be available for you to buy. If you love wine and you live in one of those areas (you know who you are), take comfort in the fact that a) you have a vote; b) freedom of choice lies just across the border; and c) if the Berlin Wall could topple and Communist Russia could change, there's hope for your local government, too.

We'll assume a healthy, open-minded, free-market economy for wine in our discussion of retail wine sales. We hope that scenario applies where you live, because your enjoyment of wine will blossom all the more easily if it does.

Supermarkets

In truly *open* wine markets, you can buy wine in supermarkets, like any other food product. Supermarkets make wine accessible to everyone. If you can buy what it takes to make a meal, you can buy a bottle of wine to drink with the meal.

When wine is sold in supermarkets, the mystique surrounding the product evaporates. (Who can waste time feeling insecure about a wine purchase when there are much more critical issues at hand, such as how much time is left before the kids turn into monsters and which is the shortest line at the checkout?) And the prices, especially in large stores, are usually quite reasonable.

We know for a fact that some people in the wine business disapprove of the straightforward attitude toward wine in supermarkets; to them, wine is sacrosanct and should always be treated like an elite beverage. At least you won't run into *them* as you browse the wine aisles in your supermarket.

Discount warehouses and superstores

Some stores sell wine on the scale of a supermarket, but they aren't supermarkets, strictly speaking. Most discount warehouse chains fall into this category. Along with your wine, you can pick up any spirits, beer, carbonated beverages, snack foods, or party supplies that you need. The stores are large and their prices are usually quite good.

If you choose to buy your wine at a supermarket or discount warehouse, you'll usually enjoy a large selection, a no-nonsense attitude, and affordable prices — maybe even the best prices in town.

On the downside, you might feel shortchanged in terms of service. In large, self-service operations, you can have difficulty finding someone to provide knowledgeable advice. More likely than not, you are on your own.

To guide you on your solo journey, there will be plenty of *shelf-talkers* (small signs on the shelves that describe individual wines). But the shelf-talkers should be taken with a large grain of salt. They are usually provided by the company selling the wine, which is more interested in convincing you to grab a bottle than in offering you information to help you understand the wine. Flowery phrases, hyperbolic adjectives, and safe, common-denominator stuff like "delicious with chicken" (*any* chicken, cooked in *any* way?) are what you're most likely to find. The information will be biased and of limited value.

Another downside of supermarkets and discount warehouses is that the seemingly limitless selection of wines is often actually somewhat limited. Most of the wines in these stores are wines produced in large enough quantities to support chain stores sales. Nothing is wrong with that, unless you're looking for one of those special, limited production wines that wine lovers spend hours discussing in hushed tones. (Of course, those special wines just wouldn't taste as good anyway if they were purchased someplace that didn't shroud them with elitism!)

The bottom line is that supermarkets and discount warehouses can be great places to buy everyday wine for casual enjoyment. But if what you really want is to learn about wine as you buy it, or if you want an unusually interesting variety of wines to satisfy your rapacious curiosity, you will probably find yourself shopping elsewhere.

Of course, exceptions do exist: The Wine Club in San Francisco (and other locations) and Wine House in Los Angeles are two large discount stores that do offer knowledgeable service as well as an excellent variety of fine wines at reasonable prices. And a few more such high-end discount stores are starting to appear across the U.S.

Wine specialty shops

Wine specialty shops are small- to medium-sized stores that sell wine and liquor and sometimes wine books, corkscrews (see Chapter 8 for more on those), wine glasses, and maybe a few specialty foods. The foods sold in wine shops tend to be gourmet items rather than just run-of-the-mill snack foods.

If you decide to pursue wine as a serious hobby, shops like these are the ones where you'll probably end up buying your wine because they offer many advantages that larger operations cannot. For one thing, wine specialty shops almost always have some wine-knowledgeable staffer on the premises. Also, you can usually find an interesting, varied selection of wines at all price levels.

Supermarket survival tips

If you're shopping in a supermarket where there's no one to turn to for advice, do one of the following:

1. Try to remember the names of the recommended wines in the last wine article you read. Bring the article or list with you. Or better yet, bring a copy of our buying guide, *Wine Buying Companion For Dummies,* published by IDG Books Worldwide, Inc., which describes over 500 recommended wines. It's small enough to carry with you (see the sidebar "Going armed to the wine shop — the wine buying guide" just ahead).

2. Go to the telephone and call a wine-knowledgeable friend, or, better yet, bring him or her with you (assuming that his or her palate and yours get along).

3. Buy the wine with the prettiest label. What have you got to lose?

Inside the wine shop

Wine shops often organize their wines by country of origin and — in the case of classic wine countries, such as France — by region (for example, Bordeaux, Burgundy, Rhône, and so on). Red wines and white wines are often in separate sections within these country areas. There might be a special section for Champagnes and other sparkling wines and another section for dessert wines.

In some wine shops, there is a special area (or even a special *room*) for the *finer* or more expensive wines. In some stores, it's a locked vault-like room. In other stores, it's the whole back area of the store.

Over in a corner somewhere, often right by the door to accommodate quick purchases, there's usually a *cold box,* a refrigerated cabinet with glass doors where bottles of best-selling white and sparkling wines sit. Unless you really *must* have an ice-cold bottle of wine *immediately* (the two of you have just decided to elope, the marriage minister is a mile down the road, and the wedding toast is only ten minutes away), avoid the cold box. The wines in there are usually too cold and therefore might not be in good condition.

Near the front of the store you might also see boxes or bins of special *sale* wines. These sale displays are usually topped with *case cards* — large cardboard signs that stand above the open boxes of wine — or similar descriptive material. Our words of caution on the credibility of shelf-talkers apply to case cards, too; but because case cards are a lot bigger, there's more of a chance that some useful information might appear on them.

> ## Going armed to the wine shop — the wine buying guide
>
> You might feel more secure if you arm yourself for wine shopping — with a *wine buying guide,* a book with descriptions and ratings of specific wines that you can buy.
>
> A number of fine wine buying guides are available, not only in book stores, but also in some wine shops. Our favorite? Naturally, it's our own *Wine Buying Companion For Dummies* (IDG Books Worldwide, Inc.). It looks exactly like this book, but it's smaller, 5¹/₂-x-8¹/₂ inches, so that you can conveniently tuck it in your purse or briefcase. In it, we describe and rate 540 of our favorite wines from around the world; chapters are divided by price categories, wine regions, and type (red, white, or sparkling), and a useful index lists all of the wines in the book, for quick reference.
>
> Wine-buying guides are particularly useful if you have no expert to rely on in your local shop — but they're also fun to use in planning your wine purchases before you even get to the shop.

Choosing the Right Wine Merchant

It's as simple to size up a wine merchant as it is to size up any other specialty retailer. The main criteria are *price, selection, expertise,* and *service.* Also, the conditions in which a shop stores its wines are paramount.

No such species in your neighborhood? In Chapter 17, we talk about the advantages and disadvantages of buying wine by catalog, telephone, mail, or the Internet, which can be good alternatives if you don't have access to a decent wine shop where you live.

Price

When you're a novice wine buyer, your best strategy is to shop around with an eye to service and reliable advice more than to price. After you've found a merchant who has suggested several wines that you've liked, stick with him, even if he doesn't have the best prices in town. It makes better sense to pay a dollar or so more for wines that are recommended by a reliable merchant (wines that you'll probably like) than to buy wines in a cut-rate or discount store and save a buck, especially if that store has no special wine adviser or if the advice you receive is suspect.

When you have more knowledge of wine, you'll have enough confidence to shop at stores with the best prices. But even then, price must take a backseat to the storage conditions of the wine (see "Wine storage conditions" later in this chapter).

Selection

You won't necessarily know on your first visit whether a particular store's selection is adequate for you. If you notice many wines from many different countries at various prices, give the store's selection the benefit of the doubt. If you outgrow the selection as you learn more about wine, you can seek out a new merchant at that point.

Expertise

Don't be too ready to give a merchant the benefit of the doubt when it comes to expertise. Some retailers are not only extremely knowledgeable about the specific wines they sell, but also extremely knowledgeable about wine in general. But some retailers know less than their customers. Just as you expect a butcher to know his cuts of meat, you should expect a wine merchant to know a lot more about wine than most of his customers do! Be free with your questions (such as, "Can you tell me something about this wine?" or "How are these two wines different?") and judge how willing and able he is to answer them.

Expect a wine merchant to have *personal* knowledge and experience of the wines he sells. These days, lots of retailers use the ratings of a few critics as a crutch in selling wines. They plaster their shelves with the critics' scores (usually a number like 90 on a scale of 100) and advertise their wines by these numbers (see "Wine magazines" and "Wine newsletters" in Chapter 18). We agree that selling by the numbers is one quick way of communicating an approximate sense of the wine's quality (remember, that doesn't mean you'll *like* the wine!). But the retailer's knowledge and experience of the wines simply must go beyond the critic's scores, or he's not doing his job properly.

Service

Most knowledgeable wine merchants pride themselves in their ability to guide you through the maze of wine selections and help you find a wine that you will like. Trust a merchant's advice at least once or twice and see if his choices are good ones. If he's not flexible enough — or knowledgeable enough — to suggest wine that suits your needs, obviously you need another merchant. All it will have cost you is the price of a bottle or two of wine. A bit less costly than choosing the wrong doctor or lawyer!

Speaking of service, any reputable wine merchant will accept a bottle back from you if he has made a poor recommendation or if the wine seems damaged. After all, he wants to keep you as a customer. But with the privilege comes responsibility: Be reasonable. You should only return an *open* bottle if you think the wine is defective (and then the bottle should be mostly full!). Hold on to the store's receipt. And don't wait several months before returning an unopened bottle of wine. By that time, the store might have a hard time getting its money back from the wholesaler. After a week or two, it's yours — whether you like it or not.

Wine storage conditions

Here's a fact about wine that's worth learning early on: Wine is a perishable product. It doesn't go moldy like cheese, and it can't host e-coli bacteria, as meat can. In fact, some wines — usually the more expensive ones — can get better and better as they get older. But if wine is not stored properly, its flavor can suffer. (For advice on storing wine in your own home, see "Creating a Healthy Environment for Your Wines" in Chapter 21.)

In sizing up a wine shop, especially if you plan to buy a lot of wine or expensive wine, check out the store's wine storage conditions. What you don't want to see is an area that's warm — for example, wines stored near the boiler so that they cook all winter or wines stored on the top floor of the building where the sun can smile on them all summer. The very best shops will have climate-controlled storerooms for wine — although frankly these shops are in the minority. If a shop does have a good storage system, the proprietor will be happy to show it off to you because he'll be rightfully proud of all the expense and effort he put into it.

In better wine shops, you'll see most of the bottles (except for the inexpensive, large bottles with screw caps) lying *in a horizontal position,* so that their corks remain moist, ensuring a firm closure. A dry cork can crack and let air into the bottle, which will spoil the wine.

Unfortunately, the problem of wine spoilage doesn't begin at the retail outlet. Quite frequently, the *wholesaler* or *distributor* — the company from which the retailer purchases his wine — doesn't have proper storage conditions, either. And there have certainly been instances when wine has been damaged by extremes of weather even before it got to the distributor, for example, while sitting on the docks in the dead of winter (or the dead of summer) or while traveling through the Panama Canal. A good retailer will check out the quality of the wine before he buys it, or he will send it back if he discovers the problem after he has already bought the wine. He'll also take back your damaged merchandise. (For more information on ideal wine storage conditions, see Chapter 21.)

Strategies for Wine Shopping

When you get beyond all the ego-compromising innuendos associated with buying wine, you can really have fun in wine shops. We remember when we first caught the wine bug. We spent countless hours on Saturdays, visiting

How to avoid encounters with poorly stored wine

If you don't know how a wine has been stored — and let's face it, most of the time you won't — you can do two things to minimize the risk of getting a bad bottle.

First, patronize retailers who seem to care about their products and provide their customers with good service. Second, be attentive to seasonal weather patterns when buying wine or when having it shipped to you. We're very cautious about buying wine at the end of, or during, a very hot summer, unless the store has a good climate-control system.

And we never have wine shipped to us (other than quick deliveries from our local shop) at the height of summer or the dead of winter.

Another way of knowing that the wine you are buying is sound is just to buy the best-selling, most popular wines — assuming you don't mind being a slave to taste trends. Wines that move through the distribution chain very quickly have less opportunity to be damaged along the way. Sometimes we wonder if the wines that sell the most just sell the most because they sell the most. . . .

different wine stores near our home (to a passionate wine lover, 30 miles can be near). Trips to other cities offered new opportunities to explore. So many wines, so little time. . . .

We discovered good, reliable stores — and stores that we would Recommend Only To Our Worst Enemies (ROTOWE). Naturally, we made our share of mistakes along the way, but we learned a lot of good lessons.

See a chance, take it

When we first started buying wine, our repertoire was about as broad as a two-year-old child's vocabulary. We'd buy the same brands again and again because they were safe choices, we knew what to expect from them, and we liked them well enough — all good reasons to buy a particular wine. But in retrospect, we let ourselves get stuck in a rut because we were afraid to take a chance on anything new.

If wine was really going to be fun, we realized, we had to be a little more adventuresome.

If you want to experience the wonderful array of wines in the world, experimenting is a must. New wines can be interesting and exciting. Now and then you might get a lemon, but at least you'll learn not to buy *that* wine again!

Ten clues for identifying a store where you should NOT buy wine

1. The dust on the wine bottles is more than 1/8-inch thick.

2. Most of the white wines are light brown in color.

3. The most recent vintage in the store is 1987.

4. The colors on all the wine labels have faded from bright sunlight.

5. It's warmer than a sauna inside.

6. Most of the bottles are standing up.

7. *All* of the bottles are standing up!

8. Three-quarters of the bottles have screw caps.

9. The July wine of the month has a picture of Santa Claus on the label.

10. The owner resembles Darth Vader.

Explain what you want

The following scene — or something very much like it — occurs in every wine shop every day (and ten times every Saturday):

Customer: I remember that it's got a beige label. I had it in this little restaurant last week.

Wine Merchant: Do you know what country it's from?

Customer: No, but I think it has a flower on the label.

Wine Merchant: Do you recall the vintage?

Customer: I think it's young, but I'm not sure. Maybe if I walk around, I can spot it.

Needless to say, most of the time that customer never finds the wine he or she is looking for.

When you come across a wine you like in a restaurant or at a friend's house, write down as much specific information about the wine from the label as you can. Don't trust your memory. By the time you arrive in your wine store, you might not recall many details about the wine if you haven't written them down. If your wine merchant can see the name, he can give you that wine or — if he doesn't have that exact wine — he might be able to give you something very similar to it.

It's clearly to your advantage to be able to tell your wine retailer anything you can about the types of wine that you have liked previously or that you want to try. Often, telling him about the food you are planning to have with the wine is helpful, too (see Chapter 20, "Marrying Wine with Food").

In-store wine tastings

In general, we're all for tasting wines before buying them, whenever possible. But the wine tastings that some retailers arrange in their stores do have their limitations. In addition to the fact that you usually get a miniscule taste of wine in a little plastic cup more suited to dispensing pills in a hospital, you get to taste only the wines that the wine merchant (or one of his suppliers) happens to be "pushing" that day. Sometimes it's a wine that the store made an especially good buy on (translation: The store is making a good profit), or a wine that a local distributor is particularly interested in selling. You might like or not like the wine, but in either case you might feel some pressure to buy it after trying it. Our advice to you is not to succumb to any conscious or unconscious sales pressure. Buy the wine only if you really like it — and even then, only buy one bottle to start. The wine might taste completely different to you when you're having dinner that night. If it tastes even better than you thought, you can always buy more bottles later.

Name your price

Because the price of a bottle of wine can range from $2 or $3 to — literally — hundreds of dollars, it's a good idea to decide approximately how much you want to spend and to tell your wine merchant. A good retailer with an adequate selection should be able to make several wine suggestions in your preferred price category.

A good wine merchant is more interested in the repeat business he'll get by making you happy than he is in trading you up to a bottle of wine that's beyond your limits. If all you want to spend is $6 a bottle, just say so, and stand firm, without embarrassment. There are plenty of decent, enjoyable wines at that price.

Five questions you should ask in a wine shop

1. If a wine is over $10: What kind of storage has this wine experienced? Hemming and hawing on the part of the wine merchant should be taken to mean, "Poor."

2. How long has this wine been in your store? (This is especially important if the store does not have a climate-control system.)

3. What are some particularly good buys this month? (Provided you trust the wine merchant, and you don't think he's dumping some overstocked, close-out wine on you.)

4. If applicable: Why is this wine selling at such a low price? (The merchant might know that the wine is too old, or is otherwise defective; unless he comes up with a believable explanation, assume that's the case.)

5. Will this wine go well with the food I'm planning to serve?

Five questions you should *not* ask in a wine shop

1. Do you have a nice, fruity wine? (Too vague.)

2. Does this wine have a nice, oaky taste? (If the retailer thinks you want an oaky wine, he'll very likely give you an over-oaked monster of a wine, which might be *too* oaky for you.)

3. Can you give me a wine without any sulfites? (*All* wines contain a tiny amount of sulfites — a preservative that does far more good to the wine than it does harm to the great majority of drinkers, especially in the tiny amounts used in wine; it is said that only one-quarter of one percent of the population, usually those with severe asthma, has justifiable concern over sulfites in wine; see Chapter 22, "Are there any wines without sulfites?")

4. Can you give me a cold bottle from the fridge? (In some stores, the wine may have been in that fridge for months. It could be *numb* — without expression, just like a numb limb — or if it's supposed to be bubbly, it could be flat. You're better off chilling the wine yourself.)

5. What's your most highly rated wine? (According to whom? You first have to trust the palate of the person who's doing the rating!)

Four easy steps to getting a wine you like

Step One

Decide how much you want to spend on a bottle

a) For everyday purposes (this figure might change over time; the $5 to $6 range you started with often rises to $10 to $15 as you discover better wines)

b) For special occasions

Tell your wine merchant your price range; this will narrow the arena of wines to consider.

Step Two

Describe to your wine merchant the kind of wine you like in clear, simple terms. For example, for white wine, you might use such words as "crisp, dry," or "fruity, ripe, oaky, buttery, full-bodied." For red wines, you might say "big, rich, tannic," or "medium-bodied, soft." (Turn to Chapter 2 to learn other helpful descriptors.)

Step Three

Tell your wine merchant what kind of food you plan to have with the wine, if you know. This will narrow down your choices even more. The wine you drink with your filet of sole is probably not the one you want with spicy chili! A good wine merchant is invaluable in helping you match your wine with food.

Step Four

Ask for tasting samples, if they are available where you shop. (Stores often have wine samples available for tasting every Saturday, where legal.) Of course, the sample will probably come to you in a plastic cup and the temperature might not be the best for that particular wine; therefore, the sample might not be truly indicative of the quality or taste of that wine. But at least you'll get a general idea of whether or not it's your cup of tea.

Chapter 7

Navigating a Restaurant Wine List

● ●

In This Chapter

▶ Showing the wine list who's boss

▶ Choosing the right wine

▶ Surviving the wine presentation ritual

▶ Experimenting on foreign shores

● ●

*W*hen you buy a bottle of wine in a restaurant, you get to taste it right then and there: instant gratification. If you've chosen well, you can bask in the compliments of your family and friends during the whole meal and go home feeling good about yourself. If you haven't chosen well   well, we all know *that* feeling. self-defensive statements marching through your head, over-tipping to compensate for your vague feelings of inadequacy. At least you can take comfort in the thought that next time you won't order *that* bottle of wine!

Buying Wine in a Restaurant

Here and there, you might come across a restaurant with a retail wine shop on the premises, a useful hybrid of a place where you can look over all the bottles, read the labels, browse through wine books and magazines, and then carry your chosen bottle to your table. Unfortunately, such establishments are rarer than four-leaf clovers. In most restaurants, you have to choose your wine from a menu that tells you only the names of the wines and the price per bottle — and manages to make even that little bit of information somewhat incomprehensible. Welcome to the *restaurant wine list*.

Restaurant wine lists can be infuriating: They don't tell you enough about the wines, or they tell you nonsense. Often, either there's nothing worth drinking, or the choice is so huge that you're immobilized. All too frequently, the lists simply are not accurate; you spend ten good minutes of your life deciding which wine to order, only to discover that it's "not available tonight" (and probably hasn't been for months).

When you eat out, you might not feel like wading through the restaurant's wine list at all, knowing that it can be an ego-deflating experience. But don't give up without a fight. With a little guidance and a few tips, you can navigate the choppy waters of the wine list.

How Wine Is Sold in Restaurants

Believe it or not, restaurateurs really do want you to buy their wine. They usually make a sizable profit on every sale, their servers earn bigger tips and become happier employees, and you enjoy your meal more, going home a happier customer.

Traditionally, however, mainly due to a lack of awareness on the restaurateur's part, many restaurants have done more to hinder wine sales than to encourage them. Fortunately, the old ways are changing. (*Un*fortunately, they're changing slowly.)

Wines available for sale in a restaurant these days generally fall into four categories (not all restaurants offer wines in all four categories, though):

- ✔ The *house wines:* usually one white and one red, sometimes also a sparkling wine; can be purchased *by the glass* or in a *carafe* (a wide-mouthed handle-less pitcher)
- ✔ *Premium* wines available by the glass: a wider selection than the house wines, and usually better quality (these wines are also usually available by the bottle)
- ✔ Wines available by the bottle from the restaurant's *regular,* or standard, *wine list*
- ✔ Older or rarer wines available by the bottle from a special wine list, sometimes called a *reserve wine list*

The choice of the house

The wine list looks so imposing that you finally give up laboring over it. You hand it back to the server and say (either a bit sheepishly, because you're acknowledging that you can't handle the list, or with defiant bravado, signifying that you're not going to waste your time on this nonsense), "I'll just have a glass of white wine." Smart move, or big mistake?

You'll probably know the answer to this question as soon as the house wine hits your lips. It could be just what you wanted — and with less than half the effort of plowing through that list. But in theory, we'd say, "Mistake."

Usually, a restaurant's *house wines* are some inferior stuff that the restaurant owner is making an enormous profit on. (Cost-per-ounce is a restaurant owner's main criterion in choosing a house wine.) House wines can range in price from $3 to $4 up to $9 a glass (with an average of $5 to $6). Often, the entire bottle costs the proprietor the price of one glass, or less! No wonder the "obliging" server fills your glass to the brim.

By the way, you usually will save money if you buy the house wine by the carafe—if it's offered that way. On the other hand, you might not want an entire carafe of the house wine!

We've found that only a small percentage of better restaurants — and wine-conscious restaurants, often located in enlightened places like Napa or Sonoma — offer a house wine worth drinking. And it's practically never a good value. Under most circumstances, avoid the house wine.

If circumstances are such that a glass of wine makes the most sense to you (if you're the only one in your group who's having wine with dinner, for example), ask the server what the house wine is. Don't be satisfied with the response, "It's Chardonnay;" ask for specifics. Chardonnay from where? What brand? Ask to see the bottle. Either your worst fears will be confirmed (you've never heard of the wine, or it has a reputation for being inferior), or you'll be pleasantly surprised (you *have* heard of the wine, and it has a good reputation). And at least you'll know what you're drinking, for future reference.

Premium pours

The word *premium* is used very loosely by the wine industry. You might think that it refers to a rather high-quality wine, but when annual industry sales statistics are compiled for the U.S., *premium* indicates any wine that sells for more than $3 a bottle in stores!

As used in the phrase, *premium wines by the glass,* however, *premium* usually does connote better quality. These are red and white wines that a restaurant offers at a higher price than its house wines. (Oh, we get it: You pay a premium for them!) Premium wines are usually in the $6 to $12 price range per glass.

A restaurant might offer just one premium white and one red, or it might offer several choices. These premium wines are not anonymous beverages, like the house red and white, but are identified for you somehow — on the wine list, on a separate card, verbally, or sometimes even by a display of bottles. (Why would you ever pay a premium for them if you didn't know what they were?) In some informal restaurants, wines by the glass are listed on a chalkboard.

Why aren't there more wines by the glass?

You might be wondering why more restaurants don't offer a larger selection of wines by the glass; a larger selection could enhance your pleasure so much ("Let's see, we'll have one of these, and a glass of that one, and . . ."). The problem for the restaurateur is preserving the wine in all of those open bottles. The more wines a restaurant manager offers by the glass, the greater the odds that there will be wine left over in each bottle at the end of the evening, and those wines won't be fresh enough to serve the next day.

Unless he has a wine preservation system — often an attractive console that injects inert gas into the open bottles to displace oxygen — or unless he's lucky enough to finish every bottle every night, the restaurateur will waste an enormous amount of wine. His wine profits will go right down the drain! (Or into the stew!)

Ordering premium wines by the glass is a fine idea, especially if you want to have only a glass or two or if you and your guests want to experiment by trying several wines. Sometimes we order a glass of a premium white wine as a starter and then go on to a bottle of red wine.

Of course, there's a catch. Only a small percentage of restaurants — the "wine-conscious" ones — offer premium wines by the glass. Also, you'll end up paying more for the wine if you order a bottle's worth of individual glasses than you would if you ordered a whole bottle to begin with.

If two or three of you are ordering the same wine by the glass — and especially if you might want refills — ask how many ounces are poured into each glass (usually five or six ounces) and compare the price with that of a 25.4-ounce (750 ml) bottle of the same wine. (You do usually have the option of buying an entire bottle.) Sometimes, for the cost of only three glasses you can have the whole bottle.

Special, or reserve, wine lists

Some restaurants — only a few, and usually the fanciest — offer a special wine list of rare wines to supplement their regular wine list. These special lists appeal to two types of customers: very serious wine connoisseurs and "high rollers." If you're not in either category, don't even bother asking if the restaurant has such a list. Then again, if you're not paying for the meal or if you seriously want to impress a client or a date, you might want to look at it! Try to get help with the list from some knowledgeable person on the restaurant staff, though: Any mistake you make could be a costly one.

The (anything but) standard wine list

Most of the time, you'll probably end up turning to the restaurant's standard wine list to choose your wine. Lucky you.

We use the term *standard wine list* to distinguish a restaurant's basic wine list from its special, or reserve, wine list. Unfortunately, there's nothing standard about wine lists at all. They come in all sizes, shapes, degrees of detail, degrees of accuracy, and degrees of user-friendliness (the latter usually ranging from moderate to nil).

If you're still hung up on the emotional-vulnerability potential of buying wine, don't even pick up a wine list. (Instead, turn to Chapter 6 and reread our pep talk about wine buying in the section, "Buying Wine Can Intimidate Anyone.") When you're ready, read the following section to get a wine you'll like with minimum angst.

How to Scope Out a Wine List

Your first step in the dark encounter between you and the wine list is to size up the opposition. You can do this by noting how the wine list is organized.

When the restaurant doesn't have an alcohol license — BYOB

In most places, establishments that sell alcohol beverages — both retail stores and restaurants — must be licensed by the government to assure that all appropriate taxes are paid and to aid in the enforcement of local laws. Sometimes a restaurant doesn't have a liquor license due to circumstance or choice, and it therefore cannot sell wine. In those restaurants, you can BYOB (bring your own bottle of wine) to enjoy with your meal. (If you're not sure of the restaurant's policy on BYOB, call ahead.)

Many Chinese restaurants fall into this category, for example. (Although it can be difficult to match Asian cuisine with wine, we have found that Champagne and sparkling wine generally go well, as does German or Alsace Gewurztraminer.) Other examples include restaurants that have recently opened and have not yet received their liquor licenses, or restaurants that for some reason do not qualify for a license (they may be located too close to a school or a church, for example).

Read the headings on the wine list the way you'd read the chapter titles in a book that you were considering buying. Figure out how the wines are categorized and how they are arranged within each category. Notice how much or how little information is given about each wine. Check out the style of the list: Does it seem pretentious or straightforward? Estimate the number of wines on it — there could be 12 or 200. (An indirect benefit of this procedure is that the purposeful look in your eyes as you peruse the list will convince your guests that you know what you're doing.)

Sizing up the organization of the list

There's no way of predicting exactly what you'll find on the list, other than prices. Generally speaking, though, you may discover the wines arranged in the following categories:

- Champagne and sparkling wines
- (Dry) white wines
- (Dry) red wines
- Dessert wines

After-dinner drinks like Cognac, Armagnac, single-malt Scotches, or liqueurs usually will not appear on the list, or if they do, they'll have their own section near the back of the list.

Some restaurants further subdivide the wines on their list according to country, especially in the white and red wine categories: French red wines, Italian red wines, American reds, and so on. These country segments might then be subdivided by wine region. France, for example, might have listings of Bordeaux, Burgundy, and possibly Rhône all under *French red wines. USA reds* may be divided into California wines, Oregon wines, and Washington wines.

Or you might find that the categories under white wines and red wines are the names of grape varieties — for example, a Chardonnay section, a Sauvignon Blanc section, and a miscellaneous *other dry whites* section, all under the general heading of white wines. If the restaurant features a particular country's cuisine, the wines of that country might be listed first (and given certain prominence), followed by a cursory listing of wines from other areas.

We've noticed two recent trends in wine-conscious restaurants, and we applaud them both, because they make ordering easier and more fun.

Wine list power struggles

In many restaurants, the servers don't give you enough time to study the wine list. (Really good restaurants recognize that choosing a bottle of wine can take some time and, therefore, don't put you in this position.) If your waiter asks, somewhat impatiently, "Have you selected your wine yet?" simply tell him (firmly) that you need more time. Don't let him bully you into making a hasty choice.

Usually, your table will receive only one wine list. An outmoded convention dictates that only the host (the masculine is intentional) needs to see the list. (It's part of the same, outmoded thinking that dictates that females should receive menus with no prices on them.) At our table of two, there are *two* thinking, curious, decision-making customers. We ask for a second wine list.

Invariably, the wine list is handed to the oldest or most important-looking male at the table. If you are a female entertaining business clients, this situation can be insulting and infuriating. Speak up and ask for a copy of the wine list for yourself. If it's important enough to you, slip away from the table and inform the server that you are the host of the table.

✔ **The so-called progressive wine list, in which wines appear in a progressive sequence under each category heading.** For example, under "Chardonnays," the wines are arranged by weight and richness, progressing from the lightest wines to the most intense, regardless of price.

✔ **Lists that use wine styles as their basic form of organization.** In these lists, the category headings are neither varietal nor regional, but describe the taste of the wines in each category, such as "Fresh, crisp, unoaked whites," or "Full-bodied, serious reds."

No two wine lists are exactly alike, unless both restaurants are part of the same chain or unless they've both surrendered control of their list to the same local wine distributor, who has loaded the list with his own wines presented his own way.

Sometimes, you'll discover that the list is very small, with hardly any wines on it. It's tough to look purposeful for very long when you're studying a list like that.

Getting a handle on the pricing setup

Often you'll find that within each category, the wines are arranged in ascending order of price with the least expensive wine first. The restaurateur is betting that you won't order that first wine out of fear of looking

---

The lowdown on high prices

Most restaurateurs count on wine and liquor sales to provide a disproportionate percentage of their business profit. The typical restaurant, therefore, charges two to two-and-a-half (sometimes three!) times the retail store price for a bottle of wine. That means that the restaurant is earning *three to four times* the price it paid for the bottle.

Admittedly, restaurateurs incur costs for wine storage, glasses, breakage, service, and so on. But those costs don't justify such extraordinary markups in the eyes of most wine drinkers.

Some savvy restaurateurs have discovered that by marking up their wines less, they actually sell *more* wine and make *more money* in the end. We try to patronize *those* restaurants.

If you frequent restaurants in Canada, you should know that restaurateurs there have a serious disadvantage (except in the province of Alberta): They must purchase their wines from the provincial liquor control authorities *at the same price as you would purchase the wines* for drinking in your own home. There's no such thing as wholesale for them — and prices will reflect that fact.

---

cheap. He figures you'll go for the second, third, or fourth wine down the price column or even deeper if you're feeling insecure and need the reassurance that your choice is a good one. (Meanwhile, nothing is wrong with that least expensive wine.)

What the wine list should tell you

The more serious a restaurant is about its wine selection, the more information it gives you about each wine.

Here's some information that's likely to be on the wine list:

- An *item number* for each wine. These are sometimes called *bin numbers,* referring to the specific location of each wine in the restaurant's cellar or wine storage room.

  Item numbers make it easier for the server to locate and pull the wine quickly for you, after you order it. They're also a crutch to help the server bring you the right wine in case he doesn't have a clue about wine. They're also a crutch for *you* in ordering the wine in case you don't have a clue how to pronounce what you've decided to drink. (And you can always pretend that you're using the number for the waiter's benefit.)

✔ The name of each wine. These names might be grape names or place-names (see Chapter 5), but they had better also include the name of each producer (Château this or that, or such-and-such Winery), or you'll have no way of knowing exactly which wine any listing is meant to represent.

✔ A vintage indication for each wine — the year that the grapes were harvested. If the wine is a blend of wines from different years, it might say *NV,* for *non-vintage.* (Chapter 9 tells you why non-vintage wines exist.) Sometimes, you'll see *VV,* which means that the wine is a vintage-dated wine, but you're not allowed to know *which* vintage it is unless you ask. The restaurateur just doesn't want to bother changing the vintage on the list when the vintage changes. We're always annoyed when we see lists with an attitude like that.

✔ Sometimes, a brief description of the wines — but this is unlikely if dozens of wines are on the list.

✔ Sometimes restaurateurs suggest certain wines to go with their entrées on the dinner menu; in our experience, this information is helpful at times, but you might not always like — or agree with — their wine suggestion.

✔ There will *always* be a price for each wine.

Rating the list's style

Once upon a time, the best wine lists consisted of hand-lettered pages inside heavy leather covers embossed with the words *Carte des Vins* in gold. Today, the best wine lists are more likely to be laser-printed pages or cards that more than make up in functionality what they sacrifice in romance.

The more permanent and immutable a wine list seems, the less accurate its listings are likely to be — and the less specific. Such lists suggest that no one is really looking after wine on a day-to-day basis in that restaurant. Chances are that many of the wines listed will be out of stock.

The world's most complicated wine list

We've heard that there's a restaurant in Colorado whose wine list is like this:

1. White wine

2. Red wine

3. Rosé wine

To avoid confusing the waiter, please order your wine by number."

Sometimes, the list of wines is actually included on the restaurant's menu, especially if the menu is a computer-printed page or two that changes from week to week or from month to month. Restaurants featuring immediate, up-to-date wine listings like this can be a good bet for wine.

How to Ask for Advice

If after sizing up the wine list, you decide that you are not familiar with most of the wines on it, ask for help with your selection.

If the restaurant is a fancy one, ask if there's a *sommelier* (pronounced *sōm-mel-yay*) — technically, a specially trained, high-level wine specialist who is responsible for putting the wine list together and for making sure that the wines offered on the list complement the cuisine of the restaurant. (Unfortunately, only a few restaurants employ one — usually the most wine-conscious.)

If the restaurant is not particularly fancy, ask to speak with the wine specialist. Often someone on the staff, frequently the proprietor, knows the wine list well.

If someone on the restaurant staff knows the wine list well, this person is your best bet to help you select a wine. He or she will usually know what wines go best with the food you are ordering. He will also be extremely appreciative of your interest in the list. For these reasons, even though we are familiar with wine, we often consult the sommelier, proprietor, or wine specialist for suggestions from the wine list.

Here are some face-saving methods of getting help:

✔ If you are not sure how to pronounce the wine's name, point to it on the list, or use the wine's item or bin number (if there is one).

✔ Point out two or three wines on the list to the sommelier or server and say, "I'm considering these wines. Which one do you recommend?" This is also a subtle way of communicating your price range.

Timing counts

As soon as your server comes to the table, ask to see the wine list. Besides communicating to the server that you feel comfortable with wine (whether it's true or not), your asking for the list quickly gives you more time to examine the list.

Order the wine at the same time that you order the food — if not sooner; otherwise, you might be sipping water with your first course.

✔ Ask to *see* one or two bottles; the labels might help you make up your mind.

✔ Ask if there are any half-bottles (375 ml) or 500 ml bottles available (sometimes they're not listed). Smaller bottles give you wider possibilities in ordering: For example, a party of four might drink one half-bottle of white wine and a half or full (750 ml) bottle of red wine.

✔ Mention the food you plan to order and ask for suggestions of wines that would complement the meal.

How to Bluff Your Way through the Wine Presentation Ritual

In many restaurants, the wine presentation occurs with such solemnity and ceremony that you'd think you were involved in high church or temple services. The hushed tones of the waiter, the ritualized performance — the seriousness of it all can make you want to laugh (but that seems wrong — like laughing in church). At the very least, you might be tempted to tell your waiter, "Lighten up! It's just a bottle of fermented fruit juice!"

Actually, though, there's some logic behind the Wine Presentation Ritual.

Step by step, the Ritual (and the logic) goes like this:

1. **The waiter or sommelier presents the bottle to you (assuming that you are the person who ordered the wine) for inspection.**

   The point of this procedure is to make sure that it *is* the bottle you ordered. Check the label carefully. In our experience, 15 to 20 percent of the time it's the wrong bottle. Feel the bottle with your hand, if you like, to determine whether it seems to be the correct temperature. (This is also a good time for you to pretend to recognize something about the label, as if the wine is an old friend, even if you've never seen it before.)

2. **The server then pulls the cork and either hands it to you or places it in front of you.**

   The purpose of this step is for you to determine, by smelling and visually inspecting the cork, whether the cork is in good condition, and whether the cork seems to be the legitimate cork for that bottle of wine.

   In rare instances, a wine may be so corky (see Chapter 2) that the cork itself will have an unpleasant odor. On even rarer occasions, the cork might be totally wet and shriveled or very dry and crumbly — either situation suggesting that air may have gotten into the wine and spoiled it.

Once in your life, you might discover a vintage year or winery name on your cork that is different from the label. (Quick! Call the wine fraud police!) But most of the time, the presentation of the cork is inconsequential.

If the cork does raise your suspicions, you should still wait to smell or taste the wine itself before rejecting the bottle.

Once, when one of our wise-guy friends was presented the cork by the server, he proceeded to put it into his mouth and chew it, and then he pronounced to the waiter that it was just fine!

3. **If your wine needs decanting, the server will decant it at this point.**

(For more information on decanting, see "How to Aerate Your Wine" in Chapter 8.)

4. **The server pours a small amount of wine into your glass and waits.**

At this point, you're *not* supposed to say, "Is that all you're giving me?!" You're expected to take a sniff of the wine, perhaps a little sip, and then either nod your approval to the waiter or murmur, "It's fine." Actually, this is an important step of the Wine Presentation Ritual because if something is *wrong* with the wine, *now* is the time to return it (not after you've finished half of the bottle!). For a review of wine-tasting technique, turn to Chapter 2 before you head out to the restaurant.

If you're not really sure whether the condition of the wine is acceptable, ask for someone else's opinion at your table and then make a group decision; otherwise, you risk feeling foolish by either returning the bottle later when it's been declared defective by one of your guests, or by drinking the stuff when you know there's something wrong with it. Either way, you suffer. Take as long as you need to on this step.

If you do decide that the bottle is out of condition, describe to the server what you find wrong with the wine, using the best language you can. (*Musty* or *dank* are descriptors that are easily understood.) Be sympathetic to the fact that you're causing more work for him but don't be overly apologetic (why should you be; you didn't make the wine!). Let him smell or taste the wine himself if he would like. But don't let him make you feel guilty.

Depending on whether the sommelier or captain agrees that it's a bad bottle or whether he believes that you just don't understand the wine, he might bring you another bottle of the same, or he might bring you the wine list so that you can select a different wine. Either way, the Ritual begins again from the top.

5. **If you do accept the wine, the waiter will pour the wine into your guests' glasses and then finally into yours. Now you're allowed to relax.**

If You Are Truly on Your Own

If no one is available in the restaurant who knows any more than you do about the wine list, follow a few simple guidelines in deciding which wine will go best with your meal:

- Choose a wine that won't overpower the food — or be overpowered by it. For example, choose a relatively low-tannin red wine, such as a Pinot Noir or French Burgundy, with light meat dishes, poultry, or full-flavored fish, such as salmon. A light-bodied white wine, such as a Soave or a French Chablis, would be fine with lighter fish or shellfish dishes. A full-bodied Chardonnay would be good with lobster and richer fish dishes. (See Chapters 10 through 14 for a discussion of these wines.)

- Some foods, like chicken or pasta, are equally at home with white or red wines. Look to see what sauce accompanies the dish to give you a clue about the appropriate wine. The texture and weight of the sauce will be determining factors. For example, a pasta with a meaty tomato sauce probably would be better with a red wine, whereas a pasta with vegetables or a cream sauce would go well with a white or sparkling wine.

- Full-flavored dishes, such as stews, roasts, game, duck, and so on usually go best with full-bodied red wines.

- Spicy dishes, such as the ones you find in Chinese, Indian, or Mexican cuisine, are great with Champagne or other sparkling wines, off-dry white wines like Riesling or Gewürztraminer (or beer).

- All of the preceding "rules" are guidelines. Follow your instincts and maintain a spirit of adventure.

Twice the price

A few profit-minded restaurateurs train their servers to maximize wine sales in every way possible — even at the customers' expense. For example, some servers are trained to refill wine glasses liberally so that the bottle is emptied before the main course arrives (this can happen all the more easily when the glasses are large). Upon emptying the bottle, the server asks, "Shall I bring another bottle of the same wine?" Depending on how much wine is in everyone's glass and how much wine your guests tend to drink, you might not *need* another bottle, but your tendency will be to say yes to avoid looking stingy.

An even trickier practice is to refill the glasses starting with the host, so that the bottle runs dry before each of the guests has had a refill. How can you refuse a second bottle at the expense of your guest's enjoyment?! You'll have to order that second bottle — and you should let the manager know how you feel about it when you leave. (But remember, these nefarious restaurant practices are the exception rather than the rule.)

Safe wine choices in a restaurant

White Wine:

Soave, Pinot Grigio, or Sancerre (if you like crisp, dry wines that aren't too flavorful)

Sauvignon Blanc from South Africa and New Zealand (if you like dry, fairly light-bodied white wines with assertive flavor)

Mâcon-Villages or Pouilly-Fuissé (if you prefer a medium-bodied, dry white wine with medium intensity of flavor)

Californian or Australian Chardonnay (if you want a full-bodied, rich white wine)

Meursault (if a dry, full-bodied wine with a honeyed, nutty character sounds good to you)

Chenin Blanc, Vouvray, or German Riesling (medium-dry wines, for times when you don't want a wine that's very dry)

Red Wine:

Beaujolais (especially from a reputable producer, like Louis Jadot or Georges Duboeuf, when you want an easy-drinking, inexpensive red)

California red Zinfandel (when you need a versatile, relatively inexpensive red that can even stand up to spicy food)

Oregon or California Pinot Noir (for a lighter red that is delicious young)

Bourgogne Rouge (the basic French version of Pinot Noir)

Barbera or Dolcetto (widely available in Italian restaurants; dry, light, grapey and relatively inexpensive)

Chianti Classico (a very dry, medium-bodied red wine that's great with food)

For more information on all these wines, refer to Chapters 10 through 14.

For more information on pairing wine and food, turn to Chapter 20, or consult our nifty wine-and-food pairing chart in our book *Wine Buying Companion For Dummies,* published by IDG Books Worldwide, Inc.

Restaurant Wining Tips

There are so many decisions to make about wine in restaurants that you really do need a guidebook. Should you leave the wine in an ice bucket? What should you do if the wine is bad? And can you bring your own wine? Let the following tips guide you:

> ✔ **Can you kick the ice-bucket habit?** Usually, an ice bucket is assumed to be necessary to chill white wines and sparkling wines. But sometimes the bottle is already so cold when it comes to you that the wine would be better off warming up a bit on the table. If your white wine goes into an ice bucket but you think it's getting *too* cold, remove it from the bucket or have the waiter remove it. Just because that ice

bucket is sitting there on your table (or next to your table) doesn't mean that your bottle has to be in it!

Sometimes, a red wine that is a bit too warm can benefit from five or ten minutes in an ice bucket. (But be careful! It can get too cold very quickly. And if the server acts as if you're nuts to chill a red wine, ignore him.)

✔ **Do I have to use these tiny glasses?** When various glasses are available, you can exercise your right to choose a different glass from the one you were given. If the restaurant's red wine glass is quite small, a stemmed water glass might be more appropriate for the red wine.

✔ **Should the wine "breathe"?** If a red wine you ordered seems to need aeration to soften its harsh tannins (see Chapter 8), merely pulling the cork will be practically useless in accomplishing that (the air space at the neck of the bottle is too small). Decanting the bottle or pouring the wine into glasses is the best tactic.

✔ **Where's my bottle?** We prefer to have our bottle of wine on or near our table, not out of our reach. We can look at the label that way, and we don't have to wait for the server to remember to refill our glasses, either. (Okay, call us controlling.)

✔ **What if the bottle is bad?** Refuse any bottle that tastes or smells unpleasant (unless you brought it yourself!). A good restaurateur will always replace the wine, even if he thinks there's nothing wrong with it.

✔ **May I bring my own wine?** Some restaurants allow you to bring your own wine — especially if you express the desire to bring a special wine, or an older wine. Restaurants will usually charge a *corkage* fee (a fee for wine service, use of the glasses, and so on) that can vary from $5 to even $25 a bottle, depending on the attitude of the restaurant. You should never bring a wine that is already on the restaurant's wine list; it's cheap and it's insulting. (Call and ask the restaurant when you're not sure whether the wine is on its list.) Anyway, you certainly should call ahead to determine whether or not it's possible to bring wine (in some places, the restaurant's license prohibits it) and to ask what the corkage fee is.

Normally corkage is expressed as a fee per bottle, but exceptions do exist. A friend of ours brought a bottle of aged white Burgundy to a fancy French restaurant in New York City, thinking that the corkage fee was $30. When he got the bill, the corkage was $120: $30 a person times four people! We're still angry on his behalf.

When Traveling Abroad

If you journey to countries where wine is made, such as France, Italy, Germany, Switzerland, Austria, Spain, or Portugal, by all means try the local wines. They will be fresher than the imports, in good condition, and the best values on the wine list. It would not be a very good idea to order French wines, such as Bordeaux or Burgundy, in Italy, for example. Or California Cabernets in Paris. Among other reasons, you'll have to pay the built-in charge of importing the wines into that country.

Wine bars

Wine bars are fairly popular in London, Italy, and Paris. They are establishments that offer an extensive choice of wines by the glass — from 12 to 100 — as well as simple food to accompany the wines. The wine bottles are usually either hooked up to an inert-gas injection system, which keeps the wine fresh, or are topped up with inert gas from a free-standing dispenser after each serving. The former system often makes a dramatic center-piece behind the bar.

In wine bars, you are sometimes offered a choice of two different *sizes* of wines by the glass. You can have a *taste* of a wine (about two-and-a-half ounces) for one price, or a *glass* of a wine (often five ounces) for another price.

Wine bars haven't really caught on in much of the United States, but there are a few in major cities such as New York, Chicago, and San Francisco. Wine bars are the ideal way to try lots of different wines by the glass — an educational as well as a satisfying experience. Hopefully, their numbers will increase with the years.

Chapter 8

How to Open a Bottle — and What to Do Next

*H*ave you ever broken a cork while trying to extract it from the bottle, or taken an unusually long time to remove a stubborn cork, while your guests smiled at you uneasily? This has certainly happened to us from time to time and probably to just about everyone else who has ever pulled a cork out of a bottle of wine.

In wine shops, we've noticed some people opting for either screw-top bottles of wine or for bag-in-a-box wines (large boxes that hold the equivalent of four or five bottles of wine in a collapsible plastic sack; you pour the wine through a nozzle near the bottom of the box). Wines packaged like this are inexpensive, and that's one good reason to buy them. But we strongly suspect that many people buy screw-top bottles or bag-in-a-box wines not just for value, but because, lurking in their minds, there is an actual fear of opening a bottle of wine that has a cork in it.

Maybe an unsuccessful encounter with an unyielding cork during their formative wine-drinking years has traumatized the screw-top and bag-in-a-box drinkers, causing them to develop *corkophobia*. If so, they have our sympathy. Besides the emotional trauma they've experienced, corkophobics have deprived themselves of most of the world's best wines — because just about all of those wines come with a cork in the bottle. The solution? Be armed with the right tools.

The First Step: Uncovering the Cork

The bigger the winery, the more time and money it spends creating attractive bottles that grab your eye as you walk down the aisle of the wine shop or supermarket. Part of the fetching package is the *capsule*, a colorful covering over the cork end of the bottle. The good news is that it's pretty; the bad news is that some coverings are difficult to remove.

These days, most wineries use colored foil or plastic capsules rather than the traditional lead capsules because of the potential risk of lead poisoning. In keeping with the sheerness trend in fashion, some wineries use a transparent cellophane covering that lets the cork show through; usually, the sheer look is found on special *flange-top* bottles, a fancy wine bottle with a protruding, flat lip at the top.

Whatever the material, we usually remove the entire capsule, for sanitary reasons, so that no wine can possibly come into contact with the covering. (That's one moment when we actually appreciate the old lead capsules — they're easier to remove than the plastic ones!)

After removing the capsule (usually we use a small knife, which is part of many corkscrews), we wipe clean the top of the bottle with a damp cloth because sometimes the cork is dark with mold that developed under the capsule. (That's actually a good sign; it means that the wine has been stored in humid conditions. See Chapter 21 for information on humidity and other aspects of wine storage.)

SNOB ALERT

Why is my cork blue?

Have you ever opened a bottle of wine and discovered that the "cork" is not cork at all, but plastic — and brightly colored, to boot?

While we appreciate the touch of whimsy that an orange or blue cork contributes, we must admit that we are not fans of plastic corks. We can understand winemakers' disillusion with real cork, due to its potential to taint a wine with off-aromas. But if you're going to invent an alternative to cork, why invent yet another closure that sits in the bottle's neck as a rude barrier between wine drinkers and their wine; demands the same, complicated tool as a cork does; and can be even more difficult to remove? This is progress?

Instead of imitation cork, we'd prefer to see real screw caps on most wine bottles. For wines that are consumed young, as the majority of wines are, screw caps are perfectly sound closures, technically speaking.

Sometimes wine lovers just can't bring themselves to remove the whole capsule out of respect for the bottle of wine that they are about to drink. (In fact, traditional wine etiquette dictates that you do not remove the entire capsule.) Some wine drinkers use a handy gizmo called a foil cutter that sells for about $6 or $7 in wine shops, kitchen stores, or specialty catalogs. The problem is that the foil cutter does not cut the foil (or the lead capsule) low enough, in our opinion, to prevent wine from dripping over the edge of the foil into your glass. If you want to leave the capsule on, cut the foil with a knife under the second lip of the bottle, which is approximately three-fourths of an inch below the top of the bottle.

Getting the Cork Out

Corkophobia or not, anyone can conquer most corks with a good corkscrew.

We suspect it's probably wise not to mention that we actually use three different corkscrews, each for certain situations, or that there are some corkscrews we would use only in desperation, as a last resort before drinking screw-top or bag-in-a-box wine. We don't want to sound like snobs or fanatics. After all, who cares what kind of corkscrew you use as long as you can extract the cork and drink the wine?

We agree that getting to the wine is the important thing. But the voyage to the wine is much smoother sailing with a good corkscrew. And struggling over a puny piece of cork with a second-rate corkscrew will surely put you in a miserable mood before you even get to the wine.

The corkscrew not to use

The one corkscrew we absolutely avoid happens to be the most common type of corkscrew around. We don't like it for one very simple reason: It mangles the cork, almost guaranteeing that brown flakes will be floating in your glass of wine. (We also don't like it because it offends our sense of righteousness that an inferior product should be so popular.)

That corkscrew is the infamous Wing Type Corkscrew, a bright silver-colored, metal device that looks something like a pair of pliers; when you insert this corkscrew into a cork, two "wings" spread out from the side of the corkscrew. The major shortcoming of this device is its very short worm, or *auger* (the curly prong that bores into the cork), which is too short for many corks and overly aggressive on all of them. Unfortunately, the Wing Type is the most commonly found corkscrew in most stores. No wonder people have trouble with corks!

Rather than finding out the hard way that this corkscrew just doesn't cut it (or, literally, cuts it too much!), as we did, invest a few dollars in a decent corkscrew right off the bat. The time and hassle you'll save will be more than worth the investment. Of the many types of wine openers available, we recommend the three described in the following sections.

The corkscrew to buy

The one indispensable corkscrew for every household is the Screwpull. It was invented in the early 1980s by a renowned Houston scientist, Dr. Herbert Allen, who was apparently tired of having a ten-cent piece of cork get the better of him.

The Screwpull is about six inches long. It consists of an arched piece of plastic (which looks like a clothespin on steroids) straddling an inordinately long, five-inch worm that's coated with Teflon® (see Figure 8-1). To use this corkscrew, you simply place the plastic over the bottle top (having removed the capsule), until a lip on the plastic is resting on the top of the bottle. Hold on to the plastic firmly while turning the lever atop the worm clockwise. The worm descends into the cork. Then you simply keep turning the lever in the same clockwise direction, and the cork magically emerges from the bottle. To remove the cork from the Screwpull, simply turn the lever counterclockwise while holding on to the cork.

Figure 8-1:
The
Screwpull
corkscrew.

The Screwpull comes in many colors — burgundy, black, and China red being the most common — and costs in the $15 to $20 range in wine shops, kitchen stores, and specialty catalogs. It's very simple to use, does not require a lot of muscle, and is our corkscrew of choice for over 95 percent of the corks that we encounter.

Other corkscrews worth owning

Did we say 95 percent? Well, you see, that's why we have two other corkscrews for the remaining 5 percent of the corks that the Screwpull can't remove (or threatens to break itself on; after all, it is mostly plastic, and $20 is $20). Flange-top bottles, for example, really challenge the Screwpull because of their unusual width at the top of the bottle.

Our two alternative corkscrews are smaller devices that — besides working better now and then — can conveniently fit into your pocket or apron. Their size is one reason that they are favored by servers in restaurants.

The two-pronged type that they use in California

One is called, unofficially, the Ah-So because (according to legend, anyway) when people finally figure out how it works, they say, "Ah, so that's how it works!" (Some people also refer to it as the Butler's Friend, but who has a butler these days?)

It's a simple device made up of two thin, flat metal prongs, one slightly longer than the other (see Figure 8-2). To use it, you slide the prongs down into the tight space between the cork and the bottle (inserting the longer prong first), using a back-and-forth seesaw motion until the top of the Ah-So is resting on the top of the cork. Then you twist the cork while you gently pull it up.

One advantage of the Ah-So is that it delivers an intact cork, without a hole in it, that can be reused to close bottles of homemade vinegar, to maintain the integrity of the cork for collectors, or to make cutesy bulletin boards.

Although more difficult to operate than the Screwpull, the Ah-So really comes into its own with very tight-fitting corks when no other corkscrews, including the Screwpull, seem to be able to budge the cork. Also, the Ah-So can be effective with old, crumbly corks in which other corkscrews cannot get a proper grip.

The Ah-So is useless with loose corks that move around in the bottle neck when you try to remove them. The Ah-So just pushes those corks down into the wine. At that point, you'll need another tool called a *cork retriever* (which we describe in the "Waiter, there's cork in my wine!" section, later in this chapter).

Figure 8-2:
The Ah-So
corkscrew.

The Ah-So sells for around $6 to $8. It seems to be especially favored in California for no particular reason that we have ever been able to figure out.

The most professional corkscrew of them all

Our final recommended corkscrew, probably the most commonly used corkscrew in restaurants all over the world, is simply called the Waiter's Corkscrew. A straight metal base holds three other pieces of metal that fold into it, like a Swiss Army knife: a lever; a small, two-inch worm; and a little knife (see Figure 8-3). The latter is especially handy for removing the capsule from the bottle.

Using the Waiter's Corkscrew requires some practice. (Could that be another reason for corkophobia?) First, wrap a fist around the top of the bottle. The trick then is to guide the worm down through the center of the cork through an opening in your fist so that the worm goes right through the middle of the cork. After the worm is fully descended into the cork, place the lever on the lip of the bottle and push against the lever while lifting the cork up. Give a firm pull at the very end or wiggle the bottom of the cork out with your hand.

If your cork ever breaks and part of it gets stuck in the neck of the bottle, the Waiter's Corkscrew is indispensable for removing the remaining piece. Use the method we just described, but insert the worm at a 45-degree angle instead. In most cases, you will successfully remove the broken cork.

Figure 8-3:
The
Waiter's
Corkscrew.

The Waiter's Corkscrew sells for about $7.

Waiter, there's cork in my wine!

Every now and then, even if you've used the right corkscrew and used it properly, you can still have pieces of cork floating in your wine. They can be tiny dry flakes that crumbled into the bottle, actual chunks of cork, or even the entire cork.

Before you start berating yourself for being a klutz, you should know that Floating Cork Syndrome has happened to all of us at one time or another, no matter how experienced we are. Cork won't harm the wine. And besides, there's a wonderful instrument called a *cork retriever* (no, it's not a small dog from the south of Ireland!) available in specialty stores and in catalogs, although it's considerably more difficult to find than a corkscrew.

The cork retriever consists of three ten-inch pieces of stiff metal wire with hooks on the ends. This device is remarkably effective in removing floating pieces of cork from the bottle. We have even removed a whole cork from the neck with a cork retriever (fearing the whole time that the bottle neck would explode when we tried to force the cork *and* the retriever back up through that tiny neck).

What genius thought of using corks in the first place?

We confess to not knowing the name of the genius who first closed a bottle of wine with a piece of cork, but we believe that the French monk, Dom Pérignon, was the genius who popularized the cork as a closure for Champagne.

It was a stroke of genius that endures to this day. The bark of the cork tree, has enviable properties — such as compressibility (which enables the cork to be squeezed into the tiny neck of a bottle) and elasticity (which enables it to expand again and hug that tiny neck from the inside) — that make it nearly ideal for keeping the air out of wine bottles and keeping the wine in for long periods of time.

But corks aren't perfect for two reasons: They can sometimes develop a moldiness that spoils the wine, and they are a frustrating barrier between us and the wine. For wines that are intended to be consumed young — like most white wines — a screw cap would be less risky, simpler to remove, and just as effective in keeping out the air. But traditions die hard, and the cork will probably be the closure of choice even on young wines for some time to come.

Alternatively, you can just pick out the offending piece(s) of cork with a spoon after you pour the wine into your glass. (That's one occasion when it's rude to serve your guest first, because the first glass has more cork pieces in it.) Or you can pour the wine through a paper coffee filter (preferably rinsed with hot water, to remove the chemicals) into a decanter or pitcher to catch the remaining pieces of cork.

A Special Case: Opening Champagne and Sparkling Wine

Opening a bottle of sparkling wine is often an exciting occasion. Who doesn't enjoy the ceremony of a cold glass of bubbly? Is there a more festive beverage in the world? If there is, we haven't found it.

Forget how the victors do it in locker rooms

Part of the fun of sparkling wine for us is in the opening. If the bottle has just traveled, though, let it rest for a while, preferably a day. Controlling the cork is difficult when the carbonation has been stirred up. (Hey, you wouldn't open a large bottle of soda that's warm and shaken up, either, would you? Sparkling wine has much more carbonated pressure than soda, and so it needs more time to settle down.)

If you're in the midst of a sparkling wine emergency and need to open the bottle anyway, one quick solution is to calm down the carbonation by submerging the bottle in an ice bucket for 20 to 30 minutes. (Fill the bucket with one-half ice cubes and one-half ice-cold water.)

In any case, be careful when you remove the wire cage, which is twisted around the top of the bottle, helping to hold the cork in place. (We have a hole in our kitchen ceiling from one encounter with a flying cork.) As a precaution, keep one hand on top of the cork while removing the wire and be sure to point the bottle away from people and other fragile objects.

Never, ever use a corkscrew on a bottle of sparkling wine. The pressure of the trapped carbonation, when suddenly released, could send the cork and corkscrew flying right into your eye.

A sigh is better than a pop

If you like to hear the sparkling wine pop, just yank the cork out. When you do that, however, you'll lose some of the precious wine, which will froth out of the bottle top as foam. Also, the noise could interfere with your guests' conversation. Besides, it ain't too classy!

Removing the cork from sparkling wine with just a gentle sigh rather than a loud pop is fairly easy. Simply hold the bottle at a 45-degree angle with a towel wrapped around it if it's wet. (Try positioning the base of the bottle on your hipbone.) Twist the bottle while holding on to the cork so that you can control the cork as it emerges. When you feel the cork starting to come out of the bottle, *push down against the cork* with some pressure as if you don't want to let it out of the bottle. In this way, the cork will emerge slowly with a hissing or sighing sound rather than a pop.

Every once in a while, you'll come across a really tight cork that doesn't want to budge. Try running the top of the bottle under warm water for a minute or two, or wrapping a towel around it to create friction. Either one of these actions usually loosens the cork enough for you to remove it.

Or you could purchase some fancy gadget resembling a pair of pliers (there are actually three gadgets: Champagne Pliers, a Champagne Star, and a Champagne Key) that you place around the part of the cork that's outside the bottle. (Sparkling wine corks have a mushroom-shaped head that protrudes from the bottle.) Or you could probably try using regular pliers, although lugging in the toolbox will surely change the mood of the occasion.

The good doctor makes a bubbly bumble

We'll never forget a party that a doctor friend of ours threw to celebrate his baby girl's birth. At an appropriate moment with all the guests watching, he clamped the Champagne bottle between his legs to remove the cork. The cork popped out with more gusto than he anticipated, propelling the bottle backward through his legs and across the floor in a zig-zag motion, spilling Champagne everywhere. We were all on the verge of laughter until his disapproving stepmother proclaimed chillingly, "You don't know how to do anything right, do you?" Our friend stood there with a frozen grin on his face.

Does Wine Really Breathe?

Most wine is alive in the sense that it changes chemically as it slowly grows older. Wine absorbs oxygen and, like our own cells, it oxidizes. When the grapes turn into wine in the first place, they give off carbon dioxide, just like us. So we suppose you could say that wine breathes, in a sense.

But that's not what the server means when he asks, "Shall I pull the cork and let the wine breathe, sir (or madam)?" The term *breathing* usually refers to the process of aerating the wine, exposing it to air. Sometimes a wine that is very young will display an enhanced aroma or flavor if it is aerated. But just pulling the cork out of the bottle and letting the bottle sit there is a truly ineffective way to aerate the wine. The little space at the neck of the bottle is way too small to allow your wine to breathe very much.

How to aerate your wine

If you really want to aerate your wine, do one or both of the following:

1. Pour the wine into a *decanter* (a fancy word for a container — usually glass — that is big enough to hold the contents of an entire bottle of wine).

2. Pour the wine into large glasses at least ten minutes before you plan to drink it.

Practically speaking, it doesn't matter what your decanter looks like or how much it costs. In fact, the very inexpensive, wide-mouthed carafes are fine. For example, low-priced Paul Masson-brand wines come in such decanters.

Which wines need aerating?

Many red wines but only a few white wines — and some dessert wines — can benefit from aeration. Most white wines can be consumed upon pouring, unless they're too cold, but that's a discussion for later.

Young, tannic red wines

Young red wines, especially those that are high in tannin (see Chapter 2 for more on tannin) — such as Cabernet Sauvignons, many red Zinfandels, Bordeaux, many wines from the Rhône Valley, and many Italian wines — actually taste better with aeration because their tannins soften and the wine becomes less harsh.

The younger and more tannic the wine is, the more time it needs to breathe. As a general rule, most tannic, young red wines soften up with one hour of aeration. A glaring exception to the one-hour rule would be many young Barolos or Barbarescos (red wines from Piedmont, Italy, which you can read about in Chapter 11); these wines are frequently so tannic that they can practically stand up by themselves without a decanter. They often can benefit from three or four hours of aeration.

Older red wines with sediment

Many red wines develop *sediment* (tannin and other particles in the wine that solidify over time and drop to the bottom of the bottle) usually after about eight years of age. The sediment can taste a bit bitter (remember, it's tannin). Also, the dark particles floating in your wine, usually near the bottom of your glass, don't look very appetizing.

To remove sediment, keep the bottle of wine standing upright at least a day or two before you plan to open it so that the sediment settles at the bottom of the bottle. Then decant the wine into a decanter: Pour the wine out of the bottle slowly while watching the wine inside the bottle as it approaches the neck. You watch the wine so that you can stop pouring when you see cloudy wine from the bottom of the bottle making its way to the neck.

To actually see the wine inside the bottle as you pour, you need to have a bright light shining up through the bottle's neck. Candles are commonly used for this purpose, and they are romantic, but a flashlight standing on end works even better. (It's brighter, and it doesn't flicker.) Stop pouring the wine into the decanter when you reach the sediment, which should be toward the bottom of the bottle.

The older the wine, the more delicate it can be. Don't give old, fragile-looking wines excessive aeration. (Look at the color of the wine through the bottle before you decant; if it looks pale, the wine could be pretty far along its maturity curve.) The flavors of really old wines will start fading rapidly after 10 or 15 minutes of being exposed to air. Remember what happened to the people who left the Hidden Valley of Shangri-La in *Lost Horizon?* They withered into wizened ancients in a matter of minutes!

If the wine needs more aeration after decanting (that is, it still tastes a bit harsh), let it breathe in the open decanter. If the wine has a dark color, chances are that it is still quite youthful and will need to breathe more. Conversely, if the wine has a brick red or garnet color, it probably has matured and might not need much more aeration.

A few white wines

Some very good, dry white wines — such as full-bodied white Burgundies and white Bordeaux wines, as well as the best Alsace whites — also get better with aeration. For example, if you open up a young Corton-Charlemagne (a great white Burgundy), and it doesn't seem to be showing much aroma or flavor, chances are that it needs aeration. Decant it and try it again in a half hour. (If the room is relatively cool, no need to put the decanter in the refrigerator.) In most cases, your wine will dramatically improve.

Vintage Ports

One of the most famous fortified wines is vintage Port (properly called "Porto"). We discuss this wine and others like it in more detail in Chapter 16.

For now, we'll just say that, yes, vintage Port needs breathing lessons, very much so indeed! Young vintage Ports are so brutally tannic that they demand many hours of aeration (eight would not be too much). Even older Ports will improve with four hours or more of aeration. Older vintage Ports require decanting, also, because they are chock-full of sediment (often, filling the bottom 10 percent of the bottle). Keep vintage Ports standing for several days before you open them.

Exceptions to the "decant your red wines and Ports" rule

The exceptions prove the rule. The majority of red wines you drink do not require decanting, aeration, or any other special preparation other than pulling the cork out and having a glass handy.

The following red wines *do not* need decanting:

 ✔ Lighter-bodied, less tannic red wines, such as Pinot Noirs, Burgundies, Beaujolais, Côtes du Rhônes; lighter red Zinfandels; and lighter-bodied Italian reds, such as Dolcettos, Barberas, and lighter Chiantis. These wines don't have much tannin and, therefore, don't need much aeration.

✔ Inexpensive (less than $8) red wines. Same reason as preceding.

✔ Tawny ports — in fact, any other Ports except vintage Ports. These wines should be free from sediment (which stayed behind in the barrels where the wine aged) and are ready to drink when you pour them.

Does the Glass Really Matter?

If you are just drinking wine as refreshment with your meal and you are not thinking about the wine much as it goes down, the glass you use probably doesn't matter in the least. A jelly glass? Why not? Plastic glasses? We've used them dozens of times on picnics, not to mention in airplanes (where the wine's quality doesn't demand great glasses, anyway).

But if you have a good wine, a special occasion, friends who want to talk about the wine with you, or the boss for dinner, *stemware* (glasses with stems) is called for. And it's not just a question of etiquette and status: Good wine will taste better out of good glasses. Really.

Compare wine glasses to stereo speakers. Any old speaker brings the music to your ears, just like any old glass brings the wine to your lips. But (assuming that you can tell the difference and that you care to notice it) can't you appreciate the sound so much more, aesthetically and emotionally, from good speakers? The same principle holds true with wine and wine glasses. You can appreciate wine's aroma and flavor complexities so much more out of a fine wine glass. The medium is the message.

First, the right color

Unless you're playing some kind of perverse game on your wine expert friends, your wine glasses should be clear. (It's okay for jelly glasses to have pictures of the Flintstones on them, as long as the background is clear.) Those pretty pink or green glasses may look nice in Aunt Betty's china cabinet, but they mess up your ability to distinguish the true colors of the wine. Those opaque black glasses that were popular a while ago may be appropriate for a devil-worshipping ceremony, but certainly not for wine appreciation.

Now the size, thickness, and shape

Believe it or not (we didn't always), the taste of a wine changes when you drink the wine out of different types of glasses. A riot almost broke out at one wine event we organized because the tasters thought we served them different wines in each glass and that we had just pretended that it was the same wine, to fool them — so different did the wine taste in different glasses. We learned that three aspects of a glass are important: its size, its shape, and the thickness of the glass.

Size

For dry red and white wine, small glasses are anathema — besides that, they're a pain in the neck. You just can't swirl the wine around in those little glasses without spilling it, which makes appreciating the aroma of the wine almost impossible. And furthermore, who wants to bother continually refilling them? Small glasses can work adequately only for sherries or dessert wines, which have strong aromas to begin with and are generally consumed in smaller quantities than table wines. But in most cases, larger is usually better.

✔ For red wines, your glass should hold a minimum of 12 ounces; many of the best glasses have capacities ranging from 16 to 24 ounces, or more.

✔ For white wines, 10 to 12 ounces should be the minimum capacity.

✔ For sparkling wines, a capacity ranging from 8 to 12 ounces is fine.

Thickness and shape

Very thin, fine crystal costs a lot more than normal, thick glass. That's one reason why many people don't use it (and one reason why some people do).

The better reason for using fine crystal is that the wine tastes better out of it. We're not sure whether the elegant crystal simply heightens the aesthetic experience of the wine drinking or whether there's some more scientific reason.

Tulips, flutes, balloons, and other picturesque wine-glass names

You thought that a tulip was a flower and a flute was a musical instrument? Well, the tulip also happens to be the name of the ideally shaped glass for sparkling wine (see Figure 8-4). It is tall, elongated, and more narrow at the rim than in the middle of the bowl. This shape helps hold the bubbles in the wine longer, not allowing them to escape freely (the way the wide-mouthed, sherbet-cuplike, so-called champagne glasses do).

The flute is also a good sparkling wine glass because of its narrow, elongated shape (see Figure 8-5); but it is less ideal than the tulip because it does not narrow at the mouth. The trumpet actually widens at the mouth, making it less suitable for sparkling wine but very elegant looking (see Figure 8-6).

The balloon glass is ideal for aerating many red wines, such as Burgundies, Barolos, and so on, because of its ample shape.

Figure 8-4:
The tulip glass for sparkling wine.

Figure 8-5:
The flute glass for sparkling wine.

Figure 8-6:
The trumpet glass for sparkling wine.

An oval-shaped bowl that is narrow at its mouth (see Figure 8-7) is ideal for many red wines, such as Bordeaux, Cabernet Sauvignons, Merlots, Chiantis, and Zinfandels. On the other hand, some red wines, such as Burgundies, Pinot Noirs, and Barolos, are best appreciated in wider-bowled, apple-shaped glasses (see Figure 8-8).

Half empty or half full?

"Fill 'er up" might be fine for your service station attendant, but not for the person pouring the wine. It always annoys us when servers fill our glasses to the top. We guess they don't want to bother repouring the wine too often. Or maybe they want to give us our money's worth. But how can we stick our noses into full glasses without looking like idiots? Once a kid at a nearby table blurted out, "Look, Mom, that man is drinking with his nose!"

To leave some margin of safety for swirling and smelling the wine, fill the glass only partially. One-third capacity, at the most, is the best fill-level for serious red wines. (This goes back to that idea of aerating the wine.) White wine glasses can be filled halfway, while sparkling wines can be three-quarters full. On the other hand, if you're using paper cups or jelly glasses, you might as well "Fill 'er up."

Figure 8-7:
The
Bordeaux
glass.

Figure 8-8:
The
Burgundy
glass.

How many glasses do I need, anyway?

So what's a wine lover to do: Buy different glasses for each kind of wine? Fortunately, some all-purpose red and white wine glasses combine the best features of all glasses. And you don't have to pay a fortune for decent wine glasses. A company called St. George Crystal makes crystal glasses in all sizes and shapes that sell for $3 to $4 a glass. They are available in most wine stores.

If you want something finer, try Riedel Crystal. Riedel is an Austrian glass manufacturer that specializes in making the right wine glass for each kind of wine. Riedel has done a good deal of research to discover which glass shapes are best suited for major types of wine, for example, Bordeaux, Burgundy, Chardonnay, Champagne, and so on.

Riedel produces three lines of wine glasses: the relatively inexpensive ($8 or $9 per glass) Overture series, the medium-priced ($17 to $24 per glass) Vinum series, and its state-of-the-art, hand-blown Sommelier glasses for serious connoisseurs (at $35 to $60 a glass, you'd better be serious!). Riedel is widely available in catalogs and in wine stores.

The more you care to pay attention to the flavor of the wine, the more you really and truly appreciate and enjoy wine from a good wine glass. If you just don't have an ear for music, that's okay, too.

Washing your crystal glasses

Detergents often leave a filmy residue in glasses, which can affect the aroma and flavor of your wine. We strongly advise that you clean your good crystal glasses by hand, using washing soda or baking soda (washing soda is the better of the two; it doesn't cake up, like baking soda). Neither product leaves any soapy, filmy residue in your glass. Washing soda can be found in the soap/detergent section of supermarkets. Buy the least expensive store brand. It won't have any added, perfumey aromas.

Serving Wine Not Too Warm, Not Too Cold

Just as the right glass will enhance your wine experience, serving wine at the ideal temperature is a vital factor in your enjoyment of wine. Frequently, we have tasted the same wine at different temperatures (and, believe it or not, at different barometric pressures) and have loved the wine on one occasion but disliked it the other time!

Most red wines are at their best at cool room temperature, 62° to 65°F (16 to 18°C). Once upon a time, in drafty old English and Scottish castles, that was simply room temperature (actually it was probably *warm, high noon room temperature*!). Today when you hear room temperature, you think of a room that's about 70°F (21°C), don't you? Red wine served at this temperature can taste flat, flabby, lifeless, and often too *hot* — a burning sensation from the alcohol.

Fifteen or twenty minutes in the fridge will do wonders to revive red wines that have been suffering from heat prostration. But don't let the wine get too cold. Red wines served too cold taste overly tannic and acidic, decidedly unpleasant. Light, fruity red wines, such as Beaujolais, are most delightful when served slightly chilled at about 58° to 60°F (14° to 15.5°C).

Are you wondering how to know when your bottle is 58° to 60°F? You could buy a nifty digital thermometer that wraps around the outside of the bottle and gives you a color-coded reading. Or you could buy something that looks like a real thermometer that you place into the opened bottle (in the wine's mouth, you might say). We have both of those, and we never use them. Just feel the bottle with your hand and take a guess. Practice makes perfect.

Just as many red wines are served too warm, most white wines are definitely served too cold, judging by the service that we have received in many restaurants. The higher the quality of a white wine, the less cold it should be so that you can properly appreciate its flavor.

✔ Fine white wines are best between 58° and 62°F (14° and 16.5°C).

✔ Simpler, inexpensive, quaffing-type white wines are best served colder, between 50° and 55°F (10° and 12.8°C).

✔ Rosés and blush wines can be served at the same temperature as inexpensive white wines.

✔ Inexpensive sweet wines should be served cold, similar to inexpensive dry white wines.

✔ Finer dessert wines, such as a good Sauternes or Port, taste their best at the same temperature as better white wines (for Sauternes, 58° to 62°F, 14° to 16.5°C) and better red wines (for Port, 62° to 65°F, 16° to 18°C).

✔ Champagnes and sparkling wines are at their best when cold, about 45°F (7°C).

To avoid the problem of warm bubbly, keep an ice bucket handy. Or put the bottle back in the refrigerator between pourings.

Storing Leftover Wine

A sparkling-wine stopper, a device that fits over the opened bottle and keeps it closed, is really effective in keeping any remaining Champagne or sparkling wine fresh (often for several days) in the refrigerator. But what do you do when you have red or white wine left in the bottle?

You can put the cork back in the bottle if it still fits, and put the bottle into the refrigerator. (Even red wines will stay fresher there; just take the bottle out to warm up an hour or so before serving it.) But three other methods are more reliable in keeping your remaining wine from oxidizing:

✔ If you have about half a bottle of wine left, you can simply pour the wine into a clean, empty half-sized wine bottle and recork the smaller bottle. We sometimes buy wines in half-bottles, just to make sure that we have the empty half-bottles around.

✔ There is a handy, inexpensive, miniature pump that you can buy in any wine store, called a Vac-U-Vin. This pump removes the oxygen from the bottle, and the rubber stoppers that come with it keep additional oxygen from entering the bottle. It's supposed to keep your wine fresh for up to a week, but it doesn't work with all wines.

✔ You can buy small cans of inert gas in some wine stores. Just squirt a few shots of the gas into the bottle through a skinny straw, which comes with the can, and put the cork back in the bottle. The gas acts as a layer between the wine and the oxygen in the bottle, thus protecting the wine from oxidizing. Simple and effective. Private Preserve is one of the better brands; it is highly recommended.

An aside about atmospheric pressure

File this under FYI ("For Your Information") — or maybe under "Believe It or Not."

A few years ago, we were enjoying one of our favorite red wines, an Italian Barbera, in the Alps. It was a perfect summer day in the mountains — crisp, clear, and cool. The wine was also perfect — absolutely delicious with our salami, bread, and cheese. A couple of days later, we had the very same wine at the seashore, on a cloudy, humid, heavy-pressure day. The wine was heavy, flat, and lifeless.

What had happened to our wonderful mountain wine? We made inquiries among some of our wine-drinking friends and discovered that they had had similar experiences. For red wines, at least, atmospheric pressure apparently influences the taste of the wine: thin, light pressure, for the better; heavy pressure, heavy humidity, for the worse. So the next time one of your favorite red wines doesn't seem quite right, check the air pressure! Believe it or not.

To avoid all this bother, just drink the wine! Or, if you're not too fussy, just place the leftover wine in the refrigerator and drink it in the next day or two — before it goes into a coma.

Chapter 9
Judging a Wine by Its Label

- -

In This Chapter

▶ The language of the wine label

▶ The truth behind impressive terms like *reserve* and *estate-bottled*

▶ The difference between regions, districts, and communes

▶ Vintage versus nonvintage wines

▶ AOC, DOC, DO, QbA, QWPSR, and other strange designations

- -

*W*e're standing at the immigration desk in some foreign airport, and a distrustful officer is studying our passports. We're disheveled after six hours of trying to sleep in seats too small to sit in. He needs to make a judgment about us, and all he has to go on is the sketchy information in our passport and our tired faces.

Do you sometimes feel like that immigration officer when you stand in front of an array of wine bottles and attempt to make a judgment about which to buy? To the untrained eye, the labels hardly say more than a passport, and the pretty pictures on the labels are even less relevant to what's inside the bottles than passport photos are to a traveler's true appearance.

The Wine Label and What It Tells You

Every bottle of wine must have a label, and that label must provide certain information about the wine. Some of the information on a wine label is required by the country where the wine is *made*. Other items of information are required by the country where the wine is *sold*. When the requirements are different in the two places, life can get very, very complicated for label writers!

The forward and backward of wine labels

Many wine bottles have two labels. The front label names the wine and grabs your eye as you walk down the aisle, and the back label gives you a little more information, ranging from really helpful suggestions like "this wine tastes delicious with food" to oh-so-useful data such as "this wine has a total acidity of 6.02 and a pH of 3.34."

Now, if you're on your toes, you might be thinking: How can you tell the difference between front and back on a round bottle?

The government authorities in the U.S. apparently haven't thought that one through yet. They (and other governments) require certain information to appear on the front label of all wine bottles — basic stuff, such as the alcohol content, the type of wine (usually *red table wine* or *white table wine*), and the country of origin — but they don't define *front label*. So sometimes producers put all that information on the smaller of two labels and call that one the front label. Then the producers place another larger, colorful, dramatically eye-catching label — with little more than the name of the wine on it — on the *back* of the bottle. Guess which way the back label ends up facing when the bottle is placed on the shelf?

We don't feel at all outraged about this situation. We'd rather look at colorful labels on the shelf than boring information-laden ones any day. And we're not so lazy that we can't just pick up the bottle and turn it around to find out what we need to know. Besides, we enjoy the idea that wine producers and importers — whose every word and image on the label is scrutinized by the authorities to make sure that there are no sexual connotations or even the slightest suggestion that wine is healthful (regardless of medical findings) — have found one small way of getting even with the government.

Contains sulfites? Whose government warning?

Ironically, two items of label information (both of them dear to politicians' hearts) required for wines sold in the U.S. — the words "Contains Sulfites" and the government warning regarding alcohol consumption during pregnancy or while using heavy machinery — *cannot* appear on U.S. wine labels when the wine is exported to any country in the European Union (EU). The way the European labeling laws work, anything that is not explicitly permitted to appear on the label is forbidden. Sorry, surgeon general.

The mandatory sentence

The federal government mandates that certain items of information appear on labels of wines sold in the U.S. (see Figure 9-1). Such items are generally referred to as *the mandatory.* These include

- ✔ A brand name

- ✔ Indication of class or type (table wine, dessert wine, or sparkling wine)

- ✔ The percentage of alcohol by volume (unless it is implicit in the class; for example, the statement "table wine" implies an alcohol content of less than 14 percent; see the section, "Table wine" in Chapter 1)

- ✔ Name and address of the bottler

- ✔ Net contents (expressed in milliliters; the standard wine bottle is 750 ml, which is 25.6 ounces)

- ✔ The phrase *Contains Sulfites* (with very, very few exceptions)

- ✔ The government warning (that we won't dignify by repeating here; just pick up any bottle of wine and you'll see it)

American Viticultural Area (AVA)

GOBBLEDYGOOK

Brand name

Sonoma Valley
Nonna's Vineyard

Select Reserve — Quality designation
Estate-Bottled — Estate-bottled designation

Chardonnay — Wine name
White table wine — Type
Net contents 750ml - 13.5% alcohol — Alcohol by volume
Vinted and bottled by Gobbledygook Winery, Healdsburg, CA
CONTAINS SULFITES

Bottler information

Vineyard designation

Figure 9-1: The label of an American varietal wine.

Will the real producer please stand up?

Although U.S. and Canadian labeling laws require wine labels to carry the name and address of the bottler or dealer, respectively, this information doesn't necessarily tell you who made the wine.

Of the various phrases that may be used to identify the bottler on labels of wine sold in the U.S., only the words *produced by* or *made by* indicate the name of the company that actually fermented 75 percent or more of the wine (that is, who really *made* the wine); words such as *cellared by* or *vinted by* mean only that the company subjected the wine to cellar treatment (holding it for a while, for example).

On labels of wine sold in Canada, the dealer whose name and address must be indicated is the person for whom or by whom the wine is produced for sale. The person might or might not be the actual producer of the wine.

Labels on wines that are made outside the U.S. but sold within the U.S. must also carry the phrase *imported by* as well as the name and business location of the importer.

Canadian regulations are similar. Those regulations require wine labels to indicate the *common name* of the product (that is, *wine*), the net contents, the percentage of alcohol by volume, the name and address of the producer, the wine's country of origin (although only 75 percent of the grapes or wine must come from that country), and the container size. Many of these items must be indicated in both English and French.

The European mandate

Some of the mandatory information on American and Canadian wine labels is also required by the European Union's wine authorities to appear on labels of wines produced or sold in the EU. But additional label items are prescribed by the EU for wines produced in its member countries.

The most important of these additional items is an indication of a wine's so-called quality level — which really means the wine's status in the EU's hierarchy of place-names. In short, every wine made in an EU member country *must* carry one of the following items on the label:

- ✔ A registered place-name, along with an official phrase that confirms that the name is in fact a registered place-name (see the following section for a listing of those official phrases)

- ✔ Or, a phrase indicating that the wine is a *table wine,* a status lower than a registered place-name

For U.S. wines, the *table wine* category encompasses all non-sparkling wines that contain up to 14 percent alcohol. This is a distinctly different use of the term *table wine.*

Appellations of origin

A registered place-name is called an *appellation of origin.* In fact, each EU place-name defines far more than just the name of the place that the grapes come from: The place-name connotes the wine's grape varieties, grape-growing methods, and winemaking methods. Each appellation is, therefore, a definition of the wine as well as the wine's name. European governments regulate their wine appellations in various ways to determine that wines carrying registered place-names conform to the legal definitions of those names.

European wines with official place names fall into a European category called QWPSR (Quality Wine Produced in a Specific Region). You see the following phrases on European labels that confirm that a wine is a QWPSR wine and that its name is therefore a registered place-name:

- **France:** *Appellation Contrôlée* or *Appellation d'Origine Contrôlée* (AC or AOC, in short), translated as *regulated name* or *regulated place-name.* Also, on labels of wines from places of slightly lower status, the initials AO VDQS, standing for *Appellation d'Origine — Vins Délimités de Qualité Supérieure;* translated as *place-name, demarcated wine of superior quality.*

- **Italy:** *Denominazione di Origine Controllata* (DOC), translated as *regulated place-name;* or for certain wines of an even higher status, *Denominazione di Origine Controllata e Garantita* (DOCG), translated as *regulated and guaranteed place-name.*

- **Spain:** *Denominación de Origen* (DO), translated as *place-name;* and *Denominación de Origen Calificada* (DOCa), translated as *qualified-origin place-name* for regions with the highest status (of which there is only one, Rioja).

- **Portugal:** *Denominação de Origem Controlada* (DOC), translated as *regulated place-name* for the major place-names; and *Indicação de Proveniencia Regulamentada* (IPR), translated as *regulated place indication* for other registered place-names.

- **Germany:** *Qualitätswein bestimmter Anbaugebiete* (QbA), translated as *quality wine from a specific region;* or *Qualitätswein mit Prädikat* (QmP), translated as *quality wine with special attributes,* for the best wines. (Read more about Germany's complex appellation system in Chapter 12.)

Table 9-1 lists the European wine designations for easy reference.

Table 9-1	European Wine Designations at a Glance		
Country	*QWPSR Designation(s)*	*Table Wine Designation with Geographic Indication*	*Table Wine Designation without Geographic Indication*
France	AOC VDQS	Vin de pays	Vin de table
Italy	DOCG DOC	IGT Vino da tavola (and geographic name)	Vino da tavola
Spain	DOCa DO	Vino de la tierra	Vino de mesa
Portugal	DOC IPR	Vinho de mesa regional	Vinho de mesa
Germany	QmP QbA	Landwein	Deutscher tafelwein

Phrases on European labels that indicate that a wine is a table wine vary according to country. Each country has two such phrases, one for table wines with a geographic indication (actually Italy has two phrases in this category), and one for table wines with no geographic indication smaller than the country of production. These phrases are

- **France:** *Vin de pays* (country wine) followed by the name of an approved area; *vin de table*

- **Spain:** *Vino de la tierra* (country wine) followed by the name of an approved area; *vino de mesa*

- **Italy:** *Indicazione Geografica Tipica* (translated as *typical geographic indication* and abbreviated as *IGT*) and the name of an approved area, or *vino da tavola* (table wine) followed by a the name of a geographic area; *vino da tavola*

- **Germany**: *Landwein* (country wine) and the name of an approved area; *Deutscher tafelwein*

- **Portugal**: *Vinho regional* (regional wine) and the name of an approved area; *vinho de mesa*

Figure 9-2 shows a European wine label, as it would appear in the U.S.

Alcohol by volume

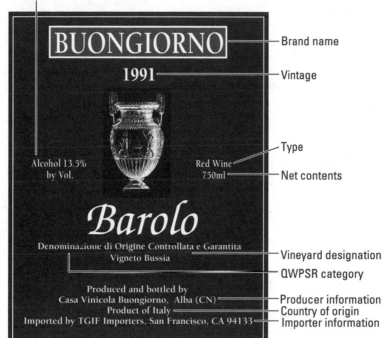

Brand name

Vintage

Type

Net contents

Vineyard designation

QWPSR category

Producer information
Country of origin
Importer information

Figure 9-2:
The label of
a European
wine to
be sold in
the U.S.

TIP

The phrase for a registered place-name in the U.S. is *American Viticultural Area* (AVA). But the phrase does *not* appear on wine labels (refer to Figure 9-1). Nor does any such phrase appear on labels of Australian or South American wines.

Some Optional Label Terms

Besides the mandatory information required by government authorities, all sorts of other words can appear on wine labels. These words can be meaningless phrases designed to make you think that you're getting a special quality wine, or words that provide useful information about what's in the bottle. Sometimes the same word can fall into either category, depending on the label. This ambiguity occurs because some words that are strictly regulated in some producing countries are not at all regulated in others.

The EU hierarchy of wine

Although each country within the European Union makes its own laws regarding the naming of wine, these laws must fit within the framework of the larger European Union law. This framework provides two levels into which every single EU-produced wine (every French wine, Italian wine, Spanish wine, and so on) must fit:

✔ **Quality wine:** Wines with official appellations of origin. (Each appellation law defines the geographic area, the grapes that may be used, grape-growing practices, winemaking and aging techniques, and so on.) This category is abbreviated as QWPSR in English (Quality Wine Produced in a Specific Region) or VQPRD in several other European languages. All AOC, DOC, DO, and QbA wines — to use the abbreviations mentioned previously in this chapter — fall into this category.

✔ **Table wine:** All other wines produced within the EU — in other words, any wine produced in France, Italy, Spain, Germany, and so forth that does not carry an official appellation of origin. The table wine category is subdivided into two categories: Table wines that carry a precise geographic indication on their labels, such as French *vin de pays* or Spanish *vino de la tierra* wines; and table wines with no geographic indication except the country of origin. These latter wines may not carry a vintage or a grape name.

All other wines sold in the EU fall into a third category:

✔ **Wine:** Wines produced by countries outside the EU, such as the U.S., Canada, or Australia. If a wine has a geographic indication smaller than the country of origin, it enjoys higher status than otherwise.

Vintage

The word *vintage* followed by a year, or the year listed alone without the word *vintage,* is the most common optional item on a wine label (refer to Figure 9-2). Sometimes the vintage appears on the front label, and sometimes it has its own small label above the front label.

The *vintage year* is nothing more than the year in which the grapes for a particular wine were harvested. But there is an aura surrounding vintage-dated wine that causes many people to believe that any wine with a vintage date is by definition better than a wine without a vintage date. *In fact, there is no correlation between the presence of a vintage date and the wine's quality.* (Because a vintage date is *perceived* as an indication of quality by consumers, however, the EU denies simple table wines the privilege of listing a vintage date.)

Most of the wines you'll find in wine shops, supermarkets, and restaurants are *vintage wines* in the sense that 95 percent or more of that wine came from grapes harvested in a single year — the official U.S. definition for a vintage wine. (*Nonvintage* wines are blends of wines whose grapes were harvested in different years.) Most wines are also *vintage-dated wines* — they state the year on the bottle — because vintage-dated wines sell better (thanks to that aura).

Vintage wines can vary in style and quality from one vintage to the next because the weather (which affects the grapes) is different every year (naturally). But generally speaking, *what* vintage a wine is — that is, whether the grapes grew in a year with perfect weather or whether the grapes were meteorologically challenged — is an issue you need to consider a) only when you buy top quality wines, and b) mainly when those wines come from parts of the world that experience significant variations in weather from year to year — in a nutshell, Europe. Vintage variation does exist in California and Australia, but the swing in quality from year to year is less dramatic than for most European wines. In the case of less expensive wines — those that sell for up to about $10 a bottle retail — differences from year to year are usually insignificant.

Reserve

Reserve is our favorite meaningless word on American wine labels. The term is used to convince you that the wine inside the bottle is something special. This trick usually works because the word *does* have specific meaning and *does* carry a certain amount of prestige on labels of wines from many other countries. So *reserve* ends up carrying positive connotations when it appears on U.S. wines, even when it means nothing.

In Italy and Spain, for example, the word *reserve* (or its foreign language equivalent, which looks something like *reserve*) indicates a wine that has received extra aging at the winery before release. Implicit in the extra aging is the idea that the wine was better than normal and, therefore, worthy of the extra aging. So a Chianti Classico Riserva is considered a better and more expensive wine than the same producer's basic Chianti Classico. A Rioja Gran Reserva (Spain even has *degrees* of reserve) is better than the same producer's Rioja Reserva, which is better than that producer's regular Rioja. You get the picture.

In some other countries, like France, the use of *reserve* is not regulated. However, its use is generally consistent with the notion that the wine is better in quality than a given producer's norm.

Why not vintage?

There are really just two situations in which producers might be inclined to blend wines from two or more years and create a nonvintage wine. If a winery is situated in a climatic zone where full ripeness of the grapes is a best-case scenario rather than the norm (parts of Germany, for example, or Champagne — both cool, northerly areas), the producer might choose to hold back wine from one year to blend in with the next year's wine in case he has a poor crop the next year.

The decision is as much financial as qualitative: He needs to guarantee that he will have a product to sell the next year.

The second reason for creating a nonvintage blend is price. When a winery purchases wine on the bulk market (as large wineries do, to supplement their own production), it gets a better price by buying grapes from different vintages.

In the U.S., the word *reserve* has historically been used in the same sense — as in Beaulieu Vineyards Georges de Latour Private Reserve, the best Cabernet that Beaulieu Vineyards makes. But these days, the word is bandied about so much that it no longer has meaning. For example, there are California wines labeled *Proprietor's Reserve* that sell for $6 a bottle. Those wines are not only the *least* expensive wines in a particular producer's lineup, but also some of the least expensive wines, period. There are Special Reserve wines, Vintage Reserve wines, Vintner's Reserve wines, and Reserve Selection wines — all utterly meaningless phrases.

Estate-bottled

Estate is a genteel word for a wine farm, a combined grape-growing and wine-making operation. The words *estate-bottled* on a wine label indicate that the company that bottled the wine also grew the grapes and made the wine. In other words, *estate-bottled* suggests accountability from the vineyard to the winemaking through to the bottling. The winery does not necessarily have to own the vineyards, but it has to control the vineyards and perform the vineyard operations.

Estate-bottling is an important concept to those of us who believe that you can't make good wine unless the grapes are as good as they can possibly be. If *we* made wine, we'd sure want to control our own vineyards.

We wouldn't go so far as to say that great wines *must* be estate-bottled, though. Ravenswood Winery — to name just one example — makes some terrific wines from the grapes of small vineyards owned and operated by private landowners. And some large California landowners, such as the Sangiacomo brothers, are quite serious about their vineyards but do not make wine themselves (they sell their grapes to various wineries). None of those wines would be considered estate-bottled.

Sometimes French wine labels carry the words *domaine-bottled* or *château-bottled* (or the phrase *mis en bouteille au château/au domaine*). The concept is the same as estate-bottled, with *domaine* and *château* being equivalent to the American term *estate*.

Vineyard name

Wines in the medium-to-expensive price category — those that cost about $15 or more — might carry on the label the name of the specific vineyard where the grapes for that wine grew. Sometimes one winery will make two or three different wines that are distinguishable only by the vineyard name on the label. Each wine is unique because the *terroir* of each vineyard is unique. (For an explanation of *terroir*, see Chapter 5.) These single vineyards might or might not be identified by the word *vineyard* next to the name of the vineyard.

Italian wines, which are really into the single-vineyard game, will have *vigneto* or *vigna* or sometimes the French word *cru* on their labels next to the name of the single vineyard. Or they won't. It's optional.

Other optional words on the label

You'll be pleased to know that we have just about exhausted our list of terms that you might find on a wine label (not to mention exhausting ourselves — and probably you — in the process).

One additional expression on some French labels is *Vieilles Vignes (vee yay veen),* which translates as *old vines.* Because old vines produce a very small quantity of fruit compared to younger vines, the quality of their grapes and of the resulting wine is considered to be very good. The problem is, the phrase is unregulated. Anyone can claim that his vines are old.

The word *superior* can appear in French *(Supérieure)* or Italian *(Superiore)* as part of an AOC or DOC place-name (refer to the section, "The mandatory sentence," earlier in this chapter for a refresher on these acronyms). It means the wine attained a higher alcohol level than the nonsuperior version of the same wine. Frankly, it's a distinction not worth losing sleep over.

The word *Classico* appears on the labels of some Italian DOC and DOCG wines when the grapes come from the heartland of the named place.

Part III
Around the World of Wine

The 5th Wave   By Rich Tennant

"Well, I'm enough of a wine expert to know that if the boat were sinking, there'd be several cases of this Bordeaux that would go into a lifeboat before you would."

In this part . . .

We're flattered if you've gotten to this point by reading every word we've written so far. But we realize that you might have landed here by skipping lots of stuff earlier in the book. That's okay with us — the meat and potatoes of the book are right here.

The seven chapters in this part are chock-full of information about the major wines of the world, including our recommendations on specific wines to buy. We devote one entire chapter each to the wines of France, Italy, and the U.S., because these are such important wine countries. We also give a whole chapter to Champagne and other sparkling wines, and end with dessert — a chapter on fortified and dessert wines. Happy drinking!

Chapter 10

Doing France

• •

In This Chapter

▶ *Crus,* classified growths, *chateaux,* and *domaines*

▶ Why Bordeaux wines are legendary

▶ The scarcity issue in fine Burgundy

▶ Robust red Rhônes

▶ White gems of the Loire and Alsace

• •

*F*rance. What comes to mind when you hear that word? Strolling along Paris's grand boulevard, the Champs Elysées? Romance? The beautiful, blue water and golden sun on the French Riviera?

When we think of France, we think of wine. Bordeaux, Burgundy, Beaujolais, Chablis, Champagne, and Sauternes are not only famous wines — they are also places in France where people live, work, eat, and drink (wine, of course!). France has the highest per capita wine consumption of any country in the world. They have set a good example for the rest of us.

The French Model

Why has France become the most famous place in the world for wine? For one thing, the French have been doing it for a long time — making wine, that is. Centuries before the Romans conquered Gaul and planted vineyards, the Greeks arrived with their vines.

Equally important is French *terroir,* that magical combination of climate and soil that, when it clicks, can yield grapes that give us breathtaking wines. And what grapes! France is the home of almost all the renowned varieties in the world — Cabernet Sauvignon, Chardonnay, Merlot, Pinot Noir, Syrah, and Sauvignon Blanc, just to name a few. (See Chapter 4 for more information on these grape varieties.)

France is the model, the standard setter, for all the world's wines: Most countries that produce wine now make their own versions of Cabernet Sauvignon, Chardonnay, Merlot, Pinot Noir, and so on, thanks to the success of these grapes in France. If imitation is the sincerest form of flattery, French winemakers have had good reason to blush for a long time now.

Understanding French wine law

French lawmakers have reason to blush, too. France's system of defining and regulating wine regions — the *Appellation d'Origine Contrôlée,* or AOC (translated as *regulated place name* or *regulated origin name*) system, established in 1935 — has been the legislative model for most of the other European countries. The European Union's (EU's) framework of wine laws, within which the AOC system now operates, is also modeled on the French system.

To understand French wines and wine laws, you need to know five things:

✔ Most French wines are named after places. (These are not arbitrary places; they are places registered and defined under French wine law.) When we talk about French wines and the regions they come from, most of the time the region and the wine have the same name (as in Burgundy, from Burgundy).

✔ The French wine system is hierarchical. Some wines (that is, the wines of some places) officially have higher rank than other wines.

✔ Generally, the smaller and more specific the place for which a wine is named, the higher the rank.

✔ Just because a wine carries a high rank doesn't necessarily mean that it's better than the next wine; it just means that it should be better. The laws rank the potentiality of the place where the wine comes from, and are not infallible indications of actual quality.

✔ The wine's rank or grade is always stated on the label, usually in small letters underneath the name of the wine.

There are four possible ranks of French wine, according to French wine law. You can determine the rank of a French wine at a glance by seeing which of the following French phrases appears on the label. (Wines of higher rank generally cost more.) From highest to lowest, the rankings are

✔ **Appellation Contrôlée,** or AOC (or AC), the highest grade. On the label, the place-name of the wine usually appears between the two French words, as in Appellation Bordeaux Contrôlée.

✔ **Vins Délimités de Qualité Supérieure,** or VDQS wines (translated as *demarcated wine of superior quality*). These words appear on the label immediately below the name of the wine.

> ✔ **Vins de pays,** meaning *country wines*. On the label, the phrase is always followed by a place-name, such as Vins de Pays *de Jardin de France,* which indicates the area where the grapes grew; the places or regions are generally much larger than the places or regions referred to in the two higher rankings.
>
> ✔ **Vins de table,** ordinary French table wines that carry no geographic indication other than France. By law, they also have no grape variety nor vintage indicated. (See Chapters 1 and 9 for more about table wines.)

Here's how these four categories of French wines fit within the European Union's two-tier system described in Chapter 9:

> ✔ All AOC and VDQS wines fall into the EU's higher tier, QWPSR (Quality Wine Produced in a Specific Region, or simply *quality wine*).
>
> ✔ All *vins de pays* and *vins de table* fall into the EU's lower tier, table wines.

Fine distinctions in the ranks

France's system of place-naming its wines is actually a bit more complex than the four neat categories described in the preceding section might imply, however. Although all AOC wines/places hold exactly the same legal status — they're all generals in the French wine army, let's say — the market accords some AOCs higher regard (and higher prices) than others, based on the specificity of their *terroir*. Some of the generals have silver stars.

Imagine three concentric circles. Any wines produced from grapes grown within the entire area of the three circles may carry a particular AOC place-name, such as Bordeaux (assuming that the proper grape varieties are used and the wine conforms to the law for Bordeaux in all other respects); but wines whose grapes come from the territory of the two smaller circles are entitled to a different, more specific AOC name, such as Haut-Médoc. And wines whose area of production is limited to the smallest circle can use yet another AOC name, such as Pauillac. (They're all generals, but some have better credentials than others.)

The more specific the place described in the wine name, the finer the wine is generally considered to be in the eyes of the market, and the higher the price the winemaker can ask. Naturally, a winemaker will use the most specific name to which his wine is entitled.

In increasing order of specificity, an AOC name can be the name of

- ✔ A region (Bordeaux or Burgundy, for example)
- ✔ A district (Haut-Médoc or Côte de Beaune)
- ✔ A subdistrict (Côte de Beaune-Villages)
- ✔ A village or commune (Pauillac or Meursault)
- ✔ A specific vineyard (Le Montrachet)

Unfortunately, unless you are an expert at French geography and place names, you won't know which type of place an AOC name refers to by looking at the label. You can sometimes gauge how specific the place is by knowing the wine's price relative to other wines from the same region (a wine whose appellation is the name of a broad *region,* such as Bordeaux, usually costs less than a wine whose appellation represents a *district within that region,* such as Haut-Médoc, for example). And some names you just have to memorize.

France's Wine Regions

We single out five of France's ten wine regions for detailed discussion in this chapter: Bordeaux, Burgundy, the Rhône, the Loire, and Alsace. Historically, these are France's most important wine regions. Each region specializes in certain grape varieties for its wines, based on climate, soil, and local tradition. Table 10-1 provides a quick reference to the grapes and wines of these five regions.

Two other major wine regions of France are Provence and Languedoc-Roussillon. Sunny Provence, in southeastern France, is the home of many rosé, red, and white wines, most of which are uncomplicated, easy-drinking wines that are delightful accompaniments to the grilled fish and seafood of the region. Provence is especially known for its dry rosé wines, which are excellent for warm weather or casual enjoyment (other dry French rosés can be found in the Rhône and the Loire regions).

Languedoc-Roussillon *(lahn gweh doc roo see yon)* has become so important in the world wine market recently that we discuss this wine region separately in a sidebar in this chapter.

Cahors, Madiran, and Bergerac are wine zones in southwest France producing good-value wines that are now of better quality than ever. Cahors and Madiran are renowned for their full-bodied red wines, while Bergerac is best known for its inexpensive white and dessert wines.

Table 10-1   **The Wine Regions of France and Their Wines**

Red Wines	White Wines	Grape Varieties
Bordeaux		
Bordeaux		Cabernet Sauvignon, Merlot, Cabernet Franc, Petite Verdot, Malbec*
	Bordeaux Blanc	Sauvignon Blanc, Sémillon, Muscadelle*
Burgundy		
Burgundy		Pinot Noir
	White Burgundy	Chardonnay
Beaujolais		Gamay
	Chablis	Chardonnay
Rhône		
Hermitage		Syrah
Côte-Rôtie		Syrah, Viognier*
Châteauneuf-du-Pape		Grenache, Mourvèdre, Syrah, (many others)*
Côtes du Rhône		Grenache, Mourvèdre, Carignan, Syrah, (many others)*
	Condrieu	Viognier
Loire		
	Sancerre; Pouilly-Fumé	Sauvignon Blanc
	Vouvray	Chenin Blanc
	Muscadet	Melon de Bourgogne, alias Muscadet
Alsace		
	Riesling	Riesling
	Gewurztraminer	Gewurztraminer
	Tokay-Pinot Gris	Pinot Gris
	Pinot Blanc	Pinot Blanc

* Wines are blended from several grape varieties

France's bargain basement: Languedoc-Roussillon

The sunny, dry Languedoc-Roussillon area in southern France, also known as the Midi *(mee dee)*, has long been the country's largest wine-producing area (more than half of France's red wines come from here). Until about ten years ago, much of the wine from Languedoc-Roussillon had been of unremarkable quality, and it was usually not exported. But the technological wine revolution reached southern France, leading to improvements in the grapes of the area as well as the wines made from them. Now, even large American wineries such as Kendall-Jackson and Robert Mondavi are capitalizing on the wine potential in Languedoc-Roussillon.

In this region, look especially for the red wines from the specific AOC zones of Corbières, Minervois, Fitou, and Costières de Nîmes. In addition, many wines labeled with the appellation Vin de Pays d'Oc, made from grapes that can come from anywhere in the Languedoc-Roussillon region, are often good values.

Traditionally, the robust red wines of Languedoc-Roussillon were made from lesser-known grape varieties, such as Carignan, Cinsault, and Grenache. But in the last decade, better-known (and probably better quality) varieties such as Syrah, Cabernet Sauvignon, and Merlot have become popular with wineries. These grapes appear on their own, as varietal wines, or in blends.

The best news is that almost all of these wines are under $15, and many of them are under $10! Two of the better-known brands of varietal wines (with the Vin de Pays d'Oc appellation) in the Languedoc-Roussillon region are Fortant de France and Réserve St. Martin.

Bordeaux: The Incomparable

You must know French wine to know wine — French wines are that important in the wine world. Likewise, you must know Bordeaux to know French wine.

Bordeaux, a wine region in western France named after the fourth-largest French city (see Figure 10-1), produces 10 percent of all French wine and 26 percent of all AOC wine. Most Bordeaux wines are dry reds; 15 percent of the region's production is dry white, and 2 percent is sweet white wine, such as Sauternes.

The Bordeaux region, situated on the Atlantic coast, has a maritime climate, with warm summers and fairly mild winters. But the maritime weather also brings rain, often during harvest time. The variable weather accounts for the variability of vintage character and quality; when all goes well, such as in 1989 and 1990, great wines are produced.

Figure 10-1:
The wine
regions of
France.

Bordeaux produces wines at many levels of price and quality. Prices, for example, range from $6 a bottle for simple Bordeaux to well over $300 a bottle for Château Pétrus, one of the most expensive red Bordeaux wines (*old* vintages of Pétrus cost even *more!*). Most of the finer Bordeaux wines, both red and white, begin selling at about $20 a bottle when they are first released, two or three years after the vintage.

Bordeaux's reputation as one of the greatest wine regions in the world revolves around the legendary red wines of Bordeaux — *grands vins* (great wines) made by historic *châteaux* (wine estates) and capable of improving for many decades (see Chapter 21). These wines sit at the top of a red Bordeaux pyramid; quantitatively speaking, they are only a small facet of the region's reds. Many middle-level Bordeaux reds are made to be consumed within 10 to 15 years of the harvest, and other Bordeaux reds are meant to be enjoyed young, within two to five years of the vintage date.

The taste of really great Bordeaux

When young, the finest red Bordeaux wines have a deep cranberry hue, with aromas of blackcurrants, plums, spice, cedar, and cassis. For the first ten years or so, they can be very dry, almost austere, with tannin masking the fruit flavors. Eventually, these wines turn slightly garnet, develop an extraordinarily complex bouquet and flavor, and soften in tannin. The very finest red Bordeaux wines will frequently take 20 years or more before reaching their maturity; some have lasted well over 100 years (see Chapter 21).

The subregions for red Bordeaux

Two distinct red wine production zones exist with the Bordeaux region; these two areas have come to be called the Left Bank and the Right Bank — just like Paris. While many of the least expensive Bordeaux reds are blended from grapes grown all through the Bordeaux region — and thus they carry the region-wide AOC, Bordeaux — the better wines come from from specific AOC *districts* or AOC *communes* that are located in either the Right Bank or the Left Bank.

The Left Bank vineyards lie west of the Garonne River (the more southerly of the two rivers depicted in the Bordeaux inset of Figure 10-1) and the Gironde Estuary into which the Garonne empties. The Right Bank vineyards lie east and north of the Dordogne River (the more northerly of the two rivers depicted in the same inset), and east of the Gironde Estuary. (The middle ground in between the two rivers is more important for white wine than for red.)

Of the various wine districts on the Left Bank and the Right Bank, four (two on each bank) are the most important for red wine:

Left Bank (the western area)   *Right Bank (the eastern area)*

Haut-Médoc   St-Emilion
Graves/Pessac-Léognan   Pomerol

The Left Bank and the Right Bank differ mainly in soil composition: on the Left Bank, gravel predominates, whereas clay prevails on the Right Bank. As a result, Cabernet Sauvignon, which has an affinity for gravel, is the principal grape variety in the Médoc *(meh doc)*, the Haut-Médoc *(oh meh doc)*, and the Graves/Pessac-Léognan *(grahv/pay sac lay oh nyahn)*. Merlot, happier in clay, dominates the St-Emilion *(sant em eel yon)* and Pomerol *(pohm eh roll)* wines. (Both areas grow Cabernet Sauvignon *and* Merlot, as well as Cabernet Franc and two less significant grapes. See Chapter 4 for more information on grape varieties.)

You can therefore conclude correctly that Left Bank and Right Bank Bordeaux wines are markedly different from one another. But wines from the Médoc and the Graves or Pessac-Léognan (the northern part of the Graves) are quite similar to each other; likewise, it can be difficult to tell the difference between a Pomerol and a St-Emilion.

Each bank — in fact, each of the four districts — has its avid fans. The older, more well-established Left Bank generally produces austere, tannic wines with a more pronounced blackcurrant flavor. Left Bank wines usually need many years to develop, and will age for a long time, often for decades — typical of a Cabernet Sauvignon-based wine.

Bordeaux wines from the Right Bank are better introductory wines for the novice Bordeaux drinker. Because they are dominated by Merlot, they are more approachable; you can enjoy them long before their Left Bank cousins, often as soon as five to eight years after the vintage. They are less tannic, but richer and more plummy in flavor, and contain a bit more alcohol than Left Bank reds.

The Médoc mosaic

The word *Médoc* actually has two meanings. Besides being the northernmost district of the Left Bank (refer to Figure 10-1), the name also applies to the entire area west of the wide Gironde Estuary; in other words (in the same word, actually) Médoc is often used as an umbrella term for the combined districts of Médoc and Haut-Médoc.

Of the two districts, the Haut-Médoc, in the south, is by far the more important district for wine. The Haut-Médoc itself encompasses four famous wine communes: St. Estèphe *(sant eh steff),* Pauillac *(poy yac),* St-Julien *(san jhoo lee ehn),* and Margaux *(mahr go).* Table 10-2 gives a general description of each commune's wines.

Two other communes in the Haut-Médoc (whose wines are less well known) are Listrac *(lee strahk)* and Moulis *(moo lees).* Any vineyards in the Haut-Médoc that are not located in the vicinity of these six communes have the district appellation, *Haut-Médoc,* rather than that of a specific commune.

The names of these districts and communes are part of the official name of wines made there and appear on the label.

Table 10-2 The Four Principal Communes in the Haut-Médoc

Commune	Wine Characteristics
St-Estèphe	Hard, tannic, full-bodied, earthy, acidic, chunky, slow to mature; typical wine — Château Montrose
Pauillac	Rich, powerful, firm, tannic, full-bodied; blackcurrants and cedar aromas; very long-lived; home of three of Bordeaux's most famous wines — Lafite-Rothschild, Mouton-Rothschild, and Latour
St-Julien	Rich, flavorful, medium/full-bodied; cedary bouquet; wines of elegance and finesse; typical wine — Château Léoville-Poyferré
Margaux	Perfumed, fragrant bouquet; medium-bodied, supple, complex; typical wine — Château Palmer

Classified information

Have you ever wondered what a wine expert was talking about when he smugly pronounced that a particular Bordeaux was a *second growth?* Wonder no more. He's talking about a château (as wine estates are called in Bordeaux) that got lucky over 143 years ago.

Back in 1855, when an Exposition (akin to a World's Fair) took place in Paris, the organizers asked the Bordeaux Chamber of Commerce to develop a classification of Bordeaux wines. The Chamber of Commerce delegated the task to the Bordeaux wine brokers, the people who bought and sold the wines of Bordeaux. These merchants named 61 top red wines, dividing them into five categories, known as *crus* (in Bordeaux, a *cru,* or growth, refers to a wine estate). The listing is known as the classification of 1855; to this day, these *classified growths* enjoy special prestige among wine lovers. The following list shows the five categories and lists the first growths (60 Médoc Growths; 1 Graves Growth):

- **First Growths (5 châteaux)**

   Château Lafite-Rothschild
   Château Latour
   Château Margaux
   Château Haut-Brion
   Château Mouton-Rothschild (elevated from a Second Growth in 1973)

- **Second Growths (14 châteaux)**

- **Third Growths (14 châteaux)**

- **Fourth Growths (10 châteaux)**

- **Fifth Growths (18 châteaux)**

The 61 ranked wine estates are sometimes referred to as Great Growths or *Grands Crus Classés*. To appreciate the honor attached to being one of the Great Growths, bear in mind that there are about 8,000 châteaux (and over 13,000 wine producers) in Bordeaux!

The 1855 classification has held up remarkably well over time. Certainly, a few of the 61 properties are not performing up to their classification ranking today, while other unclassified châteaux possibly deserve to be included today. But because of the politics involved, no changes in classification ranking have been made, with one dramatic exception (see "The Mouton exception" sidebar) nor are any foreseen in the near future.

Top wines to try when you're feeling flush

If you're curious to try a prestigious red Bordeaux, let this list guide you. In addition to the five first growths listed in the section, "Classified information," we recommend the following classified growths from the Médoc (second through fifth growths), as well as some wines from the three other principal subregions. Consult the "Practical-advice on drinking red Bordeaux" section just ahead before you drink the wine.

Médoc wines

Château Léoville-Las-Cases
Château Léoville-Barton
Château Rauzan-Ségla
Château Palmer
Château Cos D'Estournel
Château Léoville-Poyferré
Château Pontet-Canet
Château Haut-Batailley
Château Duhart-Milon-
Rothschild

Château Clerc-Milon
Château Gruaud-Larose
Château Pichon-Lalande
Château Lagrange
Château Pichon-Baron
Château d'Armailhac
Château Prieuré-Lichine
Château Malescot
St.-Exupéry
Château Calon-Ségur

Château Lynch-Bages
Château Montrose
Château Ducru-Beaucaillou
Château Grand-Puy-Lacoste
Château La Lagune
Château Branaire-Ducru
Château Batailley
Château Talbot

Pessac-Léognan (Graves) wines

Château La Mission-Haut-Brion
Château Pape-Clément
Château La Tour-Haut-Brion

Château Haut-Bailly
Domaine de Chevalier
Château Smith-Haut-Lafitte

Château de Fieuzal
Château La Louvière

Pomerol wines

Château Pétrus*
Château Lafleur*
Château Latour à Pomerol
Château Certan de May

Château Trotanoy
Château Clinet
Vieux-Château-Certan
Château Gazin
Château Lafleur-Pétrus

Château L'Evangile
Château La Fleur de Gay
Château La Conseillante
Château l'Eglise Clinet

* Very expensive

St-Emilion wines

Château Cheval Blanc
Château Figeac
Château Troplong Mondot
Château Clos Fourtet

Château La Dominique
Château Grand Mayne
Château Ausone
Château Magdelaine

Château Canon-La-Gaffelière
Château L'Arrosée
Château Pavie-Macquin

The value end of the Bordeaux spectrum

As you might have expected, the best buys in Bordeaux wines are not found among classified growths. For really good values (and for Bordeaux that you can drink within a few years of the vintage), look for wines that were not included in the 1855 classification. In the Médoc, about 400 red wines are now grouped under the classification *cru bourgeois*. These wines generally sell in the $10 to $23 price category; some of them are even as good as the lesser-quality classified growths. We recommend the following cru bourgeois wines:

Château Monbrison
Château Sociando Mallet
Château Poujeaux
Château de Pez
Château Les Ormes-de-Pez
Château Haut-Beauséjour
Château Labegorce-Zédé

Château Phélan-Ségur
Château Meyney
Château Chasse-Spleen
Château Gloria
Château Haut-Marbuzet
Château Bel Air
Château Monbousquet

Château d'Angludet
Château Coufran
Château Fourcas-Hosten
Château Lanessan
Château Loudenne
Château Greysac

Even less expensive is the vast group of Bordeaux wines, both red and white, that has never received any classification; these wines are informally referred to as *petits châteaux*. Such wines retail for $7 to $12, are usually light-bodied, and are drinkable upon release. *Petits châteaux* are the Bordeaux wines of choice when you are looking for a young, inexpensive, approachable Bordeaux with dinner. Of course, these wines don't say *petits châteaux* on their labels. (We never said Bordeaux would be easy.) You'll know them by their price.

The Mouton exception

The one dramatic exception to the "no changes in the 1855 classification" rule occurred in 1973 when the late Baron Philippe de Rothschild, having waged a 50-year battle with the French government to have his beloved Château Mouton-Rothschild upgraded from a second growth to a first growth, finally (and rightfully) triumphed. The Minister of Agriculture decreed that Château Mouton-Rothschild was indeed a first growth (which Bordeaux wine lovers considered it to be all along, in quality if not in status). The Baron's motto, written in French on his family crest, had to change. Before 1973, it read

> First, I cannot be; second, I do not deign to be; Mouton, I am.

The Baron changed the motto on his 1973 Château Mouton-Rothschild to read:

> First, I am; second, I was; Mouton does not change.

A postscript to this wonderful story: We adopted an adorable little kitten, a Blue Point Siamese, in 1973. Since Mouton-Rothschild is one of our favorite wines, and since our little kitten demonstrated the same firm, tenacious qualities as the wine, we named him Mouton. He was with us for 20 years, proving that he had the same quality of longevity as the wine for which he was named. He is buried in our backyard, in an old wooden crate of 1973 Mouton-Rothschild.

Practical advice on drinking red Bordeaux

Because the finest red Bordeaux wines take many years to develop, they are often not good choices in restaurants where young vintages predominate on the wine list. And when mature Bordeaux wines do appear on restaurant wine lists, they are usually extremely expensive. Order a lesser Bordeaux when you're dining out, and save the best ones for drinking at home.

Red Bordeaux wines go well with lamb, venison, simple cuts of meat, and hard cheeses, such as cheddar. If you plan to serve a fine red Bordeaux from a good but recent vintage (see Appendix C), you should decant it at least an hour before dinner and let it aerate (see Chapter 8); serve it at about 64°F to 66°F (18 to 19°C). Better yet, if you have good storage conditions (see Chapter 21), save your young Bordeaux for a few years — it will only get better.

Great recent Bordeaux vintages have been 1982, 1985, 1986, 1988, 1989, 1990, and 1995. And 1996 looks promising, judging by our preliminary tastings.

TIP

A word about the exorbitant prices of 1995 and 1996 red Bordeaux

Advertised prices for 1995 and 1996 Bordeaux wines (most 1996 red Bordeaux will be available in 1999) are the highest ever; the most sought-after 1995 Bordeaux cost 20 to 50 percent more than the 1994 wines, and the 1996 Bordeaux are 20 to 30 percent higher than the 1995s!

Although preliminary reports indicate that both the 1995 and 1996 vintages — especially the 1995 — are very good for red Bordeaux, this does not explain the insane price increases. (There have been many good, even better, vintages in the last two decades.) You can blame the unprecedented demand for "name" Bordeaux for the exorbitant price increases. This demand has been created mainly by a booming world economy, plus the emergence of new Bordeaux buyers on the world market — mainly in Asia and South America, as well as in the United States.

Of course, what goes up can come down; the recent economic downturn in the Asian economy might very well bring prices of Bordeaux wine down again. That's the reason that, generally speaking, we do not advocate buying wine "futures." (See the "Buying time" sidebar in Chapter 17.)

We advise you to buy the currently available 1994 red Bordeaux, a fine vintage whose price looks downright reasonable next to the 1995 and 1996 vintages! Most of the better 1994 red Bordeaux wines will soften and develop further with another eight to ten years of aging. For current and near-term drinking (the next four or five years), try the underrated 1993 Bordeaux wines; many are still available.

Bordeaux also comes in white

White Bordeaux wine comes in two styles, dry and sweet. White wine production is concentrated in two districts:

- The Graves district is home to the finest white wines of Bordeaux, both dry and sweet (we cover the great dessert wine from the southern Graves, Sauternes, in Chapter 16).

- The middle ground between the Garonne and Dordogne Rivers, a district called Entre-Deux-Mers *(ahn treh-douh-mare),* is also known for its dry and sweet white Bordeaux wines.

But in one area — the Pessac-Léognan subdistrict, in the northern Graves — the dry white wines are so distinguished that they rank among the greatest dry white wines of the world.

Sauvignon Blanc and Sémillon, in various combinations, are the two grape varieties that dominate the production of white Bordeaux. It is a fortunate blend, because the Sauvignon Blanc grape offers immediate charm, while the slower-developing Sémillon adds a viscous quality and depth to the wine, enabling it to age well.

The best dry white Graves are crisp and lively when they are young, but they develop a full-bodied richness and a honeyed bouquet with age. In good vintages (see Appendix C), the best white Graves need at least ten years to develop and can live many years more. (See Chapter 21 for more information on older Bordeaux.)

Table 10-3 lists the Graves district's top 12 white Bordeaux wines, in our rough order of preference, and indicates their grape blends. We've separated the wines into an A and B group because the four wines in the first group literally are in a class by themselves, quality-wise; the white Bordeaux wines in the first group possess more depth and complexity, plus they will have more longevity than other white Bordeaux. Their prices reflect that fact — the A group wines range from $50 to over $100 per bottle, whereas the B group wines are priced between $18 and $35.

Table 10-3	Top 12 White Bordeaux
Wine	*Grape Varieties*
Group A	
Château Haut-Brion Blanc	Sémillon, 50 to 55%; Sauvignon Blanc, 45 to 50%
Château Laville-Haut-Brion	Sémillon, 60%; Sauvignon Blanc, 40%
Domaine de Chevalier	Sauvignon Blanc, 70%; Sémillon, 30%
Château de Fieuzal	Sauvignon Blanc, 50 to 60%; Sémillon, 40 to 50%
Group B	
Château Pape-Clément	Sémillon, 45%; Muscadelle, 10%; Sauvignon Blanc, 45%
Château Smith-Haut-Lafitte	Sauvignon Blanc, 100%
Château Couhins-Lurton	Sauvignon Blanc, 100%
Château La Louvière	Sauvignon Blanc, 70%; Sémillon, 30%
Clos Floridene	Sémillon, 70%; Sauvignon Blanc, 30%
Château La Tour-Martillac	Sémillon, 60%; Sauvignon Blanc, 30%; other, 10%
Château Malartic-Lagravière	Sauvignon Blanc, 100%
Château Carbonnieux	Sauvignon Blanc, 65%; Sémillon, 34%; Muscadelle, 1%

Burgundy: The Other Great French Wine

Burgundy, a wine region in eastern France, southeast of Paris (refer to Figure 10-1), stands side by side with Bordeaux as one of France's two greatest regions for dry, non-sparkling wines. Unlike Bordeaux, however, Burgundy's fame is split nearly equally between its white and red wines — and the best white Burgundies, in general, are even more expensive than their red counterparts.

Also unlike Bordeaux, good Burgundy is often scarce. The reason is simple: Not counting Beaujolais (technically Burgundy, but really a separate type of wine) Burgundy produces only 25 percent as much wine as Bordeaux!

Burgundy's vineyards are smaller and more fragmented than Bordeaux's. The French Revolution in 1789 is partly to blame. Prior to the Revolution, French nobility and the Catholic Church were the major vineyard owners in Burgundy, but after the Revolution, vineyards were distributed among the populace. (Bordeaux, once owned by the English, was considered somehow less French, and was not really that affected by the Revolution.) France's Napoleonic Code, which requires all land to be equally divided among one's heirs, further fragmented each family's small vineyard holdings.

As the result of these occurrences, Burgundy (or, as the French call it, *Bourgogne,* pronounced *bor guh nyeh*) today is a region of small vineyard holdings. Where large vineyards exist, they have multiple owners, with some families owning only two or three rows of vines in a particular vineyard. (One famous Burgundy vineyard, Clos de Vougeot, has about 82 owners!) The typical Burgundy winemaker's production varies from 50 cases to 1,000 cases of wine a year, per type — far from enough to satisfy wine lovers all over the world. Compare that to Bordeaux, where the average château owner makes 15,000 to 20,000 cases of his principal wine annually.

In Burgundy, the winemaker calls his property a *domaine,* certainly a more modest name than *château,* and a proper reflection of the size of his winery.

Chardonnay, Pinot Noir, Gamay

Burgundy has a *continental* climate (warm summers and cold winters) subject to localized summer hailstorms that can damage the grapes and cause rot. The soil is mainly limestone and clay.

Burgundy's *terroir* is particularly suited to the two main grape varieties of the region, Pinot Noir (for red Burgundy) and Chardonnay (for white Burgundy). In fact, nowhere else in the entire world does the very fickle, difficult Pinot Noir grape perform better than in Burgundy.

In the southerly Beaujolais district of Burgundy, the soil becomes primarily granitic but also rich in clay, which is very suitable for the Gamay grape of this area.

Districts, districts everywhere

Burgundy has five districts, all of which make quite different wines. The districts include (from north to south) Chablis *(shah blee)*, the Côte d'Or *(coat dor)*, the Côte Chalonnaise *(coat shal oh naze)*, the Mâconnais *(mack coh nay)*, and Beaujolais *(boh jhoe lay)*. The heart of Burgundy, the *Côte d'Or* (which literally means *golden slope*), is further divided into two parts: Côte de Nuits *(coat deh nwee)* in the north and the Côte de Beaune *(coat deh bone)* in the south.

Table 10-4 lists the districts geographically from north to south, along with the grape varieties used in each region. A quick glance at Table 10-4 immediately shows that, even though Beaujolais is part of Burgundy, Beaujolais is an entirely different wine. The same is true of Mâcon Rouge — even the small amount that's made from Pinot Noir rather than from Gamay does not resemble true red Burgundy. (Actually, very little red Mâcon is exported; the world sees mainly white Mâcon.)

Table 10-4	**The Districts of Burgundy**	
Red Wine	*White Wine*	*Grape Variety*
	Chablis	
	Chablis	Chardonnay
	Côte d'Or: Côte de Nuits	
Red Burgundy		Pinot Noir
	Côte d'Or: Côte de Beaune	
Red Burgundy		Pinot Noir
	White Burgundy	Chardonnay
	Côte Chalonnaise	
Red Burgundy		Pinot Noir
	White Burgundy	Chardonnay
	Mâconnais	
Mâcon Rouge		Gamay; Pinot Noir
	Mâcon Blanc	Chardonnay
	Beaujolais	
Beaujolais		Gamay

Thus, the term *red Burgundy* refers primarily to the red wines of the Côte d'Or and also to the less well known — and less expensive — red wines of the Côte Chalonnaise. Likewise, when wine lovers talk about *white Burgundy,* they are usually referring just to the white wines of the Côte d'Or and the Côte Chalonnaise. They'll use the more precise names, Chablis and Mâcon, to refer to the white wines of those parts of Burgundy. On the other hand, when wine lovers talk about the region, Burgundy, they could very well be referring to the whole shebang, including Beaujolais, or all of Burgundy *except* Beaujolais. It's an imprecise language.

Don't ever mistake the inexpensive red California wine that calls itself *burgundy* — or the inexpensive California wine that calls itself *chablis* — for the real McCoys from France. The imposter Burgundy and Chablis are the product of various ordinary grapes grown in industrial-scale vineyards 6,000 miles away from the Côte d'Or. We'd be surprised if either one had even a drop of the true grapes of Burgundy — Pinot Noir or Chardonnay — in them. They're both medium-dry wines blended for mass appeal, and they sell fairly well. But you should know that they bear absolutely no resemblance to true (100 percent Pinot Noir) red Burgundy from Burgundy, France — or true (100 percent Chardonnay) Chablis from Chablis, France.

From the regional to the sublime

The soils of the Burgundy region vary from hillside to hillside and even from the middle of each hill to the bottom. You can find two different vineyards growing the same grape but making distinctly different wines, only two meters apart from each other across a dirt road!

In a region with such varied *terroir,* specificity of site becomes extremely relevant. A wine made from a tiny vineyard with its own particular charac-teristics is more unique, precious, and rare than a wine blended from several vineyards or a wine from a less-favored site.

The AOC structure for Burgundy wines recognizes the importance of site. While there are region-wide AOCs and district-wide AOCs and commune AOCs — just as in Bordeaux — *there are also AOC names that refer to indi-vidual vineyards.* In fact, some of these vineyards are recognized as better than others: Some of them are *premier cru (prem yay crew),* meaning first growth, while the very best are *grand cru,* meaning great growth.

The terms *premier cru* and *grand cru* are used in Bordeaux, too, but in Bordeaux, the terms generally represent status bestowed on a property by a classification outside the AOC law. In Burgundy, *premier cru* and *grand cru* are official distinctions of the AOC law. Their meaning is extremely precise.

Table 10-5 gives examples of AOC names in Burgundy, listed in increasing order of specificity. The two broadest categories — regional and district place-names — account for 65 percent of all Burgundy wines. Such wines retail for $12 to $24 a bottle. (You *can* buy affordable Burgundies at this level.) Commune (also referred to as *Village*) wines, such as Nuits-St. Georges or Chambolle-Musigny, make up 23 percent of Burgundy and are in the $25 to $40 per bottle price range. Fifty-three communes in Burgundy have their own appellations.

Premier crus, such as Meursault Les Perrières or Chambolle-Musigny Les Chaumes, account for 11 percent of Burgundy wines; there are 561 vineyards entitled to the *premier cru* appellation. The wines can range from $30 to $80 per bottle. The 30 *grand crus,* such as Chambertin, represent only *1 percent* of Burgundy's wines. Prices for *grand cru* Burgundies — both red and white — start in the $65 to $75 price range and can go up to well over $500 a bottle for Romanée-Conti, normally Burgundy's most expensive red wine.

Table 10-5	The Structure of Burgundy AOC Names
Specificity of Site	*Examples*
Region-wide	Bourgogne Rouge
District-wide	Côte de Beaune-Villages; Mâcon-Villages
Village or Commune	Pommard; Gevrey-Chambertin; Volnay
Premier Cru*	Nuits-St. Georges Les Vaucrains; Beaune Grèves; Vosne-Romanée Les Suchots
Grand Cru*	Musigny; La Tâche; Montrachet

* Refers to specific vineyard sites.

Thankfully, you can actually tell the difference between a *premier cru* and a *grand cru* Burgundy by looking at the label. *Premier cru* wines usually carry the name of their commune plus the vineyard name — usually in the same-sized lettering — on the label, and often, the words, *Premier Cru*. If the vineyard name is in smaller lettering than the commune name, often the wine is not a *premier cru* but a wine from a single-vineyard site in that commune. (Not all single vineyards are recognized as *premier cru* under the law.) *Grand cru* Burgundies carry only the name of the vineyard on the label.

If a wine is made by blending the grapes of two or more *premier crus* in the same commune, it can be called a *premier cru* but it won't carry the name of a specific *premier cru* vineyard. The label will carry a commune name and the words *premier cru*, sometimes written as *1er cru*.

Burgundy AOCs (once again, with feeling)

Burgundies with regional, or region-wide, AOCs are easy to recognize — they always start with the word *Bourgogne (boor guh nyeh)*. In the following list, read the AOC names down each column to see how the names change, becoming more specific from district to *grand cru*.

	Red Burgundy	**White Burgundy**
District:	Côte de Nuits-Villages	Côte de Beaune (also red)
Commune:	Chambolle-Musigny	Puligny-Montrachet
Premier Cru:	Chambolle-Musigny Les Amoureuses	Puligny-Montrachet Les Pucelles
Grand Cru:	Musigny	Bâtard-Montrachet; Montrachet

The Côte d'Or

The heart of Burgundy is the Côte d'Or, a narrow 40-mile stretch of land with some of the most expensive real estate in the world. This is the region where all the famous red and white Burgundies originate.

The northern part of the Côte d'Or is named the Côte de Nuits, after its most important (commercial) city, Nuits-Saint-Georges. Red Burgundies almost exclusively are made here (although one superb white Burgundy, Musigny Blanc, and a couple of other white Burgundies do exist on the Côte de Nuits). The following wine communes, from north to south, are in the Côte de Nuits:

- **Marsannay *(mahr sah nay):*** Known mainly for rosés

- **Fixin *(fee san):*** Sturdy, earthy, firm red wines

- **Gevrey-Chambertin *(jehv ray sham ber tan):*** Full-bodied, rich, red wines; eight *grand crus*, such as Chambertin, Chambertin Clos de Bèze

- **Morey-Saint Denis *(maw ree san d'nee):*** Full, sturdy red wines; *grand crus* are Bonnes Mares (part), Clos de la Roche, Clos Saint-Denis, Clos de Tart, Clos des Lambrays

- **Chambolle-Musigny *(shom bowl moo sih nyee):*** Soft, elegant red wines; *grand crus* include Musigny and Bonnes Mares (part)

- **Vougeot *(voo joe):*** Medium-bodied red wines; *grand cru* is Clos de Vougeot

The taste of fine red Burgundy

The Pinot Noir grape does not have nearly as much color as the Cabernet Sauvignon or Merlot grapes. Red Burgundy, therefore, is paler than Bordeaux, ranging in color from garnet to cherry or ruby. It's medium-bodied to full-bodied in terms of its alcohol and is relatively low in tannin. The characteristic aroma is small red fruits — cherries and berries — and woodsy, damp-earth, or mushroomy scents. When a red Burgundy ages, it often develops a silky texture, richness, and a natural sweetness of fruit flavors; sometimes a bouquet of leather, coffee, and well-hung game emerges.

With some exceptions (for example, a powerful wine from a great vintage, such as 1990 or 1995), red Burgundy should be consumed within ten years of the vintage — and even sooner in a weaker vintage (see Appendix C).

- ✔ **Vosne-Romanée *(vone roh mah nay):*** Elegant, rich, velvety red wines; *grand crus* include Romanée-Conti, La Tache, Richebourg, Romanée-Saint-Vivant, La Romanée, and La Grand Rue

- ✔ **Flagey-Échézeaux *(flah jhay eh sheh zoe):*** Hamlet of Vosne-Romanée; *grand crus* are Grands-Échézeaux and Échézeaux

- ✔ **Nuits-Saint-Georges *(nwee san johrjes):*** Sturdy, earthy, red wines; no *grand crus*; fine *premier crus*

All these red wines are made entirely with the Pinot Noir grape. The different characteristics of the wines are due to their individual *terroirs.*

The southern part of the Côte d'Or, the Côte de Beaune, is named after its most important city, Beaune (the commercial and tourist center of the Côte d'Or). Both white and red Burgundies are made in the Côte de Beaune, but the white Burgundies are more renowned. The following communes, from north to south, make up the Côte de Beaune:

- ✔ **Ladoix *(lah dwah):*** Seldom-seen, inexpensive red and white wines; part of the *grand crus*, Corton (red) and Corton-Charlemagne (white) are in this commune

- ✔ **Pernand-Vergelesses *(per nahn ver jeh less):*** Little-known red and white wines; good buys

- ✔ **Aloxe-Corton *(ah luss cortohn):*** Full, sturdy wines; several red *grand crus* that all include the name Corton and one magnificent white *grand cru* (Corton-Charlemagne) are here

- ✔ **Chorey-lès-Beaune *(shor ay lay bone):*** Mainly good-value red wine, and a little white wine, here

- **Savigny-lès-Beaune** *(sah vee nyee lay bone):* Mostly red wines; fine values here, too

- **Beaune** *(bone):* Soft, medium-bodied reds; some whites; fine *premier crus* here

- **Pommard** *(pohm mahr):* Sturdy, full red wines; some good *premier crus* (Rugiens and Epénots)

- **Volnay** *(vohl nay):* Soft, elegant red wines; good *premier crus* (Caillerets and Clos des Ducs)

- **Auxey-Duresses** *(awe see duh ress),* **Monthélie** *(mon tel lee),* **Saint-Romain** *(san roh man),* **Saint-Aubin** *(sant oh ban):* Four little-known villages producing mainly red, but some white wines; excellent values

- **Meursault** *(muhr so):* First important white Burgundy commune; full-bodied, nutty wines; some excellent *premier crus* (Les Perrières and Les Genevrières)

- **Puligny-Montrachet** *(poo lee nyee mon rah shay):* Home of elegant white Burgundies; *grand crus* include Montrachet (part), Chevalier-Montrachet, Bâtard-Montrachet (part)

- **Chassagne-Montrachet** *(shah sahn nyah mon rah shay):* A bit sturdier than Puligny; the rest of the Montrachet and Bâtard-Montrachet *grand crus*; also, some earthy, rustic reds

- **Santenay** *(sant nay):* Light-bodied, inexpensive red wines here

- **Maranges** *(ma rahnj):* Little-known, mainly red, inexpensive wines

Tables 10-6 and 10-7 list the best Burgundy producers and their greatest wines. For our specific recommendations on good, less expensive Burgundies to buy, and descriptions of specific wines, see our buying guide, *Wine Buying Companion For Dummies,* published by IDG Books Worldwide, Inc.

Table 10-6	Best Red Burgundy Producers and Their Greatest Wines
Producer	*Recommended Wines*
Domaine Leroy*	Musigny, Richebourg, Chambertin (*all* of Leroy's *grand crus* and *premier crus* recommended)
Domaine de la Romanée-Conti*	Romanée-Conti; La Tâche; Richebourg; Grands Echézeaux
Georges et Christophe Roumier	Musigny; Bonnes Mares; Chambolle-Musigny Les Amoureuses

Producer	*Recommended Wines*
Ponsot	Clos de la Roche (Vieilles Vignes); Chambertin; Clos St-Denis (Vieilles Vignes); Griotte-Chambertin
Armand Rousseau	Chambertin (*all* of his *grand crus*); Gevrey-Chambertin Clos St-Jacques
Domaine des Chézeaux	Griotte-Chambertin; Clos St. Denis Vieilles Vignes
Méo-Camuzet	Vosne-Romanée *premier crus* (any of his three); Clos de Vougeot; Richebourg; Corton
Hubert Lignier	Clos de la Roche; Charmes-Chambertin
Jean-Jacques Confuron	Romanée St.-Vivant; Clos de Vougeot
Anne Gros	Richebourg; Clos de Vougeot
Domaine Dujac	Clos de la Roche; Bonnes Mares
Joseph Roty	Any of his *grand cru* Chambertins
Domaine Comte de Vogüé	Musigny (Vieilles Vignes); Bonnes Mares
Mongeard-Mugneret	Richebourg; Grands Échézeaux
Jayer-Gilles	Échézeaux; Nuits-St.-Georges Les Damodes
Louis Jadot	Romanée-St-Vivant; Chambertin Clos de Beze; Musigny
Chopin-Groffier	Clos de Vougeot
Domaine Maume	Mazis-Chambertin; Charmes-Chambertin
Michel Lafarge	Any of his Volnay *premier crus*; Beaune Les Grèves
Domaine Robert Chevillon	Nuits-St.-Georges Les St.-Georges; Nuits-Georges Les Vaucrains
Domaine Albert Morot	All Beaune *premier crus*
Jacques-Fréderick Mugnier	Musigny; Bonnes Mares
Daniel Rion	Vosne-Romanée Les Beaux Monts
Christian Serafin	Charmes-Chambertin; Gevrey-Chambertin Vieilles Vignes
Tollot-Beaut	Corton; Corton Les Bressandes; Beaune Les Grèves

* These wines are very expensive.

Table 10-7	Best White Burgundy Producers and Their Greatest Wines
Producer	***Recommended Wines***
Domaine Ramonet*	Montrachet; Bâtard-Montrachet; Bienvenue-Bâtard-Montrachet; any of his Chassagne-Montrachet *premier crus*
Coche-Dury*	Corton-Charlemagne; Meursault *premier cru* (any)
Domaine des Comtes Lafon	Meursault *premier crus* (any); Le Montrachet
Domaine Leflaive	Chevalier-Montrachet; Bâtard-Montrachet; Puligny-Montrachet *premier crus* (any)
Michel Niellon	Bâtard-Montrachet; Chevalier-Montrachet; Chassagne-Montrachet Les Vergers
Domaine Étienne Sauzet	Bâtard-Montrachet; Bienvenue-Bâtard-Montrachet; Puligny-Montrachet Les Combettes
Verget	Bâtard-Montrachet; Chevalier-Montrachet; Meursault *premier crus* (any)
Guy Amiot	Chassagne-Montrachet *premier crus* (any)
Louis Latour	Corton-Charlemagne; Puligny-Montrachet *premier crus* (any)
Louis Carillon	Bienvenue-Bâtard-Montrachet; Puligny-Montrachet *premier crus* (any)
Colin-Delégér	Chassagne-Montrachet *premier crus* (any); Puligny-Montrachet *premier crus* (any)
Jean-Noël Gagnard	Chassagne-Montrachet *premier crus* (any)
Louis Jadot	Corton-Charlemagne; Chassagne-Montrachet Les Caillerets; Beaune Grèves; Puligny-Montrachet *premier crus* (any)
Domaine François Jobard	Meursault *premier crus* (any)
Domaine Bernard Morey	Chassagne-Montrachet Les Caillerets; Puligny-Montrachet La Truffierè
Domaine Marc Morey	Chassagne-Montrachet *premier crus* (any)

* These wines are very expensive.

Practical advice on buying and drinking Burgundy

Nice of the Burgundians to make everything so stratified and clear, isn't it? *Premier cru* Burgundies are always better than commune wines, and *grand crus* are the best of all, right? Well, it ain't necessarily so! In order of importance, these are the criteria to follow when you are buying Burgundy:

- **The producer's reputation:** Based on wines he has made in recent years

- **The vintage year:** There are great fluctuations in quality from year to year

- **The appellation:** The name of the commune or vineyard and its specificity

The producer and the vintage are *considerably* more important than the appellation in Burgundy. Good vintages for red Burgundy are 1996, 1995, 1993, 1991, and 1990. For white Burgundy, 1996, 1995, 1992, 1989, and 1986 are quite good.

Red Burgundy is a particularly good wine to choose in restaurants. Unlike Bordeaux and other Cabernet Sauvignon-based wines, it is usually approachable when young because of its softness, along with its enticing aromas and flavors of red fruits.

Moreover, red Burgundy, like all Pinot Noirs, is a versatile companion to food. It's the one red wine that can complement fish or seafood; it is ideal with salmon, for example. Chicken, turkey, or ham are also good matchups for Burgundy. For fuller-styled red Burgundies, beef and game birds (such as duck, pheasant, rabbit, or venison) all go well.

Red Burgundy is at its best when served at cool temperatures — about 60° to 62°F (17°C). It should *not* be decanted (even older Burgundies seldom develop much sediment), but poured straight from the bottle. Too much aeration would cause you to lose the wonderful Burgundy aroma, which is one of the greatest features of this wine.

On the other hand, white Burgundy often benefits from decanting, especially *grand cru* and *premier cru* white Burgundies from younger vintages (five years or younger). Great young white Burgundies, such as Corton Charlemagne, really have not evolved completely in their first few years; the extra aeration will help bring out their aromas and flavors. And remember, don't serve them too cold! The ideal temperature range for serving the better white Burgundies is 58° F to 62° F (15° to 17° C).

The taste of fine white Burgundy

White Burgundy combines a fullness of flavor — peaches, hazelnuts, and honey in Meursault; floweriness and butterscotch in a Puligny or Chassagne-Montrachet — with lively acidity and a touch of oak. With age, even more flavor complexity develops. The wine finishes on the palate with a lingering reminder of all its flavors. Chardonnay wines from other regions and countries can be good, but there's nothing else quite like a great white Burgundy.

Bargain Burgundies: The Côte Chalonnaise

The sad fact about Burgundy is that most of the good wines are costly. But one of Burgundy's best-kept secrets is the wines of the Côte Chalonnaise (the district which lies directly south of the Côte d'Or). Five villages here are home to some very decent Burgundies. True, the Côte Chalonnaise Burgundies are not so fine as the Côte d'Or Burgundies (they're a bit earthier and coarser), but we're talking $15 to $25 retail per bottle here. Four villages or communes whose names appear as appellations on wine labels are the following:

- ✔ **Mercurey** *(mer cure ay):* Mostly red; a small amount of white; the best wines of the Chalonnaise come from here, also the most expensive ($20 to $25); two of the better producers of Mercurey are Faiveley and Antonin Rodet

- ✔ **Rully** *(rue yee):* About half red and half white wines; the whites, although a bit earthy, are significantly better than the reds; look for the wines of the producer Antonin Rodet

- ✔ **Givry** *(gee vree):* Mostly red; a small amount of white; reds are better than the whites (but quite earthy); Domaine Joblot's Givry is especially worth seeking out

- ✔ **Montagny** *(mon tah nyee):* All white wines (Chardonnay); look for Antonin Rodet's and Louis Latour's Montagny

Another village specializes in the Aligoté grape (a second white grape permitted in Burgundy) that makes a particularly crisp and lively wine.

- ✔ **Bouzeron** *(boo zer ohn):* Aubert de Villaine is the quality producer here; try his Bourgogne Rouge, Bourgogne Blanc (made from Pinot Noir and Chardonnay respectively), or Bourgogne Aligoté de Bouzeron

Chablis: A unique white wine

The village of Chablis, northwest of the Côte d'Or, is the closest Burgundian commune to Paris (about a two-hour drive). Although Chablis' wines are 100 percent Chardonnay — just like the white Burgundies of the Côte d'Or — they are quite a different style from Côte d'Or whites. Whereas almost all of the Côte d'Or white Burgundies use oak barrels both in fermentation and aging, most Chablis producers now use only stainless steel. Also, Chablis' climate is cooler than that of the Côte d'Or, producing wines that are intrinsically lighter-bodied, austere, and more acidic. Chablis is very dry and sometimes flinty, without quite the rich, ripe flavors of Côte d'Or white Burgundies.

Chablis is an ideal companion to seafood, especially oysters. Like all other white Burgundies, it should be served cool (58 to 60°F, or 15°C), not cold.

The Chablis worth trying

Chablis is at its best on the *grand cru* and *premier cru* level. Simple village Chablis is priced in the $15 to $20 price range, but, frankly, at that price better white wines can be found in Mâcon, in the Chalonnaise, or in the Côte d'Or (Bourgogne Blanc).

The seven *grand cru* Chablis are Les Clos, Valmur, Les Preuses, Vaudésir, Grenouilles, Bougros, and Blanchot.

Another Chablis, La Moutonne, is actually a part of the Vaudésir and Les Preuses *grand cru* vineyards, but does not have a *grand cru* appellation on its own. *Grand cru* Chablis range in price from $30 to $75, depending on the producer. *Grand cru* Chablis from good vintages (see Appendix C) can age and improve for 15 years.

There are 22 *premier cru* Chablis appellations, but the six most well known are Fourchaume, Montée de Tonnerre, Vaillons, Mont de Milieu, Montmains, and Les Forêts (also known as Forest).

Premier cru Chablis range in price from $20 to $45, depending on the producer, and can age up to ten years in good vintages.

Four outstanding producers of Chablis

Four producers really stand out in Chablis. You should try to buy their *grand* or *premier cru* Chablis for a true understanding of this underrated wine. *Try* is the operative word here. These are small producers whose wines are available only in better stores:

- **Francois Raveneau and René et Vincent Dauvissat:** Both still use oak for fermenting and aging their wine.
- **Louis Michel:** Uses stainless steel exclusively.
- **Jean Dauvissat:** Uses mainly stainless steel.

Mâcon: Affordable whites

If you're thinking that $20 or more sounds like too much to spend for a bottle of white Burgundy or Chablis for everyday situations, we have an alternative white wine for you: the white wines of Mâcon. Many of the best white wine buys — not only in France, but in the world, as well — come from the Mâconnais district, which lies directly south of the Chalonnaise and north of Beaujolais.

The Mâconnais has a milder, sunnier climate than the Côte d'Or to the north. Wine production is centered around the city of Mâcon, a gateway city to Provence and the Riviera. In northern Mâcon, you can find a village called Chardonnay, for which the famous grape was perhaps named. The hills in the Mâconnais contain the same chalky limestone beloved by Chardonnay that can be found in Burgundy districts to the north.

Mâcon's white wines, in fact, are 100 percent Chardonnay. Most of them are simply called *Mâcon* or *Mâcon-Villages* (a slightly better wine than Mâcon, because it comes from specific villages); the wines retail for $8 to $14 a bottle. Often better are Mâcons that come from just one village. The name of the village is added to their appellation (such as Mâcon-Lugny or Mâcon-Viré).

Mâcon whites are medium-bodied, crisp, fresh, and lively wines that are usually unoaked. They should be consumed while they are young, generally within three years of the vintage.

The best Mâcon whites come from the southernmost part of the district and carry their own appellations — Pouilly-Fuissé *(pwee fwee say)* and Saint-Véran *(san ver ahn)*.

- ✔ Pouilly-Fuissé is a richer, fuller-bodied wine than a simple Mâcon, is often oaked, and is a bit more expensive (around $18 to $22; up to $40 for the best examples). To try an outstanding example of Pouilly-Fuissé, buy Château Fuissé, which, in good vintages, compares favorably with more expensive Cote d'Or white Burgundies.

- ✔ Saint-Véran is very possibly the best-value wine in all of Mâcon ($12 to $16). Especially fine is the Saint-Véran of Verget, who is one of the best producers of Mâconnais wines.

Beaujolais: As delightful as it is affordable

Are you surprised that Beaujolais is in the Burgundy region? Beaujolais is so famous that it stands on its own. It even has its own red grape: the Gamay.

The Beaujolais district is situated south of the Mâconnais, in the heart of one of the greatest gastronomic centers of the world; good restaurants abound in the area, as well as in the nearby city of Lyon.

Beaujolais and *Beaujolais Supérieur* (one percent higher in alcohol) are district-wide AOCs, but actually they come from the southern part of Beaujolais where the soil is mainly clay. They are fresh, fruity, uncomplicated, light-bodied wines that sell for $6 to $9 and are at their best a year or two after the vintage. They are excellent wines for warm weather, when a heavier, more tannic red wine would be inappropriate.

If you're a white wine, White Zinfandel, or rosé wine drinker (or even a non-wine drinker!), Beaujolais is the *ideal* first red wine to drink — a bridge, so to speak, to more serious red wines. It's delicious, has lots of fruity character (although it's a dry wine), and doesn't require serious contemplation. Beaujolais is truly a fun wine.

Beaujolais has its serious side, too. The best Beaujolais are made in the northern part of the Beaujolais district where the soil is granite-based. *Beaujolais-Villages* is a wine blended from (some of) 39 designated villages that produce fuller, more substantial wine than simple Beaujolais. It costs a dollar or two more, but it's well worth the difference.

Even higher quality Beaujolais comes from ten specific areas in the north. The wines of these areas are known as *cru* Beaujolais, and only the name of the cru appears in large letters on the label. (The wines are not actually named Beaujolais.) *Cru* Beaujolais have more depth, and, in fact, need a little time to develop; some of the *crus* can age and improve for four or five years or more. They range in price from about $9 to $15. Table 10-8 lists the ten *cru* Beaujolais as they are geographically situated, from south to north, along with a brief description of each *cru*.

Almost all of Beaujolais is sold by large *négociants* — firms that buy grapes and wine from growers and blend, bottle, and sell the wine under their own labels. Two of the largest and most reliable Beaujolais négociants are Georges Duboeuf and Louis Jadot.

Celebration time: Beaujolais Nouveau

Each year on the third Thursday in November, the new vintage of Beaujolais — called Beaujolais Nouveau — is released all over the world with great fanfare. This youngster — only six weeks old! — is a very grapey, easy-to-drink wine with practically no tannin but lots of fruitiness. Beaujolais Nouveau is particularly popular in the U.S., where it is served with many Thanksgiving dinners because of the timing of its annual debut. It sells for $5 to $8, and is at its best within the first year of the vintage.

Table 10-8	The Ten *Cru* Beaujolais
Cru	*Description*
Brouilly (broo yee)	The largest *cru* in terms of production and the most variable in quality; light and fruity; drink within three years
Côte de Brouilly	Distinctly better than Brouilly, fuller and more concentrated; vineyards are higher in altitude; drink within three years
Regnié (ray nyay)	The newest village to be recognized as a *cru;* very similar to Brouilly; not quite as good as Côte de Brouilly
Morgon (mor gohn)	At its best, full and earthy; can age for five to seven years; look for Duboeuf's Morgon *(Domaine Jean Descombes)*
Chiroubles (sheh roob leh)	One of our favorites; the quintessential, delicate, delicious perfumed Beaujolais; tastes of young red fruits; very pretty; drink it within two years of the vintage
Fleurie (flehr ee)	Medium-bodied, rich, with a velvety fruitiness; the most popular *cru* (and, along with Moulin-á-Vent, the most expensive, at $13 to $15); quite reliable; can age for four years
Moulin-à-Vent (moo lahn ah vahn)	Clearly the most powerful, concentrated *cru,* and the one that can age the longest (ten years or more); this is one Beaujolais that really needs three or four years to develop
Chénas (shay nahs)	Bordering Moulin-à-Vent (in fact, much of it can be legally sold as the more famous Moulin-à-Vent); what is sold as Chénas is usually well priced; drink within four years
Juliénas (jhool yay nahs)	The insider's Beaujolais; often the most consistent and the best of the *crus;* full-bodied and rich, can last five years or more; seldom disappoints
Saint-Amour (sant ah more)	The most northerly *cru* in Beaujolais; perfectly named for lovers on Valentine's Day (or any other day); soft, light to medium-bodied, delicious berry fruit; drink within two or three years

TIP

> ## Beaujolais in action
>
> To really get a feeling for being in France, visit a bistro in Paris or Lyon and order a carafe of young Beaujolais with your charcuterie, pâté, or cold chicken. No wine slides down the throat as easily!
>
> Young, uncomplicated Beaujolais should *definitely* be served chilled, at about 55°F (13°C), to capture their fruity exuberance. The fuller *cru* Beaujolais, on the other hand, are best at about the same temperature as red Burgundy (60°F to 62°F; 17°C).

The Hearty Rhônes of the Valley

For a good, reliable dry red wine that costs about $8 to $11, look no farther than the Rhône *(rone)* Valley and its everyday red wine, Côtes du Rhône. The Rhône Valley makes more serious wines — mostly red, and some white and dry rosé as well — but Côtes du Rhône is one of the best inexpensive red wines in the world.

The Rhône Valley is in southeastern France, south of Beaujolais, between the city of Lyon and the region of Provence. The growing season is sunny and hot. The wines reflect the weather: the red wines are full, robust, and high in alcohol. Even some of the white wines tend to be full and earthy. But the wines from the southern part of the Rhône are distinctly different from those in the northern Rhône Valley.

Generous wines of the south

Most (in fact, over 90 percent of) Rhône wines come from the southern Rhône. They are generally inexpensive and uncomplicated. The dominant grape variety in the southern Rhône is the prolific Grenache, which makes wines that are high in alcohol and low in tannin.

Besides Côtes du Rhône, other southern Rhône wines to look for are

- Côtes du Ventoux *(vahn too)*, which is similar, but a bit lighter than Côtes du Rhône
- Côtes du Rhône-Villages (50 villages making fuller and a bit more expensive wines than Côtes du Rhône, 16 of which are entitled to use their names on the label, such as "Cairanne — Côtes du Rhône-Villages")
- The single-village wines, Gigondas *(jhee gon dahs)* and Vacqueyras *(vah keh rahs)*

The last two wines are former Côtes du Rhône-Villages wines that graduated and are now entitled to their own appellations. Gigondas, which sells in the $15 to $25 range, is particularly rich and robust, and can live for ten years or more in good vintages. Vacqueyras is lighter-bodied and less robust than Gigondas, but also less expensive (about $12 to $15). The 1995 vintage, by the way, is a truly excellent one for Gigondas wines. Look for it!

Two dry rosé wines of interest in the southern Rhône are Tavel *(tah vel)* and Lirac *(lee rahk);* the latter is less well known and therefore less expensive. (Tavel costs about $15 to $18, Lirac a little less.) Both are made mainly from the Grenache and Cinsault grapes; they can be delightful on hot, summer days or at picnics. As with most rosé wines, they are best when they are very young.

But Châteauneuf-du-Pape *(shah toe nuf doo pahp)* is the king in the southern Rhône. Its name recalls the 14th century, when nearby Avignon (not Rome) was the home of the Popes. Almost all Châteauneuf-du-Pape is a blended red wine: As many as 13 grape varieties can be used, but Grenache, Mourvèdre, and Syrah predominate. At its best, Châteauneuf-du-Pape is full-bodied, rich, round, and rather high in alcohol. In good vintages, it will age well for 15 to 20 years. Most red Châteauneuf-du-Pape wines (a little white Châteauneuf-du-Pape is also made; very earthy) retail in the $20 to $30 price range, but the very best ones can cost over $50. The two finest Châteauneuf-du-Papes are clearly *Château Rayas* (100 percent Grenache, very old vines) and *Château Beaucastel* (can age 20 years or more).

Noble wines of the north

The two best red wines of the entire Rhône, Côte-Rôtie *(coat roe tee)* and Hermitage *(er mee tahj),* are produced in the northern Rhône Valley. Both are made from the noble Syrah grape (a bit of white Viognier wine is sometimes used in Côte Rôtie).

Although both are rich, full-bodied wines, Côte-Rôtie is the more subtle of the two. It has a wonderfully fragrant aroma, which always reminds us of green olives and raspberries, and soft, fruity flavors. In good vintages, Côte Rôtie can age for 20 years or more (1995 and 1991 were particularly fine for Côte-Rôtie). Most Côte-Rôties are in the $25 to $50 price range.

The most famous producer of Côte-Rôtie is Guigal; his single-vineyard Côte-Rôties — La Mouline, La Landonne, and La Turque — are legendary, but particularly expensive (well over $100 a bottle!).

Red Hermitage is clearly the most full-bodied, longest-lived Rhône wine. It is a complex, rich, tannic wine that needs several years before it begins to develop, and it will age easily for 30 years or more in good vintages (1995, 1991, 1990, 1989, and 1988 were all excellent vintages in the northern Rhone; 1989 was especially great for Hermitage). The best red Hermitages sell today for $45 to $60, and a few are even over $100, although lesser Hermitages are as low as $25 to $30 a bottle.

The three best producers of Hermitage are Jean Louis Chave, Chapoutier, and Paul Jaboulet Aîné (for his better Hermitage, La Chapelle).

Jaboulet also makes a less expensive little brother to Hermitage, a Crozes-Hermitage (a separate appellation) called Domaine de Thalabert. It's as good as — if not better than — many Hermitages, can age and improve for 10 to 15 years in good vintages, and is reasonably priced at $21 to $23: a wine to buy.

A small amount of white Hermitage is produced from the Marsanne and Roussanne grape varieties. White Hermitage is traditionally a full, heavy, earthy wine that needs eight to ten years to fully develop. Chapoutier's fine Hermitage Blanc, Chante-Alouette, however, is all Marsanne (about $40), and made in a more approachable style. The other great white Hermitage is Chave's. About $60, it is complex, rich, and almost as long-lived as his red Hermitage.

Condrieu *(cohn dree oo),* made from 100 percent Viognier, is the other white wine to try in the northern Rhône. It's one of the most fragrant, floral wines in existence. Its flavors are delicate but rich, with delicious fresh apricot and peach undertones; it makes a wonderful accompaniment to fresh fish. Condrieu (which sells in the $40 to $60 range) must be consumed young, however. In addition, Condrieu is a small appellation, and therefore the best Condrieu wines are hard to find. Look for them in the finer wine shops and the better French restaurants.

The Loire Valley: White Wine Heaven

Have you been Chardonnay-ed out yet? If you're looking for white-wine alternatives to Chardonnay, discover the Loire *(l'wahr)* Valley wine region. Lots of white wines come from there, but none of them are Chardonnay! For the record, you can find red wines and some dry rosés, too, in the Loire, but the region is really known for its white wines.

The Loire Valley stretches across northwest France, following the path of the Loire River from central France in the east to the Atlantic Ocean in the west. The rather cool climate, especially in the west, produces relatively light-bodied white wines.

In the eastern end of the Valley, just south of Paris, are the towns of Sancerre and Pouilly-sur-Loire, located on opposite banks of the Loire River. Here, the Sauvignon Blanc grape thrives, making lively, dry wines that have spicy, green-grass flavors.

The two principal wines in this area are Sancerre *(sahn sehr)* and Pouilly-Fumé *(pwee foo may)*.

- Sancerre is the lighter, drier, more lively of the two. It is perfect for summer drinking, especially when accompanied by shellfish or light, fresh water fish, such as trout.

- Pouilly-Fumé is slightly fuller and less spicy than Sancerre, and can have attractive gun-flint and mineral flavors. Pouilly-Fumé can be quite a fine wine when made by a good producer such as Didier Dagueneau or Ladoucette. Because it is fuller, Pouilly-Fumé goes well with rich fish, such as salmon, or with chicken or veal.

Most Sancerre and Pouilly-Fumé wines sell in the $15 to $20 price range, but a few of the better ones are $20 to $30. They are at their best when they're young and fresh; drink them within three or four years after the vintage.

You might get the two *Pouilly* wines, Pouilly-Fuissé and Pouilly-Fumé, confused — but they are very different wines. The Chardonnay-based Pouilly-Fuissé, from the Mâcon in Burgundy, is a more full-bodied wine. The Pouilly-Fumé, made from Sauvignon Blanc, is lighter and more acidic.

In the central Loire Valley near the city of Tours (where beautiful châteaux of former French royalty can be found), lies the town of Vouvray *(voo vray)*. The Chenin Blanc grape makes better wine here than it does anywhere else in the world. The wines of Vouvray come in three styles: dry, medium-dry, or sweet (called *moelleux*), but the sweet wines can only be made in vintages of unusual ripeness, which occur infrequently. There is also a sparkling Vouvray.

The best wines of Vouvray need several years to develop and can last almost forever, thanks to their remarkable acidity. The better Vouvrays begin at about $20. The two most respected producers are Philippe Foreau of Clos Naudain and Gaston Huet.

Less expensive Vouvrays, priced at $10 to $15, are pleasant to drink young. Even the drier versions are not really bone dry and are a good choice for you if you cannot tolerate very dry wines. They go well with chicken or veal in a cream sauce or with fruit and cheese after dinner.

The third wine district of the Loire Valley is called the Pays Nantais _(pay ee nahn tay),_ after the city of Nantes, right where the Loire River empties into the Atlantic Ocean. The vineyard area around Nantes is home of the Muscadet grape (also known as the Melon). The wine, also called Muscadet _(moos cah day),_ is light and very dry — a perfect accompaniment to clams, oysters, and river fish (and, naturally, ideal for summer drinking).

The best news about Muscadet is the price. You can buy a really fine Muscadet in the $7 to $10 range. Buy the youngest one you can find because Muscadet is at its best within one to two years of the vintage. It is not an ager.

The best Muscadet comes from the Sèvre-et-Maine region, and those words appear on the label. Frequently you will also see the term _sur lie,_ which means that the wine was aged on its _lees_ (fermentation yeasts) and bottled straight from the tank. This procedure gives the wine liveliness, freshness, and sometimes a slight prickle of carbon dioxide on the tongue.

Alsace Wines: French, Not German

It's understandable that much of the wine-drinking populace confuses the wines of Alsace _(ahl zas)_ with German wines. Alsace, in northeastern France, is just across the Rhine River from Germany. Originally a part of Germany, Alsace became French in the 17th century. Germany took the region back in 1871 only to lose it to France again as a result of World War I (1919). To complicate things further, both Alsace and Germany grow some of the same grapes (Riesling and Gewurztraminer). But there is where the similarity ends: Alsace wines are _dry,_ whereas most German wines are medium-dry or sweet.

Alsace's identity crisis has hurt her wines in the international marketplace. As a result, the wines of Alsace are a very good value.

Alsace wines are unique among French wines in two ways. All Alsace wines come in a tall, thin bottle called a _flûte._ And almost all Alsace wines carry a grape variety name _and_ a place-name, which is simply Alsace.

Considering Alsace's northerly latitude, you'd expect the region's climate to be cool. But thanks to the protection of the Vosges Mountains to her west, Alsace's climate is quite sunny and temperate and one of the driest in France — in short, perfect weather for grape growing.

Although some light-bodied Pinot Noir is made, 93 percent of Alsace's wines are white. Four are particularly important: Pinot Blanc, Riesling, Pinot Gris, and Gewurztraminer. Although each reflects the characteristics of the grape from which it is made, they all share a certain aroma and flavor, sometimes called a spiciness, that can only be described as the flavor of Alsace.

Alsace Pinot Blanc is the lightest of the four wines. In a slight reinterpretation of traditional Alsace style, some producers make their Pinot Blanc medium-dry to appeal to wine drinkers who are unfamiliar with the region's wines. Other producers make it bone dry. Either way, it's at its best in its youth. Pinot Blanc is quite inexpensive, selling in the $10 to $14 range.

Riesling is the king of Alsace wines (remember: it's a *dry* wine here). Alsace Riesling has a flowery nose, but firm, dry, almost steely, flavors. Although it can be consumed young, like most Alsace wines, a Riesling from a good vintage is easily capable of aging and improving for ten years or more. Rieslings are in the $15 to $30 price range.

Tokay-Pinot Gris is an Alsace wine whose name resembles a famous Hungarian dessert wine, Tokaji — but there is no relationship. Tokay-Pinot Gris is made from Pinot Gris, the same variety that you find in Italy as Pinot Grigio. Here in Alsace, it is a rich, spicy, full-bodied wine with a lot of character. It is relatively low in acidity and high in alcohol. Alsace's Pinot Gris retails in the $15 to $20 range; it goes well with spicy meat dishes.

The Gewurztraminer grape has such an intense, pungent, spicy aroma and flavor that it's a love it or leave it wine (one of us loves it — the other leaves it!). But it certainly has its followers. And it is clearly at its best in Alsace. If you haven't tried an Alsace Gewurztraminer yet, you haven't tasted one of the most unique wines in the world. It's quite low in acidity and high in alcohol, a combination which gives an impression of fullness and softness. It goes best with *foie gras* and strong cheeses, and some people like it with spicy Asian cuisine. Gewurztraminer sells for about the same price as Riesling but doesn't age quite as well.

Chapter 11
Italy, the Heartland of Vino

• •

In This Chapter

▶ Italy's Big "B" wines

▶ Chianti: Still famous after all these years

▶ Three gentlewines from Verona

▶ The *vino bianco* quality revival

• •

More than 2,000 years after Julius Caesar conquered Gaul, the Italians continue to take the world by storm. With passion, artistic flair, impeccable taste, and flawless workmanship as their weapons, the Italians have infiltrated the arenas of fashion, film, food, and of course, wine.

Thanks to the popularity of Italian restaurants, most of us have frequent opportunities to enjoy the best-selling Italian wines such as Soave, Pinot Grigio, Valpolicella, and Chianti. But Italy makes other wines, too — many of them among the greatest wines on earth. And every one of Italy's thousand-something wines is terrific with food, because Italian wines are made specifically to be enjoyed during a meal. That's how the Italians drink wine.

We focus on Italy's three most renowned wine areas — Piedmont, Tuscany, and the northeast — in this chapter. We also give you a snapshot of some of the other Italian wine regions whose wines you are likely to find in your wine shop or ristorante.

The Vineyard of Europe

Tiny, overachieving Italy — 60 percent the size of France, three-quarters the size of California — makes, along with France, two-thirds of the world's wines! Wine is the lifeblood of the Italian people. Vines grow everywhere, and no meal could possibly occur without a bottle of wine on the table.

The downside of wine's omnipresence in Italy is that wine is often taken for granted. Italy took 28 years longer than France to develop a wine classification system, for example; and still today, 35 years after creating that system, Italy has yet to incorporate official recognition of her best vineyard sites (*crus*) into her wine laws, as the French have done in Burgundy. Italy's casual attitude toward wine has slowed the acceptance of even the top Italian wines by many serious wine lovers around the world.

Another handicap of Italian wines, in the eyes of some wine drinkers in other countries, is that most Italian wines are made from native grape varieties that don't exist elsewhere (and when transplanted, they don't perform nearly as well as in Italy). Grapes such as Nebbiolo, Sangiovese, Aglianico and Barbera, to name just a few, can make outstanding wine in Italy, but their names are unfamiliar to many wine lovers around the world. Table 11-1 lists the grape varieties behind some wines of Italy's most important wine regions.

On the upside, Italy is blessed with such a variety of soils and climates — from Alpine foothills in the north to Mediterranean coastlines in the south — that the range of her wines is almost endless. (A curious wine lover could keep busy for a lifetime exploring the hundreds of wines in Italy!) Italy's hilly landscape provides plenty of high-altitude relief for grapevines even in the warm south, and many craggy slopes with poor soil challenge vines to perform small miracles.

The ordinary and the elite

Italy's wines, as we outside of Italy know them, fall into two distinct groups:

- ✔ Inexpensive red and white wines often sold in large value-priced bottles for everyday drinking with meals in the casual Italian fashion
- ✔ The better wines, which range from good to great in quality

One of the best-known Italian wines in the first category is Lambrusco, a frothy, slightly sweet (and delicious) red wine that has been a first wine for many wine drinkers outside Italy. In the second category is the drier version of Lambrusco that is drunk in the home market, the Italian wines we describe in this chapter, and many other wines that space does not permit us to mention.

The wine regions of Italy

Italy is said to have 20 wine regions, which correspond exactly to her political regions (see Figure 11-1). (In other words, wine is produced everywhere in Italy.) What we would call a wine region in France, such as Burgundy or Alsace, we refer to as a wine *zone* in Italy to avoid confusion with the larger political region.

Table 11-1   The Non-Varietal Wines of Italy's Main Regions

Red Wine	White Wine	Grape Variety
Piedmont		
Barolo		Nebbiolo
Barbaresco		Nebbiolo
Gattinara		Nebbiolo, Bonarda*
	Gavi	Cortese
	Roero Arneis	Arneis
Tuscany		
Chianti, Chianti Classico		Sangiovese, Canaiolo and others*
Brunello di Montalcino		Sangiovese Grosso
	Vernaccia di San Gimignano	Vernaccia
Vino Nobile di Montepulciano		Sangiovese, Canaiolo, and others*
Carmignano		Sangiovese, Cabernet Sauvignon*
Super-Tuscans**		Cabernet Sauvignon, Sangiovese, others*
Veneto		
	Soave	Garganega, Trebbiano, and others*
Valpolicella		Corvina, Rondinella, Molinara*
Amarone		(Same grapes as Valpolicella; semi-dried)
Bardolino		Corvina, Rondinella, Molinara*
	Bianco di Custoza	Trebbiano, Garganega, Tocai*
	Lugana***	Trebbiano

Blended wines, made from two or more grapes.

** *Untraditional wines produced mainly in the Chianti district; see the discussion under Tuscany.*

*** *Much of the Lugana wine zone is actually in Lombardy.*

Many of the finest wines come from the north: the Piedmont region in the northwest, Tuscany in north-central Italy, and the three regions (informally called the Tre Venezie) of northeastern Italy.

Figure 11-1:
The wine
regions
of Italy.

Categories of Italian wine, legally speaking

Because Italy is a member of the European Union (EU), her official system of categorizing wines and naming wines (her *appellation* system) must conform to the two-tier EU categorization of wines: QWPSR wines (Quality Wines Produced in a Specific Region) on the top tier and table wines on the second tier. (See "The EU hierarchy of wine" in Chapter 9 for more information.)

At the QWPSR level are

- DOCG wines *(Denominazione di Origine Controllata e Garantita)*, translated as *regulated and guaranteed place-name,* a small group of elite wines, currently 17. The long Italian phrase corresponding to the initials DOCG appears on the labels of these wines.

- DOC wines *(Denominazione di Origine Controllata),* translated as *regulated place-name,* Italy's basic QWPSR wines. As of 1997, 286 place-named wines have been recognized by the Italian government. The phrase *Denominazione di Origine Controllata* appears on the labels of these wines.

The terms DOC and DOCG refer to both wine zones and the wines of those zones. The DOC Soave, for example, is both a place (a specific production zone defined and regulated by Italian law, named after a town called Soave) and the wine of that place.

At the table wine level are

- IGT wines *(Indicazione di Geografica Tipica),* or table wines with a geographic indication on the label. Most of these wines were previously labelled as *vino da tavola* followed by a geographic designation of the producer's choosing; as IGT wines, they must carry one of the officially approved geographic designations. As of 1997, 128 such IGT designations had been recognized.

- Ordinary table wines that carry no geographical indication except "Italy."

Reds Reign in Piedmont

Piedmont's claim to wine fame is the Nebbiolo *(neb bee OH lo)* grape, a noble red variety that produces great wine only in northwestern Italy. The proof of Nebbiolo's nobility is twofold: Barolo *(bah RO lo)* and Barbaresco *(bar bah RES co)* are two of the world's great red wines. Both are DOCG wines made entirely from the Nebbiolo grape in the Langhe hills around Alba, and each is named after a village within its production zone.

Both Barolo and Barbaresco are robust reds — very dry, full-bodied, and high in tannin, acidity, and alcohol. Their aromas suggest tar, violets, roses, ripe strawberries, and (sometimes) truffles — the kind that grow in the ground, not the chocolate! Barolo is more full-bodied than Barbaresco and usually requires a bit more aging; otherwise, the two wines are very similar. Like most Italian wines, they show their best with food. Good Barolo and Barbaresco wines usually retail for $25 to over $50 per bottle.

Tradition versus "new-style"

One Barolo can differ from another (and one Barbaresco from another) quite a lot according to the production methods that the producer applies. Traditionally made wines experience longer fermentation periods during which a huge amount of tannin is extracted from the grapes, for example; they are usually then aged in large wooden casks old enough to have lost most of their oaky aromas and tannins. At the other extreme, most avant-garde Barolos and Barbarescos have short fermentation periods and are often aged in small French oak barrels (called *barriques*), at least for part of their maturation; these barrels contribute an oaky flavor to the wine, as well as tannin. The traditional wines are more tannic and need more time to develop, but typically have greater longevity than new-style wines — which in turn are fruitier in flavor but also oaky-tasting, and are ready to drink sooner.

Neither Barolo nor Barbaresco is a wine to drink young. Production rules stipulate that Barolo is not Barolo until it has aged for three years at the winery, or for five years if it is called *Riserva* (Barbaresco's minimum aging is two years, or four for *Riserva*). But both wines benefit from additional aging. When traditionally made, Barolo and Barbaresco often require 10 to 20 years' total aging, from the year of the vintage — and they usually benefit from a few hours of aeration before drinking to soften their somewhat tough nature (see Chapter 8 for instructions on aerating wine). However, some avant-garde producers are making these wines in such a way that they are enjoyable sooner, from one to five years after they appear on the market.

Both Barbaresco and especially Barolo have something in common with Burgundy in France: *You must find a good producer to really experience the wine at its best.* To guide you in that endeavor, we list whom we consider the best producers of Barolo and of Barbaresco, in our rough order of preference. Some producers — including Giacomo Conterno, both Mascarellos, both Rinaldis, and Bruno Giacosa — clearly make traditionally styled wines; others — including Gaja, Sandrone, and Voerzio — are in the modern camp; and some, such as Ceretto and Renato Ratti, combine aspects of both winemaking styles. (We prefer the traditionally made wines, but excellent producers can be found in all three stylistic camps.)

Lightning strikes twice: Three great vintages

Piedmont recently enjoyed three excellent harvests in a row (just like Bordeaux): 1988, 1989, and 1990. Almost miraculously, this string of fortune has repeated itself in 1995, 1996, and 1997.

Barolo (and many Barbaresco) wines from the last three named years will be available for purchase in 1999, 2000, and 2001, respectively. Because Barbaresco wines can legally be sold sooner than Barolo, however, you can buy some 1995, 1996, and 1997 Barbarescos in 1998, 1999, and 2000, respectively.

WORTH THE SEARCH

Barolo
Giacomo Conterno
Giuseppe Mascarello
Vietti
Bartolo Mascarello
Giuseppe Rinaldi
Bruno Giacosa
Aldo Conterno
Gaja
Caretta
Ceretto
Paolo Scavino
Renato Ratti
Marcarini
Prunotto
Luciano Sandrone
Pio Cesare
Manzone

Roberto Voerzio
Elio Altare
Marchesi di Barolo
Conterno-Fantino
Clerico
Francesco Rinaldi
Fontanafredda
Corino
Parusso

Barbaresco
Bruno Giacosa
Gaja
Ceretto
Marchesi di Gresy
Cigliuti
Moccagatta
Produttori del Barbaresco
Castello di Neive

REAL DEAL

Another good Nebbiolo-based wine, the DOCG Gattinara *(gah tee NAH rah)*, comes from northern Piedmont, where the Nebbiolo grape is called Spanna. Although Gattinara seldom gets the praise that the two Big B's (Barolo and Barbaresco) enjoy, it offers the same enticing Nebbiolo aromas and flavors in a slightly less full-bodied style. Attractively priced at $15 to $18 a bottle, Gattinara from a good producer has to be one of the world's most under-rated wines. Look for Antoniolo's and Travaglini's Gattinaras.

Weekday reds

The Piedmontese reserve serious wines like Barolo and Barbaresco for Sunday dinner or special occasions. What they drink on an everyday basis are the red wines Dolcetto *(dohl CHET to)* and Barbera *(bar BEAR ah)*. Of the two, Dolcetto is the lighter-bodied and is usually the first red wine served in a Piedmontese meal.

If you know enough Italian to translate the phrase *la dolce vita,* you might think that the name Dolcetto indicates a sweet wine. Actually, the Dolcetto grape tastes sweet but the *wine* is distinctly dry and somewhat grapey with ample tannins. Dolcetto is often compared to Beaujolais (France's easy-drinking red wine; see Chapter 10) but it is drier and more tannic than most Beaujolais wines, and it goes better with food (at least in our opinion).

Dolcetto sells in the $12 to $18 price range. The best Dolcetto wines are from the zones of Dogliani, Diano d'Alba, and Alba; wines from these areas carry the grape name, Dolcetto, along with the name of the area. Just about all of our recommended Barolo producers make a Dolcetto, usually Dolcetto d'Alba. A favorite producer of ours who happens to make only Dolcetto di Dogliani is Chionetti.

While Dolcetto is unique to Piedmont, the Barbera grape is one of the most widely planted red grape varieties in all of Italy. (Sangiovese is *the* most widely planted red variety.) But it is in Piedmont, specifically the Alba and Asti wine zones, that Barbera excels. It's a rich red wine with high acidity and generous black-cherry fruit character. Barbera d'Alba is generally a bit fuller, riper, and richer than the leaner Barbera d'Asti — but Barbera d'Asti from certain old vineyards rivals Barbera d'Alba in richness and in power. (Link the d' with the word following it when pronouncing these names: *DAL ba, DAHS tee.*) Barbera happens to be our favorite everyday wine, especially with pasta or pizza — or anything tomatoey.

Barbera is more popular in the United States than it has ever been, and we couldn't be more delighted, as it's now easier to find. Two different types of Barbera are available:

- The traditional style, aged in casks (large oak containers that impart little, if any, oak flavor to the wine), which sells in the $12 to $20 range.

- The newer, oak-influenced barrique-aged Barbera, which sells in the $20 to $40 range (somebody has to pay for those expensive oak barrels!).

As with Barolo and Barbaresco, some producers combine both styles of winemaking for their Barbera wines. Although both types of Barbera are very good, we prefer the simpler, less expensive, traditional style. (Frankly, we're getting a bit tired of all the oak flavor in wines these days.)

Two particularly good producers of Barbera d'Alba are Vietti and Giacomo Conterno. One especially fine Barbera d'Alba of Vietti's is his Scarrone Vigna Vecchia (old vines), made from 50-year-old vines in a small part of his Scarrone vineyard. At $27 to $30 a bottle, it's more expensive than Vietti's other Barberas, but it's worth the difference. Vietti's regular — and more readily available — Barbera d'Alba "Scarrone" is a fine $20 Barbera; his simpler $15 Barbera d'Alba "Tre Vigne" is also quite good.

A third weekday red from Piedmont is Nebbiolo d'Alba, a wine made from Nebbiolo grapes grown in vineyards outside the prized Barolo or Barbaresco zones. The wine is lighter in body and easier to drink than either Barolo or Barbaresco, and it sells for about $14 to $16 a bottle.

Whites in a supporting role

Almost all of Piedmont's wines are red, but two interesting whites are made here. Gavi, named for a town in southern Piedmont, is a very dry wine with pronounced acidity. Most Gavis sell for $12 to $17 (rather expensive for what it is, perhaps because Gavi has become chic), while a premium Gavi, La Scolca's Black Label, costs around $35.

Arneis *(ahr NASE)* is a white wine produced in the Roero zone near Alba from a long-forgotten grape called Arneis, which was resurrected by Vietti several years ago. Arneis is a dry to medium-dry wine with a rich texture. It's best when it is consumed within two years of the vintage; a bottle sells for $16 to $20. Besides Vietti's, look for Bruno Giacosa's and Ceretto's Arneis wines.

Tuscany the Beautiful

Florence, Siena, Michelangelo's David, the leaning tower of Pisa . . . the beautiful region of Tuscany has more than her share of attractions. Only one wine could possibly compare in fame — and that, too, comes from Tuscany: Chianti.

Here a Chianti, there a Chianti

Chianti is a large wine zone extending through much of Tuscany. The zone — all of it DOCG status, deservedly or not — is divided into seven districts. Chianti wines may use the name of the district where their grapes grew or the simpler appellation, Chianti, if their production does not qualify for a district name (if grapes from two districts are blended, for example). The district known as *Chianti Classico* is the heartland of the zone, the best area, and — lucky for us — the one district whose wines are widely available. The only other Chianti district that can rival Chianti Classico in quality is *Chianti Rufina (ROO fee nah),* whose wines are also quite available (especially from the well-known producer, Frescobaldi).

Besides varying according to their district of production, Chianti wines vary in style according to their aging: *Riserva* wines are quite often aged in French oak, may be released only after two years or more at the winery, and have potential for longer life. Chianti wines can also vary according to their grape blend — although, in practice, most Chiantis are made almost entirely from the Sangiovese grape.

Chianti is a very dry red wine (there's no such animal as *white* Chianti) that, like most Italian wines, tastes best with food. It ranges from light-bodied to almost full-bodied, often has an aroma of cherries and sometimes violets, and its taste is reminiscent of tart cherries. The best Chianti wines have very concentrated fruit character and usually taste best from five to eight years after the vintage — although in good vintages they have no problem aging for ten or more years. The best recent years for Chianti have been the 1985, 1988, 1990, and 1995 vintages.

These days, Chianti is better than ever. From simple $6 Chianti to the more substantial Chianti Classico (generally priced between $12 and $18), Chianti remains one of the wine world's great values. Even Chianti Classico Riservas are good values, with most of them priced about $5 or $6 more than regular Chianti Classico.

Chianti is more consistent in quality than Barolo, especially in the classico district, but it's still smart to know the good producers. Here is an alphabetical list of some of our favorites. (If 35 favorite producers seems excessive, remember that Chianti is a fairly large area with many thousands of growers and winemakers.)

Great Chianti Producers

Badia a Coltibuono	Castello di Volpaia	Monte Vertine
Carpineto	Cecchi (Villa Cerna)	Nozzole
Castellare	Dievole	Podere Il Palazzino
Castell'in Villa	Fattoria di Felsina	Renzo Masi
Castello d'Albola	Fontodi	Rocca di Castagnoli
Castello dei Rampolla	Frescobaldi	Ruffino
Castello di Ama	Isole e Olena	San Felice
Castello di Brolio	Lilliano	San Giusto a Rentennano
Castello di Cacchiano	Marchesi Antinori	Selvapiana
Castello di Fonterutoli	La Massa	Villa Cafaggio
Castello di Gabbiano	Melini	Viticcio
Castello di Verrazzano	Monsanto	

Brunello di Montalcino, overnight celebrity

While Chianti has been famous for centuries, another great Tuscan wine, Brunello di Montalcino, exploded on the scene only recently — and became an overnight success with staying power.

South of the Chianti zone sits the fortress town of Montalcino. The local wine, Brunello di Montalcino *(brew NEL lo dee mon tahl CHEE no)*, originated in the last century but was pretty much unheard of outside Tuscany until 1970 when the Biondi-Santi family, a leading producer in Montalcino, presented some of its oldest wines to writers. The 1888 and 1891 vintages were still drinking well. (In fact, they were in excellent shape!) The rest is history, as they say. Today, Brunello di Montalcino, a DOCG wine, is considered one of the greatest, long-lived red wines in existence, with a price-tag to match ($30 to $50 and up).

This stalwart cousin to Chianti is an intense, concentrated, tannic wine that demands aging (up to 20 years) when traditionally made and benefits from several hours of aeration before serving. Lately, some producers in Montalcino have been making a more approachable version of Brunello.

Rosso di Montalcino is a less expensive ($15 to $20), ready-to-drink wine made from the same grapes and grown in the same production area as Brunello di Montalcino. Rosso di Montalcino from a good Brunello producer is a great value, offering you a glimpse of Brunello without breaking the bank.

To really appreciate Brunello di Montalcino, seek out one of the producers recommended in the following list (in our rough order of preference). Brunellos from traditional winemakers, such as Biondi-Santi, Costanti, and Pertimali, need at least 15 to 20 years of aging in good vintages (1975, 1985, 1988, 1990, 1995, and 1997 are recent great vintages for Brunello, but the 1997's will not be available until 2002). Brunellos from modern-style producers, such as Caparzo, Altesino, and Col d'Orcia, can be enjoyed within ten years. Younger than ten years — drink Rosso di Montalcino.

Great Brunello di Montalcino Producers

Case Basse of Soldera (very expensive)
Biondi-Santi (very expensive)
Altesino (especially Montosoli vineyard)
Costanti
Pertimali di Livio Sassetti
Pertimali di Angelo Sassetti
Poggio Antico
Il Poggione
Ciacci Piccolomini

Two reds and a white

Three more Tuscan wines of note include two reds, Vino Nobile di Montepulciano *(NO be lay dee mon tay pul chee AH no)* and Carmignano *(car mee NYAH no)*, and Tuscany's best white wine, Vernaccia di San Gimignano *(ver NAH cha dee san gee mee NYAH no)* — all three DOCG wines.

The Montepulciano wine zone, named after the town of Montepulciano, is located southeast of the Chianti zone. Vino Nobile's principal grape is the Prugnolo Gentile (alias Sangiovese). From a good producer, Vino Nobile di Montepulciano can rival the better Chianti Classicos. Eight producers we recommend are Poderi Boscarelli, Fattoria del Cerro, Avignonesi, Lodola Nuova, La Braccesca, Dei, Fassati, and Poliziano. Vino Nobile producers now also make a lighter, readier-to-drink wine than Vino Nobile, Rosso di Montepulciano.

The Carmignano wine region is directly west of Florence. What distinguishes Carmignano from Chianti is that, although Sangiovese is the main grape, Cabernet Sauvignon is one of the traditional grapes that can be used in the wine. As a result, Carmignano's taste can be described as "a Chianti with the finesseful touch of a Bordeaux." Two outstanding producers of Carmignano are Villa di Capezzana and Ambra.

Vernaccia di San Gimignano is named for the medieval walled town of San Gimignano, west of the Chianti Classico zone. Vernaccia is generally a fresh white wine with a slightly oily texture and an almondy flavor, and it is meant to be drunk young. For an unusual interpretation, try Teruzzi & Puthod's oak-aged riserva, Terre di Tufo, a pricey but very good Vernaccia (about $20). Most other Vernaccias are in the $8 to $10 range. In addition to Teruzzi & Puthod, producers to look for are Montenidoli (especially the wine called Fiore) and Falchini.

Super-Tuscans

When Chianti fell into an economic slump in the 1970s, progressive producers caught the attention of the world by creating new wines that are today collectively known as super-Tuscans. The pioneering examples include Sassicaia *(sas ee KYE ah)*, from Marchese Incisa della Rocchetta, and Tignanello *(tee nyah NEL loh)* and Solaia *(so LYE ah)* from Piero Antinori. These red wines could not be called Chianti either because they were produced outside the Chianti zone or because their grape blend (generally Cabernet Sauvignon, Cabernet Franc, and/or Sangiovese) did not conform to DOC requirements for Chianti.

Today, dozens of super-Tuscan wines exist. Their actual grape blends vary from wine to wine, some producers using Merlot or even Syrah with their Sangiovese, others using only native Tuscan grapes. What these wines have in common is that they are expensive, ranging from $30 to $50 on up to $75 to $100 per bottle. The most famous super-Tuscan wines, Sassicaia and Solaia, prized by wine collectors, can cost $200 in good vintages such as 1985.

The super-Tuscan wines vary greatly in flavor because of differing grape varieties and microclimates; they can range in style from a very good Chianti-like wine to a Bordeaux-type or California Cabernet-type wine, depending on the varying amounts of Sangiovese, Cabernet Sauvignon, Merlot, and so on.

Now that Chianti has reestablished itself in the world market, these expensive new wines have become less prominent — but most major Chianti producers still make a super-Tuscan wine.

Sangiovese at the table

Lighter Chianti wines go well with pasta, prosciutto, and roast chicken or squab. With Chianti Classicos and riservas, lamb, roast turkey, veal, steak, and roast beef are fine accompaniments. For the robust Brunello di Montalcino and super-Tuscan wines, try pheasant, steak, game, or chunks of fresh Parmesan cheese. Serve these wines at cool room temperature, 64° to 66° F (19° C).

In addition to Sassicaia, Solaia, and Tignanello, five of our favorite super-Tuscans are

- ✔ Le Pergole Torte, made by Monte Vertine entirely from Sangiovese grapes

- ✔ Ornellaia (made by Piero Antinori's younger brother, Lodovico Antinori, at a separate estate), a blend of Cabernet Sauvignon and Merlot

- ✔ Sammarco, from Castello dei Rampolla, 75 percent Cabernet Sauvignon and 25 percent Sangiovese

- ✔ I Sodi di San Niccolò, from Castellare, primarily Sangiovese

- ✔ Percarlo from San Giusto a Rentennano, 100 percent Sangiovese

For us, these are among Italy's finest wines. Vintages to look for: 1985, 1988, 1990, and 1995 (the latter becoming available in 1999).

Decant young (less than ten years old) super-Tuscan wines several hours before serving.

A Cornucopia of Wines from the Northeast

The three regions in the northeastern corner of Italy (refer to Figure 11-1) are often referred to as the *Tre Venezie* — the Three Venices — because they were once part of the Venetian Empire. Colorful historical associations aside, each of these regions produces red and white wines that are among the most popular Italian wines outside of Italy — as well as in their own regions.

Doing Romeo and Juliet proud

Chances are that if your first Italian wine wasn't Chianti, it was one of Verona's big three: the white Soave *(so AH vay)* or the reds, Valpolicella *(val po lee CHEL lah)* or Bardolino *(bar do LEE noh)*. These enormously popular wines hail from northeast Italy around the picturesque city of Verona — Romeo and Juliet's hometown — and the beautiful Lake Garda.

Of the two Veronese reds, Valpolicella is the fuller; the lighter Bardolino is a pleasant summer wine when served slightly cool. (Bolla and Masi are two of the largest producers of both.) Valpolicella, Bardolino, and Soave are attractively priced in the $6 to $10 range, as are two other white wines of the region, Bianco di Custoza and Lugana (Santi is one of the leading producers of these two). Recommended producers of Veronese wines include

- ✔ **Soave:** Gini, Pieropan, Anselmi, Santa Sofia
- ✔ **Valpolicella:** Allegrini, Le Ragose, Guerrieri-Rizzardi, Alighieri, Tommasi, Masi
- ✔ **Bardolino:** Guerrieri-Rizzardi, Cavalchina

Amarone della Valpolicella (also simply known as Amarone), one of Italy's most full-bodied red wines, is made from the same grapes as Valpolicella (refer to Table 11-1), but the ripe grapes are dried on mats for several months before fermentation, thus concentrating their sugar and flavors. The resulting wine is a rich, potent (14 to 16 percent alcohol), velvety, long-lasting wine, perfect for a cold winter night and a plate of mature, hard cheeses. Some of the best producers of Amarone are Quintarelli, Bertani, Masi, Tommasi, Le Ragose, Allegrini, Dal Forno, Zenato, Sartori, and Bolla.

The Austrian-Italian alliance

If you have traveled much in Italy, you probably realize that in spirit Italy is not one unified country but 20 or more different countries linked together politically. Consider Trentino-Alto Adige. Not only is this mountainous region (the northernmost in Italy; refer to Figure 11-1) dramatically different from the rest of Italy, but also the mainly German-speaking Alto Adige (or South Tyrol) in the north is completely different from the Italian-speaking Trentino in the south. (Before World War I, the South Tyrol was part of the Austro-Hungarian Empire.) The wines of the two areas are different, too — yet the area is considered a single region!

Although red wine is made in Alto Adige, most of it goes to Germany, Austria, and Switzerland. The rest of the world sees Alto Adige's white wines: Pinot Grigio, Chardonnay, Pinot Bianco, Sauvignon, and Gewürztraminer, which are priced mainly in the $10 to $15 range.

But one local red wine to seek out is Alto Adige's Lagrein, from the same-named grape variety. It is a robust, hearty wine, somewhat rustic in style, but it offers a completely unique taste experience. Hofstätter is a producer who makes a particularly good Lagrein.

Along with nearby Friuli, this region produces Italy's best white wines. Four producers to look for are Alois Lageder, Hofstätter, Tiefenbrunner, and Peter Zemmer. Here are some highlights of each brand:

- Lageder's Pinot Bianco from the Haberlehof vineyard and his Sauvignon from the Lehenhof vineyard are exceptional examples of Pinot Blanc and Sauvignon, and are among the best wines that we've tasted from these two grape varieties.

- Hofstätter's Gewürztraminer, from the Kolbenhof vineyard, is as fine a wine as you can find from this tricky grape variety. Hofstätter also makes Italy's best Pinot Nero (Pinot Noir), called Villa Barthenau.

- Tiefenbrunner's Müller Thurgau *(MULE lair TOOR gow)* from his Feldmarschall Vineyard (the region's highest altitude vineyard) could well be the wine world's best example of this often lackluster grape variety.

- Peter Zemmer produces reliable Chardonnay and Pinot Grigio wines in the $9 to $10 price range.

Trentino, the southern part of the Trentino-Alto Adige region, is not without its own notable wines. Some excellent Chardonnays come from Trentino, for example; two of the best are made by Pojer & Sandri and Roberto Zeni. (In fact, we recommend any of the wines from these two producers.) A Trentino producer who specializes in red wines made from the local variety, Teroldego *(teh ROLL day go)* Rotaliano, is Elisabetta Foradori. Her red wine called Granato, based on Teroldego, always causes a sensation among those who taste it. Also, one of Italy's leading sparkling wine producers, Ferrari, is based in Trentino. (See Chapter 15 for more information on sparkling wine producers.)

The far side: Friuli-Venezia Giulia

Italy has been justifiably known in the wine world for its red wines. But in the last 20 years, the northeastern region of Friuli-Venezia Giulia (refer to Figure 11-1), led by the pioneering winemaker, Mario Schiopetto, has made the world conscious of Italy's white wines as well.

Near the region's eastern border with Slovenia, the districts of Collio and Colli Orientali del Friuli produce Friuli's best wine. Red wines exist here, but the white wines have given these zones their renown. In addition to Pinot Grigio, Pinot Bianco, Chardonnay, and Sauvignon, two local favorites are Tocai Friulano and Ribolla Gialla (both fairly rich, full, and viscous).

An admirable white wine made here is Silvio Jermann's Vintage Tunina, a blend of five varieties, including Pinot Bianco, Sauvignon, and Chardonnay. Vintage Tunina is a rich, full-bodied, long-lived white of world-class status. It sells in the $35 to $40 range and, frankly, it's worth the money. Give the wine eight to ten years to age and then try it with rich poultry dishes or pasta.

The following list shows you our recommended producers in Friuli, in rough order of preference.

Great Producers in Friuli

Jermann	Russiz Superiore
Volpe Pasini	Conti Formentini
Borgo Conventi	Marco Felluga
Girolamo Dorigo	Puiatti
Livio Felluga	Castello di Spessa
Gravner	Vigne dal Leon
Doro Princic	Plozner
Abbazia di Rosazzo	Pighin
Mario Schiopetto	Castelcosa
Walter Filiputti	Francesco Pecorari
Sant' Elena	Ronco del Gnemiz

Cameo Appearances from the Rest of Italy

Italy's wines are not confined to the five regions that we discuss individually. A quick tour of some of Italy's other regions will prove the point. Refer to Figure 11-1 for the location of each of the following regions:

- ✔ **Lombardy:** In the northern part of this region, near the Swiss border, the Valtellina wine district produces four light-bodied red wines from the Nebbiolo grape: Sassella, Inferno, Grumello, and Valgella. All of these wines are inexpensive (about $9 to $14) and, unlike Barolo or Barbaresco, can be enjoyed young.

- ✔ **Emilia-Romagna:** The home of Lambrusco, one of Italy's most successful wines on the export market. For a different Lambrusco experience, try one without the screw cap if you can find it. (You might have to go to Emilia-Romagna for that — but, hey, that's not so bad. Bologna and Parma, two gastronomic meccas, are in this region.)

- ✔ **Marches** (also known as **Marche**): Verdicchio, a dry, inexpensive white wine that goes well with fish, is widely available, and quality increases with every vintage. Try the Verdicchio dei Castelli di Jesi from Fazi-Battaglia or Umani Ronchi, great values at $8.

- ✔ **Umbria:** This is the region of Perugia and Assisi. Umbria makes some good red and white wines. Orvieto, a white wine, is widely available for around $9 or $10 from Tuscan producers such as Antinori and Ruffino. Two interesting red wines are Torgiano, a Chianti-like blend (try

Lungarotti's Rubesco Riserva DOCG), and Sagrantino di Montefalco DOCG, a medium-bodied, elegant wine made from a local grape variety (Sagrantino) that has been a well-kept secret outside of Umbria. Two producers of Sagrantino di Montefalco to look for are Arnaldo Caprai and Rocca di Fabbri.

- ✔ **Latium:** This region of Rome makes the ubiquitous, inexpensive Frascati, a light, neutral wine from the Trebbiano grape; Fontana Candida is a popular brand.

- ✔ **Abruzzo:** Montepulciano d'Abruzzo, a very inexpensive, easy-drinking, low tannin, low-acid red wine, comes from here; it's a terrific everyday red if you like the style.

- ✔ **Campania:** Here, near Naples, the most serious wines in southern Italy are produced. The full-bodied, tannic Taurasi, a DOCG wine from the Aglianico grape, is one of the great, long-lived red wines in Italy. The outstanding producer is Mastroberardino; his single-vineyard Taurasi, called *Radici,* is especially worth trying. Mastroberardino also produces two unique white wines, Greco di Tufo and Fiano di Avellino. The Greco is a full-flavored, viscous wine with a great aging capacity. It sells in the $17 to $18 range. The Fiano has a flowery, delicate nose with a flavor of hazelnuts. It needs a few years to develop, but can age for 15 years or more. It sells for about $20. Another fine producer of the wines of Campania is Feudi di San Gregorio.

- ✔ **Basilicata:** The instep of the Italian boot, Basilicata has one important red wine, Aglianico del Vulture. It's similar to Taurasi, but not quite so intense and concentrated. D'Angelo is the leading producer.

- ✔ **Apulia:** More wine is made here than in any other region in Italy. An important wine is Salice Salentino, an inexpensive, full-bodied red. Cosimo Taurino is a leading producer.

- ✔ **Sicily:** Two producers of note in Sicily are Corvo and Regaleali. The latter makes wines from grapes grown at high altitudes to counteract Sicily's warm climate. Regaleali's best red wine is called Rosso del Conte; Regaleali also makes a delicious, dry rosato (rosé) that sells for about $12. Corvo is the brand name for wines made by the Duca di Salaparuta winery. The everyday white and red wines sell for around $10 and are particularly popular in Italian restaurants. But the Duca Enrico — a rich, velvety, full-bodied, concentrated red wine with an intense bouquet (made from the local Nero d'Avola grape) — is the star performer of Duca di Salaparuta. Introduced in 1989, Duca Enrico has already established itself internationally as one of the great red wines of Italy. It sells in the $45 to $50 price range.

- ✔ **Sardinia:** This large island off the eastern coast of Italy makes delicate white wines and characterful reds from native grape varieties as well as international varieties such as Cabernet Sauvignon. Sella & Mosca and Argiolas are two leading producers. Two of their interesting wines made from local varieties are the white Vermentino and the red Cannonau, both of which sell for under $10.

TIP

Sixteen white wines you should try at least once

Wine	Grape Varieties	Country of Origin	Price
Chablis, '95/'96 (Louis Michel)	Chardonnay	France (Chablis)	$22; Premier Cru, $30
Riesling Kabinett, '95/'96 (Dr. Loosen)	Riesling	Germany (Mosel-Saar-Ruwer)	$12 to $13
Gewürztraminer (Hofstätter) (Most recent vintage)	Gewürztraminer	Italy (Alto Adige)	$20
Chardonnay, '95 (Hanzell Vineyards)	Chardonnay	U.S. – California (Sonoma)	$33
Sancerre, '95/'96 (Lucien Crochet)	Sauvignon Blanc	France (Loire Valley)	$18
Sauvignon Blanc, '96 (Cakebread Cellars)	Sauvignon Blanc	U.S. – California (Napa Valley)	$17
Pinot Gris, '95/'96 (Eyrie Vineyards)	Pinot Gris	U.S. – Oregon (Willamette Valley)	$16
Chassagne- Montrachet, '95/'96 (Louis Jadot)	Chardonnay	France – Burgundy (Côte de Beaune)	$39 (Les Caillerets or Morgeot)
Tocai Friulano, '96 (Livio Felluga)	Tocai Friulano	Italy (Friuli)	$18
Riesling, '94/'95 (Trimbach)	Riesling	France (Alsace)	$14 ('92 Cuvée Frédéric Émile, $28)
Albariño, '96 (Lusco or Morgadío)	Albariño	Spain – Galicia (Rías Baixas)	$18
Greco di Tufo, '95/'96 (Mastroberardino)	Greco	Italy (Campania)	$18
Viognier, '96 (Calera)	Viognier	U.S. – California (San Benito – Mt. Harlan)	$33
Viognier Estate, '96 (Alban Vineyards)	Viognier	U.S. – California (San Luis Obispo – Edna Valley)	$29
Pinot Bianco, '96 (Alois Lageder)	Pinot Blanc	Italy (Alto Adige)	$11 (Haberlehof, $17)
Bourgogne Aligoté '96 (A. & P. deVillaine)	Aligoté	France – Burgundy (Bouzeron)	$18

Chapter 12
Elsewhere in Europe

. . . .

. . . .

*T*en years ago, we never used the phrase *European wine* in talking generally about the wines of France, Italy, Spain, Portugal, and Germany. The wines had nothing in common.

But today, two factors have changed the way we look at the wines of these countries. First, Europe has unified, and the wines of the European Union member countries now exist under a common legislative umbrella. Second, non-European wines — from California, Australia, and South America — have inundated the U.S. market, popularizing a nomenclature (varietal names, such as Chardonnay) and flavors (fruity, fruitier, fruitiest) foreign to the European, or *Old World*, model.

When we compare Europe's wines to non-European, or *New World,* wines, we notice that the diverse wines of Europe have many things in common after all. Most European wines are usually named for their place of production instead of their grape (see Chapter 5); European winemaking is tethered to tradition; the wines reflect local tastes more than international trends; and the wines are relatively low in fruitiness. European wines embody the traditions of the people who make them and the flavors of the earth from which they grow, compared to New World wines, which embody grape variety.

Despite these similarities among European wines, the countries of Europe each make distinctly different wines. France's and Italy's importance have earned each of these two countries a whole chapter, while the rest of Europe shares the spotlight here.

Intriguing Wines from Old Spain

Spain is a hot, dry, mountainous country with more land under vines than any other country in the world. It ranks third in the world in wine production, after France and Italy.

Spain's wine image has been one of inexpensive, unremarkable red wines. Spain's evolution in quality began in the late 1950s in Spain's most famous red wine region, Rioja *(ree OH ha)*. Besides Rioja, the following regions are an important part of the wine quality picture in Spain today (see Figure 12-1):

- ✔ Ribera del Duero *(ree BEAR ah dell DWAIR oh)*, also famous for red wines, has helped to excite world interest in Spanish wines other than Sherry (for more on Sherry, see Chapter 16).

- ✔ The Rías Baixas *(REE ahse BYCE ahse)* region of Galicia *(gah LEETH ee ah)* has lately become recognized by wine lovers for its exciting white wine, Albariño.

- ✔ Navarra, an area long known for its dry rosé wines, is now an important emerging red wine region.

- ✔ Penedés is important for both its red and white wines.

- ✔ Another region, Rueda, is known for white wine only.

Like Italy's, Spain's wine laws provide for a bilevel QWPSR category: *Denominaciónes de Origen* (DO) and a higher classification, *Denominaciónes de Origen Calificada* (DOCa), the latter created in 1991. So far, the only DOCa is Rioja, Spain's classic red wine from the region of the same name. Wines that do not qualify as DO fall into the table wine category *Vino de la Tierra* (equivalent to the French *Vins de Pays*).

Rioja rules

Rioja, in north-central Spain (see Figure 12-1), has historically been the major red wine region in the country (even if today Ribera del Duero is catching up). Three-quarters of Rioja's wine is red, 15 percent *rosado* (rosé), and 10 percent white.

The principal grape in Rioja is Tempranillo *(tem prah NEE yoh)*, clearly Spain's greatest red variety; but another three varieties are permitted by law for red Rioja (Garnacha, Graciano, and Mazuelo), and the wine is typically a blend of two or more varieties.

Figure 12-1:
The wine
regions of
Spain.

The Rioja region has three districts, the cooler Rioja Alavesa and Rioja Alta and the warmer Rioja Baja. Most of the best Riojas are made from grapes in the two cooler districts, but some Riojas are blended from grapes of all three districts.

Traditional production for red Rioja involved many years of aging in small barrels of American oak before release, which created pale, gentle, some-times tired and oaky-tasting wines that lacked fruitiness. The trend has been to replace some of the cask aging with bottle aging, resulting in wines that are now much fresher and better than ever. In the cellars of the more progressive winemakers, barrels of American oak, which give Rioja its characteristic vanilla aroma, now share the stage with barrels made of French oak. (See Chapter 3 for a discussion of oak barrels.)

Red Riojas have several faces. Sometimes the wine receives no oak aging at all and is released young; sometimes the wine is aged (in oak and in the bottle) for two years at the winery and is labeled *crianza;* some wines are aged for three years and carry the designation *reserva;* and the finest wines age for five years or even longer, earning the status of *gran reserva.*

Prices start at around $10 for crianza reds and go up to $35 for some of the gran reservas. The best recent vintages for Rioja are 1994, 1989, and 1982 followed by 1995, 1993, 1990, 1988, and 1981.

The following producers have been particularly consistent in quality for their red wines:

- CVNE (Compañia Vincola del Norte de España)
- Bodegas Muga
- R. Lopez de Heredia
- Bodegas Remelluri
- La Rioja Alta
- Bodegas Montecillo
- Marqués de Murrieta Ygay
- Marqués de Riscal

Most white Riojas these days are merely fresh, neutral, inoffensive wines, but Marqués de Murrieta still makes a traditional white Rioja, golden-colored and oak-aged, from a blend of local white grape varieties, predominantly Viura. We find the Murrieta white fascinating: lots of flavor, voluptuous, capable of aging, with attractive traces of oxidation. It's not everybody's cup of tea, true, but the wine sure has character! It has so much body that it can go with foods normally associated with red wine, as well as traditional Spanish food, such as paella or seafood. The Murrieta white sells for about $14 or $15.

Ribera del Duero challenges

Ribera del Duero, north of Madrid, is Spain's fastest growing wine region. For many years, it was dominated by one producer, the legendary Vega Sicilia. In fact, Spain's single most famous wine is Vega Sicilia's Unico (mainly Tempranillo, with 20 percent Cabernet Sauvignon) — an intense, concentrated, tannic red wine with enormous longevity; it is aged for ten years in casks and then sometimes further aged in the bottle.

But Vega Sicilia is no longer the only renowned red wine in Ribera del Duero. Alejandro Fernández's Pesquera, made from 100 percent Tempranillo, has been gaining high praise in wine circles. Pesquera is a big, rich, oaky, tannic wine with intense fruit character. The Reserva sells for about $29, while the younger Pesquera is $22. Two other producers to watch in Ribera del Duero are Bodegas Mauro and Téofilo Reyes, who are making red wines that rival Pesquera.

Four other Spanish regions to watch

The action in Spanish wines — especially when value is your concern — definitely doesn't end with Rioja and Ribera del Duero. Penedés, Navarra, Rueda, and Rías Biaxas (in Galicia) are all hotbeds for interesting wines.

Penedés

The Penedés *(pen eh DAIS)* wine region is in Catalonia, south of Barcelona (refer to Figure 12-1). It is home to most of Spain's sparkling wines, which are discussed in Chapter 15.

One producer dominates the non-bubbly wine business in this region: Torres. The Torres line includes many wines made from French grape varieties (Cabernet Sauvignon, Chardonnay, and so on) as well as local grapes, such as Tempranillo.

All of the Torres wines are clean, well made, reasonably priced, and widely available. Wines start in the $8 to $9 range (for the red Sangre de Toro and Coronas and the white Viña Sol) while the top-of-the-line Gran Coronas Mas La Plena Black Label, a Cabernet Sauvignon, sells for $35.

Navarra

Once upon a time, the word *Navarra* in wine circles conjured up images of inexpensive, easy-drinking dry rosé wines (or, to the more adventurous, memories of running the bulls in Pamplona, Navarra's capital city). Nowadays, Navarra, just northeast of Rioja, is rapidly becoming known as an alternative source of red wines that are somewhat less expensive than the more famous wines of Rioja.

Red Navarra wines in many cases rely on Rioja's — and Spain's — most famous grape variety, Tempranillo, along with Garnacha (Grenache), but you can also find Cabernet Sauvignon, Merlot, and various blends of all four varieties in the innovative Navarra region. Look for the wines of the following three Navarra producers: Bodegas Julian Chivite *(HOO lee ahn cha VEE tay)*, Bodegas Guelbenzu *(gwel BEN zoo)*, and Bodegas Magana.

The Verdejo from Rueda

The Rueda region, west of Ribera del Duero, produces one of Spain's best white wines from the Verdejo grape. The wine is clean, elegant, has good fruit character, and sells for an affordable $8. The Rioja producer Marquis de Riscal makes one of the leading and most available examples.

The white wine from Galicia

Galicia, in northwest Spain, next to the Atlantic Ocean and Portugal (refer to Figure 12-1) was not a province known for its wine. But from an area with the unlikely name of Rías Baixas *(REE ahse BYCE ahse)*, an exciting new, white wine has emerged — Albariño. It is a wine of very high acidity (and therefore will not be to everyone's taste), a floral nose, and an apricoty, delicate flavor that is not unlike Condrieu (from the Rhône Valley; see Chapter 10).

Two fine examples of Albariño are made by Lusco and Bodegas Morgadío; they sell for about $18. There are inexpensive Albariño available, but they cannot compare to those of Lusco and Morgadío.

Some Spanish wine terms

You will see some of the following terms on a Spanish wine label:

Blanco: White

Bodega: Winery

Cosecha *(coh SAY cha)* or **Vendimia** *(ven DEE me yah):* The vintage year

Crianza *(cree AHN zah):* For red wines, this means that the wine has been aged for at least two years, including a period in oak; for white and rosé wines, Crianza means that the wines are at least one year old.

Gran Reserva: Wines produced only in exceptional vintages; red wines must be aged for at least five years in wood and bottle; white *gran reservas* must be aged at least four years before release, including six months in oak.

Reserva: Wines produced in the better vintages; red *reservas* must be aged in oak and bottle a minimum of three years; white *reservas* must be aged for two years, including six months in oak.

Tinto *(TEEN toe):* Red

Viña *(VEEN yah):* Vineyard

Viejo *(vee AY ho):* Old

Portugal: More Than Just Port

Portugal is justifiably famous for its great dessert wine, Port (discussed in Chapter 16). And millions of wine drinkers have enjoyed the medium-dry, slightly effervescent Portuguese rosés, Mateus and Lancer's. But lately, Portugal has shown a new face to wine drinkers around the world: Thanks to a campaign of serious modernizing in her vineyards and winemaking practices, better table wines, especially red wines, are beginning to emerge. We can look forward to Portugal's well-priced wines playing a larger role in world wine markets as we enter the 21st century.

Portugal's highest rank for wines is the *Denominação de Origen Controlada* (DOC), which has been awarded to the wines of only 11 regions. The next-highest rank, similar to France's VDQS (a secondary level within the QWPSR category), the *Indicação de Proveniência Regulamentada* (IPR), has been awarded to 32 regions (DOCs-in-waiting). The table wine category includes *Vinho de Mesa Regional*, equivalent to France's *Vin de Pays*. All other wines are classified simply as *Vinho de Mesa*.

Portugal's "green" white

On hot summer evenings, the most appropriate wine can be a bottle of cold, slightly effervescent, white Vinho Verde *(VEEN yo VAIRD)*. The high acidity of Vinho Verde has a bracing, cleansing effect on the palate. It is an especially good wine to accompany grilled fish or seafood.

The Minho region, where Vinho Verde is made, is in the northwest corner of Portugal, directly across the border from the Rías Baixas wine region of Spain. (The region is particularly verdant because of the rain from the Atlantic Ocean — one theory behind the wine's name.)

Two quality levels of white Vinho Verde exist on the market place. The most-commonly found brands (Aveleda and Casal Garcia) sell for about $6. These brands are medium-dry wines of average quality and are best served cold.

The more expensive Vinho Verdes ($15 to $20) are made from the Alvarinho grape (same grape as Rías Baixas's Albariño). They are a more complex, longer-lasting version of Vinho Verde and are Portugal's best white wines. Unfortunately, the more expensive Vinho Verdes are more difficult to find than the inexpensive ones; look for them in finer wine shops or in Portuguese neighborhoods (or on your next trip to Portugal!).

There is also a red Vinho Verde — in fact, the majority of wines from this DOC region are red. It is a *highly* acidic wine — you definitely need to acquire a taste for it (which we haven't acquired yet!).

Noteworthy Portuguese red wines

The best red wine in Portugal, Barca Velha, comes from the Douro region, where Port (officially known as *Porto*) is made. The Ferreira Port house makes this wine from the same local grapes used to make Port and only in good vintage years.

Barca Velha is a full-bodied, intense, concentrated wine that needs years to age — Portugal's version of Vega Sicilia's Unico, but at a much lower price (the 1985 costs about $35). Like Vega Sicilia, not much is made, and consequently, Barca Velha is hard to find.

Fortunately, the Port house of Ramos Pinto (recently acquired by Roederer Champagne) is now making some inexpensive, top-quality, dry red Douro wines that are more readily available. The 1993 *Duas Quintas* has ripe, plummy, velvety fruit; it is a surprisingly rich but supple wine, drinkable now and selling at about $9. The more full-bodied, intense *1991 Duas Quintas Reserva* needs a few years to age; it is an outstanding wine at any price — at $18, this Douro red is an amazing value.

Other good red Portuguese wines to look for include the following:

- ✔ **Quinta do Carmo:** This estate in the Alentejo in southern Portugal was recently purchased by Château Lafite-Rothschild's owners. A rich, full-bodied wine, the 1995 sells for about $24. Domaine Martinho is a second-label wine from the estate; the 1995 sells for $12.

- ✔ **Quinta de la Rosa:** This is another Port house in the Douro region that makes a fine dry red wine. The 1996 Quinta de la Rosa table wine, made from the same, local grapes used for Port, sells for a reasonable $12.

- ✔ **Quinta de Pancas:** One of the few Cabernet Sauvignons in Portugal, the Quinta de Pancas comes from the Alenquer region, north of Lisbon; the 1995 sells for about $11 or $12.

- ✔ **Quinta de Parrotes:** Made from the local Castelão Frances grape variety, the 1996 Quinta de Parrotes, from the same estate in Alenquer as the Quinta de Pancas, is a steal at $8.

- ✔ **Quinta da Bacalhôa:** An estate-bottled Cabernet Sauvignon made by the esteemed Portuguese winemaker, Joào Pires, in Azeito (south of Lisbon); the Bacalhôa has the elegance of a Bordeaux; the 1995 sells for about $14.

- ✔ **The red wines of J.M. da Fonseca Successores** (no relation to the Fonseca Port house): This firm is producing some of the best red wines in Portugal. Look for *Quinta da Camarate, Morgado do Reguengo, Tinto Velho Rosado Fernandes,* and all of da Fonseca's *Garrafeiras.*

Recent great vintages for Portuguese red wines are the 1994, 1992 (superb), and 1991.

Portuguese wine terms

The following terms might appear on Portuguese wine labels:

Adega *(ah DAY gah):* Winery

Colheita *(col YAY tah):* Vintage year

Garrafeira *(gar rah FAY rah):* A reserva that has been aged at least two years in a cask and one in a bottle for a red wine; six months in a cask, six months in a bottle for a white wine

Quinta *(KEEN ta):* Estate or vineyard

Reserva: A wine of superior quality from one vintage

Seco *(SAY coh):* Dry

Tinto *(TEEN toe):* Red

Vinho *(VEEN yo):* Wine

Germany: Europe's Individualist

German wines march to the beat of a different drum. They come in mainly one color: white. They are fruity in style, often off-dry or sweet, low in alcohol, and they are rarely oaked — the antithesis of current taste trends. Their labels carry grape names, which is an anomaly in Europe. And their classification system is not based on the French AOC system, as most other European wines are.

Germany is the northernmost major wine-producing country in Europe — which means that its climate is cool. Except in warmer pockets of southern Germany, red grapes don't ripen adequately (by the standards of the rest of the wine world) in Germany; about 85 percent of Germany's wine production is therefore white wine. The climate is also erratic from year to year, meaning that vintages do matter for fine German wines.

Germany's finest vineyard sites are situated by rivers like the Rhine and the Mosel, which temper the extremes of the weather and aid the grapes in ripening fully.

Riesling and its cohorts

In Germany's cool climate, the noble Riesling grape finds true happiness. But Riesling ripens successfully and predictably year after year only in Germany's best vineyards (the best locations, climatewise). Thus, Riesling represents only 21 or 22 percent of Germany's vineyard plantings.

The grape variety, which until recently has been the most planted variety in Germany, is Müller-Thurgau (pronounced *MULE lair TOOR gow*), a crossing purportedly between the Riesling and Silvaner (or possibly Chasselas) grapes. Müller-Thurgau ripens early, thus taking much of the anxiety out of harvest season for its growers. Its wines are softer than Riesling with less character and little potential for greatness.

After Müller-Thurgau and Riesling, a number of grapes make up the balance of Germany's white vineyard plantings: Silvaner, Kerner, Scheurebe *(SHOY reb beh),* and Ruländer (Pinot Gris) being the most important. Among Germany's red grapes, Spätburgunder (Pinot Noir) is the most widely planted, mainly in the warmer parts of the country.

Germany's wine laws: Ripeness is king

Like most European wines, German wines are named after the places they come from — usually a combination of a village name and a vineyard name, such as Piesporter (town) Goldtröpfchen (vineyard).

Unlike most European wines, however, the grape name is also usually part of German wine names (as in Piesporter Goldtröpfchen *Riesling*). And the finest German wines have yet another element in their name — a *Prädikat* (*PRAY di cat*), an indication of the ripeness of the grapes (as in Piesporter Goldtröpfchen Riesling *Spätlese*). Wines with a *Prädikat* hold the highest rank in the German wine system.

Germany's system of assigning the highest rank to the ripest grapes is completely different from the concept behind most other European appellation systems, which is to bestow the highest status on the best vineyards or districts. Germany's system underscores the country's grape growing priorities: Ripeness — never guaranteed in a cool climate — is the highest goal.

There are six *Prädikat* levels. From the least ripe to the ripest (that is, from the lowest to the highest), they are

- Kabinett (*KAB ee net*)
- Spätlese (*SHPATE lay seh*)
- Auslese (*OUSE lay seh*)
- Beerenauslese (*BEER en OUSE lay seh*)
- Eiswein (*ICE vine*)
- Trockenbeerenauslese (*TROH ken BEER en OUSE lay seh*)

At the three highest *Prädikat* levels, the amount of sugar in the very ripe grapes is so high that the wines are inevitably sweet. Many people, therefore, mistakenly believe that the *Prädikat* level of a German wine is an indication of the wine's sweetness. In fact the *Prädikat* is an indication of the amount of sugar in the *grapes at harvest,* not the amount of sugar in the resulting wine. At lower *Prädikat* levels, the sugar in the grapes can be fermented fully, to dryness; and for those wines there is *no direct correlation between Prädikat level and sweetness of the wine.*

Wines whose (grape) ripeness earns them a *Prädikat* are categorized as QmP wines (*Qualitätswein mit Prädikat),* translated as *quality wines with special attributes* (their ripeness). They are QWPSR wines in the eyes of the EU (see Chapter 9). When the ripeness of the grapes in a particular vineyard is insufficient to earn the wine a *Prädikat* name, the wine can still qualify as a "quality wine" in Germany's second QWPSR tier, called QbA (*Qualitätswein bestimmter Anbaugebiet*), translated as *quality wine from a special region.* Often the term *Qualitätswein* alone will appear on labels of QbA wines.

Less than 10 percent of Germany's wine production falls into the table wine categories *Landwein* (table wines with geographic indication) or *Deutscher Tafelwein.*

Fooling Mother Nature

Unfortunately for Germany, codifying ripeness levels into wine law does nothing to change the reality of Mother Nature's cool climate. In reality, even grapes that are ripe enough to qualify as *Kabinett* can still have such high acid levels and low sugar levels that the wine made from them is destined to be very light-bodied and tart — not necessarily well-balanced or pleasurable in the eyes of many wine drinkers.

Somewhere along the way, however, German wine producers found a way to mimic the ripeness that Mother Nature denies them. By making many of their wines in a medium-dry to sweet style, they change the balance in their wines, creating wines that most wine drinkers consider delicious and pleasurable.

In the mouth, acidity counterbalances — and is counterbalanced by — sweetness and alcohol. If a white wine has high alcohol or has sweetness, its acidity is perceived as lower than it actually is, and even a wine with very high acidity can then taste relatively soft.

A way that the Germans devised to keep some sweetness in their wines is called the *süssreserve* (or sweet reserve) method. In this method, a winemaker ferments his wine fully dry, ending up with a low-alcohol, high-acid dry wine. Before fermentation, however, he holds back a small quantity of his grape juice and does not ferment it. Later, he blends this grape juice with his dry wine. The unfermented grape juice (the *süssreserve*) contributes its natural, juicy sweetness to the wine. Many of Germany's best producers prefer instead to ferment their juice slowly, letting the fermentation stop whenever it does naturally, with or without sweetness left in the wine.

Dry, half-dry, or gentle?

Most inexpensive German wines, such as Liebfraumilch, are produced with *süssreserve*. They are light-bodied, fruity wines with pleasant sweetness — wines that are easy to enjoy without food. The German term for this style of wine is *lieblich,* which translates as gentle — a poetic but apt descriptor.

Germany's most famous wine

The light, fresh style of German wines makes them particularly appropriate for people just beginning to enjoy wine. One German wine, in fact, has single-handedly introduced millions of people to the pleasures of wine. That wine is Liebfraumilch *(LEEB frow milsh)*.

Liebfraumilch, translated as milk of the virgin, takes its name from a vineyard in Worms, in the Rheinhessen region, which surrounds a majestic church named for the Virgin Mary.

Liebfraumilch today is a wine blended from several grape varieties, mainly Müller-Thurgau, and sometimes a little Riesling, Silvaner and/or Kerner. It can be produced in four of Germany's wine regions: the Rheinhessen, the Pfalz (these two accounting for the great majority of its production), the Nahe, and the Rheingau.

Liebfraumilch is, by definition, a medium-dry, QbA-level wine; it is usually low in alcohol and should be enjoyed as young as possible.

In recent years, wine drinkers in Germany have begun to favor dryer wines, especially for drinking with meals. The very driest German wines are called *trocken* (dry). Wines that are sweeter than trocken but dryer than lieblich are called *halbtrocken* (half-dry). These words sometimes appear on the label, but not always.

What's noble about rot?

No matter how much of a dry tooth German consumers develop, they will undoubtedly admit that the greatest wines of their country are the sweet wines. Wine connoisseurs all over the world, in fact, recognize Germany's sweetest wines as among the greatest wines on the face of the earth.

Oddly enough, Germany's great sweet wines do not owe their sweetness to *süssreserve* but rather to the same Mother Nature who so often denies the rest of Germany's wines adequate ripeness. Although Germany has a cool climate with short summers, German autumns are long and often warm. When grapes from the best vineyard sites are allowed to hang on the vine longer than usual, they can become infected by the ugly but magical fungus known as *botrytis cinerea,* commonly called *noble rot.*

Noble rot dehydrates the berries, concentrating their sugar and their flavors in the process. When these infected berries are used for the production of wine, the wine they give is sweet, amazingly rich, and complex beyond description. It can also be expensive: $100 a bottle or more!

Wines of the *Prädikat* levels *Beerenauslese* (abbreviated as BA) and *Trockenbeerenauslese* (abbreviated as TBA) are usually made entirely from grapes infected with noble rot (called *botrytised* grapes) and are generally richly textured and sweet. *Auslese* level wines often are made with some partially botrytised grapes, and when they are, they are likely to be sweet, although never to the extent of a BA or TBA.

Another way that Nature can contribute unusual sweetness to German wines is by freezing the grapes on the vine late in the autumn or in early winter. When the grape grower harvests the frozen grapes and crushes them, much of the water in the berries separates out as ice. The juice that is left to ferment is concentrated in sugar and flavor and makes a lush sweet wine that carries the *Prädikat Eiswein* (literally, ice wine). *Eisweins* differ from BAs and TBAs because they lack a certain flavor that derives from botrytis, sometimes described as a honeyed character.

Both botrytised wines and *Eisweins* are referred to as *late-harvest wines,* not only in Germany but all over the world, because the special character of these wines comes from conditions that normally occur only when the grapes are left on the vine beyond the usual point of harvest.

Germany's wine regions

With the reunification of Germany, Germany has 13 wine regions — 11 in the west and another 2 in the eastern part of the country (see Figure 12-2).

The most famous of these 13 are the Mosel-Saar-Ruwer region, named for the Mosel River and two of its tributaries, along which the region's vineyards lie; and the Rheingau region along the Rhine River.

Mosel-Saar-Ruwer: The Mosel-Saar-Ruwer (*MO zel zar Roo ver*) is a dramatically beautiful region, its vineyards rising steeply along the slopes of the twisting and turning Mosel River. The wines of the region are among the lightest in Germany (usually containing less than 10 percent alcohol); they are generally delicate and charming, often containing a slight amount of carbon dioxide, which accentuates their freshness and their liveliness. Riesling dominates the Mosel-Saar-Ruwer with 55 percent of the plantings. Wines from this region are instantly recognizable because they come in green bottles rather than the brown bottles that other German wines use.

Figure 12-2:
The wine regions of Germany.

The Mosel boasts dozens of excellent winemakers who produce really exciting Riesling wines. Some of our favorites include, in alphabetical order

- Dr. Fischer
- Friedrich Wilhelm Gymnasium
- Karlsmühle
- Dr. Loosen
- Maximin Grünhauser
- Merkelbach
- Meulenhof
- Egon Müller
- J.J. Prüm
- Reichsgraf Von Kesselstatt
- Willi Schaefer
- Selbach-Oster
- Zilliken

Rheingau: The Rheingau (*RYNE gow*) is among Germany's smaller wine regions. It, too, has dramatically steep vineyards bordering a river, but here the river is Germany's greatest wine river, the Rhine. The Riesling grape occupies more than 80 percent of the Rheingau's vineyards, many of which are south-facing slopes that give the Riesling an extra edge of ripeness. Rheingau wine styles tend toward two extremes, *trocken* wines on the one hand and sweet late-harvest and *Eisweins* on the other. Recommended Rheingau producers include

- Georg Breuer
- Knyphausen
- Franz Küntsler
- Schloss Schönborn
- Robert Weil

A secret code of German place-names

If you don't speak German and you don't know German geography intimately, you'll surely find deciphering German wine names tricky. But here's a bit of information that can help. In German, the possessive is formed by adding the suffix *er* to a noun. When you see names like Zeller or Hochheimer — names that end in *er* — on a wine label, the next word is usually a vineyard area that "belongs" to the commune or district with the *er* on its name (Zell's Swartze Katz, Hochheim's Kirchenstück). You still have to learn what the *Prädikats* mean, though.

Rheinhessen: The Rhine River lends its name to three other German wine regions, Rheinhessen (*RYNE hess ehn*), the Pfalz (until recently called the Rheinpfalz), and the tiny Mittelrhein region. The Rheinhessen is Germany's largest wine region, producing huge quantities of simple wines for everyday enjoyment. Liebfraumilch originated here, and it is one of the most important wines of the region today — although now it can by law be produced in three other regions, as well. Numerous grape varieties grow in the Rheinhessen, with Müller-Thurgau and Silvaner at the top of the list. Many of the region's vineyards extend far away from the Rhine River, but the Rheinhessen's highest quality wines come from the Rheinterrasse, a vineyard area along the river. Particularly good producers include

- ✔ Gunderloch
- ✔ Heyl Zu Herrnsheim
- ✔ Strub

Pfalz: Almost as big as the Rheinhessen, the Pfalz (*fallz*) has earned somewhat more respect from wine lovers for its fairly rich and full-bodied white wines and its very good red wines — all of which owe their style to the region's relatively warm climate. Müller-Thurgau, Riesling, Silvaner, and Kerner are among the most planted grape varieties of the Pfalz, but qualitatively Scheurebe and Blauburgunder (Pinot Noir) are important. To experience the best of the Pfalz, look for wines from

- ✔ Dr. Bürklin-Wolf
- ✔ Rainer Lingenfelder
- ✔ Müller-Catoir
- ✔ Basserman-Jordan

Nahe: One other German region of importance for the quality of its wines is the Nahe (*NAH heh*), named for the Nahe River and situated west of the Rheinhessen. The Riesling wines here are relatively full and intense. Favorite producers include

- ✔ Diel
- ✔ Kruger-Rumpf
- ✔ Prinz zu Salm-Dahlberg
- ✔ Dönnhoff

Switzerland: Stay-at-Home Wines

Nestled between Germany, France, and Italy, Switzerland is in a perfectly logical location for growing grapes and making fine wine. In fact, Switzerland has a small but proud wine industry: Vineyards grace the country's three faces — French-speaking, German-speaking, and Italian-speaking. But few wine lovers outside of Switzerland have much opportunity to taste Swiss wines because the production is small and because the wines are so popular within Switzerland itself.

About half of Switzerland's wines are white; most are made from Chasselas — a grape cultivated with much less distinction in Germany, eastern France, and the Loire Valley. In Switzerland, Chasselas wines tend to be dry, fairly full-bodied, and unoaked, with mineral and earthy flavors. Other white grapes include Pinot Gris, Sylvaner, Marsanne, Petit Arvine, and Amigne — the latter two indigenous to Switzerland. Merlot is an important red grape (especially in the Italian-speaking Ticino region), along with Pinot Noir and Gamay.

As a country with varied terrain (hills of varying altitudes, large lakes, sheltered valleys), numerous microclimates contribute to many wine styles, from relatively full-bodied red and white wines to more delicate, crisp white wines.

Switzerland's major wine regions include the Vaud, along Lake Geneva; Valais, to the east, along the Rhône River; Neuchâtel, in western Switzerland, north of the Vaud; Ticino, in the south, bordering Italy; and Thurgau in the north, bordering Germany.

When you do find a bottle of Swiss wine, you might be surprised to discover how costly it is — $18 to $30 in the U.S., reflecting high production costs. If you buy a bottle of white Swiss wine in Switzerland, you might also be surprised to find a screw cap closure — one of Switzerland's more courageous contributions to the art of wine enjoyment, considering the poor image of screw cap wines.

Austria: A New Quality Direction

Austria makes twice as much wine as Switzerland, all of it coming from the eastern part of the country, where the Alps recede into hills.

Austria's wine industry has transformed itself in the past 12 years and now shows a fresh face: dedicated young winemakers, private estates bottling their own production, and quality dry wines appropriate for a quality-conscious world market. Critical praise for Austrian wine in recent years is due directly to the seriousness of the country's producers.

The ratio of white to red wines in Austria is 80/20, the red wines being produced mainly in the region of Burgenland bordering Hungary, one of the warmest parts of the country. The red wines are medium- to full-bodied, often engagingly spicy with moderate tannin and vivid fruit. Many of the red wines are based on unusual grape varieties such as Blauer Zweigelt, rarely found elsewhere.

Austria's white wines occupy two camps: dry, firm whites ranging from light- to full-bodied, and lush late-harvest whites, made from botrytised grapes or extremely ripe grapes. While the excellence of Austria's sweet whites has long been recognized, her dry whites and reds are just beginning to gain recognition.

The country's single most important grape variety is the white Grüner Veltliner, which Austria can claim as her very own. Its wines are full-bodied yet crisp, with herbal and sometimes spicy-vegetal flavors (especially green pepper). Müller-Thurgau and Welschriesling are tied for second in plantings. Welschriesling, a grape popular in Eastern Europe for inexpensive commercial wines, reaches its finest quality in Austria.

Of Austria's four wine regions, Lower Austria, in the north, produces the largest quantity, mainly along the plain of the Danube River. Burgenland, in the east, ranks second; Styria, a southern region bordering Slovenia, and the tiny region of Vienna are the other two.

Austria's wine laws are based on the German system, with QWPSR wine divided into *Qualitätswein* and *Prädikatswein* categories. The *Prädikat* levels are the same as in Germany, except that Prädikatswein begins at *Spätlese* (*Kabinett* wine falls into the *Qualitätswein* group). The minimum ripeness requirements for each level are also higher in Austria than in Germany, and the wines are higher in alcohol.

In some parts of Austria, for example in the Wachau district of Lower Austria, wines are named in the German system — a town name ending in -*er* followed by a vineyard name and a grape variety — while in other parts, such as Burgenland, the wine names are generally a grape name followed by the name of the region.

Chapter 13

The Brave New World of Wine

*W*hat do the wines of North America, South America, Africa, and Australia have in common? For one thing, none of them are produced in Europe. In fact, you could say that they are the wines of "Not Europe."

The name most often used in wine circles for Not Europe is the *New World*. Undoubtedly this phrase, with its ring of colonialism, was coined by a European. Europe, home of all the classic wine regions of the world, producer of two-thirds of the wines in the world, is the Old World. Everything else is nouveau riche.

When we first heard the expression *New World* applied to wines, we thought it was absurd. How can you lump together wine regions as remote as Napa Valley, the Finger Lakes, Coonawarra, and Santiago? (It's a bit like saying that Thailand, the U.S., and Liechtenstein are all the same because they're countries.)

But then we started thinking about it. In Europe, they've been making wines for thousands of years. Which hillsides to plant, which grapes should grow where, how dry or sweet a particular wine should be — these decisions were all made long ago, by the grandparents and great-great-grandparents of today's winemakers. In Not Europe, the grape growing and winemaking game is wide open; every winery owner gets to decide for himself where to grow his grapes, what grape variety to plant, and what style of wine to make. The wines of the New World do have that in common.

The more we thought about it, the more similarities we found among New World wine regions as compared to Europe. Finally, we concluded that the New World is an actual winemaking entity whose legislative reality, spirit, and winemaking style are unique from those of the Old World — as generalizations go.

We could easily fill 400 pages on the wines of the U.S., Canada, South America, Australia, New Zealand, and South Africa alone, if only we had the space. Fortunately, New World wines are easy for you to explore without a detailed road map: In the New World, there's very little encoded tradition to decipher and very little historical backdrop against which the wines need to be appreciated. Think of New World wines as modern art; you can approach them and enjoy them at face value without ever having studied art history. They come at you loud and clear.

In this chapter, we explore the wines of Chile, Argentina, Australia, New Zealand, and South Africa. We devote the next chapter to the wines of the United States, with a short look at Canada, too.

The old and the new

In wine terms, the New World is not just geography but also an attitude and approach to wine. Some winemakers in Europe approach wine the liberated New World way, and some winemakers in California are certainly dedicated Old World traditionalists. Keep that in mind as you look over the following comparison between the Old and the New. And remember, we're talking generalizations here — and generalizations are never always true.

New World	Old World
Innovation	Tradition
Wines named after grape varieties	Wines named after region of production
Expression of the fruit is the winemaking goal	Expression of *terroir* (the particular place where the grapes grow, with its unique growing conditions) is the winemaking goal
Technology is revered	Old-fashioned methods are favored
Wines are flavorful and fruity	Wines are subtle and less-fruity
Grape-growing regions are broad and flexible	Grape-growing regions are relatively small and fixed
Winemaking resembles science	Winemaking resembles art
Winemaking processes are controlled	Intervention in winemaking is avoided as much as possible
The winemaker gets credit for the wine	The vineyard gets the credit

The Old and the New of Chile

Chile's wine industry wears the designation *New World* somewhat uncomfortably. Vineyards were first established in Chile in the mid-16th century by the Spanish, and the country has maintained a thriving wine industry for several centuries, producing traditional wines for the home market from the common, red Pais grape. Nothing new about that. What *is* new about Chile, however, is the growth of her wine industry since the mid-1980s. And what's "worldly" is her sudden development of a strong export market led by inexpensive varietal wines, and the strong shift of the viticulture toward French grape varieties such as Cabernet Sauvignon, Merlot, Sauvignon Blanc, and Chardonnay — with an almost-forgotten red Bordeaux variety called Carmenère also in the running, on the outside post position.

Blessed isolation

With the Pacific Ocean to the west and the Andes Mountains to the east, Chile is an isolated country. Viticulturally, this isolation has its advantages: Phylloxera doesn't exist in Chile, and vinifera vines can therefore grow on their own roots. (For an explanation of phylloxera, see Chapter 4.) Chile's other viticultural blessings include a range of mountains along the coast, which blocks the ocean dampness from most vineyards, and the ocean's general tempering influence on a relatively hot climate (considering Chile's fairly northerly latitude within the southern hemisphere).

Most of Chile's vineyards are in the Central Valley, which lies between the coastal range and the Andes. Growing conditions there vary from east to west. The eastern area near the Andes is sunnier and drier, and the western area is more damp. Four wine regions occupy this area. From north to south within the Central Valley, they are

- ✔ **Aconcagua:** North of Santiago, the warmest area for fine grapes
- ✔ **Maipo:** A region where many of the major wineries are based
- ✔ **Rapel:** A region which includes the renowned Colchagua district; this is a cooler region than Maipo
- ✔ **Maule:** Where the Curicó district is located, cooler and less dry than Rapel; parts of this region grow Pais

Another of Chile's wine regions, Casablanca, technically a part of Aconcagua, is slightly north of Santiago, but close to the coast, and not in the Central Valley. This cool-climate, up-and-coming region has exciting potential for white grapes such as Chardonnay.

Foreign flavor

In recent years, Chile's natural resources and the popularity of the country's wines on export markets have spurred foreign investment in new vineyards. These new vineyards are planted mainly with Cabernet Sauvignon, Merlot, and Chardonnay. Some of these grape varieties have existed in Chile for more than 100 years, but their acreage has increased dramatically. Another two white grapes, so-called Sauvignon and Sémillon, are also well established in Chile's vineyards, but the true identity of these grapes is uncertain.

Wineries and winemakers from France, Spain, and the U.S. now play a major role in the Chilean wine industry. Château Lafite-Rothschild, for example, is an owner of the Los Vascos winery. Two other prominent Bordeaux producers, Bruno Prats of Château Cos d'Estournel, and Paul Pontallier of Château Margaux, have collaborated on a Chilean winery called Viña Aquitania. France's renowned oenologist, Michel Rolland, is a consultant at Casa Lapostolle, a Chilean winery owned by the French family that makes Grand Marnier liqueur. The Miguel Torres winery in Curicó is Spanish owned. Augustin Huneeus of Franciscan Vineyards in California has a property called Veramonte in Chile's Casblanca region. And the Robert Mondavi Winery has established a partnership with the producers of the Caliterra wines of Chile.

The face and taste of the wines

Like most New World wines, Chile's wines are generally named for their grape varieties; they carry a regional (or sometimes a district) indication, too. Their reasonable prices — mainly from $4 to $15 in the U.S. — have made these wines extremely attractive values to many wine buyers outside of Chile.

Stylistically, Chile's wines lack the exuberant fruitiness of Californian and Australian wines. The whites can be quite dilute and watery — probably the result of very high yields or perhaps the grapes' doubtful pedigrees; fortunately, the quality is beginning to improve. The red wines are finer, but Chilean reds have no track record yet at the highest end of the quality spectrum. Some wines that exemplify Chile's quest to become a producer of world-class high quality red wines, however, include Concha y Toro's "Don Melchor" Cabernet Sauvignon, Casa Lapostolle's premium Merlot and Cabernet Sauvignon wines named Cuvée Alexandre, Cousiño Macul's wine called Finis Terrae, a wine called "M" made by Montes, and the new Seña wine produced by the Robert Mondavi joint venture.

In the meantime, inexpensive varietals remain Chile's strong suit. The most important wineries for the export market include Concha y Toro, Santa Rita, Santa Carolina, Cousiño Macul, Errazuriz, Los Vascos, Undurraga, Carmen, Casa Lapostolle, and Caliterra.

Argentina, a Major Player

Argentina produces about four times as much wine as Chile does, or approximately as much as the U.S. It boasts the largest wine production in South America, the fourth or fifth largest wine production in the world (Argentina and the U.S. interchange positions frequently), and one of the highest levels of wine consumption per capita in the world. Considering what a major player these statistics make Argentina on the international wine scene, the country's wine industry has been very old-fashioned up until very recently, and Argentina's wines are little known on export markets.

Wine grapes have grown in Argentina since the mid-16th century, as they have in Chile. But Argentina's source of vines has been more diverse. For example, many vines were brought over by Italian immigrants.

White grapes include a grape called Pedro Giménez, Moscatel, the Spanish Torrontés, Chenin Blanc, Sémillon, Riesling, Chardonnay, and others. The most important red grapes are Malbec — a French variety, from the Bordeaux region — and the Italian Bonarda. Other red grapes include Tempranillo, Barbera, Sangiovese, Lambrusco, Cabernet Sauvignon, Pinot Noir, Syrah, and others.

The red wines made from the little-known Malbec grape variety are probably Argentina's greatest claim to international wine fame today. Malbec might have found its most appropriate home in the warm, dry vineyards of Mendoza, Argentina's largest wine region.

Argentina's vineyard regions are situated mainly in the country's interior, where the Andes mountains divide Argentina from Chile. High altitude tempers the climate, but the vineyards are still very warm by day, cool by night, and desert dry. Rivers originating in the Andes flow through the area and provide water for irrigation.

The vast majority of Argentina's vineyards are in the state of Mendoza, roughly at the same latitude as Santiago, Chile. (One of Mendoza's wine districts is Maipú, not to be confused with Maipo in Chile.)

The huge Peñaflor winery — second largest in the world, after Gallo — dominates wine production in Argentina and is leading the country's movement toward modernization of winemaking. Peñaflor now runs the smaller Trapiche winery, whose wines are commonly seen abroad. Other wineries that export include Santa Ana, Weinert, Catena, Etchart, Finca Flichman, Bodega Norton, Pasquale Toso, Navarro Correas, Santa Julia, Bianchi, and Canale, with Bodega Weinert leading the way in truly high-quality red wines. Argentina's wines are generally even less expensive than Chile's.

Foreign investors have discovered Argentina's wine industry, but they are committing themselves on a smaller scale than in Chile. Donald Hess of California's The Hess Collection winery recently purchased the old Bodega Norton winery in Argentina, for example, and Kendall-Jackson makes wine in Argentina under the Mariposa label. Michel Rolland, one of France's great oenologists, now consults at Trapiche. Things are starting to boom in the Southern Hemisphere's sleeping giant, Argentina.

Winemaking Thunder Down Under

Make no mistake about it: Australia is one of the World Powers of wine. In the course of just a few decades, the wine industry of Australia has cata-pulted itself from purveyor of mainly sweet and fortified wines into perhaps the most technologically advanced, forward-thinking wine nation on earth.

Vinifera grapevines came to Australia from the Cape of Good Hope and Europe in the late 18th and early 19th centuries (the country has no native vines). As recently as 1960, most Australian wines were rich and sweet, many of them fortified (styles typical of a warm climate) — a far cry from the fresh red and white table wines of today. In 1980, Chardonnay produc-tion was negligible; now Chardonnay is Australia's top white grape for fine wine. The fruity, well-priced, well-made wines that Australia has forged in the past two decades have rapidly earned fans as far away as the U.S., the U.K., and Sweden.

Approximately the same size as the continental U.S., Australia has about 850 wineries but produces less than 30 percent as much wine as California. (Yet per capita wine consumption in Australia is double that of the U.S.) Australia's wine regions are mainly in the southern, cooler, part of the country, with many of them clustered in the state of Victoria, the southern part of South Australia, and the cooler parts of New South Wales.

Winemaking, grapes, and terroir

Australia's number one grape for fine wine is Syrah, locally called *Shiraz,* followed by Cabernet Sauvignon, Chardonnay, Riesling, and Semillon. The wines are generally labeled with the name of their grape variety, which must constitute at least 85 percent of the wine. An Australian peculiarity is to blend two grapes and name a wine after both, with the dominant variety first, as in Shiraz/Cabernet Sauvignon or Cabernet Sauvignon/Shiraz.

Shirazes are particularly interesting because they are made in numerous styles, from very light, quaffable wines brimming with fresh strawberry fruit (delicious but simple) to serious, complex wines that need time to evolve. Another very interesting variety is Semillon (pronounced *SEM eh lon* in Australia, as opposed to the French *sem ee yon* elsewhere in the world), especially from the Hunter Valley. Some are aged in oak, similar to Chardonnay, while a few unoaked Semillons, simple when young, take on a fascinating nutty, honey, orange marmalade flavor with age.

The success of Australia's wines stems from a generally warm, dry climate (which provides winemakers with excellent raw material for their work) and from the winemakers' embrace of technology to achieve wines that preserve the intense flavors of their grapes and are soft and pleasant to drink from an early age. Australian wines epitomize user-friendliness.

Those who know a lot about Australian wine can describe the country's wine regions in great detail, differentiating stylistic nuances from one area to the next the way that Francophiles distinguish the villages of the Côte de Nuits. But for wine drinkers outside of Australia, the whole discussion of Australian wine regions is academic. The vast majority of wines from Australia in export markets are labeled simply *South Eastern Australia,* meaning that the grapes could have come from any of four states, a huge territory. It's the taste that you drink, not the place, mate.

We mention some of the more famous regions of Australia, state by state, in the following section. If you're interested in learning about these regions — and the many others that we don't mention — in more detail, read James Halliday's excellent *Wine Atlas of Australia and New Zealand* (Angus & Robertson, 1991).

Odd couples

Although winemakers all over the world make blended wines — wines from more than one grape variety — generally the grape combinations follow the classic French models: Cabernet Sauvignon with Merlot and Cabernet Franc, for example, or Sémillon with Sauvignon Blanc. Unencumbered by foreign tradition, Australia has invented two completely original formulas:

- Shiraz with Cabernet Sauvignon
- Semillon with Chardonnay

The grape in the majority is listed first on the wine label, and the percentages of each grape are usually indicated.

Australia's wine regions

Australia's most important state for wine production is South Australia, whose capital is Adelaide (see Figure 13-1). South Australia makes 58 percent of Australia's wine, and its vineyards are phylloxera-free. While many vineyards in South Australia produce inexpensive wines for the thirsty home market (much of it sold in 4.5 liter boxes), vineyards closer to Adelaide make wines that are considered among the country's finest. Among these fine wine regions are

- **Barossa Valley:** North of Adelaide, one of Australia's oldest areas for fine wine; it's a relatively warm area famous especially for its robust Shiraz and Cabernet Sauvignon, as well as rich Semillon

- **Clare Valley:** Farther north, a climatically diverse area that makes the country's best Rieslings in a dry, crisp style, as well as many other white and red wines, including Cabernet Sauvignon and Shiraz

- **McLaren Vale:** South of Adelaide, a moderate climate influenced by the sea, and particularly admired for its Sauvignon Blanc, as well as Shiraz and Cabernet Sauvignon

- **Adelaide Hills:** Situated partially within the Adelaide city limits, this fairly cool region sits between the Barossa and McLaren Vale areas, and is increasingly the home to rather good Pinot Noir, Chardonnay, and Riesling

- **Coonawarra:** About 200 miles southeast of Adelaide, a cool region famous for its red soil and its Cabernet Sauvignon

- **Padthaway:** North of Coonawarra, a cool area known for its white wines, particularly Chardonnay and Sauvignon Blanc

Adjoining South Australia is Victoria, a smaller state but important viticulturally, making 14 percent of Australia's wines. While South Australia is home to most of Australia's largest wineries, Victoria has *more* wineries; most of them are small. Nonetheless, Victoria does make its share of everyday wines, mainly in the northwestern area along the Murray River. Victoria's fine wine production ranges from rich, fortified dessert wines to delicate Pinot Noirs. Principal regions include

- **Rutherglen:** In the northeast; long-established, warm climate zone that is an outpost of traditional winemaking and home of an Australian specialty, fortified Muscats and Tokays

- **Goulburn Valley:** In the center of the state, known especially for its Marsanne as well as Shiraz

- **Yarra Valley:** A region close to Melbourne, the capital, with a cool climate suitable for fine Pinot Noir, Chardonnay, and sparkling wine

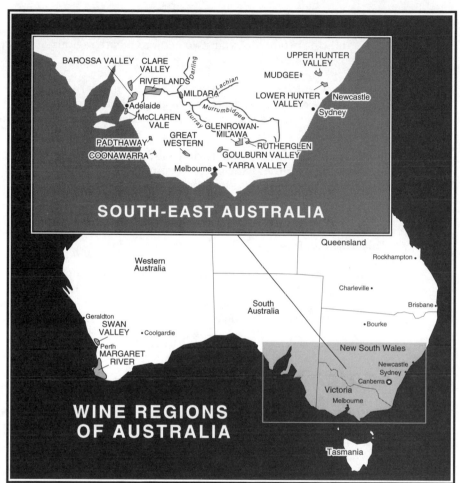

Figure 13-1:
The wine
regions of
Australia.

The first Australian state to grow vines was New South Wales, which today makes 27 percent of Australia's wine. High-volume production of everyday wines comes from an interior area called the Riverina (we get a kick trying to pronounce its alternate name, the Murrumbidgee Irrigation Area). Fine wine comes from three other areas:

- **Lower Hunter Valley:** An historic grape-growing area less than 100 miles north of Sydney with a very warm, damp climate and heavy soils; Semillon, Shiraz, and Chardonnay are important.

- **Upper Hunter Valley:** A drier climate north of the Hunter River and farther from the coast; good Chardonnay and Semillon are produced here.

- **Mudgee:** An interior area near the mountains; this area specializes in Chardonnay, Merlot, and Cabernet Sauvignon.

Western Australia makes little wine compared to the preceding three states, but quality is high. The warm, dry Swan Valley is the state's historic center of wine production, but two cooler climate regions are becoming increasingly important:

- **Margaret River:** This relatively cool region near the Indian Ocean makes excellent Cabernet Sauvignons, Chardonnays, and Semillons, especially from such fine wineries as Leeuwin Estate and Cape Mentelle.

- **Great Southern:** A large region with lots of untapped potential. Intense, austere Cabernet Sauvignons are produced here, as well as increasingly fine Shiraz; crisp, age-worthy Riesling is also a specialty.

Australia's *true* cool climate region is Tasmania, an island south of Victoria, where a few producers have begun to prove what potential exists for delicate Pinot Noirs and Chardonnays.

For a listing of Australia's leading wineries, see our books *Red Wine For Dummies,* Chapter 9, and *White Wine For Dummies,* Chapter 9; for some specific Australian wines that we recommend, see *Wine Buying Companion For Dummies.* (All three books are published by IDG Books Worldwide, Inc.)

New Zealand

The history of fine winemaking in New Zealand has been relatively short. As in the U. S., conservative attitudes towards alcohol deterred progress until recently.

New Zealand, situated farther south than Australia, is a cooler wine area, whose climate is greatly influenced by the ocean. Of the two large islands that comprise New Zealand, the North Island is the warmer, producing red wines around Auckland and Hawkes Bay (especially known for its Cabernet Sauvignon), as well as various white wines from the Müller-Thurgau, Chardonnay, and Sauvignon Blanc grape varieties.

On the South Island, Marlborough — the country's largest and most important wine region — only discovered its grapegrowing potential in 1973. This region is the top production zone for Chardonnay and, especially, Sauvignon Blanc.

New Zealand whites are generally unoaked wines with rich flavor and high acidity. New Zealand Sauvignon Blanc is so distinctive — pungent and intense, with a flavor that could be compared to asparagus, limes, or cut green grass — that it has become recognized almost overnight as a new prototype of Sauvignon Blanc. One winery in particular, Cloudy Bay, has received worldwide acclaim for its intensely flavored Sauvignon Blanc; remarkably, its first vintage took place as recently as 1985!

For the names of New Zealand's leading wineries, see our *White Wine For Dummies,* Chapter 9; for some specific New Zealand white wines that we recommend, see *Wine Buying Companion For Dummies,* Chapters 6 and 8.

New Hope in South Africa

With the election of President Nelson Mandela in 1994, and the abolition of *apartheid* a few years before, South Africa boasts new energy and a positive outlook. Its wine industry's future, in particular, has never looked better, especially for its table wines. In our opinion, South Africa's wine industry is the most improved of any country in the world over the last 12 years.

Vines came to South Africa in the 1650s with the Dutch, the first European settlers. By the end of the 18th century, South Africa was producing a world famous, luscious, dessert wine called Constantia, which became sought after in European royal courts.

South Africa has only recently begun focusing on table wine production. Traditionally, most of the country's nearly 5,000 grape growers would take their grapes to one of the 70 cooperatives run by the KWV a giant semi-national wine cooperative, where over half of the crop would be turned into distilled alcohol or grape concentrate; the remaining grapes were used mainly for sherry or port. Today, in response to a worldwide demand for table wines, more of those grapes are being used to make dry, unfortified wine.

The South African wine industry continues to be dominated by large firms. In addition to the KWV, the Stellenbosch Farmers' Winery Group (SFW) is a conglomerate that is the leading producer of table wines in the country. The highly regarded Nederburg Estate is part of the SFW. Another important table wine firm is the Bergkelder Group; 18 wine estates, including some of South Africa's best, are affiliated with the Bergkelder Group.

Today, South Africa ranks between sixth and eighth (depending on the year, over the last five years) in the world in wine production. It exports about 20 percent of its wine, with the U.K. as its biggest customer.

South African style: Old World meets New World

Although we technically place South Africa's wines in the New World, we must admit that the styles of these wines are rather reminiscent of European wines. The taste of a South African Cabernet Sauvignon, for example, might remind you of a French wine — but not quite. On the other hand, it doesn't really resemble a New World red from California or Australia, either. South African wines manage to combine the subtlety and leanness of French wines along with some of the voluptuous ripeness of California wines. In short, they are somewhat between both worlds — or, you might say, they are uniquely South African.

South Africa's principal wine regions

Although there are some cooler microclimates, especially around the southern coast (near the Cape of Good Hope) and in higher altitudes, the climate in most of South Africa's wine regions is warm and dry. Irrigation is often necessary.

South Africa's Wine of Origin legislation in 1973 created ten wine districts (and a number of subdistricts). Almost all the vineyards are near the southwestern coast, in Cape Province (within 90 miles of Cape Town, the country's most fascinating and picturesque city). These vineyards are referred to as the Coastal Region vineyards.

The five major districts — all part of the Coastal District area — are

- ✔ **Constantia:** The oldest wine producing area in the country (located south of Cape Town)

- ✔ **Durbanville:** Noted for its rolling hills and well-drained soils; north of Cape Town

- ✔ **Stellenbosch:** East of Cape Town; the most important wine district in quantity and quality

- ✔ **Paarl:** North of Stellenbosch; home of the KWV and the beautiful Nederburg Estate; second-most important wine district

- ✔ **Franschhoek Valley:** (Subdistrict of Paarl); many innovative winemakers here

The small Hermanus/Walker Bay subdistrict (part of the Overberg district), southeast of Cape Province and bordering the Indian Ocean, is also showing promise with Pinot Noir and Chardonnay, led by the innovative Hamilton Russell Winery.

About 10 percent of South Africa's wines qualify as Wine of Origin (WO). Wine of Origin regulations are based on the French *Appellation Contrôlée* laws. These laws strictly designate vineyards, allowable grape varieties, vintage-dating, and so on. Varietal wines must contain at least 75 percent of the named variety; exported wines (complying with the stricter European Union regulations) must contain 85 percent of the named variety.

Steen, Pinotage, and company

The most common wine grape variety in South Africa is Chenin Blanc. Locally called *Steen,* this grape accounts for almost 30 percent of total plantings. The versatile Chenin Blanc is used primarily to make medium-dry to semi-sweet wines, but it also makes dry wines, sparkling wines, late harvest botrytis wines, and rosés. Cinsaut (the same as Cinsault, the Rhône variety), formerly called Hermitage in South Africa, is still the leading red variety.

But things are starting to change. Cabernet Sauvignon and Merlot (and, to a lesser extent, Pinot Noir and Shiraz) are becoming increasingly important among the red varieties, while Sauvignon Blanc and Chardonnay are becoming the popular white varieties. Cabernet Sauvignon and Sauvignon Blanc do particularly well in South Africa's climate. (A very assertive version of Sauvignon Blanc is produced here.)

And then you have Pinotage. Uniquely South African, Pinotage is a grape born when Pinot Noir was crossed with Cinsaut back in 1925. However, Pinotage didn't appear as a wine until 1959. Pinotage wine combines the cherry fruit of a Pinot Noir with the earthiness of a Rhône wine. It can be a truly delicious, light- to medium-bodied red wine that makes for easy drinking (especially suitable as a warm-weather red wine). Good examples of Pinotage can be found in the $9 to $15 price range. Look especially for Kanonkop or Simonsig; Pinotage is a specialty of these wineries; their Pinotage wines are richer and denser than most other producers'.

South Africa's best bets

While Pinotage is a pleasant wine, certainly worth trying, we believe South Africa's future is with Cabernet Sauvignon and Merlot (and blends of these grapes) for its red wines and Sauvignon Blanc and Chardonnay for its whites. Some of the producers that we recommend, along with their wines and districts, are the following (listed according to preference):

- **Grangehurst (Stellenbosch):** Sensational new winery; try the Cabernet-Merlot Reserve especially, but also the Cabernet Sauvignon, Merlot, and Pinotage

- **Plasir de Merle (Paarl):** One of the country's best Cabernet Sauvignons; Chardonnay and Sauvignon Blanc also quite fine

- **Meerlust (Stellenbosch):** Especially the Rubicon (mainly Cabernet Sauvignon blend); but also, the Cabernet Sauvignon and Merlot

- **Rust En Vrede (Stellenbosch):** Cabernet Sauvignon, Estate (Cabernet blend), Shiraz

- **La Motte Estate (Franschhoek Valley):** Millennium (Cabernet Sauvignon/Merlot blend), Cabernet Sauvignon, Shiraz, Sauvignon Blanc

- **Rozendal (Stellenbosch):** Mainly Merlot blend

- **Klein Constantia (Constantia):** Marlbrook (Bordeaux-type blend), Cabernet Sauvignon, Sauvignon Blanc; also, Chardonnay

- **Warwick Estate (Stellenbosch):** Another new winery to watch; fine Trilogy (Bordeaux-type blend), Cabernet Sauvignon, Pinotage

- **Zonnebloem (Stellenbosch):** Lauréat (Bordeaux-type blend), Merlot

- **Stellenryck (Coastal Region):** Cabernet Sauvignon

- **Backsberg Estate (Paarl):** Klein Babylonstoren (Merlot-Cabernet Sauvignon blend), Merlot, Cabernet Sauvignon, Pinotage, Chardonnay, Sauvignon Blanc

- **Villiera Estate (Paarl):** Cru Monro (60/40 Cabernet Sauvignon/Merlot blend)

- **Boschendal Estate (Paarl):** Shiraz, Merlot, Sauvignon Blanc, Semillon, Chardonnay

- **Glen Carlou (Paarl):** Grande Classique (Bordeaux-type blend)

- **Hamilton Russell (Walker Bay):** Pinot Noir, Chardonnay

- **Kanonkop Estate (Stellenbosch):** Pinotage, Cabernet Sauvignon

- **L'Ormarins Estate (Franschhoek Valley):** Optima (Bordeaux-style blend), Cabernet Sauvignon, Shiraz, Chardonnay

- **Thelema Mountain (Stellenbosch):** Cabernet Sauvignon, Cabernet-Merlot, Sauvignon Blanc, Chardonnay

- **Lievland Estate (Stellenbosch):** Cabernet Sauvignon, Shiraz, DVB (Bordeaux-style blend)

- **Groot Constantia (Constantia):** Cabernet Sauvignon, Sauvignon Blanc, Chardonnay

- **Middelvlei Estate (Stellenbosch):** Pinotage, Cabernet Sauvignon

- **Simonsig Estate (Stellenbosch):** Tiara (Cabernet Sauvignon-Merlot blend), Pinotage

- **Louisvale (Stellenbosch):** Chardonnay, Sauvignon-Chardonnay

- **Neil Ellis (Coastal Region; Elgin):** Sauvignon Blanc, Chardonnay

- **Mulderbosch (Stellenbosch):** Sauvignon Blanc

- **Nederburg (Paarl):** Sauvignon Blanc (Private Bin D234); Prelude (a 70/30 bend of Sauvignon Blanc and Chardonnay — unusual, but it works), Chardonnay

The red wines in the preceding list are in the $10 to $25 price range; the white wines are in the $10 to $20 price range. Sauvignon Blancs and Pinotage wines are the best values.

As in other predominantly warm-climate regions, vintages are rather consistently good in South Africa. You do find some variability in the Coastal Districts, however. The best recent vintages for red wines have been 1995, 1992, 1991, 1989, 1987, and 1986. For white wines, 1995, 1993, 1992, and 1991 all have been quite good. The best wines in South Africa have been made from the 1986 vintage on.

Sixteen red wines you should try at least once

Wine	Country of Origin	Approximate Price
Barbera d'Alba,' 95/'96 (Vietti or G. Conterno)	Italy (Piedmont)	$15 (Vietti), $22 (Conterno)
Bourgogne Rouge, '95 (Leroy or deVillaine)	France (Burgundy)	$20 to $22
Cabernet Sauvignon, '94/'95 (Swanson Vineyards)	U.S. (Napa Valley)	$24
Rioja, '89,'90,'91 (Muga Reserva or Cune Imperial Gran Reserva)	Spain	$15 (Muga), $33 (Cune)
Juliénas (Georges Duboeuf)	France (Beaujolais)	$11
Barolo, '91/'93 (Caretta or G. Mascarello)	Italy (Piedmont)	$22 (Caretta), $34 (Mascarello)
Pinot Noir, '95/'96 (Ponzi, Rex Hill, Sokol Blosser, or Elk Cove)	U.S. (Oregon)	$18; $25 or more, Reserve
Bordeaux, '94/'95 (Ch. Bel Air, Haut-Médoc)	France (Bordeaux)	$11 to $12
Chianti Classico, '94/'95 (Ruffino "Santedame" or Castello dei Rampolla)	Italy	$15 (Ruffino), $20 (Rampolla)
Cabernet Sauvignon, '91/'95 (Meerlust or Plasir de Merle)	South Africa	$21
Merlot, '95 (Estancia Estates)	U.S. (Alexander Valley)	$16 to $17
Crozes-Hermitage, '95 (Dom. A. Belle, Cuvée Louis Belle)	France (Rhône Valley)	$20
Cabernet/Merlot, '96 (Hedges Cellars)	U.S. (Washington)	$11 to $12
Chaleur Estate, '95 (DeLille Cellars)	U.S. (Washington)	$38
Rosso di Montalcino, '96 (Argiano or Il Poggione)	Italy (Tuscany)	$18
Zinfandel, '95/'96 (Marietta Cellars, Elyse, or Frog's Leap)	U.S. (Marietta in Sonoma; Elyse, Frog's Leap in Napa)	$15 (Marietta), $20 (Elyse/Frog's Leap)

Chapter 14

America, America

• •

In This Chapter

▶ California comes of age

▶ The Golden Gate to Napa, Sonoma, and beyond

▶ Oregon's Pinots

▶ Mister Red comes to Washington

▶ Islands, rivers, and lakes of New York wine

▶ Icewine from Canada

• •

*W*hen the *conquistadores* came to the New World of America in search of gold, Spanish missionaries accompanied them and planted the first wine grapevines in what is now called the United States, in southern California. These "Mission" grapes, as they were called, still exist, but they have been supplanted by the noble grape varieties — Cabernet Sauvignon, Chardonnay, and the rest of the gang — to produce today's fine wines. The one thing that hasn't changed is that California is still the focus of the American wine industry, although most of the wine business has moved north; southern California is now mainly filled with cars and people!

In this chapter we cover the American wine scene, giving extra attention to California's special wine regions — Napa Valley and Sonoma — but also including other wine regions in California, as well as some in Oregon, Washington State, and New York. We end with a quick look at Canada's up-and-coming wine regions.

The New World of American Wine

Even though some wine was made commercially in the last century, the United States wine industry arrived big time only in the past generation. Prohibition from 1920 to 1933, the Great Depression, and WW II were serious blows to the wine business — and recovery was slow.

The 1970s began the Wine Rush Era in California. Before 1970, only a few dozen operating wineries existed in the state; today, California has more than 800 bonded wineries (about a dozen or so "giants," but mainly small, family-owned operations) — and the numbers are growing.

California's growth has stimulated interest in wine all across the country. Today, wineries exist in 47 of the 50 United States. But wine production is an important industry in only four states: California (the largest wine producing state, by far), Washington, Oregon, and New York. The U.S. currently fluctuates between fourth and fifth in world wine production — although well behind the two leaders, France and Italy (Spain is a distant third).

Home-grown ways

The wines of the U.S. — especially California — are the essence of New World wine-think. Winemakers operate freely, planting whatever grape variety they wish — wherever they wish to plant it. They blend wines from different regions together as they wish. (Blending among states is trickier, because of federal rules.)

U.S. wines have elevated grape varieties to star status. Until California began naming wines after grapes, Chardonnay, Merlot, Pinot Noir, and Cabernet Sauvignon were just behind-the-scenes ingredients of wine — but now they *are* the wine. Lest anyone think that all wines from a particular grape are the same, however, winemakers have emerged as celebrities who put their personal spin on the best wines. In the California scenario especially, the land — the *terroir* — has been secondary, at least up until recently.

American winemakers have made technology their ally in their efforts to create wines that taste like fruit. California's two important universities for winemaking — California State University at Fresno and, especially, the University of California at Davis — have become world leaders in the scientific study of wine. Even European winemakers now make pilgrimages to California to study at U.C. Davis.

Playing by their own rules

An appellation system for wines does exist in the U.S., and like the classic French model, it defines the vineyard regions. But the U.S. system of American Viticultural Areas (AVAs) establishes only the geographical boundaries of wine zones; it does not stipulate which grape varieties can be planted, the maximum yield of grapes per acre (see "Vine growing vernacular" in Chapter 3), or anything else that would link the geography to a particular type of wine. AVA names, the name of the region of production, therefore have secondary importance on wine labels after the name of the grape.

A smorgasbord of AVAs

In naming their wines, winemakers often choose to use a less specific AVA designation rather than a smaller, more specific one, in order to widen their options in buying grapes and wine. A winery in Alexander Valley, within Sonoma County, for example, might use the broader *Sonoma County* AVA instead of Alexander Valley if it buys grapes from (or owns vineyards in) other areas of the county and wishes to use those grapes in its wine. It could use the larger *North Coast* AVA if it blends in grapes or wine from neighboring counties, like Napa; and if low price is a goal, the winery will use the even broader *California* AVA in order to buy less expensive grapes from the industrial vineyards of the Central Valley (the San Joaquin Valley) or other parts of the state where grapes and wine are less expensive than in Sonoma County. Sometimes the *California* appellation is used to give the winery complete freedom to use grapes from throughout the state for its better wines as well. (This practice doesn't occur in smaller viticultural areas, such as southern Pennsylvania, where there are few alternative sources of grapes.) While specificity of place is admired, on the one hand, making a good wine at a good price through geographical blending is also admired. The relative merits depend on who's doing the admiring.

Traditional or not, America's way of making wine and naming wine sits just right with wine drinkers in the U.S.: American wines now account for nearly 85 percent of all wine sales in the United States.

Wines labeled with the name of a grape variety in the U.S. must be made at least 75 percent from that grape variety, according to federal law. Wines with an AVA indication must derive 85 percent of their grapes from that AVA. Wines with vintage years must derive at least 95 percent from the named vintage.

California, USA

When you think about American wine, you think of California. That's not surprising — the wines of California make up almost 89 percent of U.S. wine production.

California's Gallo winery is the largest winery by far — in fact, it is the largest winery in the world — producing one out of every four bottles of wine sold in the U.S. If Gallo were a separate country, it would rank about 13th or 14th in the world for wine production, with an output roughly equivalent to Chile's — if not higher (but without a national debt).

It was the Robert Mondavi Winery, however, that provided the stimulus to produce fine wine in the U.S. When Robert Mondavi left his family's winery (Charles Krug Winery) to start his own winery in 1966, a winery dedicated to making premium wines, his move symbolized the beginning of an age of awareness of better-quality wines in the U.S. These finer wines would be varietally named Cabernet Sauvignon, Chardonnay, and so on — a reaction to the nondescript jug wines labeled with names borrowed from Europe's wine regions, such as Burgundy and Chablis. Today, even Gallo is very much in the varietal wine business.

Where California wines grow

In sunny California, there's no lack of warm climate for growing grapes. For fine wine production, the challenge is to find those areas that are cool enough, with poor enough soil, so that grapes don't ripen too quickly, too easily, without full flavor development (see "Vine growing vernacular" in Chapter 3). Nearness to the Pacific coast and/or altitude are important determinants of climate in California — more so than latitude. Premium wines are, therefore, made up and down almost the whole length of the state.

The most important fine wine regions and districts include the following (see Figure 14-1):

- ✓ **North Coast Region:**
  Napa Valley
  Sonoma County
  Mendocino and Lake Counties

- ✓ **North-Central Coast Region:**
  Livermore and Santa Clara Valleys (San Francisco Bay area)
  Santa Cruz Mountains
  Monterey County

- ✓ **Sierra Foothills Region**

- ✓ **South-Central Coast Region:**
  San Luis Obispo County
  Santa Barbara County

When the wines are good

Weather variations from year to year are far less dramatic in California than they are in most European wine regions. One important reason for the lack of variation is that rain doesn't fall during the growing season in much of

California (rain at the wrong time is the usual cause of Europe's poorer vintages). Using irrigation, winemakers in effect control the rain themselves. Ironically, one factor that can cause vintage variation in California is lack of water for irrigation: drought.

Wine lovers who are interested in making fine distinctions of quality will be happy to know that California has enjoyed an amazing streak of seven excellent vintages, from 1990 to 1996 (1990, 1991, and 1994 being the best for red wines, 1992 and 1995 for whites). Among older vintages, 1984, 1985, and 1987 were good red wine vintages, while 1986 and 1988 were fine years for white wines.

Figure 14-1:
The wine regions of California.

Chardonnay rules the roost — for now

Chardonnay, the sales leader among varietal wines in the U.S. for the last 10 years or so, still rules the market, followed by White (really pink) Zinfandel. But two red wines are beginning to catch up: Cabernet Sauvignon and Merlot. In fact, Merlot has become so popular in the past five years that American producers can hardly grow the grapes fast enough; some large California wineries have even resorted to importing Merlot and other red wines from Chile, France, and Italy, and distributing these wines themselves, sometimes under their own brand names. The increased popularity of varietal red wines is attributed to Americans' increased awareness of wine, and to media coverage of medical studies suggesting favorable health and longevity benefits from wine consumption. Red wine sales, in particular, have benefited from these medical reports.

Napa Valley: As Tiny as It Is Famous

Napa Valley is about a ninety minute drive northeast of the beautiful bay city of San Francisco. Many of California's most prestigious wineries — and certainly its most expensive vineyard land — are in the small Napa Valley, where nearly 300 wineries have managed to find space. (In 1960, there were only 25 Napa Valley wineries.) The region's size is actually much tinier than its reputation: Napa produces less than five percent of California's wine grapes.

The southern part of the Valley, especially the Carneros district, is the coolest area, thanks to ocean breezes and mists from the San Pablo Bay. Carneros — which extends westward into Sonoma County — has become the vineyard area of choice for grape varieties that enjoy the cool climate: Chardonnays, Pinot Noirs, and grapes for sparkling wines. North towards Calistoga — away from the bay influence — the climate gets quite hot (but always with cool nights).

Wineries and vineyards are located throughout Napa Valley, many on the valley floor, some in the hills and mountains to the west (the Mayacamas Mountains), and some in the mountains to the east (especially Howell Mountain). Napa winemakers and grape growers have established nine AVAs besides the broad Napa Valley AVA itself and the Carneros AVA, which Napa and Sonoma share. These other nine are

- Spring Mountain and Mt. Veeder (both in the western mountains)
- Howell Mountain, Stags Leap District, Atlas Peak (all hilly or mountainous areas), and Wild Horse Valley, all in the eastern part of Napa
- Rutherford, Oakville, and St. Helena, on the valley floor

TIP

From $6 to $60

You can find Chardonnays and Cabernets from California at retail store prices as low as $6 a bottle. Better wines are in the $15 to $35 range, however. The *reserves, single-vineyard wines,* and *special selection wines* generally cost from $30 to $60 and up.

Most good Pinot Noirs and Merlots start at about $20 and can go as high as $40 (a few even higher).

Sauvignon Blancs — somewhat less in demand — are the best values among California's premium wines. You can find many good ones for around $10, although a few are priced as high as $20. Red Zinfandels are also still a bargain, but their prices are climbing as they become more popular. You can still find many red Zins from $12 to $18, although a few premium Zinfandels are over $20. If you like White Zinfandels, which are distinctly sweeter than the reds, you can save yourself a bundle; they're in the $5 to $7 range.

The words *reserve, special selection, private reserve, barrel select, vintners reserve, classic,* and so on have no legal definition in the U.S. Although many premium wineries use one of these terms to indicate their special or better wines, most of the larger wineries use the same terms on their inexpensive bottlings as marketing tools (see the "Reserve" section in Chapter 9).

The grapes of Napa

Almost everyone in Napa who makes table wine makes a Cabernet Sauvignon and a Chardonnay, and many Napa producers are now also making Merlot. Softer, less tannic, and more approachable than Cabernet Sauvignon, Merlot has become the hot, new red wine in the U.S., especially with consumers who are just getting into red wine.

The six most important wines in Napa are the two whites, Chardonnay and Sauvignon Blanc (often labeled Fumé Blanc), and the four red wines, Cabernet Sauvignon, Merlot, Pinot Noir (mainly from cool Carneros), and Zinfandel. But blended wines have become increasingly important in the last ten years. If red, these blends are usually made from red Bordeaux varieties (Cabernet Sauvignon, Cabernet Franc, Merlot, and sometimes even Malbec and Petit Verdot). If white, they're usually made from the white Bordeaux grapes (Sauvignon Blanc and Sémillon). Some of these blends are referred to as Meritage wines — not just in Napa but across the U.S. — although few carry the word *Meritage* on their labels.

Who's who in Napa (and for what)

If just about every winery in Napa makes a Chardonnay and a Cabernet Sauvignon, how can you distinguish the various wineries from one another? Good question — and there's no easy answer. The following alphabetical list indicates some of the better wine producers in Napa Valley, as well as their best wines, and could help steer you in the right direction. We know the list looks overwhelming, but . . . that's Napa!

Our list includes Napa classics as well as some personal favorites. Sparkling wine producers are covered under "California" in Chapter 15. Some of our favorite California wines — from Napa and elsewhere — are described in our *Wine Buying Companion For Dummies* (IDG Books Worldwide, Inc.).

Although all the wineries in the following list are situated in Napa Valley, their wines are not necessarily made with Napa-grown grapes; the appellation, or geographic name, indicated on the bottle can provide a clue to the vineyard locations for any specific wine.

- **Acacia Winery:** Pinot Noir, Chardonnay
- **S. Anderson Vineyard:** Cabernet Sauvignon, Chardonnay
- **Anderson's Conn Valley:** Cabernet Sauvignon, Chardonnay
- **Araujo Estate:** Cabernet Sauvignon (Eisele Vineyard)
- **Atlas Peak Vineyards:** Sangiovese, Cabernet Savignon
- **Beaulieu Vineyard:** Cabernet Sauvignon Private Reserve (Georges de Latour), Cabernet Sauvignon (Rutherford)
- **Beringer Vineyards:** Cabernet Sauvignon Private Reserve, Chardonnay Reserves
- **Bryant Family Vineyard:** Cabernet Sauvignon (small winery; scarce)
- **Burgess Cellars:** Zinfandel, Cabernet Sauvignon
- **Cafaro Cellars:** Cabernet Sauvignon, Merlot
- **Cain Cellars:** Cain Five (a blend of five Bordeaux varieties)
- **Cakebread Cellars:** Cabernet Sauvignon, Sauvignon Blanc, Chardonnay
- **Carneros Creek:** Pinot Noir (especially Signature Reserve)
- **Caymus Vineyard:** Cabernet Sauvignon (especially *Special Selection*)
- **Chappellet:** Chenin Blanc, Cabernet Sauvignon
- **Chateau Montelena:** Cabernet Sauvignon, Chardonnay, Zinfandel
- **Chateau Potelle:** Cabernet Sauvignon, Chardonnay, Zinfandel
- **Chateau Woltner:** Chardonnay

- **Chimney Rock:** Élevage (blend of Cabernet/Merlot)

- **Clos du Val:** Cabernet Sauvignon, Merlot, Sémillon

- **Clos Pegase:** Cabernet Sauvignon

- **Conn Creek:** Anthology (blend of Merlot/Cabernet)

- **Corison:** Cabernet Sauvignon

- **Cuvaison:** Chardonnay, Cabernet Sauvignon

- **Dalla Valle:** Cabernet Sauvignon, Maya (blend of Cabernet Franc/Cab Sauvignon)

- **Diamond Creek:** Cabernet Sauvignon

- **Dickerson Vineyard:** Zinfandel, Merlot

- **Dominus Estate:** Dominus (mainly Cabernet Sauvignon)

- **Duckhorn:** Merlot (especially Three Palms Vineyard), Cabernet Sauvignon, Sauvignon Blanc

- **Dunn Vineyards:** Cabernet Sauvignon (especially Howell Mountain)

- **El Molino:** Chardonnay, Pinot Noir

- **Elyse Vineyards:** Zinfandel (especially Howell Mountain)

- **Étude:** Pinot Noir, Cabernet Sauvignon

- **Far Niente:** Cabernet Sauvignon, Chardonnay

- **Flora Springs:** Trilogy (blend of Cab Sauvignon, Merlot, Cab Franc), Cabernet Sauvignon Reserve

- **Forman Vineyard:** Chardonnay, Cabernet Sauvignon

- **Franciscan Vineyards:** Chardonnay, Merlot, Cabernet Sauvignon

- **Franus Winery:** Zinfandel

- **Freemark Abbey:** Cabernet Sauvignon (Bosché and Sycamore Vineyards)

- **Frog's Leap Winery:** Cabernet Sauvignon, Zinfandel, Sauvignon Blanc

- **Girard Winery:** Chardonnay, Cabernet Sauvignon Reserve

- **Grace Family Vineyards:** Cabernet Sauvignon (small production; mailing list only)

- **Green and Red Vineyard:** Zinfandel

- **Grgich Hills Cellar:** Chardonnay, Cabernet Sauvignon, Zinfandel, Fumé Blanc

- **Groth Vineyards:** Cabernet Sauvignon (especially Reserve)

- **Harlan Estate:** Cabernet Sauvignon (small winery; very scarce)

- **Harrison Vineyards:** Cabernet Sauvignon, Chardonnay

- **Havens Wine Cellars:** Merlot
- **Heitz Wine Cellars:** Cabernet Sauvignon (Martha's and Bella Oaks Vineyards), Grignolino
- **Hess Collection Winery:** Cabernet Sauvignon, Chardonnay
- **Jarvis Estate:** Cabernet Sauvignon, Chardonnay
- **Charles Krug:** Cabernet Sauvignon (Vintage Selection), Chardonnay (Carneros Reserve)
- **La Jota Vineyard:** Cabernet Sauvignon, Viognier
- **Lamborn Family Wine Company:** Zinfandel
- **Lewis Cellars:** Cabernet Sauvignon, Chardonnay
- **Livingston:** Cabernet Sauvignon
- **Long Vineyards:** Chardonnay, Riesling, Pinot Grigio
- **Markham Vineyards:** Chardonnay, Merlot, Cabernet Sauvignon
- **Louis M. Martini:** Cabernet Sauvignon (Monte Rosso Vineyard)
- **Mayacamas Vineyards:** Cabernet Sauvignon, Chardonnay, Sauvignon Blanc
- **Merryvale Vineyards:** Chardonnay Reserve, Profile (Cabernet blend)
- **Robert Mondavi:** Cabernet Sauvignon (especially the Reserve), Pinot Noir Reserve, Fumé Blanc Reserve, Chardonnay Carneros
- **Monticello Cellars:** Chardonnay (Corley Reserve)
- **Mount Veeder:** Meritage Reserve (Cabernet Sauvignon blend)
- **Newton Vineyard:** Cabernet Sauvignon, Merlot
- **Niebaum-Coppola Estate:** Rubicon (mainly Cabernet Sauvignon), Zinfandel
- **Oakville Ranch Vineyards:** Cabernet Sauvignon
- **Opus One:** Opus One (mainly Cabernet Sauvignon)
- **Pahlmeyer Winery:** Cabernet Sauvignon, Merlot
- **Paradigm:** Cabernet Sauvignon, Merlot
- **Patz & Hall:** Chardonnay
- **Robert Pecota Winery:** Cabernet Sauvignon
- **Joseph Phelps Vineyards:** Insignia (Cabernet blend), Cabernet Sauvignon (Backus Vineyard)
- **Pine Ridge Winery:** Cabernet Sauvignon (Stags Leap District)
- **Pride Mountain:** Cabernet Sauvignon
- **Kent Rasmussen Winery:** Pinot Noir, Chardonnay

- **Raymond Vineyard:** Cabernet Sauvignon Reserve
- **Ritchie Creek Vineyards:** Cabernet Sauvignon
- **Rombauer Vineyards:** Chardonnay
- **Saddleback Cellars:** Cabernet Sauvignon
- **St. Clement Vineyards:** Chardonnay, Cabernet Sauvignon, Sauvignon Blanc
- **St. Supéry Vineyard:** Cabernet Sauvignon
- **Saintsbury:** Pinot Noir (especially Carneros and Reserve), Chardonnay Reserve
- **Selene:** Merlot, Sauvignon Blanc
- **Sequoia Grove:** Cabernet Sauvignon (especially the Reserve)
- **Shafer Vineyards:** Cabernet Sauvignon (especially Hillside Select), Merlot
- **Signorello Vineyards:** Cabernet Sauvignon (especially Reserve), Sémillon
- **Silver Oak Cellars:** Cabernet Sauvignon
- **Silverado Vineyards:** Cabernet Sauvignon, Chardonnay Reserve
- **Robert Sinskey Vineyards:** Carneros Claret (blend of Merlot/Cabernet)
- **Sky Vineyards:** Zinfandel
- **Smith-Madrone:** Riesling, Chardonnay
- **Spottswoode Winery:** Cabernet Sauvignon
- **Staglin Family Vineyard:** Cabernet Sauvignon, Sangiovese
- **Stag's Leap Wine Cellars:** Cask 23 (Cab blend), Cabernet Sauvignon (Fay Vineyard and SLV), Chardonnay (especially Reserve)
- **Steltzner Vineyards:** Cabernet Sauvignon
- **Sterling Vineyards:** Reserve (Cabernet blend), Cabernet Sauvignon (Diamond Mountain)
- **Stony Hill Vineyard:** Chardonnay, Riesling
- **Storybook Mountain:** Zinfandel
- **Sullivan Vineyards:** Cabernet Sauvignon, Merlot
- **Swanson Vineyards:** Cabernet Sauvignon, Sangiovese, Merlot, Syrah, Chardonnay Reserve
- **The Terraces:** Zinfandel
- **Philip Togni Vineyard:** Cabernet Sauvignon, Sauvignon Blanc

- **Trefethen Vineyards:** Cabernet Sauvignon Reserve, Chardonnay, dry Riesling

- **Truchard Vineyards:** Syrah, Chardonnay

- **Tulocay:** Zinfandel

- **Turley Wine Cellars:** Zinfandel (all single-vineyard Zinfandels; very scarce)

- **Turnbull Vineyards** (formerly Johnson-Turnbull): Cabernet Sauvignon

- **Viader Vineyards:** Cabernet blend

- **Villa Mt. Eden:** Cabernet Sauvignon (Signature), Chardonnay (Reserve and Signature), Merlot Reserve, Pinot Blanc Reserve

- **Vine Cliff Cellars:** Cabernet Sauvignon, Chardonnay

- **Von Strasser Vineyards:** Cabernet Sauvignon

- **Whitehall Lane Winery:** Cabernet Sauvignon (especially Morisoli Vineyard and Reserve), Merlot

- **Z D Winery:** Cabernet Sauvignon, Chardonnay

Down-to-Earth in Sonoma

If you leave San Francisco over the beautiful Golden Gate Bridge, you'll be in Sonoma in an hour. The differences between Napa and Sonoma are remarkable. Whereas many of Napa's wineries are showy (and downright luxurious), most of Sonoma's are rustic, country-like, and laid back. The millionaires bought into Napa; Sonoma is just folks (with some exceptions, of course).

On the other hand, Sonoma _is_ the home of the famously successful Sebastiani, Glen Ellen, Korbel, Kendall-Jackson, Gallo-Sonoma, Simi, and Jordan wineries — not exactly small time operations! E. & J. Gallo, for one, has been moving into Sonoma in a _big_ way. We have the sneaking impression that if we visit Sonoma in 15 or 20 years, it will bear a striking resemblance to Napa. But we hope not; we like it just the way it is.

Sonoma's AVAs

Sonoma is larger and more spread out than Napa. Its climate is similar to Napa's, except that some areas near the coast are definitely cooler. Although there is plenty of Chardonnay, Cabernet Sauvignon, and Merlot in Sonoma, the region's varied microclimates and terrain have allowed three other varieties to excel — Pinot Noir, Zinfandel, and Sauvignon Blanc.

The viticultural areas (AVAs) of Sonoma County and their principal grape varieties (and wines) are the following:

- ✔ **Sonoma Valley:** Chardonnay (to a lesser extent, Pinot Noir, Cabernet Sauvignon, Zinfandel)

- ✔ **Sonoma Mountain:** Cabernet Sauvignon

- ✔ **Russian River Valley:** Pinot Noir, Chardonnay, sparkling wine, Zinfandel

- ✔ **Sonoma-Green Valley** (within Russian River Valley): Sparkling wine, Chardonnay, Pinot Noir

- ✔ **Chalk Hill** (within Russian River Valley): Chardonnay, Sauvignon Blanc

- ✔ **Dry Creek Valley:** Zinfandel, Cabernet Sauvignon

- ✔ **Alexander Valley:** Cabernet Sauvignon, Chardonnay, Sauvignon Blanc

- ✔ **Knight's Valley:** Cabernet Sauvignon, Sauvignon Blanc

Sonoma County has two more AVAs: Northern Sonoma, a patchwork area encompassing Russian River Valley, Alexander Valley, Dry Creek Valley, and Knight's Valley; and Sonoma Coast, a hodgepodge of land in western Sonoma, along the coast.

The following AVA is shared with Napa Valley:

- ✔ **Carneros:** Pinot Noir, Chardonnay, sparkling wine, Merlot

Pinot Noir lovers should look for wine from Russian River Valley producers, such as Williams & Selyem, Rochioli, Gary Farrell, and Dehlinger. We agree with the many wine critics who say that the Russian River Valley is the source of some of the best Pinot Noir in the entire New World.

Recommended Sonoma producers and wines

The following list includes some of Sonoma's better producers, listed alphabetically, along with their best wines. It's *slightly* less staggering than the Napa list.

Although these wineries are all based in Sonoma County, their wines might be made from grapes grown elsewhere. Cline Cellars, for example, uses grapes mainly from Contra Costa County east of San Francisco.

- ✔ **Alderbrook Winery:** Zinfandel, Gewürztraminer

- ✔ **Alexander Valley Vineyards:** Cabernet Sauvignon, Merlot

- ✔ **Arrowood Vineyards:** Chardonnay, Cabernet Sauvignon, Late Harvest Riesling

Make my Zinfandel *red*

In most wine stores, not a day goes by without the following scene taking place.

Customer: Where is your Zinfandel?

Salesperson: Do you want red or white?

Customer (with puzzled look and hesitation): Er, white. You know, the pink one. (Pause) You mean it comes in red, too?!

When Bob Trinchero of Napa's Sutter Home Winery decided to make a pink wine out of his red Zinfandel grapes in 1972 and call it White Zinfandel, he made a brilliant marketing decision. Red Zins were not selling well at the time; few Americans had developed a taste for dry red wine — and those who *did* drink dry red wine drank Cabernet Sauvignon or European reds. But millions of Americans drank Coke, Pepsi, and other sweet soft drinks.

The slightly sweet, fruity taste of White Zinfandel suited their taste just right. White Zinfandel became the hottest wine in the U.S.

Actually, red Zinfandel is *the* California wine. The Zinfandel grape variety hardly exists outside of California. Red Zinfandel is a wonderful, exuberant wine, one of our favorites. It smells and tastes of berry-cherry fruit, it's rich, and it has a velvety texture. Red Zinfandel is at its best when it's young (in its first six years), but it's also capable of aging. And Zinfandel is not expensive. The best examples come from Dry Creek and Russian River Valleys in Sonoma, especially from the old Zinfandel vines that Italian immigrant farmers planted 80 to 100 years ago. (See our list of recommended Sonoma producers in the following section.)

- **Belvedere Winery:** Cabernet Sauvignon, Chardonnay
- **Benziger Family Winery:** Cabernet Sauvignon, Chardonnay (Carneros)
- **Davis Bynum Winery:** Pinot Noir, Zinfandel
- **Carmenet Vineyard:** Cabernet Sauvignon (Moon Mountain Estate), Meritage (mainly Cabernet Sauvignon)
- **Chalk Hill Winery:** Chardonnay, Sauvignon Blanc
- **Chateau St. Jean:** Chardonnay (Robert Young and Belle Terre Vineyards), Cabernet Sauvignon (Cinq Cépages), Johannisberg Riesling (Late Harvest)
- **Chateau Souverain:** Cabernet Sauvignon, Merlot, Chardonnay, Zinfandel, Sauvignon Blanc
- **Cline Cellars:** Oakley Cuvée (Rhône blend), Mourvèdre, Zinfandel
- **Clos du Bois:** Chardonnay, Cabernet Sauvignon, Marlstone (Cabernet-based blend)
- **B. R. Cohn:** Cabernet Sauvignon (Olive Hill Vineyard)
- **H. Coturri:** Zinfandel
- **Dehlinger Winery:** Pinot Noir, Chardonnay, Syrah

✔ **De Loach Vineyards:** Chardonnay, Cabernet Sauvignon, Zinfandel

✔ **Dry Creek Vineyards:** Zinfandel

✔ **Gary Farrell Wines:** Pinot Noir, Chardonnay, Zinfandel

✔ **Ferrari-Carano:** Chardonnay, Fumé Blanc, Cabernet Sauvignon, Merlot, Zinfandel

✔ **Field Stone Winery:** Petite Sirah, Sauvignon Blanc

✔ **Fisher Vineyards:** Chardonnay (especially Whitney's Vineyard), Cabernet Sauvignon

✔ **Foppiano Vineyards:** Petite Sirah, Cabernet Sauvignon, Merlot

✔ **Gallo-Sonoma:** Chardonnay (Laguna Ranch), Zinfandel (Frei Ranch)

✔ **Geyser Peak Winery:** Cabernet Sauvignon, Merlot, Syrah, Semchard (75 percent Sémillon)

✔ **Gundlach-Bundschu Winery:** Cabernet Franc, Cabernet Sauvignon

✔ **Hanna Winery:** Sauvignon Blanc, Cabernet Sauvignon

✔ **Hanzell Vineyards:** Chardonnay

✔ **Hartford Court:** Pinot Noir, Zinfandel

✔ **Paul Hobbs Cellars:** Cabernet Sauvignon (Hyde Vineyard), Pinot Noir (Hyde Vineyard), Chardonnay

✔ **Hop Kiln:** Zinfandel, Chardonnay

✔ **Jordan Vineyard:** Cabernet Sauvignon, Chardonnay

✔ **Kendall-Jackson:** Cabernet Sauvignon, Chardonnay, Zinfandel, Pinot Noir, Syrah

✔ **Kenwood Vineyards:** Cabernet Sauvignon (Artist Series), Zinfandel

✔ **Kistler Vineyards:** Chardonnay (all vineyards and selections), Pinot Noir (all vineyards)

✔ **Kunde Estate:** Chardonnay, Cabernet Sauvignon, Viognier

✔ **La Crema:** Chardonnay (especially Reserve)

✔ **Landmark Vineyards:** Chardonnay (especially Two Williams Vineyard)

✔ **Laurel Glen Vineyard:** Cabernet Sauvignon (all selections)

✔ **Limerick Lane Cellars:** Zinfandel

✔ **Marcassin:** Chardonnay (all vineyards; very scarce; by mailing list)

✔ **Marietta Cellars:** Cabernet Sauvignon, Zinfandel, Old Vine Red—Lot 18 (Zin blend)

✔ **Mark West Vineyards:** Chardonnay

✔ **Matanzas Creek Winery:** Chardonnay, Sauvignon Blanc, Merlot

- **Peter Michael Winery:** Chardonnay (all selections)

- **Mill Creek Vineyards:** Chardonnay, Cabernet Sauvignon, Sauvignon Blanc

- **Murphy-Goode Estate Winery:** Fumé Blanc, Cabernet Sauvignon, Chardonnay, Pinot Blanc

- **Nalle Winery:** Zinfandel

- **Pezzi King:** Cabernet Sauvignon, Chardonnay, Zinfandel

- **Preston Vineyards:** Zinfandel, Barbera, Syrah, Marsanne

- **Quivira Vineyards:** Zinfandel, Dry Creek Cabernet Cuvée (mainly Cabernet Sauvignon), Sauvignon Blanc

- **Rabbit Ridge Vineyards:** Zinfandel (especially Reserve), Chardonnay Reserve (Russian River Valley)

- **A. Rafanelli Winery:** Zinfandel, Cabernet Sauvignon (very scarce; by mailing list)

- **Ravenswood:** Zinfandel (especially single-vineyards), Merlot (especially Sangiacomo Vineyard), Pickberry (Cabernet Sauvignon/Merlot blend)

- **J. Rochioli Vineyard:** Pinot Noir, Sauvignon Blanc, Chardonnay (especially Reserve wines), Zinfandel

- **St. Francis Winery:** Chardonnay, Merlot, Cabernet Sauvignon (especially Reserve wines)

- **Scherrer:** Zinfandel

- **Sausal Winery:** Zinfandel, White Zinfandel

- **Seghesio Winery:** Zinfandel, Vitigno Toscano (Sangiovese)

- **Simi Winery:** Chardonnay, Cabernet Sauvignon (especially Reserve)

- **Sonoma-Cutrer Vineyards:** Chardonnay (all selections)

- **Sonoma-Loeb:** Chardonnay (especially Private Reserve)

- **Stonestreet:** Legacy (Cabernet blend), Chardonnay, Merlot

- **Rodney Strong:** Cabernet Sauvignon, Zinfandel (Old Vines)

- **Joseph Swan Vineyards:** Zinfandel (all selections)

- **Marimar Torres Estate:** Chardonnay, Pinot Noir

- **Trentadue Winery:** Zinfandel, Petite Sirah, Old Patch Red (Carignane blend)

- **William Wheeler:** Chardonnay, Zinfandel

- **Williams & Selyem Winery:** Pinot Noir (all), Zinfandel, Chardonnay (all wines very scarce; by mailing list)

Mendocino and Lake Counties

If you have a chance, it's worth your while to drive up the beautiful California coastline from San Francisco on Route 1 to the quaint, old town of Mendocino — perhaps with a side trip to view the magnificent, giant redwoods of the Pacific Coast. Tourists are more scarce up here than in Napa or Sonoma, and that makes it all the nicer: You'll be genuinely welcomed at the wineries. Lake County, dominated by Clear Lake, is Napa's neighbor to the north, while Mendocino County is directly north of Sonoma.

The cool Anderson Valley in Mendocino County is ideal for growing Chardonnay, Pinot Noir, Gewurztraminer, and Riesling, and for the production of sparkling wine. The wily Roederer Champagne house bypassed Napa and Sonoma to start its sparkling wine operation here and has been doing extremely well in a short time — as have Scharffenberger (new name, Pacific Echo) and Handley, two other successful sparkling wine producers in Anderson Valley (see Chapter 15 for sparkling wine producers).

The following list includes recommended producers and their best wines. Producers are listed alphabetically by county. Most of the wineries listed produce their wines from locally grown grapes, but some, such as Steele, buy grapes from other areas of California.

Mendocino County

- ✔ **Brutocao Cellars:** Sauvignon Blanc, Chardonnay, Zinfandel
- ✔ **Edmeades:** Zinfandel (especially single-vineyards), Chardonnay
- ✔ **Fetzer Vineyards:** Chardonnay (Bonterra), Zinfandel (especially Reserve)
- ✔ **Gabrielli Winery:** Zinfandel, Chardonnay
- ✔ **Greenwood Ridge Vineyards:** Riesling, Pinot Noir, Zinfandel
- ✔ **Handley Cellars:** Chardonnay, Gewürztraminer, Sauvignon Blanc
- ✔ **Hidden Cellars:** Zinfandel, Alchemy (Sémillon-Sauvignon Blanc blend)
- ✔ **Husch Vineyards:** Gewürztraminer, Pinot Noir, Sauvignon Blanc
- ✔ **Lazy Creek Vineyards:** Gewürztraminer, Pinot Noir
- ✔ **Lolonis Winery:** Chardonnay, Zinfandel (Private Reserves)
- ✔ **McDowell Valley Vineyards:** Syrah (Estate), Viognier
- ✔ **Navarro Vineyards:** Gewürztraminer, Chardonnay (Reserve)
- ✔ **Whaler Vineyard:** Zinfandel

Lake County

- **Guenoc Winery:** Cabernet Sauvignon, Chardonnay (especially Reserves), Langtry Meritage Red (Cabernet blend), Petite Sirah
- **Steele Wines:** Chardonnay, Zinfandel, Pinot Noir, Pinot Blanc
- **Wildhurst Vineyards:** Chardonnay, Zinfandel, Merlot

San Francisco Bay Area

The San Francisco Bay area includes wine regions north, south, and east of the city: Marin County to the north; Alameda and Livermore to the east, and the Santa Clara Valley and San Mateo to the south.

The urban spread, from Palo Alto to San Jose (Silicon Valley) and eastward, has taken its toll on vineyards in both the Livermore and Santa Clara Valleys. These two growing regions, both cooled by breezes from the San Francisco Bay, are therefore relatively small.

In Livermore, directly east of San Francisco, Sauvignon Blanc and Sémillon have always done well. In Santa Clara Valley, south of San Francisco with the Santa Cruz Mountains on its western side, Chardonnay, Cabernet Sauvignon, and Merlot are the three big grape varieties (and wines).

In the following listing of recommended producers, we include two wineries located in Marin County — Kalin Cellars and Sean H. Thackrey. The winemakers, Terry Leighton and Sean Thackrey, get their grapes from diverse areas, including Livermore, and in the case of Thackrey, Napa. We also include two wineries located in Alameda County, just east of San Francisco — Edmunds St. John and Rosenblum Cellars. The first of these sources its grapes from throughout the state, while the latter uses mainly Sonoma Valley and Napa Valley fruit.

We list our recommended wineries alphabetically, by locality.

Marin County

- **Kalin Cellars:** Sauvignon Blanc, Sémillon, Chardonnay, Pinot Noir
- **Sean H. Thackrey:** Orion (Syrah), Sirius (Petite Sirah), Taurus (Mourvèdre)

Alameda County

- ✔ **Edmunds St. John:** Syrah, Zinfandel, Viognier, Les Côtes Sauvages (Rhône blend)
- ✔ **Rosenblum Cellars:** Zinfandel (especially single-vineyards), Cabernet Sauvignon (George Hendry Vineyard)

Livermore Valley

- ✔ **Concannon Vineyard:** Sauvignon Blanc, Petite Sirah
- ✔ **Wente Bros.:** Chardonnay, Riesling, Sauvignon Blanc

San Mateo County

- ✔ **Cronin Vineyards:** Chardonnay (various vineyards and selections)
- ✔ **Thomas Fogarty Winery:** Gewürztraminer, Chardonnay, Pinot Noir

Santa Clara Valley

- ✔ **Jory Winery:** Red Zeppelin (Zinfandel, Carignane, Cabernet Franc), Black Zeppelin (Mourvèdre-Syrah blend)
- ✔ **J. Lohr Winery:** Cabernet Sauvignon (Paso Robles), Chardonnay
- ✔ **Mirassou Vineyards:** Pinot Blanc (Harvest Reserve and "White Burgundy")
- ✔ **Sarah's Vineyard:** Chardonnay

Santa Cruz Mountains

Standing atop one of the isolated Santa Cruz Mountains, you quickly forget that you are only an hour's drive south of San Francisco. The rugged, wild beauty of this area has attracted quite a few winemakers, including some of the best in the state. (Paul Draper of Ridge Vineyards and Randall Grahm of Bonny Doon are but two.) The climate is basically cool, especially on the ocean side, where Pinot Noir thrives. On the San Francisco Bay side, Cabernet Sauvignon is the important red variety. But Chardonnay is the dominant grape on both sides.

The following is a list of recommended producers in the Santa Cruz Mountains (listed alphabetically), along with their best wines. Some of these wineries, notably Page Mill, purchase their grapes throughout California.

- ✔ **Ahlgren Vineyard:** Chardonnay, Cabernet Sauvignon, Sémillon

- ✔ **Bargetto:** Chardonnay, Cabernet Sauvignon, Gewürztraminer, fruit wine

- ✔ **Bonny Doon Vineyard:** Le Sophiste, Le Cigare Volant (white and red Rhône-type blends), dessert wines

- ✔ **David Bruce Winery:** Pinot Noir (Santa Cruz Mountains, especially Reserve), Zinfandel (Paso Robles)

- ✔ **Cinnabar Vineyard:** Chardonnay, Cabernet Sauvignon

- ✔ **Kathryn Kennedy Winery:** Cabernet Sauvignon

- ✔ **Mount Eden Vineyards:** Chardonnay (especially Santa Cruz Mountains), Cabernet Sauvignon, Pinot Noir

- ✔ **Page Mill Winery:** Chardonnay (Bien Nacido Vineyard), Pinot Noir, Sauvignon Blanc

- ✔ **Ridge Vineyards:** Cabernet Sauvignon (especially Monte Bello), Geyserville (Zin blend), Zinfandel, Chardonnay

- ✔ **Santa Cruz Mountain Vineyard:** Pinot Noir, Cabernet Sauvignon, Merlot

- ✔ **Storrs Winery:** Chardonnay

Down in Old Monterey

Monterey County has a little bit of everything — a beautiful coastline, the chic town of Carmel, some very cool (as in temperature, not chicness) vineyard districts, some very warm areas, mountain wineries and Salinas Valley wineries, a few gigantic wine firms, and lots of small ones. The wineries have had their growing pains, such as learning how to avoid vegetal flavors in their wines, determining where the best areas for the various grape varieties are located, and figuring out how to cope with the phylloxera louse (see Chapter 4 for more information on phylloxera).

Chardonnay leads the way here — as it does in most of the state. But the cooler parts of Monterey are also principal sources for Riesling and Gewürztraminer. Cabernet Sauvignon and Pinot Noir are the leading red varieties in the mountain areas.

The following are our recommended producers in Monterey County (and one producer from neighboring San Benito County), along with their best wines (listed alphabetically):

- ✔ **Bernardus Winery:** Chardonnay, Sauvignon Blanc, Marinus (a blend, but mainly Cabernet Sauvignon)

- ✔ **Calera** (San Benito County): Pinot Noir (especially single-vineyard selections), Viognier, Chardonnay

- **Chalone Vineyard:** Chardonnay, Pinot Blanc
- **Chateau Julien:** Merlot
- **Durney Vineyard:** Cabernet Sauvignon
- **Estancia Estates:** Chardonnay, Cabernet Sauvignon, Merlot, Pinot Noir, Sauvignon Blanc
- **Jekel Vineyards:** Riesling
- **Lockwood Vineyard:** Pinot Blanc, Sauvignon Blanc
- **The Monterey Vineyard:** Chardonnay, Cabernet Sauvignon
- **Morgan Winery:** Cabernet Sauvignon, Pinot Noir (both Carneros and Monterey Reserves)
- **Paraiso Springs Vineyard:** Pinot Blanc, Chardonnay, Riesling
- **San Saba Vineyard:** Cabernet Sauvignon, Merlot, Chardonnay
- **Smith & Hook Vineyards:** Merlot, Cabernet Sauvignon
- **Robert Talbott Vineyards:** Chardonnay (Diamond T and Monterey)
- **Ventana Vineyards:** Chardonnay, Riesling, Sauvignon Blanc

Thar's Wine in Them There Foothills

No wine region in America has a more romantic past than the Sierra Foothills. The Gold Rush of 1849 carved a place in history for the Foothills. It also brought vineyards to the area to provide wine for the thirsty miners. One of the wines brought to the region at this time was certainly Zinfandel — still the region's most famous wine. Indeed, many of the oldest grapevines in the U.S., some over 100 years old — and mainly Zinfandel — are here in the Sierra Foothills.

In fact, very little has changed in the Sierra Foothills over the years. This is clearly the West Coast's most rustic wine region — perhaps the country's. Therein lies its charm. A visit to the Foothills is like a trip into the past, when life was simple.

The Sierra Foothills is a sprawling wine region east of Sacramento, centered in Amador and El Dorado Counties, but spreading north and south of both. Two of its best-known viticultural areas are Shenandoah Valley and Fiddletown. Summers can be hot, but many vineyards have been planted in high altitudes, such as around Placerville in El Dorado. Soil throughout the region is mainly volcanic in origin.

The following are our recommended producers in the Sierra Foothills (listed alphabetically), along with their best wines:

- ✔ **Amador Foothill Winery:** Zinfandel
- ✔ **Boeger Winery:** Zinfandel, Barbera, Merlot
- ✔ **Chatom Vineyards:** Sauvignon Blanc, Sémillon
- ✔ **Granite Springs Winery:** Zinfandel, Petite Sirah
- ✔ **Karly:** Zinfandel, Syrah, Petite Sirah
- ✔ **Lava Cap Winery:** Cabernet Sauvignon, Merlot
- ✔ **Madrona Vineyards:** Chardonnay, Cabernet Sauvignon
- ✔ **Monteviña:** Barbera, Zinfandel
- ✔ **Nevada City Winery:** Zinfandel, Chardonnay
- ✔ **Renaissance Vineyard:** Cabernet Sauvignon (especially Reserve), Riesling, Sauvignon Blanc
- ✔ **Renwood Winery:** Barbera, Zinfandel (especially Grandpère Vineyard)
- ✔ **Sierra Vista Winery:** Syrah, Zinfandel, Cabernet Sauvignon (Reserve)
- ✔ **Sobon Estate:** Syrah, Zinfandel, Viognier
- ✔ **Stevenot Winery:** Cabernet Sauvignon (Reserve)

San Luis Obispo: Mountain Meets Maritime

San Luis Obispo County is another region made up of vastly diverse viticultural areas ranging from the warm, hilly Paso Robles region (north of the town of San Luis Obispo) where Zinfandel and Cabernet Sauvignon reign, to cool, maritime Edna Valley and Arroyo Grande (south of the town), home of some very good Pinot Noirs and Chardonnays. The areas are so different that we have grouped the producers separately.

The following producers (listed alphabetically), along with their best wines, are recommended in San Luis Obispo:

Paso Robles

- ✔ **Adelaida Cellars:** Cabernet Sauvignon, Chardonnay, Zinfandel
- ✔ **Claiborne & Churchill:** Chardonnay, Pinot Noir, Riesling
- ✔ **Creston Vineyards:** Pinot Noir, Zinfandel
- ✔ **Eberle Winery:** Zinfandel, Syrah, Cabernet Sauvignon, Chardonnay

- **Justin Winery:** Isosceles (Cabernet blend), Cabernet Sauvignon, Cabernet Franc, Chardonnay
- **Meridian Vineyards:** Chardonnay (especially Reserve), Syrah
- **Peachy Canyon Winery:** Zinfandel (especially "Westside"), Cabernet Sauvignon
- **Tobin James:** Zinfandel, Cabernet Sauvignon, Chardonnay
- **Wild Horse Winery:** Pinot Noir, Chardonnay, Merlot, Zinfandel, Cabernet Sauvignon, Malvasia Bianca, Tocai Friulano, Pinot Blanc

Edna Valley and Arroyo Grande

- **Alban Vineyards:** Viognier (Estate), Syrah, Grenache
- **Corbett Canyon Vineyards:** Cabernet Sauvignon Reserve (and other good value wines)
- **Edna Valley Vineyard:** Chardonnay (especially Reserve), Pinot Noir
- **Saucelito Canyon Vineyard:** Zinfandel
- **Talley Vineyards:** Pinot Noir, Chardonnay

Santa Barbara, California Paradise

Clearly, the most exciting new viticultural areas in California — if not in the entire country — are in Santa Barbara County. We say *new* even though we are aware that the Spanish missionaries had vineyards planted there 200 years ago. But in modern times, it was as late as 1975 before the first major winery (Firestone Vineyards) opened for business. In light of what we now know — that is, how well-suited Santa Barbara is for grapegrowing — 1975 was a late start.

The cool Santa Maria, Santa Ynez, and Los Alamos Valleys, which lie north of the city of Santa Barbara, run east to west, opening towards the Pacific Ocean and channeling in the cool ocean air. The climate is ideal for Pinot Noir and Chardonnay. In the Santa Maria Valley, one of the main sources of these varieties, the average temperature during the growing season is a mere 74°F. Further south, in the Santa Ynez Valley, Riesling also does well.

The Pinot Noir grape has earned Santa Barbara much of its acclaim as a wine region. Santa Barbara is now generally recognized as one of the five great American wine regions for the difficult to grow Pinot Noir — the other four being Carneros, the Russian River Valley, Anderson Valley (in

Mendocino County), and the Willamette Valley (in Oregon). In Santa Barbara, Pinot Noir wines seem to burst with luscious strawberry fruit, laced with herbal tones. These wines tend to be precocious, delicious in their first four or five years — not the *keepers* that the sturdier, wilder-tasting Russian River Pinot Noirs seem to be. But why keep them when they taste so good?

The following are some recommended producers in Santa Barbara (listed alphabetically), along with their best wines:

- ✔ **Au Bon Climat:** Pinot Noir, Chardonnay (especially single-vineyard bottlings of both), Pinot Blanc
- ✔ **Babcock Vineyards:** Pinot Noir (especially Estate), Sauvignon Blanc
- ✔ **The Brander Vineyard:** Sauvignon Blanc
- ✔ **Byron Vineyard:** Chardonnay (especially Reserve), Sauvignon Blanc
- ✔ **Cambria Winery:** Chardonnay, Pinot Noir (Julia's Vineyard), Syrah
- ✔ **Chimère Winery:** Pinot Noir (especially Bien Nacido Vineyard), Chardonnay
- ✔ **Cottonwood Canyon:** Pinot Noir
- ✔ **Firestone Vineyard:** Chardonnay, Riesling (Select Harvest)
- ✔ **Foxen Vineyard:** Pinot Noir, Chardonnay, Cabernet Sauvignon, Chenin Blanc
- ✔ **The Gainey Vineyard:** Chardonnay, Pinot Noir (especially Santa Ynez Limited Selections), Cabernet Franc, Sauvignon Blanc
- ✔ **Daniel Gehrs:** Dry Chenin Blanc ("Le Chenière"), Sauvignon Blanc
- ✔ **Richard Longoria:** Chardonnay, Pinot Noir, Merlot
- ✔ **The Ojai Vineyard:** Syrah
- ✔ **Fess Parker Winery:** Chardonnay, Riesling, Syrah
- ✔ **Qupé Cellars:** Syrah, Chardonnay, Marsanne, Los Olivos Cuvée (Syrah, Mourvèdre), Viognier
- ✔ **Sanford Winery:** Pinot Noir (especially Sanford & Benedict Vineyard), Chardonnay, Sauvignon Blanc
- ✔ **Santa Barbara Winery:** Pinot Noir Reserve, Chardonnay (Reserve and Lafond Vineyard)
- ✔ **Lane Tanner:** Pinot Noir (especially Sanford & Benedict Vineyard)
- ✔ **Zaca Mesa Winery:** Chardonnay

Elsewhere in California

Two interesting wineries in California's Central Valley, one in the Dunnigan Hills (north of the Central Valley) and a couple in southern California complete our portrait of recommended California wineries. Although these locations are normally too warm for growing grapes for fine wine, variables such as altitude or — in the case of southern California, cool ocean breezes — often create microclimates conducive to the production of fine wine.

Central Valley

> ✔ **Bogle Vineyards:** Petite Sirah, Zinfandel, Merlot
>
> ✔ **Fiddlehead Cellars:** Pinot Noir (from Santa Maria Valley grapes)

Dunnigan Hills (Yolo County)

> ✔ **R. H. Phillips Vineyard:** Syrah (EXP), Viognier (EXP), Sauvignon Blanc, Mourvèdre (EXP), Chardonnay Estate (Toasted Head)

Southern California

> ✔ **Callaway Vineyard:** Chardonnay ("Calla-Lees"), Sweet Nancy (late-harvest Chenin Blanc)
>
> ✔ **Moraga:** Cabernet Sauvignon

Mini-trends in California wine

Experimentation is a constant in California. Although Chardonnay, Cabernet Sauvignon, and Merlot are the anointed grape varieties at the moment, winemakers can never know whether they're missing the boat on some other important grape — unless they try growing it.

Some producers have become enchanted with the grape varieties from France's Rhône Valley — the red grapes Syrah, Grenache, Mourvèdre, and Cinsault and the white Viognier. These producers are collectively referred to as the Rhône Rangers. Other producers are riding the wave called Cal-Ital, growing Italian grapes such as Sangiovese, Dolcetto, and Nebbiolo. (Some Italian grapes, like Barbera, have been grown in California since the days of the Italian immigrants in the last century.) And next year — who knows? — the new grape could be Spain's Tempranillo. Stay tuned.

Oregon, A Tale of Two Pinots

Because Oregon is north of California, most people rightfully assume that Oregon's wine regions are cool. The main reason for Oregon's cool climate, though, is that there are no large mountains standing between the Pacific Ocean and the vineyards. Along with cool temperatures, the ocean influence brings rain. Grape growing and winemaking are really completely different in Oregon than in California.

Winemaking is a fairly new industry in Oregon, but it is growing rapidly. From a handful of wineries in the early 1970s, the state now has well over 100, and that number increases every year.

Oregon first became recognized in wine circles for its Pinot Noir, a grape that needs cool climates to perform at its best (see "Red Grape Varieties" in Chapter 4). The Eyrie Vineyards released the state's first Pinot Noir in 1970, but Oregon really began to grab national attention for its wines only after the excellent 1983 and 1985 vintages. Today Pinot Noir is still Oregon's flagship wine; a vast majority of the state's wineries make a Pinot Noir. And Oregon has had a string of good vintages for the difficult-to-grow Pinot Noir, beginning with 1988 on up to 1994, with 1996 looking promising at this point.

Oregon's other Pinot

Because Chardonnay is the companion grape to Pinot Noir in the Burgundy region and because the grape (and its wine) is hugely popular in America, Chardonnay is a fairly important grape variety in Oregon. However, a second white grape variety has emerged to challenge Chardonnay's domination: Pinot Gris.

David Lett, founder and winemaker of The Eyrie Vineyards and Oregon's Pinot Noir pioneer, is also the man who made Oregon's first Pinot Gris in the early 1970s, followed by Ponzi Vineyards and Adelsheim Vineyards. Today, about 50 wineries in Oregon make Pinot Gris. While a few wineries in California and Washington also produce wine from this variety, so far Pinot Gris has been an Oregon story in the U.S. (Pinot Gris's two other renowned homes are Alsace, France, and northeastern Italy, where it's called Pinot Grigio.)

Pinot Gris has many things going for it. Because it doesn't particularly need oak aging to give it complexity (but it takes to oak well when that's the winemaker's preference), Pinot Gris can be ready to drink six months after the vintage.

Pinot Gris is medium-bodied; its color ranges from a light golden yellow to a copper-pink, its aromas are reminiscent of pears and apples, sometimes of melon, and it has surprising depth and complexity. It's an excellent food wine, especially with seafood and salmon, just the kind of food that it's paired with in Oregon. And the best news is the price. Most of Oregon's Pinot Gris cost around $15 in retail stores.

Who's who in Willamette Valley

The main home of Pinot Noir and Pinot Gris in Oregon is the Willamette *(will AM ett)* Valley. Directly south of the city of Portland in northwest Oregon, the cool Willamette Valley has established itself in the last 25 years as the most important wine region in Oregon.

The Willamette Valley wine region is a convenient wine destination to visit because the wonderful city of Portland, with all its fine restaurants, hotels, and shops, is within 30 minutes.

The huge Willamette Valley encompasses several counties. Yamhill County, directly southwest of Portland, has the greatest concentration of wineries, all of which produce Pinot Noir. But quite a few wineries are located in Washington County, west of Portland, and in Polk County, south of Yamhill.

Here are some of the better producers in the Willamette Valley, primarily for Pinot Noir and Pinot Gris (but sometimes also Chardonnay or Riesling), listed alphabetically:

Acme Wineworks (a.k.a. John Thomas)
Adelsheim Vineyard
Amity Vineyards
Archery Summit
Argyle (for sparkling wines)
Beaux Frères
Benton Lane Winery
Bethel Heights Vineyard
Brick House Vineyards
Broadley Vineyards
Cameron Winery
Chehalem
Cooper Mountain Vineyards
Cristom Vineyards
Domaine Drouhin Oregon

Domaine Serene
Edgefield Winery
Elk Cove Vineyards
Erath Vineyards
Evesham Wood Winery
The Eyrie Vineyards
Hinman Vineyards (a.k.a. Silvan Ridge)
Ken Wright Cellars
King Estate Winery (located just south of Willamette Valley)
Kramer Vineyards
Lange Winery
McKinlay Vineyards
Montinore Vineyards
Oak Knoll Winery
Panther Creek Cellars

Ponzi Vineyards
Redhawk Vineyard
Rex Hill Vineyards
Sokol Blosser Winery
St. Innocent Winery

Torii Mor Winery
Tualatin Vineyards
Willakenzie Estate
Willamette Valley Vineyards
Witness Tree Vineyard

Two other Oregon wine regions

Two other wine regions of note in Oregon are both in the southwest part of the state: the Umpqua Valley (around the town of Roseburg) and farther south, next to California's northern border, the Rogue River Valley.

Considerably warmer than Willamette, the Umpqua Valley is the site of Oregon's first winery, Hillcrest Vineyard, founded in 1962. The main grape varieties in Umpqua are the Pinot Noir, Chardonnay, Riesling, and Cabernet Sauvignon. Besides Hillcrest Vineyard, which is known primarily for its Riesling, the other major wineries are Henry Estate and Girardet Wine Cellars, known for their Pinot Noir and Chardonnay.

The Rogue River Valley is warmer still; therefore, Cabernet Sauvignon and Merlot often perform better than Pinot Noir here. Chardonnay is the leading white wine, but Pinot Gris is becoming popular. Bridgeview Vineyards, the region's largest winery, is doing an admirable job with Pinot Gris as well as Pinot Noir. Three other vineyards to watch are Ashland Vineyards, Valley View Winery, and Foris Vineyards — the latter a specialist in Merlot and Cabernet Sauvignon.

Wine on the Desert: Washington State

Although Washington and Oregon are neighboring states, their wine regions have vastly different climates due to the location of the vineyards relative to the Cascade Mountains, which cut through both states from north to south.

On Washington's western, or coastal, side, the climate can be described as maritime — cool, plenty of rain, and lots of vegetation. (In Oregon, almost all the vineyards are located on the coastal side.) East of the mountains, the climate in Washington is continental, with hot, very dry summers and cold winters. Most of Washington's vineyards are situated in this area, in the vast, sprawling Columbia and Yakima Valleys.

Washington's winemakers have found that with irrigation, many grapes can flourish in the Washington "desert." The Bordeaux varieties — Merlot, Cabernet Sauvignon, Cabernet Franc, Sauvignon Blanc, and Sémillon — are the name of the game, along with Syrah and the ever-present Chardonnay. Washington has become particularly well known for the quality of its Merlots. One brand, Columbia Crest, is the largest-selling Merlot in the

United States in the over-$10 price category. But Cabernet Sauvignon also does extremely well here.

Washington does have a few vineyards west of the Cascades, around Puget Sound, where Riesling grows well. In fact, many of the larger wineries, such as Chateau Ste. Michelle and Columbia Winery, are located in the Puget Sound area, near the thriving city of Seattle (but they obtain almost all of their grapes from the Columbia and Yakima Valleys). Selling wine in Seattle is a bit easier than in the desert! Chateau Ste. Michelle, along with the even larger Columbia Crest (both part of the same corporate ownership — Stimson Lane), are the giants in the state; they account for over 50 percent of all of Washington's wines at present. Two other large Washington wineries are The Hogue Cellars and Washington Hills Cellars.

Like Oregon, Washington got off to a late start in the wine business. With the exception of Chateau Ste. Michelle and Columbia Winery, both founded in the 1960s, practically none of the current wineries existed as late as 1980. Remarkably, within the past two decades, almost 100 wineries have opened in Washington.

Vintage-wise, three great years for Washington have been the 1983, 1989, and 1994, but 1992 and 1996 are also quite good.

Washington's wine regions

Washington has three major viticultural areas, two very large regions and one tiny one (just getting started but huge with potential). The three regions are

- ✔ **Columbia Valley:** The largest in terms of acreage, this region accounts for over half of Washington's *vinifera* varieties. A large percentage of the state's wineries, even those located in the Puget Sound/Seattle area, use grapes from this region.

- ✔ **Yakima Valley:** Though this region is the second largest in acreage, more wineries are actually located here than in the huge Columbia Valley.

- ✔ **Walla Walla Valley:** Although only 5 percent of the state's *vinifera* grapes grow here, this fast-growing region in the southeast corner of Washington is home to some of the state's premium wineries, such as Leonetti Cellar, Woodward Canyon, Waterbrook Winery, Canoe Ridge Vineyard, and L'Ecole # 41.

A Washington oddity

When was the last time you had a Lemberger? No, we don't mean the cheese! Lemberger is a little-known grape variety from Germany that's also grown in Austria, where it's called Blaufränkisch. Don't feel bad if you haven't heard of it, because few people in the United States — outside of Washington — have tasted it. Lemberger is a hardy red variety that does well in the Yakima Valley; it makes a fruity but dry, inexpensive wine in the Beaujolais or Dolcetto school, but is uniquely its own. Hoodsport, Covey Run, Kiona Vineyards, and Hogue Cellars are four good producers of Lemberger — the wine!

Who's who in Washington

No, we're not talking about cabinet members and senators here! The following are our recommended producers in Washington, grouped alphabetically, along with some of their best wines:

- ✔ **Andrew Will Cellars:** Cabernet Sauvignon, Merlot, Sorella (Cabernet-Merlot)
- ✔ **Arbor Crest Wine Cellars:** Sauvignon Blanc, Chardonnay, Riesling
- ✔ **Barnard Griffin Winery:** Sémillon, Chardonnay, Fumé Blanc, Merlot
- ✔ **Bonair Winery:** Chardonnay
- ✔ **Canoe Ridge Vineyard:** Merlot, Chardonnay
- ✔ **Chateau Ste. Michelle:** Merlot, Cabernet Sauvignon, Chardonnay (especially Cold Creek Vineyard of all three), Riesling (especially Late Harvest and Ice Wine)
- ✔ **Chinook Wines:** Sauvignon Blanc, Sémillon, Chardonnay, Cabernet Sauvignon
- ✔ **Columbia Crest Winery:** Reserve Red (Cabernet-Merlot blend), Semillon, Syrah, Merlot, Cabernet Sauvignon, Sémillon-Chardonnay
- ✔ **Columbia Winery:** Cabernet Sauvignon, Cabernet Franc, Syrah, Merlot (especially Red Willow Vineyard of all four), Chevrier (Sémillon)
- ✔ **Covey Run Winery:** Chardonnay (especially Celilo Vineyard Reserve), Lemberger
- ✔ **DeLille Cellars:** Chaleur Estate (Bordeaux-style blend), Chaleur Estate Blanc (Sauvignon Blanc-Sémillon blend), D2 (second label of Chaleur Estate), Harrison Hill (Cabernet Sauvignon)

- **L'Ecole #41:** Merlot (especially Seven Hills Vineyard), Cabernet Sauvignon, Sémillon

- **Gordon Brothers Cellars:** Chardonnay, Merlot

- **Hedges Cellars:** Red Mountain Reserve (Bordeaux-style blend), Cabernet/Merlot, Fumé/Chardonnay (Sauvignon Blanc-Chardonnay blend)

- **The Hogue Cellars:** Merlot, Cabernet Sauvignon (especially Reserves), Blue Franc (Lemberger), Dry Chenin Blanc, Sémillon-Chardonnay, Fumé Blanc, Sémillon

- **Hoodsport Winery:** Lemberger, Sémillon

- **Kiona Vineyards:** Lemberger, Cabernet Sauvignon, Merlot

- **Leonetti Cellar:** Cabernet Sauvignon (especially Seven Hills Vineyard), Merlot, Sangiovese

- **Matthews Cellars:** Merlot, Washington State Red (Bordeaux-style blend)

- **McCrea Cellars:** Chardonnay, Tierra del Sol (Syrah-Grenache blend), Syrah

- **Northstar:** Merlot

- **Portteus Winery:** Cabernet Sauvignon, Merlot, Zinfandel

- **Preston Wine Cellars:** Cabernet Sauvignon, Merlot (especially Reserves)

- **Quilceda Creek Vintners:** Cabernet Sauvignon

- **Seven Hills******:** Merlot, Cabernet Sauvignon

- **Staton Hills Winery:** Cabernet Sauvignon, Merlot

- **Stewart Vineyards:** Gewürztraminer, Riesling (both Late Harvest)

- **Tefft Cellars:** Sangiovese

- **Washington Hills Cellars:** Cabernet Sauvignon, Merlot, Chardonnay, Sémillon, Riesling (Late Harvest), Gewürztraminer, Dry Chenin Blanc, Cabernet Franc ("Apex" is this winery's premium label; it also uses the "W. B. Bridgman" label)

- **Waterbrook Winery:** Cabernet Sauvignon, Merlot, Chardonnay (Cottonwood Creek Estate), Cabernet Franc, Sauvignon Blanc

- **Wineglass Cellars:** Cabernet Sauvignon, Merlot

- **Woodward Canyon Winery:** Chardonnay (especially Estate Reserve), Cabernet Sauvignon (especially Canoe Ridge Vineyard), Merlot, Charbonneau

**Seven Hills winery is actually just across the border in Oregon, but the vineyard is in Walla Walla Valley, Washington.

The Empire State

New York City may be the capital of the world in many ways, but its state's wines do not get the recognition they deserve, perhaps because of California's overwhelming presence in the U.S. market. The oldest continuously operating winery in the United States, Brotherhood Winery, opened its doors in New York's Hudson Valley in 1839. And the second largest wine company in the United States, Canandaigua Wine Company, has its headquarters in the Finger Lakes. In fact, New York is the second largest wine producing state in the U.S.

New York's most important region by far is the Finger Lakes in western New York, where four large lakes temper the otherwise cool climate. This AVA produces approximately 85 percent of New York's wines. The other two important regions are the Hudson Valley, along the Hudson River north of New York City, and Long Island, which has two AVAs — North Fork of Long Island (the more important) and the Hamptons, on the island's south fork.

In the early days (prior to 1960), most of New York's wines were made from local *Vitis labrusca* (see Chapter 4) and other native American varieties, such as Concord, Catawba, Delaware, and Niagara as well French-American hybrid grapes (see Chapter 4) such as Seyval Blanc, Baco Noir, and Maréchal Foch.

Common wisdom held that the relatively cold New York winters could not support *Vitis vinifera* varieties. But a Russian immigrant, the late, great Dr. Konstantin Frank, proved all the naysayers wrong when he succeeded in growing Riesling (followed by many other vinifera varieties) in 1953 in Hammondsport, part of the Finger Lakes region. (The first wines from vinifera grapes were actually made in 1961 at his winery, Dr. Frank's Vinifera Wine Cellars.) Today, his son Willy Frank runs one of the most successful wineries in the state, with an entire line of fine vinifera wines and an excellent sparkling wine.

The Long Island story

This generation's wine success story in New York has taken place on Long Island. In 1973, Alec and Louisa Hargrave got the idea that Long Island's North Fork (about a two-hour drive east of New York City) had the ideal climate and soil for vinifera grapes. Today, Long Island is 24 wineries strong and growing! Like Washington state, Long Island seems particularly suited to Merlot, but Chardonnay, Riesling, Cabernet Sauvignon, Cabernet Franc and Sauvignon Blanc are also grown, plus some Gewürztraminer and Pinot Noir.

Who's who in New York

The New York wine industry has grown from 19 wineries in 1976 to well over 100 today — half of them in the Finger Lakes region and most of them small, family-run operations. The following is a list of recommended producers in New York's three major wine regions, listed alphabetically.

The Finger Lakes Region

Anthony Road Wine Company
Casa Larga Vineyards
Dr. Frank's Vinifera Wine Cellars
(and its affiliate, Chateau
 Frank, for sparkling wines)
Fox Run Vineyards
Glenora Wine Cellars (espe-
cially for sparkling wines)
Hazlitt 1852 Vineyards
Heron Hill Vineyards
Hunt Country Vineyards
King Ferry Winery
Knapp Vineyards
Lakewood Vineyards
Lamoreaux Landing Wine Cellars
Lucas Vineyards
McGregor Vineyard Winery
Prejean Winery
Standing Stone Vineyards
Swedish Hill Vineyard
Wagner Vineyards
Widmer's Wine Cellars
Hermann J. Wiemer Vineyard

Hudson River Valley Region

Adair Vineyards
Baldwin Vineyards
Benmarl Vineyard
Brotherhood America's Oldest
Winery, Ltd.
Cascade Mountain Vineyards
Clinton Vineyards
Magnanini Winery
Millbrook Vineyards
Rivendell Winery

Long Island Region

Bedell Cellars
Gristina Vineyards
Hargrave Vineyard
Jamesport Vineyards
Lenz Winery
Palmer Vineyards
Paumanok Vineyards, Ltd.
Peconic Bay Vineyards
Pelligrini Vineyards
Pindar Vineyards
Sagpond Vineyards (South Fork)

Oh, Canada

Ask just about any wine lover in the U.S. about Canadian wines, and you'll probably get a blank stare in response. Canada's wines are known mainly to Canadians, who consume the bulk of their country's production.

Wine is made in four of Canada's provinces, but Ontario has bragging rights as the largest producer by far, with 80 percent of the national production. British Columbia ranks second. Quebec and Nova Scotia also produce wine.

To identify and promote wines made entirely from local grapes (some Canadian wineries import wines from other countries to blend with local production), the provinces of Ontario and British Columbia have established an appellation system called VQA, Vintners' Quality Alliance. This system regulates the use of provincial names on wine labels, establishes which grape varieties can be used (*vinifera* varieties and certain hybrids), regulates the use of the terms *icewine, late harvest,* and *botrytised* (see the "Germany" section in Chapter 12 for an explanation of these terms), and requires wines to pass a taste test.

Ontario

Ontario's vineyards are cool-climate wine zones, despite the fact that they lie on the same parallel as Chianti Classico and Rioja, warmer European wine regions discussed in Chapters 11 and 12. Sixty percent of the production is white wine, from Chardonnay, Riesling, Gewürztraminer, Pinot Blanc, Auxerrois, and the hybrids Seyval Blanc and Vidal. Red wines come from Pinot Noir, Gamay, Cabernet Sauvignon, Cabernet Franc, Merlot, and the hybrids Maréchal Foch and Baco Noir.

Ontario's VQA rules permit the use of the appellation Ontario and also recognize three *Designated Viticultural Areas* (DVAs):

- ✔ **Niagara Peninsula:** Along the south shore of Lake Ontario
- ✔ **Pelee Island:** Eleven miles south of the Canadian mainland, in Lake Erie, Canada's most southerly vineyards
- ✔ **Lake Erie North Shore:** The sunniest of Canada's viticultural areas

Because winter temperatures regularly drop well below freezing, Icewine is a specialty of Ontario, one that is gradually earning the Canadian wine industry a modicum of international attention.

British Columbia

The small but rapidly growing wine industry of British Columbia now boasts 33 wineries. Production is about 84 percent white — from Auxerrois, Bacchus, Chardonnay, Ehrenfelser, Gewürztraminer, Pinot Gris, and Riesling — and 15 percent red, from Pinot Noir and Merlot. Bacchus and Ehrenfelser are vinifera crossings developed in Germany.

The Okanagan Valley in southeast British Columbia, where the climate is influenced by Lake Okanagan, is the center of wine production. VQA rules recognize four Designated Viticultural Areas:

- ✔ **Okanagan Valley**
- ✔ **Similkameen Valley**
- ✔ **Fraser Valley**
- ✔ **Vancouver Island**

Chapter 15

Bubbling Beauties

*I*n the universe of wine, sparkling wines are a solar system unto themselves. Sparkling wines are produced in just about every country that makes wine, and they come in a wide range of flavors, quality levels, and prices. Champagne, the sparkling wine from the Champagne region of France, is the brightest star in the sky, but by no means the only one.

Sparkling wines are distinguished (and distinguishable) from other wines by the presence of bubbles — *carbon dioxide* — in the wine. In the eyes of most governments, these bubbles must occur as a natural result of fermentation in order for a wine to be officially considered a sparkling wine.

Sparkling wines are made all over the wine world. But in a few places, sparkling wines are major business, not just another style of wine to give a winery's portfolio a bit of diversity.

At the top of that list is France's Champagne region (where sparkling wine was — if not invented — certainly made famous). Italy's Asti wine zone is another important region, as is the Loire Valley in France, northeastern Spain, and parts of California. We are now also seeing some interesting sparklers from Australia and South Africa.

The cool rule

Many sparkling wine regions are very cool areas, where grapes don't ripen sufficiently for *still* wine production. Vinified normally, the wines of these regions would be extremely high in acid, disagreeably tart, and very thin; the reds would lack color. But the elaborate process of sparkling wine production (the *traditional method* of production, described later in this chapter, as practiced in the Champagne region) turns the deficits of such grapes into virtues, and transforms the ugly duckling grapes into graceful swans.

All That Glitters Is Not Champagne

Champagne, the sparkling wine of Champagne, France, is the model for most sparkling wines for a number of reasons:

- ✔ Champagne is the most famous sparkling wine in the world; the name has immediate recognition for the general population, not just for wine drinkers.
- ✔ A particular technique for making sparkling wine was perfected in the Champagne region.
- ✔ The wines of Champagne are considered not only the finest sparkling wines in the world, but also among the finest wines in the world of any type.

For these reasons, the name *champagne* has been applied to all sorts of sparkling wines that don't come from the Champagne region. Wine producers who want to make their product more saleable name their wine champagne; most wine drinkers themselves use the word champagne indiscriminately to refer to all wines that have bubbles.

Ironically, most sparkling wine sold in the U.S. that's called champagne is not even made using the same techniques as true Champagne. Most imitation Champagnes are made by a technique that takes only a few months from beginning to end (compared to a few years to make Champagne), costs less to the producer, and works more effectively on an industrial scale.

Within the European Union, only the wines of the Champagne region in France can use the name Champagne.

Whenever we use the word Champagne, we'll be referring to true Champagne, from the region of the same name; we'll use the generic term *sparkling wine* to refer to bubbly wines collectively, as well as for sparkling wines other than Champagne.

Sparkling Wine Styles

All sparkling wines have bubbles and nearly all of them are either white or pink (far less common than white). That's about as far as broad generalizations will take us in describing sparkling wines.

Some sparkling wines are downright sweet, some are bone dry, and many fall somewhere in the middle, from medium-dry to medium-sweet. Some have toasty, nutty flavors and some are fruity; among those that are fruity, some are just nondescriptly grapey, while others have delicate nuances of lemons, apples, cherries, berries, peaches, and other fruits.

The sparkling wines of the world fall into two broad types, according to how they're made:

- ✔ Wines that express the character of their grapes; these wines tend to be fruity and straightforward, without layers of complexity.
- ✔ Wines that express complexity and flavors (yeasty, biscuity, caramel-like, honeyed) that derive from winemaking and aging, rather than expressing direct fruitiness.

Each of these styles corresponds to a particular method of making sparkling wine, described in the section, "How Sparkling Wine Happens," later in this chapter.

How sweet is it?

Nearly all sparkling wines are not completely dry in the sense that they contain measurable amounts of residual sugar, usually as the result of sweetening added at the last stage of production. But all sparkling wines don't necessarily taste sweet. The perception of sweetness depends on two factors: the actual amount of sweetness in the wine (which varies according to the wine's style) and the wine's balance between acidity and sweetness.

Here's how the balance factor operates. Sparkling wines are usually very high in acidity, because the grapes weren't particularly ripe at harvest (having grown in a cool climate). The wine's carbon dioxide compounds the acidic impression in the mouth. But the wine's sweetness counterbalances its acidity and vice versa. Depending on the particular acid/sugar balance a sparkling wine strikes, the wine might taste dry, very slightly sweet, medium sweet, or quite sweet.

Champagne itself is made in a range of sweetness levels, the most common of which is a dry style called *brut* (see "Sweetness categories" later in this chapter). Sparkling wines made by the *traditional method* used in Champagne (see "How Sparkling Wine Happens" later in this chapter) are made in the same range of styles as Champagne.

Inexpensive sparkling wines tend to be medium sweet in order to appeal to a mass market that enjoys sweetness. Wines labeled with the Italian word *spumante* tend to be overtly sweet. (See the section on Italian Spumante later in this chapter.)

How good is it?

When you taste a sparkling wine, the most important consideration is whether you like it — just as for a still wine. If you want to evaluate a sparkling wine the way professionals do, however, you have to apply a few criteria that don't apply to still wines (or are less critical in still wines than in sparkling wines). Some of those criteria are

✔ **The visual appearance of the bubbles.** In the best sparkling wines, the bubbles are tiny and float upward in a continuous stream from the bottom of your glass. If the bubbles are large and random, you have a clue that the wine is a lesser-quality sparkler. If you don't see many bubbles at all, you could have a bad bottle, or the wine could be too old.

Tiny variations in glassware can drastically affect the flow of bubbles, though — even if the two glasses appear identical. If the wine in your glass looks almost flat, but another glass from the same bottle is lively with bubbles, blame the glass and not the wine. (In this case, you should be able to *taste* the bubbles, even if you can't *see* many of them.) See Chapter 8 for our recommendations about glasses for Champagne and other sparkling wines.

✔ **The feel of the bubbles in your mouth.** The finer the wine, the less aggressive the bubbles feel in your mouth. (If the bubbles remind you of a soft drink, we hope you didn't pay more than $5 for the wine.)

✔ **The balance between sweetness and acidity.** Even if you decide that a wine is too sweet or too dry for your particular taste, you should consider its sweetness/acid balance and decide whether these two elements seem reasonably balanced.

✔ **The texture.** Traditional-method sparkling wines should be somewhat creamy in texture as a result of their extended lees aging. (See the section, "How Sparkling Wine Happens" for an explanation of *traditional method* and *lees*.)

✔ **The finish.** Any impression of bitterness on the finish of a sparkling wine is a sign of low quality.

How Sparkling Wine Happens

When yeasts convert sugar into alcohol, carbon dioxide is a natural by-product. Wine becomes sparkling when fermentation takes place in a closed container and the carbon dioxide created by the yeasts cannot escape into the air. With nowhere else to go, the carbon dioxide (CO_2) becomes trapped in the wine in the form of bubbles.

Most sparkling wines actually go through *two* fermentations: one to turn the grape juice into still wine (without bubbles) and a subsequent one to turn the still wine into bubbly wine (conveniently called the *second fermentation*). The winemaker has to instigate the second fermentation by adding yeasts and sugar to the base wine. The added yeasts convert the added sugar into alcohol and CO_2 bubbles.

Methods of trapping the CO_2 vary — and with them, the style and quality of the wine. Basically, the longer and slower the winemaking process, the more complex and expensive the sparkling wine will be. Some sparkling wines are ten years in the making; others are produced in only a few months. The former can cost more than $100 a bottle, while bubblies at the opposite end of the spectrum can sell for as little as $3.

Although you find many variations on the theme, most sparkling wines are produced in one of two ways: through *second fermentation in a tank,* or through *second fermentation in a bottle.*

Economy of scale

The quickest, most efficient way of making a sparkling wine involves conducting the second fermentation in large, closed, pressurized tanks. This method is called the *bulk method, tank method, cuve close* (meaning *closed tank* in French), or *charmat method,* after a Frenchman named Eugene Charmat, who championed this process.

Sparkling wines that are made in the charmat (pronounced *shar mah*) method are usually the least expensive because they are ready for sale soon after harvest and are usually made in large quantities. Also, the grapes used in making sparkling wine by the charmat method (Chenin Blanc, for example) are usually *far* less expensive than the Pinot Noir and Chardonnay typically used in the *traditional* or *champagne method* described in the next section.

The following occurs in the charmat method:

✔ A base wine is *seeded* with sugar and yeast and ferments. The carbon dioxide created by the fermentation becomes trapped in the wine, thanks to the closed tank, the pressure within the tank, and the cold temperature.

✔ The wine — now a dry sparkling wine with higher alcohol than the base wine had — is filtered (under pressure) to remove the solid deposits (the *lees*) from the second fermentation.

✔ Before bottling, some sweetness is added to adjust the wine's flavor, according to the desired style of the final wine.

The whole process can take just a few weeks. In some exceptional cases, it might be extended to a few months, allowing the wine to rest between the fermentation and the filtration.

Small is beautiful

The charmat method is a fairly new method of producing sparkling wines, dating back less than 100 years. The more traditional method is that of conducting the second fermentation in the individual bottles in which the wine is later sold.

Champagne has been made in this way for approximately 300 years and, according to French law, can be made in no other way. Many other French sparkling wines are made in the same way, as are the best sparkling wines from Spain, California, and other countries.

The technique of conducting the second fermentation in the bottle is called the *classic* or *traditional method* in Europe; in the U.S., it's called the *champagne method* or *méthode champenoise*.

Bottle fermentation (or, more correctly, second fermentation in the bottle) is an elaborate process in which every single bottle becomes an individual fermentation tank, so to speak. Including the aging time at the winery before the wine is sold, this process requires a minimum of fifteen months and usually takes three years or more. Invariably, sparkling wines made in this way are more expensive than those made by tank fermentation.

The elements of bottle fermentation are

✔ Each bottle is filled with a mixture of base wine and a sugar-and-yeast solution, closed securely, and laid to rest in a cool, dark cellar.

✔ Inside each bottle, the second fermentation occurs, producing carbon dioxide as well as fermentation lees inside the bottle.

✔ As the bottles continue to lie in the cellar, the wine gradually undergoes changes through interaction of the lees and the wine.

✔ Eventually — nine months to several years after the second fermentation — the bottles are put through a process of shaking and turning so that the solid lees fall to the neck of each upside-down bottle.

- The lees are flash-frozen in the neck of each bottle and expelled from each bottle as a frozen plug, leaving clear sparkling wine behind.

- A sweetening solution (called a *dosage*) is added to adjust the flavor of the wine, and the bottles are corked and labeled for sale.

The beauty of blending

Actually, the classic method as practiced in Champagne involves several steps that occur way before the second fermentation. For example, the pressing to extract the juice for the first fermentation must be conducted with meticulous care to prevent the grapeskins' bitter flavors — and their color, in the case of black grapes — from passing into the juice. Another step crucially important to the quality of the sparkling wine is the production of the base wine for the second fermentation.

Following the first fermentation, the wines of different grape varieties and different vineyards are kept separate. To create his base wine, or *cuvée,* the winemaker blends these separate wines in varying proportions, often adding some *reserve wine* (older wine purposely held back from previous vintages). From 100 to 200 different wines could go into a single base wine, each bringing its own special character to the blend. What's particularly tricky about blending the base wine — besides the sheer volume of components in the blend — is that the winemaker has to see into the future and create a blend *not* for its flavor today but for how it will taste in several years, after it has been transformed into a sparkling wine. The people who blend sparkling wines are true artists of the wine world.

Taste: The proof of the pudding

Tank-fermented sparklers tend to be fruitier than traditional-method sparkling wines. This difference occurs because in tank fermentation, the route from grape to wine is shorter and more direct than that of bottle fermentation. Some winemakers use the *charmat,* or tank, method because their goal is a fresh and fruity sparkling wine. Asti (formerly called Asti Spumante), Italy's most famous sparkling wine, is a perfect example. Charmat-method sparklers should be consumed young, when their fruitiness is at the max.

Sparkling wines produced through second fermentation in the bottle tend to be less overtly fruity than charmat-method wines. Chemical changes that take place as the wine develops on its fermentation lees diminish the fruitiness of the wine and contribute aromas and flavors such as toastiness, nuttiness, caramel, and yeastiness. The texture of the wine can also change as a result of prolonged aging on the lees, becoming smooth and creamy. The bubbles themselves tend to be tinier, and they feel less aggressive in your mouth than the bubbles of tank-fermented wines.

Champagne and Its Magic Wines

Champagne. Does any other word convey such a sense of celebration? Think of it: Anytime that anyone, in any country in the world, wants to celebrate, he or she says, "This calls for Champagne!" ("This calls for iced tea!" just isn't quite the same.)

Champagne, the real thing, comes only from the region of Champagne (*sham pahn yah*) in northeast France. Dom Pérignon, the famous monk who was cellar master at the Abbey of Hautvillers, didn't invent Champagne, but he did achieve a number of breakthroughs that are key to making Champagne as we now know it. He perfected the method of making white wine from black grapes, for example, and, most importantly, he mastered the art of blending wines from different grapes and different villages to achieve a complex base wine. (See the previous section to find out what base wine is.)

Champagne is the most northerly vineyard area in France. Most of the important Champagne *houses* (as Champagne producers are called) are located in the cathedral city of Rheims — where 17-year-old Joan of Arc had Prince Charles crowned King of France in 1429 — and in the town of Epernay, south of Rheims (French spelling, *Reims*). Around Rheims and Epernay are the main vineyard areas, where three permitted grape varieties (two black and one white) for Champagne flourish:

- The Montagne de Reims (south of Rheims), where the best Pinot Noir grows
- The Côte des Blancs (south of Epernay), home of the best Chardonnay
- The Valleé de la Marne (west of Epernay), most favorable to Pinot Meunier (a black grape) although all three grape varieties grow there

Most Champagne is made from all three grape varieties. Pinot Noir contributes body, structure, and longevity to the blend; Chardonnay offers delicacy, freshness, and elegance; and Pinot Meunier provides precocity, floral aromas, and fruitiness.

What makes Champagne special

The climate in Champagne is marginal for grape growing. With cold winters and warm (but not hot) summers, the grapes struggle to ripen sufficiently in some years. Even in warmer years, the climate dictates that the grapes will always be high in acidity (see "Worst case ripening scenarios" in Chapter 4) — a sorry state for table wine but perfect for sparkling wine.

The cool climate — combined with chalky, limestone soil — are the leading factors contributing to Champagne's excellence.

Three other elements help distinguish Champagne from all other sparkling wines:

- The number and diversity of vineyards (about 300 *crus,* or individual vineyards), which provide a huge range of individual wines for blending
- The cold, deep, chalky cellars (many built during Roman times) in which Champagnes age for many years
- The 300 years of experience the Champenois (as the good citizens of Champagne are called) have in making sparkling wine

The result is an elegant sparkling wine with myriad tiny, gentle bubbles, complexity of flavors, and a lengthy finish. Voilá! Champagne!

Nonvintage Champagne

Nonvintage (NV) Champagne — any Champagne without a vintage year on the label — accounts for 85 percent of all Champagne produced. The typical blend is two-thirds black grapes (Pinot Noir and Pinot Meunier) and one-third white (Chardonnay). Wine from three or more harvests usually goes into the blend. And remember, the wines from as many as 30 to 40 different villages from each year can also be part of the blend. The Champagne winemaker is by necessity a master blender.

Each Champagne house controls its own blend, thus creating its own house style for its nonvintage Champagne. (For example, one house may seek elegance and finesse in its wine, another might opt for fruitiness, and a third might value body, power, and longevity.) Maintaining a consistent house style is vital for Champagne producers because wine drinkers get accustomed to their favorite Champagne's style and expect to find that style in that nonvintage wine year after year.

Most major Champagne houses age their nonvintage Champagne for two and one-half to three years before selling it, even though the legal minimum for nonvintage is just 15 months. (Until the 1997 vintage, the minimum had been one year.) The extra aging prolongs the marrying time for the blend and enhances the wine's flavor and complexity. If you have good storage conditions (see Chapter 21), aging your nonvintage Champagne for a year or two after you purchase it will usually improve the flavor, in our opinion.

Most nonvintage Champagnes sell for $20 to $35 a bottle. Often, a large retailer will buy huge quantities of a few major brands, obtaining a good discount that he passes on to his customers. Seeking out stores that do a large-volume business with Champagne is worth your while.

Vintage Champagne

In four or five of every ten years, the weather in Champagne is good enough to make a vintage Champagne — that is, the grapes are ripe enough that some wine can be made entirely from the grapes of that year without being blended with reserve wines from previous years.

Champagne had exceptionally good weather in the 1980s; many houses made vintage Champagne every year from 1981 to 1990, with the exception of 1984 and 1987. The 1990s have been more typical, so far; three years, 1991, 1992, and 1994, are of unremarkable quality, while 1993, 1995, and especially 1996 are of vintage quality. The wines of the latter two vintages have not been released yet (as of 1998). The minimum aging requirement for vintage Champagne is three years, but many houses age their vintage Champagnes four to six years in order to enhance the wines' flavor and complexity.

Champagne houses decide for themselves each year whether to make a vintage Champagne. Factors such as the need to have enough reserve wines on hand for their nonvintage Champagnes (85 percent of their business, after all) and/or whether a particular vintage's style suits the "house style" of a particular Champagne house are taken into consideration when making the decision to produce a vintage-dated Champagne. For example, although 1989 was a rather good vintage, a few houses decided that Champagnes made from this vintage would be too soft (low in acidity) and/or too preco-cious (ready too soon, and lacking longevity) for them, and did not choose to make a vintage Champagne in 1989.

Vintage Champagnes fall into two categories:

- Regular vintage, with a price range of $35 to $50 a bottle; these wines simply carry a vintage date in addition to the name of the house; see "Recommended Champagne producers" later in this chapter

- Premium vintage (also known as a prestige cuvée or tête de cuvée), such as Moët & Chandon's Dom Pérignon, Roederer's Cristal, or Veuve Clicquot's La Grande Dame; the typical price for prestige cuvées ranges from $60 to well over $100 per bottle

Refrigerator blues

Don't leave your Champagne — or any other good sparkling wine — in your refrigerator for more than a few days! Its flavor will become flat from the excessively cold temperature; also vibrations of the refrigerator motor going on and off are not good for any wine — especially sparkling wine (see Chapter 21 for more on storing your wine properly).

Vintage Champagne is invariably superior to nonvintage for the following reasons:

- ✔ The best grapes from the choicest vineyards are put into vintage Champagne (this is *especially* so for prestige cuvées).

- ✔ Usually, only the two finest varieties (Pinot Noir and Chardonnay) are used in vintage Champagne. Pinot Meunier is saved for nonvintage Champagne.

- ✔ Most Champagne houses age vintage Champagnes at least two more years than the nonvintage style. The extra aging assures more complex flavors.

- ✔ The grapes all come from one year — an above average year at least, a superb one at best.

Vintage Champagne is more intense in flavor than nonvintage Champagne. It is more full-bodied, more complex, and its flavor lasts longer in your mouth. Being fuller and richer, these Champagnes are the ones to have with food. Nonvintage Champagnes — being lighter, fresher, and less complicated — are suitable as apéritifs, and they are good values. Whether a vintage Champagne is worth its extra cost or not is a judgment you have to make for yourself.

The 1990 vintage in Champagne (just as in most other wine regions in Europe) is super, and the 1988 is almost as good. Also good is 1989, yet not quite up to the 1988 or 1990. The 1986 vintage is inconsistent, but Pol Roger, Roederer, and Billecart-Salmon made fine vintage Champagnes in that year. The 1985 vintage is very good, especially for Bollinger, Dom Pérignon, Krug, and Laurent-Perrier. 1982 is a super vintage, if you can still find it; Krug and Dom Pérignon did especially well.

Blanc de blancs and blanc de noirs

A small number of Champagnes are made from just one of the three permitted grapes. That grape is Chardonnay, and that type of Champagne is called *blanc de blancs,* literally, white (wine) from white (grapes). A *blanc de blancs* can be a vintage Champagne or a nonvintage. It usually costs a few dollars more than other Champagnes in its category. Because they are lighter and more delicate than other Champagnes, *blanc de blancs* make ideal apéritifs. Not every Champagne house makes a *blanc de blancs*. Two of the best are Taittinger's Comte de Champagne and Billecart-Salmon's Blanc de Blancs.

Blanc de noirs Champagne (made from 100 percent black grapes, often just Pinot Noir) is rare but does exist. Bollinger's Blanc de Noirs *Vieilles Vignes Francaises* (old vines) is absolutely the best, but it is very expensive (about $200). The 1985 Bollinger Blanc de Noirs was one of the two best Champagnes we have ever had; the other was the 1928 Krug.

Who's drinking Champagne

Not surprisingly, France leads the world in Champagne consumption, drinking almost twice as much as the rest of the world put together. The UK and Germany are the leading export markets for Champagne. The U.S. is third, followed by Belgium, Switzerland, and Italy. But the U.S. buys the most prestige cuvée Champagne, especially Dom Pérignon.

Rosé Champagne

Rosé Champagnes — pink Champagnes — can also be vintage or nonvintage. Usually, only Pinot Noir and Chardonnay are used, in proportions that vary from one house to the next.

Rosés are made primarily by including some red Pinot Noir wine in the base wine blend, although a few houses actually vinify some of their red grapes into pink wines for rosé Champagne. Colors range from pale onion skin to salmon to rosy pink (the lighter-colored ones are usually better quality).

Rosés are fuller and rounder than other Champagnes and are best enjoyed with dinner. (Because they have become associated with romance, they're popular choices for wedding anniversaries and Valentine's Day.)

Like *blanc de blancs* Champagnes, rosés usually cost a few dollars more than regular Champagnes, and not every Champagne house makes one. Some of the best rosés are made by Roederer, Billecart-Salmon, Gosset, and Moët & Chandon (their Dom Pérignon Rosé).

For some people, rosé Champagne has a bad connotation because of the tons of sweet, insipid (inexpensive) pink wines — sparkling and otherwise — that are sold. But rosé Champagne is just as dry and has the same high quality as regular (white) Champagne.

Sweetness categories

Champagnes always carry an indication of their sweetness on the label, but the words used to indicate sweetness are cryptic: extra dry is not really dry, for example. In ascending order of sweetness, Champagnes are labeled

- **Extra Brut, Brut Nature,** or **Brut Sauvage:** Totally dry
- **Brut:** Dry
- **Extra Dry:** Medium dry
- **Sec:** Slightly sweet

✔ **Demi-Sec:** Fairly sweet

✔ **Doux:** Sweet

The most popular style of Champagne and other serious bubblies is brut. However, the single best-selling Champagne in the U.S., Moët & Chandon's White Star, actually is an extra dry Champagne. Brut, extra dry, and demi-sec are the three types of Champagne you find almost exclusively nowadays.

Recommended Champagne producers

The Champagne business — especially the export end of it — is dominated by about 25 or 30 large houses, most of whom purchase the majority of grapes they need to make their Champagne from independent growers. Of the major houses, only Roederer and Bollinger own most of the vineyards from which they get their grapes — a definite economic and quality-control advantage for them.

Moët & Chandon is by far the largest Champagne house. In terms of world-wide sales, the next-largest houses are, Veuve Clicquot, Mumm, Vranken, Laurent-Perrier, Pommery, and Lanson. The following lists name some of our favorite producers in rough order of preference, grouped according to the style of their Champagne: light-bodied, medium-bodied, or full-bodied. (For an understanding of the term, *body*, as it applies to wine, see Chapter 2.)

✔ **Light, elegant styles**

Laurent-Perrier	Bruno Paillard*
Taittinger	Perrier-Jouët
Ruinart	J. Lassalle*
Jacquesson*	de Castellane

✔ **Medium-bodied styles**

Charles Heidsieck	Deutz
Pommery	Cattier*
Pol Roger	Selosse*
Moët & Chandon	Jacques
Philipponnat	Piper-Heidsieck
Mumm	Joseph Perrier

✔ **Full-bodied styles**

Krug	Alfred Gratien*
Louis Roederer	Delamotte
Bollinger	Monopole
Gosset	Heidsieck
Veuve Clicquot	Henriot
Salon*	Paul Bara*

* Small producer; may be difficult to find.

Madame Lily Bollinger's advice on drinking Champagne

When Jacques Bollinger died in 1941, his widow, Lily Bollinger, carried her famous Champagne house through the difficult years of the German occupation of France. She ran the company until her death in 1977. Bollinger prospered under her leadership, doubling in size. She was a beloved figure in Champagne, where she could be seen bicycling through the vineyards every day. In 1961, when a London reporter asked her when she drank Champagne, Madame Bollinger replied:

"I only drink Champagne when I'm happy, and when I'm sad. Sometimes I drink it when I'm alone. When I have company I consider it obligatory. I trifle with it if I am not hungry and drink it when I am. Otherwise I never touch it — unless I'm thirsty."

The redoubtable Madame Lily Bollinger died at the age of 78, apparently none the worse for all that Champagne.

The following list names, in rough order of preference, Champagne houses whose vintage and prestige cuvées have been in top form lately, and their particularly fine vintages. (If you're going to lay out big bucks for a top-of-the-line Champagne, you might as well go for the best!)

- ✔ **Krug:** Vintage (1982, 1985, 1988); NV Rosé; Clos du Mesnil (1985)
- ✔ **Louis Roederer:** Cristal (1990, 1988, 1986, 1985)
- ✔ **Bollinger:** Vintage (1988, 1985); Blanc de Noirs Vieilles Vignes (1985, 1989)
- ✔ **Moët & Chandon:** Dom Pérignon (1990, 1988, 1985, 1982)
- ✔ **Veuve Clicquot:** La Grande Dame (1988, 1985, 1983, 1989)
- ✔ **Pommery:** Cuvée Louise (1988); Cuvée Louise Rosé (1990, 1989)
- ✔ **Gosset:** Celebris (1988); Grand Millesime (1985, 1989); Rosé (1990)
- ✔ **Philipponnat:** Clos des Goisses (1988, 1985, 1982)
- ✔ **Heidsieck Monopole:** Diamant Bleu and Rosé (1985, 1988)
- ✔ **Pol Roger:** Cuvée Sir Winston Churchill (1986, 1985)
- ✔ **Salon:** Vintage (1982, 1979)
- ✔ **Taittinger:** Comtes de Champagne (1990, 1989); Rosé (1985, 1993)
- ✔ **Billecart-Salmon:** Blanc de Blancs (1988, 1986, 1985, 1989); Cuvée Elisabeth Salmon Rosé (1990, 1989)
- ✔ **Laurent-Perrier:** Grand Siècle (1988, 1985)

- **Cattier:** Clos du Moulin (a nonvintage)
- **Jacquesson:** Signature (1985, 1988); Signature Rosé (1990, 1989)
- **Deutz:** Cuvée William Deutz (1985, 1988); Rosé (1985)
- **Perrier-Jouët:** Fleur de Champagne (1989, 1988); Rosé (1988, 1985)
- **Ruinart:** Dom Ruinart Blanc de Blancs (1988)
- **Charles Heidsieck:** Blanc des Millenaires (1985, 1983)
- **Piper-Heidsieck:** Champagne Rare (1985, 1988)

Other Sparkling Wines

Wineries all over the world have adopted the techniques used in the Champagne region to make sparkling wines that emulate Champagne. These wines differ from Champagne, however, because their grapes are not grown in the ideal conditions of the Champagne region or, in some cases, because their grapes are not even the same varieties as those used in Champagne. And some sparkling wines are made using the tank fermentation rather than the bottle fermentation method specifically to attain a certain style.

French sparkling wine

France makes many other sparkling wines besides Champagne, especially in the Loire Valley, around Saumur, and in the regions of Alsace and Burgundy. When sparkling wine is made by the traditional method (second fermentation in the bottle), it is often called *Crémant,* as in Crémant d'Alsace, Crémant de Loire, Crémant de Bourgogne, and so on. Grape varieties are those typical of each region.

Some of the leading brands of French sparkling wines are Bouvet Ladubay, Brut d'Argent, Gratien & Meyer, Kriter, Saint Hilaire, and Veuve du Vernay. These wines sell in the $9 to $12 price range and are of decent quality. They are perfect for parties and other large gatherings, when you might want to serve a French bubbly without paying a Champagne price. But remember, you can often find true nonvintage Champagnes on sale for less than $20 in large discount wine stores and supermarkets.

American sparkling wine

U.S. sparkling wine is made in almost as many states as still wine is, but the two states most famous for it are California and New York. Two fine examples of New York State sparkling wines made in the traditional method are Chateau Frank, about $18, and Fox Run, in the $14 range.

In California, sparkling wines made by wineries owned by Champagne houses have been particularly successful.

California bubbly is definitely a different wine from Champagne, even when made by a Champagne house using the same methods as in Champagne and the same grape varieties. (It tastes fruitier.) Good California sparkling wines, the ones made in the traditional Champagne method, can be purchased for as low as $10 on up to $30 and more.

Most of California's finest sparkling wines do not call themselves Champagne, but the less-expensive, best-selling ones do. Among the best-selling inexpensive sparkling wines in the U.S. that use the name Champagne, Korbel, at about $10, is the only one that is actually fermented in the bottle.

We recommend the following California sparkling wine producers, listed in our rough order of preference within each category:

U.S.-owned

- ✔ **Iron Horse:** In Green Valley, the coolest part of Sonoma (temperature, that is), Iron Horse is clearly making some of California's finest sparkling wine. Look for its better cuvées, such as the Wedding Cuvée, Russian Cuvée, and Vrai Amis, for about $25. Iron Horse's top-of-the-line sparklers, the Late Disgorged Blanc de Blancs and Late Disgorged Brut, are truly superb, comparable in quality to a fine Champagne; they are $40 or more.

- ✔ **J:** Not content with making some of America's most popular Cabernet Sauvignons and Chardonnays, the Jordan winery in Sonoma now also makes one of the best sparkling wines in the country. And the wine keeps getting better each year. Now, almost all of its grapes are coming from the cool Russian River Valley. Quite fruity and fairly delicate, the wine comes in a knockout bottle, and sells in the $25 to $30 price range.

- ✔ **S. Anderson:** In Napa Valley, S. Anderson continues to produce one of the finest lines of sparkling wines in the U.S. for about $20 to $22; look especially for its Blanc de Noirs.

- ✔ **Handley Cellars:** Up in Anderson Valley in Mendocino County, Milla Handley is making some excellent, quite dry sparkling wines; her Rosé Brut is a beauty, at about $15.

French- or Spanish-owned

- ✔ **Roederer Estate:** Louis Roederer is such a fine Champagne house that we're not surprised that its Anderson Valley winery, near the town of Mendocino, has become a smashing success. Some critics think it's California's best. Wines include a good-value Brut ($18), a delicate rosé ($21) that's worth the search, and an outstanding premium cuvée, L'Ermitage ($35).

- **Mumm Cuvée Napa:** Mumm has established itself as one of California's best sparkling wine houses. Much of its production comes from the cool Carneros District; look especially for the Winery Lake Brut and the cherry-like Blanc de Noirs. The price range is $16 to $21; the winery's premium cuvée, about $33, is called DVX, and is especially fine.

- **Domaine Carneros:** Taittinger's California winery makes an elegant, quality brut in cool Carneros, with a price range of $20 to $22. Its new premium cuvée, Le Rêve, a $30 blanc de blancs, is worth seeking out.

- **Domaine Chandon:** This winery, in the Napa Valley, part of the Moët & Chandon empire, is a must-stop for its restaurant alone. Winemaker Dawnine Dyer continues to make solid, consistent sparkling wines at reasonable prices ($15 to $18). Look especially for Chandon's longer aged Réserve Cuvées at around $24. Chandon's premium wine, Etoile ($28 to $30), deserves to be better known: It is one of the most elegant sparkling wines in the U.S.; also look for Chandon's new Etoile Rosé.

- **Gloria Ferrer:** Spain's Freixenet company has built a beautiful winery in windswept Carneros. Its wines are priced right ($15 to $17 for their least expensive) and are widely available. The winery is definitely worth a visit.

- **Codorniú Napa:** This Spanish-owned winery located in Carneros has made some impressive, good-value ($15 to $17) sparklers.

Spanish sparkling wines (Cava)

What if you want to spend less than $10 for a sparkling wine? The answer is Spain's sparkling wine, Cava, almost all of which is produced in Penedés, near Barcelona. Many of these wines sell for $8 to $10 a bottle.

Cava is made in the traditional method, fermented in the bottle. But most Cavas use local Spanish grapes. As a result, they taste distinctly different (a nicely earthy, mushroomy, rubbery flavor) from California bubblies and from Champagne. Some of the more expensive cuvées do contain Chardonnay.

Two gigantic wineries dominate Cava production — Freixenet (pronounced *fresh net*) and Codorniu. Freixenet's frosted black Cordon Negro bottle has to be one of the most recognizable bottles in the world. Other Cava brands to look for are Mont Marçal, Paul Cheneau, and Segura Viudas. Juve y Camps, a vintage-dated, upscale version of Cava, is a worthwhile buy at $15.

German sparkling wines (Sekt)

Germany makes an enormous amount of sparkling wine (called Sekt), most of which is consumed in Germany. The charmat (tank) method is used; the style of the wine is fresh and fruity. The grapes are the Riesling (for the better wines) and Müller-Thurgau.

Two of the largest brands, which are widely available, are Henkell Trocken, priced at around $16, and Deinhard Brut, at $8 to $10.

Italian spumante: Dry and sweet

Spumante is simply the Italian word for "sparkling," but it has come to refer to sweet, fruity spin-offs of Italy's classic Asti Spumante.

 The real Asti (producers have now dropped the second word, to avoid confusion with other spumante wines) is a delicious, exuberantly fruity sparkling wine made in the Piedmont region from Moscato grapes, via the tank method. It's one bubbly that you can drink with dessert (fantastic with wedding cake!). Because freshness is essential in Asti, buy a good brand that sells well. (Asti is a nonvintage wine, so there's no other way to determine how old the wine is.) We recommend Fontanafredda, Martini & Rossi, Cinzano, and Gancia (all priced around $10 to $12).

 For Asti flavor with fewer bubbles, try Moscato d'Asti, a delicate and delicious medium-dry wine that can be served as a refreshing apéritif as well as with dessert. It's also a great brunch wine. And it has less than 7 percent alcohol! Vietti makes a good one, called Cascinetta, for about $12. Again, freshness is essential. With Moscato d'Asti, let the vintage date guide you; buy the youngest one you can find.

 Using the traditional method, Italy produces a good deal of dry sparkling wine in the Oltrepò-Pavese and Franciacorta wine zones of Lombardy, as well as in Trentino. Italy's dry sparkling wines are very dry with little or no sweetening dosage. They come in all price ranges, from the affordable Castello Gancia at about $12, to the medium-priced Ferrari Brut, Berlucchi Cuvée Imperiale Brut, and Banfi Brut (all $15 to $18), to four upscale (and very good) bruts, all in the $35 price range: Bellavista, Cà del Bosco, Giulio Ferrari, and Bruno Giacosa Extra Brut. Giacosa, well known for his outstanding Barbarescos and Barolos, makes his 100 percent Pinot Noir Brut in his spare time, for kicks. Like everything else he produces, it's superb.

Southern stars

Australia and South Africa have begun to make some very fine sparkling wines in the traditional method during the last decade. Australia, especially, with its advanced winemaking technology, is now producing a number of fine bubblies. Look for Moët & Chandon's Green Point Brut, a dry, complex stunner at about $25; another superb sparkler comes from the excellent Mountadam Winery (a blend of Pinot Noir and Chardonnay) for about $35. If you're looking for a really good $10 sparkling wine, try the Seaview Brut.

The South African sparkling wine that has really impressed us comes from Cabrière Estate in the Franschhoek Valley, and is sold under the Pierre Jourdan brand. The nonvintage Pierre Jourdan Brut is a real bargain at $15. Better yet is Pierre Jourdan Vintage Brut, Vintage Blanc de Blancs (100 percent Chardonnay), and especially Pierre Jourdan Cuvée Belle Rose, a 100 percent Pinot Noir vintage-dated sparkler that sells for $23 to $24.

Serving Champagne and Sparkling Wines

Sparkling wine is at its best when it is cold, about 45°F (7° to 8°C), although some people prefer it less cold (52°F; 11°C). We like the colder temperature because the wine holds its effervescence better when cold, and the wine warms up so quickly in the glass, anyway. Older Champagnes and vintage Champagnes, being more complex, can be chilled less than young, nonvintage Champagne or sparkling wine.

Never leave an open bottle of sparkling wine on the table unless it's in an ice bucket (half cold water, half ice) because it will warm up quickly. Use a sparkling wine stopper to keep leftover bubbly fresh for a couple of days (in the fridge, of course).

If you're entertaining, you should know that the ideal bottle size for Champagne is the *magnum,* which is equivalent to two bottles. The wine ages more gently in the larger bottle. Magnums (and sometimes double magnums) are usually the largest bottles in which Champagne is fermented. All the other larger bottles have Champagne poured into them, and the wine is not as fresh as it is in a magnum or a regular bottle.

Avoid half-bottles (375 ml) and — worse yet — splits (187 ml)! Champagne in these small bottles is often not too fresh. (If you're given a small bottle of Champagne or any sparkling wine as a wedding favor, for example, open it at the first excuse; do not keep it around for a year waiting for the right occasion!)

Champagne and other good, dry sparkling wines are extremely versatile with food — and they are the essential wine for certain kinds of foods. For example, no wine goes better with egg dishes than Champagne. Indulge yourself next time that you have brunch. And the next time you're having spicy Asian cuisine, try sparkling wine. For us, no wine goes better with spicy Chinese or Indian food!

Turkey is excellent with sparkling wine. If you're having lamb (pink, not well done) or ham, pair rosé Champagne with it. For aged Champagne, chunks of aged Asiago, aged Gouda, or Parmesan cheese go extremely well.

Do not serve a dry Brut (or Extra-Dry) sparkling wine with dessert. These styles are just too dry and won't taste good with dessert. With fresh fruit, try a demi-sec Champagne. With sweeter desserts (or wedding cake!), we recommend Asti.

Ten excuses to drink Champagne (or another good sparkling wine)

1. You have a bottle on hand.

2. Your boss just left for vacation, or better yet, changed jobs.

3. The noisy neighbors next door finally moved out.

4. You finished your income taxes.

5. It's Saturday.

6. The kids left for summer camp.

7. You just found $20 in your old coat pocket.

8. You didn't get a single telephone solicitation all day.

9. The wire muzzle over the cork makes a great cat toy.

10. You have just finished revising a wine book!

Chapter 16

Wine Roads Less Traveled: Fortified and Dessert Wines

In This Chapter

▶ The world's most versatile wine

▶ 80 grapes for one wine

▶ A wine that lasts 200 years

▶ Liquid gold from rotted grapes

*T*he wines we lump together as *fortified wines* and *dessert wines* aren't mainstream beverages that you want to drink every day. Some of them are much higher in alcohol than regular wines, and some of them are extremely sweet (and rare and expensive!). They're the wine equivalent of really good candy — delicious enough that you could get carried away if you let yourself indulge daily. So you treat them as treats, a glass before or after dinner, a bottle when company comes, a splurge to celebrate the start of your diet — tomorrow.

Pleasure aside, you owe it to yourself to try these wines from a purely academic point of view. Seriously! Learning about wine is hard work, but somebody's got to do it.

Timing Is Everything

Many wines enjoyed before dinner, as apéritif wines, or after dinner, as dessert wines, fall into the category of *fortified wines* (called *liqueur wines* by the European Union, or EU; see Chapter 8 for an explanation of EU terms). Fortified wines all have alcohol added to them at some point in their production, giving them an alcohol content that ranges from 16 to 24 percent.

The point at which alcohol is added determines whether the wines are naturally sweet or dry. When fortified with alcohol *during* fermentation, the wines are sweet, because the added alcohol stops fermentation, leaving natural, unfermented sugar in the wine (see Chapter 1 for an explanation of fermentation). When fortified *after* fermentation (after all the grape sugar has been converted to alcohol), the wines are dry (unless they are subsequently sweetened).

Some of the wines we call dessert wines don't have added alcohol. Their sweetness occurs because the grapes are at the right place at the right time when noble rot strikes (see the discussion of German wines in Chapter 12). Other dessert wines are sweet because winemakers pick very ripe (but not rotten) grapes and dry them before fermentation to concentrate their juice, which is another method of turning grape juice into the nectar of the gods.

Sherry: The World's Most Misunderstood Wine

The comedian Rodney Dangerfield built a career around the line, "I get no respect!" His wine of choice should be Sherry, because it shares the same plight. We avoided Sherry like the plague until we found out how good it can be. We thought it was just a sweet, cheap wine that our elderly aunts and the British fancied. Now we realize that the British (and our elderly aunts) were on to something: Sherry is a wine of true quality and diversity; but it remains undiscovered by most of the world. In a way, we're not sorry, because the price of good Sherry is attractively low.

The Jerez triangle

Sherry is produced in the Andalucía region of sun-baked southwestern Spain. The wine is named after Jerez *(her ETH)* de la Frontera, an old town of Moorish and Arab origin where many of the Sherry *bodegas* are located. (*Bodega* can refer to the actual building in which Sherry is matured or to the Sherry firm itself.)

Actually, the town of Jerez is just one corner of a triangle that makes up the Sherry region. Puerto de Santa María, a beautiful, old coast town southwest of Jerez, and home to a number of large bodegas, is another corner. The third corner of the triangle, Sanlúcar de Barrameda (also on the coast but northwest of Jerez), is so famous for its sea breezes that the lightest and driest of Sherries, *Manzanilla,* can legally be made only there. Aficionados of Sherry swear that they can detect the salty tang of the ocean in Manzanilla *(mahn zah NEE yah).*

Traveling from Sanlúcar to Jerez, you pass vineyards with dazzling white soil. This soil is *albariza,* the region's famous chalky earth, rich in limestone from fossilized shells. Summers are hot and dry, but balmy sea breezes temper the heat.

The Palomino grape — the main variety used in Sherry — thrives only here in the hot Sherry region on *albariza* soil. Palomino is a complete failure for table wines because it makes neutral, low-acid wine, but it's perfect for Sherry production. Two other authorized grape varieties, the Pedro Ximénez *(PAY dro he MAIN ehz)* and the Moscatel (Muscat), are also used for dessert types of Sherry.

The phenomenon of the flor

All Sherry is fortified with alcohol after fermentation, but from that point the diversity begins. Sherry consists of two basic types: *fino* (light, very dry) and *oloroso* (rich and full, but also dry). Sweet Sherries are made by sweetening either type.

After fermentation, the winemaker decides which Sherries will become *finos* or *olorosos (oh loh ROH sohs)* by judging the appearance, aroma, and flavor of the young, unfortified wines. If a wine is to be a *fino,* the winemaker fortifies it lightly (until its alcohol level reaches about 15.5 percent). He strengthens future *olorosos* to 18 percent alcohol.

At this point, the special Sherry magic begins: A yeast called *flor* grows spontaneously on the surface of the wines destined to be *finos.* The flor eventually covers the surface of the wine, preventing the wine from oxidizing. The flor feeds on oxygen from the air and on alcohol and glycerin in the wine. As it lives on the wine, the flor changes the wine's character, contributing a distinct aroma and flavor and rendering the wine thinner and more delicate.

Flor doesn't grow on wines destined to become *olorosos* because of their higher alcohol content. Without the protection of the flor (and because the barrels are never filled to the brim) these wines are exposed to oxygen as they age.

Communal aging

Both the *fino* and *oloroso* types of Sherry age in a special way that is unique to Sherry making.

The young wine is not left to age on its own (as most other wines would) but is added to casks of older wine that are already maturing. To make room for the young wine, some of the older wine is emptied out of the casks and is added to casks of even older wine. To make room in those casks, some of the wine is transferred to casks of even older wine, and so on. At the end of this chain, four to nine generations away from the young wine, finished Sherry is taken from the oldest casks and is bottled for sale.

This system of blending wines is called the *solera* system. It takes its name from the word *solera* (floor), the term also used to identify the casks of oldest wine. Earlier generations of aging wine are referred to as *criaderas,* suggesting that the wine is still in nursery school.

As wines are blended — younger into older, into yet-older, and eventually into oldest — each cask is emptied less than halfway to make room for the younger wine. In theory, then, each solera contains small (and ever-decreasing) amounts of very old wine. As each wine mingles with older wine, it takes on the characteristics of the older wine; within a few months, the wine of each generation is totally indistinguishable from what it was before being refreshed with younger wine. Thus, the solera system maintains infinite consistency of quality and style in Sherry.

Because the casks of Sherry age in dry, airy bodegas above ground (rather than humid, underground cellars like most other wines), some of the wine's water content evaporates, and the wine's alcoholic strength increases. Some *olorosos* kept for more than ten years can have as much as 24 percent alcohol, compared to their starting point of 18 percent.

Two makes twelve

So far, so good: two types of Sherry — delicate *fino* aged under its protective flor, and fuller *oloroso,* aged oxidatively — and no vintages. But now Sherry begins to get a bit confusing. Those two types are about to branch into at least twelve. Sometimes the natural course of aging changes the character of a Sherry so that its taste no longer conforms to one of the two categories. Deliberate sweetening of the wine also creates different styles.

Among dry Sherries, these are the main styles:

- **Fino:** Pale, straw-colored Sherry, light in body, dry, and delicate. Fino Sherries are always matured under flor, either in Jerez or Puerto de Santa María. They have 15.5 to 17 percent alcohol. Once they lose their protective flor (by bottling), *finos* become very vulnerable to oxidation spoilage, and must therefore be stored in a cool place, drunk young, and refrigerated after opening. They're best served chilled.

- **Manzanilla:** Pale, straw-colored, delicate, light, tangy, and very dry *fino*-style Sherry made only in Sanlucar de Barrameda. (Although various styles of Manzanilla are produced, *Manzanilla Fina,* the *fino* style, is by far the most common.) The temperate sea climate causes the flor to grow thicker in this town, and Manzanilla is thus the driest and most pungent of all the Sherries. Handle it similarly to a Fino Sherry.

- **Manzanilla Pasada:** A Manzanilla that has been aged in cask about seven years and has lost its flor. It's more amber in color than a *Manzanilla Fina* and fuller-bodied. It's close to a dry amontillado (see the next item) in style, but still crisp and pungent. Serve cool.

- **Amontillado:** An aged *fino* that has lost its flor in the process of cask aging. It is deeper amber in color and richer and nuttier than the previous styles. Amontillado *(ah moan tee YAH doh)* is dry but retains some of the pungent tang from its lost flor. True *amontillado* is fairly rare, while cheaper Sherries labeled *amontillado* are common, so be suspicious if it costs less than $8 a bottle. Serve *amontillado* slightly cool and, for drinking it at its best, finish the bottle within a week.

- **Oloroso:** Dark gold to deep brown in color (depending on its age), full-bodied with rich, raisiny aroma and flavor, but dry in the finish. *Olorosos* lack the sharp pungency of *fino* (flor) Sherries. They are usually between 18 and 20 percent alcohol and can age for a few weeks because they have already been oxidized in their aging. Serve them at room temperature.

- **Palo Cortado** *(PAH loe cor TAH doh):* The rarest of all Sherries. It starts out as a *fino* with a flor and develops as an *amontillado,* losing its flor. But then, for some unknown reason, it begins to resemble the richer, more fragrant oloroso style, all the while retaining the elegance of an *amontillado.* In color and alcohol content, *palo cortado* is similar to an oloroso, but its aroma is quite like an *amontillado.* Like Amontillado Sherry, beware of cheap imitations. Serve at room temperature. It ages as long as Olorosos.

The bouquet, or aroma, of *fino* Sherry is often compared with almonds. *Amontillados* are said to smell like hazelnuts, and *olorosos* smell like walnuts. And, by the way, the named nuts make ideal accompaniments to each particular sherry.

Sweet Sherry is made by adding sweetening to dry Sherry. The sweetening can come in many forms, such as by adding the juice of Pedro Ximénez grapes that have been dried like raisins. All the following sweet styles of Sherry should be served at room temperature:

- **Medium Sherry:** *Amontillados* and light *olorosos* that have been slightly sweetened. They are light brown in color.

- **Pale Cream:** Made by blending *fino* and light a*montillado* Sherries and lightly sweetening the blend. They have a very pale gold color. Pale Cream is a fairly new but popular style that has been increasing in sales in recent years.

- **Cream Sherry:** Cream and the lighter "milk" Sherries are rich *amorosos* (term for sweetened *olorosos*). They vary in quality, depending on the *oloroso* used, and can improve in the bottle with age. These Sherries are a very popular style today.

- **Brown Sherry:** Very dark, rich, sweet, dessert Sherry, usually containing a coarser style of *oloroso*.

- **East India Sherry:** A type of Brown Sherry that has been deeply sweetened and colored.

- **Pedro Ximénez** and **Moscatel:** Extremely sweet, dark brown, syrupy dessert Sherries. Low in alcohol, the Sherries are made from raisined grapes of these two varieties. As varietally labeled Sherries, they are quite rare today. Delicious over vanilla ice cream (really!).

Wines from elsewhere in the world, especially in the U.S. and Australia, also call themselves "Sherry." Many of these are inexpensive wines in large bottles. Occasionally you can find a decent one, but usually they're sweet and not very good. Authentic Sherry is made only in the Jerez region of Spain and carries the official name, *Jerez-Xérès-Sherry* (the Spanish, French, and English names for the town) on the label (either front or back).

Serving and storing Sherry

The light, dry Sherries — *fino* and *manzanilla* — must be fresh. Buy them from stores with rapid turnover; a *fino* or *manzanilla* that has been languishing on the shelf for several months will not give you the true experience of these wines. We find that half-bottles are the practical size to buy, eliminating the problem of the wine's getting oxidized in the open bottle.

Although *fino* or *manzanilla* can be an excellent apéritif, be wary when ordering a glass in a restaurant or bar. Never accept a glass from an already-open bottle unless the bottle has been refrigerated. Even then, ask how long it has been open — more than two days is too much. Once you open a bottle at home, refrigerate it and finish it within a couple of days.

Unlike table wines, which you should always store on their sides, Sherries can be stored standing up. Try not to hold bottles of fino or manzanilla more than three months, however. The higher alcohol and oxidative aging of other types of Sherry (Amontillado, Oloroso, Palo Cortado, all the sweet Sherries) permit you to hold them for several years.

Manzanilla and *fino* Sherry are ideal with almonds, olives, shrimp or prawns, all kinds of seafood, and those wonderful tapas in Spanish bars and restaurants. *Amontillado* Sherries can accompany tapas before dinner but are also fine at the table with light soups, cheese, ham, or sausage (especially the Spanish type, *chorizo*). Dry *olorosos* and *palo cortados* are best with nuts, olives, and hard cheeses (such as the excellent Spanish sheep-milk cheese, Manchego). All the sweet Sherries can be served with desserts after dinner or enjoyed on their own.

Recommended Sherry producers

Sherries are among the great values in the wine world: you can buy decent, authentic Sherries of all types for $7 or $8. But if you want to try the best wines, you might have to spend $12 or more. The following are some of our favorite producers, according to type.

Manzanilla

  ✔ Vinícola Hidalgo's La Gitana (a great buy at $11 to $12, $6 for the half-bottle); also, Hidalgo's Manzanilla Pasada

Fino (all of these *fino* Sherries are in the $14 to $15 price range)

  ✔ González Byass's Tío Pepe *(TEE oh PAY pay)*

  ✔ Pedro Domecq's La Ina *(EEN ah)*

  ✔ Emilio Lustau's Jarana *(har AHN ah)*

  ✔ Valdespino's Inocente

Amontillado

You will find a great number of cheap imitations in this category. For a true *amontillado,* stick to one of the following brands.

  ✔ González Byass's Del Duque (the real thing at $32; hard to find)

  ✔ Emilio Lustau (any of his *amontillados* labeled Almacenista; $20 to $30)

  ✔ Vinícola Hidalgo's Napoleon (about $14)

  ✔ Osborne's La Honda, Solera Primera, or especially Solera A.O.S. (all in the $30 to $35 price range)

Oloroso

  ✔ González Byass's Apostoles (about $32)

  ✔ Emilio Lustau (any of his *olorosos* labeled Almacenista; $20 to $30)

  ✔ Osborne's "E" Very Old or Alonso Sabio; $35 to $40

  ✔ Sandeman's Royal Corregidor (rich, but a bit sweet; about $25)

Palo Cortado

You'll find many imitations in this category, too. True *palo cortados* are quite rare.

  ✔ Emilio Lustau (any of his *palo cortados* labeled Almacenista; $20 to $30)

  ✔ Vinícola Hidalgo's Jerez Cortado (about $18)

Cream

- ✔ González Byass's San Domingo (a pale cream delicate, not too sweet; about $12)
- ✔ Sandeman's Armada Cream (about $12)
- ✔ Emilio Lustau's Rare Cream Solera Reserva ($20) or Vendimia Cream ($30)

East India, Pedro Ximénez, Moscatel

- ✔ Emilio Lustau (a quality brand for all of these Sherries; all about $20)
- ✔ González Byass's Pedro Ximénez "Noe" (about $32; hard to find)

Montilla: A Sherry look-alike

Northeast of the Sherry region is the Montilla-Moriles region (commonly referred to as Montilla), where wines very similar to Sherry are made in *fino, amontillado,* and *oloroso* styles. The two big differences between Montilla *(moan TEE yah)* and Sherry are

- ✔ Pedro Ximénez is the predominant grape variety in Montilla.
- ✔ Montillas usually reach their high alcohol levels naturally (without fortification).

Alvear is the leading brand of Montilla. Reasonably priced ($9 to $10), these wines are widely available. Alvear's premium Montillas, labeled Abuelo Diego, are in the $15 to $18 price range.

Marsala, Vin Santo, and the Gang

Italy has a number of interesting dessert and fortified wines, of which Marsala is the most famous.

Marsala (named after a town in western Sicily) is a fortified wine made from local grape varieties. Marsala comes in numerous styles, all of which are fortified after fermentation, like Sherry, and aged in a form of the solera system. You can find dry, semi-dry, or sweet versions and amber, gold, or red versions, but the best Marsalas have the word *Superiore* or — even better — *Vergine,* on the label. Marsala Vergine is unsweetened and uncolored, and is aged longer than other styles.

Marco De Bartoli is the most acclaimed producer of Marsala. His 20-year-old Vecchio Samperi is an excellent example of a dry, apéritif Marsala. Pellegrino, Rallo, and Florio are larger producers of note.

Two fascinating Sicilian dessert wines are made from dried grapes on small islands that are part of Sicily. One is Malvasia delle Lipari from the late Carlo Hauner. This wine has a beautiful, orange-amber color and an incredible floral, apricot, and herb aroma. The other is Moscato di Pantelleria, a very rich dessert wine; De Bartoli is one of the best producers of this wine.

The region of Tuscany is very proud of its Vin Santo, a golden amber wine made from dried grapes and barrel-aged for several years. Vin Santo can be dry, medium-dry, or sweet. We prefer the first two, the dry style as an apéritif and the medium-dry version as an accompaniment to the wonderful Italian almond cookies called *biscotti*.

Four outstanding producers of Vin Santo (conveniently available in half-bottles as well as full bottles) are Avignonesi, Badia a Coltibuono, Castello di Cacchiano, and San Giusto a Rentennano.

Port: The Great Fortified Wine of Portugal

Port is the world's greatest fortified red wine — in our humble opinion.

The British, and subsequently the rest of the world, discovered Port thanks to one of the many wars between the British and the French, when the English could not obtain French wine and turned instead to Portugal. To insure that Portuguese wines were stable enough for shipment, a small amount of brandy was added to finished wine. The first English Port house, Warre, was established in the city of Oporto in 1670 and was followed by several others.

True Portuguese Port, by the way, is always labelled "Porto" to distinguish itself from other so-called "Ports" produced by various countries around the world. (See the "Port-O" sidebar in this chapter.)

Ironically, the French, who drove the British to Portugal, today drink three times as much Port as the British! But, of course, the French have the highest per capita consumption of wine in the world.

Home, home on the Douro

Although Port takes its name from the city of Oporto, situated where the northerly Douro River empties into the Atlantic Ocean, its vineyards are far away in the hot, mountainous Douro Valley. (In 1756, this region became one of the first wine regions in the world to be officially recognized by its government.) You can find some of the most dramatically beautiful vineyards in the world on the slopes of the upper Douro — an area so rugged and unspoiled that some of it can still be traveled only by canoe or mule.

Most Port travels from the Douro Valley to the coast after fermentation and fortification. The wine is finished and matured in the Port lodges of Vila Nova de Gaia, a suburb of Oporto. From Oporto, the wine is shipped all over the world.

To stop your wine-nerd friends in their tracks, ask them to name the more than 80 authorized grape varieties for Port. In truth, most wine lovers — even Port lovers — can't name even one variety. These grapes are mostly local and unknown outside of Portugal. For the record, the five most important varieties are *Touriga Nacional, Tinta Roriz* (Tempranillo), *Tinta Barroca, Tinto Cão,* and *Touriga Francesca.*

Many Ports for a storm

Think Sherry is complicated? In some ways, Port is even trickier. Although all Port is sweet, and most of it is red, a zillion styles exist. The styles vary according to the quality of the base wine (ranging from ordinary to exceptional), how long the wine is aged in wood before bottling (ranging from 2 to 40-plus years), and whether the wine is from a single year or blended from wines of several years.

Following is a brief description of the main styles:

- **White Port:** Made from white grapes, this gold-colored wine can be almost dry (and drunk as an apéritif) or sweet. We can't quite figure out why it exists. Sherries and Sercial Madeiras (discussed later in this chapter) are far better as apéritifs and red Ports are far superior as sweet wines.

- **Ruby Port:** This young, nonvintage style is aged in wood for about three years before being sold. Fruity, simple, and inexpensive (around $11 or $12), it's the best-selling type of Port. If labeled *Reserve* or *Special Reserve,* the wine has usually been aged about six years and costs a few dollars more. Ruby Port provides a good introduction to the Port world.

Port-O

The term Port has been borrowed even more extensively around the world than Sherry has. Many countries outside the EU, such as Australia, South Africa, and the U.S., make a sweet, red wine in the Port style and label it as Port. Some of it can be quite good, but it's never as fine as the genuine article that is made only in Portugal. The trick in identifying authentic Portuguese Port is to look for the word *Porto,* which always appears on the label.

- **Tawny Port:** Garnet or brownish red in color, simple tawnies are lighter wines that age in casks for about three years before bottling. (Some lesser tawnies are even blends of ruby Port and white Port.) The best tawny Ports are good-quality wines that acquire their pale color through long wood aging, which causes browning. They cost about $12 to $15 (compared to under $10 for the cheaper tawnies). The very best tawnies have an indication of their average age (the average age of the wines from which they were blended) on their labels — 10, 20, 30, or 40 years. Ten-year-old tawnies cost about $25 to $35, 20-year-olds sell for $40 to $45, and 30 and 40-year-old tawnies cost a lot more ($80 to well over $100). We consider 20-year-tawnies the best buy; the older ones aren't worth the extra bucks.

  A serious Tawny Port can be enjoyed in warm weather (even with a few ice cubes!) when a Vintage Port would be too heavy and tannic.

- **Vintage Character Port:** Despite its name, this wine is not single-vintage Port — it just tries to taste like one. Vintage Character Port is actually premium ruby blended from higher-quality wines of several vintages and matured in wood for about five years. Full-bodied, rich, and ready-to-drink when released, these wines are a good value at about $15 to $20. But the labels don't always say Vintage Character: They have proprietary names like Boardroom (made by Dow), Six Grapes (made by Graham), or Bin 27 (made by Fonseca). As if Vintage Character wouldn't have been confusing enough!

- **Late Bottled Vintage Port (LBV):** This type *is* from a specific vintage, but usually not from a very top year. The wine is aged in wood four to six years before bottling and is ready to drink when released, unlike Vintage Port itself. Quite full-bodied, it sells for about $17 to $20.

- **Colheita Port:** Often confused with Vintage Port because it's vintage-dated, Colheita is actually a tawny from a single vintage. In other words, it has aged (and softened and tawnied) in wood for many years. Unlike a 20-year-old tawny, though, this is the wine of a single year. Prices range according to the age of the vintage, but Colheitas usually cost $40 and up. Niepoort is one of the few Port houses that specializes in Colheita Port.

- **Vintage Port:** The pinnacle of Port production, Vintage Port is the wine of a single year blended from several of the best vineyards. It's bottled during its "Terrible Twos," before the wine has much chance to shed its tough tannins. It therefore requires an enormous amount of bottle aging; Vintage Port is usually not mature (ready to drink) until about 20 years after the vintage.

  Very rich, very tannic, and long-lived (70 or more years in good vintages), this wine throws a heavy sediment and *must* be decanted, preferably several hours before drinking (it needs the aeration).

Most good Vintage Ports sell in the $35 to $45 range when they're young and first released (and years away from drinkability). Mature Vintage Ports can sell for well over $100. Producing a Vintage Port in a particular year amounts to a declaration of the vintage on the part of an individual Port house.

✔ **Single Quinta Vintage Port:** These are Vintage Ports from a single estate *(quinta)* that is usually a producer's best property (such as Taylor's Vargellas and Graham's Malvedos). They're made in good years, but not in the best vintages, when their grapes are needed for the Vintage Port blend. Priced at about $35 to $45, they have the advantage of being readier to drink than declared Vintage Ports. They should be decanted and aerated, however. (Some Port houses, incidentally, are single estates, such as Quinta do Noval, Quinta do Infantado, and Quinta do Vesuvio. When such a house makes a vintage-dated Port, it's a Vintage Port, as well as a single quinta Port. But that's splitting hairs.)

Storing and serving Port

Treat Vintage Ports like all other fine red wines: Store the bottles on their sides in a cool place. Other Ports may be stored either on their sides (if they have a cork rather than a plastic-topped cork stopper) or standing up, because they are no longer developing. All Ports, except white and ruby, can be kept for a few weeks after opening.

You can now find Vintage Ports in half-bottles — a brilliant development for Port lovers. Enjoying a bottle after dinner is far easier to justify when it's just a half-bottle. The wine evolves slightly more quickly in half-bottles, but considering the wine's longevity, that may even be a bonus!

Port should be served at cool room temperature, 64 to 66°F (18°C), although Tawny Port can be a bracing pick-me-up when served chilled during warm weather. The classic complements to Port are walnuts and strong cheeses, such as Stilton, Gorgonzola, Roquefort, mature Cheddar, and aged Gouda.

Recommended Port producers

In terms of quality, with the exception of a few clinker producers, Port is one of the most consistent of all wines. We've organized our favorite Port producers into two categories — outstanding and very good — each in rough order of preference. As you may expect, producers in the first group tend to be a bit more expensive. Our rating is based mainly on Vintage Port, but can be generally applied to all the various Port styles of the house.

Very Good
Ramos Pinto
Warre
Quinta do Noval
Niepoort
Croft
Sandeman
Quarles Harris
Quinta do Infantado
Quinta do Vesuvio
Ferreira
Cálem
Churchill
Gould Campbell
Martinez
Osborne
Offley Boa Vista
Rebello Valente

Outstanding
Taylor-Fladgate
Fonseca
Graham
Quinta do Noval "Nacional"
(made from ungrafted, pre-
phylloxera vineyards; see
Chapter 4)
Dow
Smith-Woodhouse
Cockburn *(COH burn)*

Declarations of quality

On the average, only three or four years out of every ten are good enough to be "declared" vintages by Port houses (meaning a year when several houses decide to produce a Vintage Port). But the 1990s have been an exception, as the Douro region has been blessed with especially fine weather lately. Following is a list of the top declared vintages since 1945:

- **1994:** Will be outstanding; hold for at least 20 years; Taylor and Fonseca exceptional

- **1992:** Looks outstanding, but only a few houses, such as Taylor and Fonseca, declared

- **1991:** Very good

- **1985:** Very good to excellent

- **1983:** Very good

- **1977:** Very good to excellent

- **1970:** Very good; ready to drink

- **1966:** Very good to excellent; underrated; ready to drink

- **1963:** Outstanding, especially Quinta do Noval Nacional

- **1955:** Very good to excellent; perfect now

- **1948:** Outstanding, especially Taylor, Fonseca, and Graham; aging well

- **1945:** Classic; still needs time, especially Taylor and Graham

Madeira, M'dear

The legendary wine called Madeira is produced on the island of the same name, which sits nearer to Africa than Europe in the Atlantic Ocean. Madeira is a subtropical island whose precarious vineyards rise straight up from the Atlantic on hillsides. The island is a province of Portugal, but its wine trade has always been run by the British. Historically, Madeira could even be considered an American wine, for this is the wine that American colonists drank.

Although Madeira's fortified wines were quite the rage 200 years ago, the island's vineyards were devastated last century, first by mildew and then by the phylloxera louse. Most vineyards were replanted with lesser grapes. Madeira has been recovering a long time from these setbacks. The best Madeiras are still those from the old days, vintage-dated wines from 1920 back to 1795. Surprisingly, you can still find a few Madeiras from the last century. The prices are not that expensive, either, ($200 to $300) considering how much other wines that age, such as Bordeaux, cost. (Refer to Chapter 17 for sources of old Madeira.)

Timeless, indestructible, and tasty

Madeira comes in four styles, two fairly dry and two sweet. The sweeter Madeiras generally have their fermentation halted somewhat early by the addition of high-alcohol spirit. Drier Madeiras have alcohol added after fermentation. A curiosity of Madeira production is a baking process called the *estufagem (es too FAH jem)*, which follows fermentation. The fact that Madeira improves by heating was discovered back in the 17th century. When trading ships crossed the equator with casks of Madeira as ballast in their holds, the wine actually improved! Today, baking the wine at home on the island is a bit more practical than sending it around the world in a slow ship.

Madeira spends a minimum of three months, often longer, in heated tanks, in *estufas* (heating rooms), or exposed to the sun (the weather stays warm year round). Any sugars in the wine become caramelized, and the wine becomes thoroughly *maderized* (oxidized through heating) without developing any unpleasant aroma or taste.

Endless finish

Technically, almost all Madeira starts as white wine, but with the heating process and years of maturation, it takes on an amber color with a pale green rim. It has a tangy aroma and flavor that is uniquely its own, and as long a finish on the palate as you'll find on the planet. When Madeira is made from any of the four noble grapes of the island (see the following list), the grape name indicates the style. When Madeira doesn't carry a grape name — and most younger Madeiras don't — the words *dry, medium-dry, medium-sweet,* and *sweet* indicate the style.

Some of the most memorable wines we've ever tasted were old Madeiras, and so we're afraid we might get carried away a bit, beginning any time now. Their aroma alone is divine, and you keep on tasting the wine long after you've swallowed it. (Spitting is out of the question.) Words truly are inadequate to describe this wine.

If you can afford to buy an old bottle of vintage-dated Madeira (the producer's name is relatively unimportant), you'll understand our enthusiasm. And maybe some day when Madeira production gets back on its feet, every wine lover will be able to experience vintage Madeira. In the meantime, for a less expensive Madeira experience, look for wines labelled *15 years old, 10 years old,* or *5 years old.* Don't bother with any other type, because it will be unremarkable, and then we'll look crazy.

You never have to worry about Madeira getting too old. It's indestructible. The enemies of wine — heat and oxygen — have already had their way with Madeira during the winemaking and maturing process. Nothing you do once it's bottled can make it blink.

Vintage Madeira must spend at least 20 years in a cask, but for the old wines, the wood-aging was even longer. If a Madeira is dated, say, "Solera 1890," it is *not* a Vintage Madeira, but a blend of many younger vintages whose first barrel, or solera, dates back to 1890; Solera-dated Madeiras can be very fine, and are generally not as expensive — nor as great — as Vintage Madeiras. Vintage and Solera-dated Madeiras are made from one of the four noble grape varieties following (once there were six) and varietally labelled. Each grape variety corresponds to a specific style of wine.

✔ **Sercial:** The Sercial grape grows at the highest altitudes. Thus the grapes are the least ripe and make the driest Madeira. The wine is high in acidity, very tangy, and fairly dry. Sercial Madeira is an outstanding apéritif wine with almonds, olives, or light cheeses. Unfortunately, true Sercial is quite rare today.

✔ **Verdelho:** The Verdelho grape makes a medium-dry style, with nutty, peachy flavors and a tang of acidity. Good as an apéritif or with consommé.

✔ **Bual (or Boal):** Darker amber in color, Bual is a rich, medium-sweet Madeira with spicy flavors of almonds and raisins and a long, tangy finish. Bual should be consumed after dinner. Like Sercial, true Bual is rare today.

✔ **Malmsey:** Made from the Malvasia grape, Malmsey is dark amber, sweet, and intensely concentrated with a very long finish. Drink it after dinner.

Another Portuguese classic

One of the great dessert wines made mainly from the white Muscat grape is Setúbal *(SHTOO bahl)*. Produced in Azeitão, just south of Lisbon, Setúbal is made similarly to Port, with grape spirit added to stop fermentation. Like Port, it is a rich, long-lasting wine. The most important producer is J. M. da Fonseca.

Two disappearing varieties, whose names you may see on some very old bottles, are

- ✔ **Terrantez:** Medium-sweet, between Verdelho and Bual in style, a powerful, fragrant Madeira with lots of acidity. Drink after dinner.

- ✔ **Bastardo:** The only red grape of the noble varieties. Old Bastardos from the last century are mahogany-colored and rich, but not so rich as the Terrantez.

Sauternes and the Nobly Rotten Wines

Warm, misty autumns encourage the growth of a fungus called *botrytis cinerea* in vineyards. Nicknamed *noble rot,* botrytis concentrates the juice and sugar in the grapes, giving the winemaker amazingly rich juice to ferment. The best wines from botrytis-infected grapes are among the greatest dessert wines in the world, with intensely concentrated flavors and plenty of acidity to prevent the wine from being excessively sweet.

The greatest nobly rotten wines are made in the Sauternes district of Graves (Bordeaux) and in Germany (see Chapter 12), but they are also produced in Austria and California, among other places.

Sauternes: Liquid gold

Sauternes is a very labor-intensive wine. Grapes must be picked by hand; workers pass through the vineyard several times — sometimes over a period of weeks — selecting only the botrytis-infected grapes. Yields are low. Harvests sometimes linger until November, but now and then bad weather in October dashes all hopes of making botrytis-infected wine. Often, only two to four vintages per decade yield decent Sauternes (but the 1980s decade was exceptional).

Consequently, good Sauternes is expensive. Prices range from $30 a bottle on up to $300 (depending on the vintage) for Château d'Yquem *(d'ee kem)*. The greatest and most labor-intensive Sauternes, d'Yquem has always been prized by collectors (see Chapter 21). It was the only Sauternes given the status of *first great growth* in the 1855 Bordeaux Classification (explained in Chapter 10).

Sauternes is now widely available in half-bottles, reducing the cost somewhat. A 375 ml bottle is a perfect size for after dinner, and you can buy a decent half-bottle of Sauternes like Château Doisy-Daëne *(dwahs ee dah en)* for $15 to $18.

Mining the gold

The Sauternes wine district includes five communes in the southernmost part of Graves (one of them named Sauternes). One of the five, Barsac, makes wines that are slightly lighter and less sweet than Sauternes, and are entitled to their own appellation. The Garonne River and the Ciron, an important tributary, produce the mists that encourage the formation of *botrytis cinerea* on the grapes.

The three authorized grape varieties are Sémillon, Sauvignon Blanc, and Muscadelle — although the latter is used by only a few châteaux, and even then in small quantities. Sémillon is the king of Sauternes. Most producers use at least 80 percent of Sémillon in their blend.

Wine that is called "Sauterne" (no final s) is produced in California and other places. This semisweet, rather insipid wine is made from inexpensive grapes and usually sold in large bottles. This wine bears absolutely no resemblance to true, botrytis-infected Sauternes, from Sauternes, France. California does make late-harvest, botrytis-infected wines, mainly Rieslings, and while they are far better than Sauterne (even worth trying), they are generally not as fine as the botrytis wines of Sauternes or of Germany.

Recommended Sauternes

All of the Sauternes in the following list range from outstanding to good. In Sauternes, vintages are just as important as in the rest of Bordeaux. Check our vintage recommendations later in this chapter.

Outstanding

- ✔ **Château d'Yquem:** Can last for 100 years or more
- ✔ **Château de Fargues:** Owned by d'Yquem; almost as good as d'Yquem, at one-third the price

- **Château Climens (Barsac):** At $55 to $60, a value; near d'Yquem's level
- **Château Coutet (Barsac):** Especially the rare Cuvée Madame

Excellent

- **Château Suduiraut:** Only its inconsistency from vintage to vintage denies it an outstanding rating
- **Château Rieussec:** Rich, lush style, but not without delicacy
- **Château Raymond-Lafon:** Located next to d'Yquem

Very Good

- Château Lafaurie-Peyraguey
- Château Guiraud
- Château Latour Blanche
- Château Sigalas-Rabaud
- Château Rabaud-Promis
- Château Doisy-Dubroca (Barsac)
- Château Doisy-Daëne (Barsac)
- Château Doisy-Védrines (Barsac)

Good

- Château Lamothe-Guignard
- Château Rayne Vigneau
- Château Clos Haut-Peyraguey
- Château Bastor-Lamontagne
- Château d'Arche
- Château Filhot
- Château de Malle
- Château Nairac (Barsac)

Letting baby grow

Sauternes has such balance of natural sweetness and acidity that it can age well (especially the better Sauternes mentioned here) for an extraordinarily long time. Unfortunately, because Sauternes is so delicious, it is often consumed in its early years when it is very rich and sweet. But Sauternes is really at its best when it loses its baby fat and matures.

After about ten to fifteen years, Sauternes's color changes from light gold to an old gold-coin color, sometimes with orange or amber tones. At this point, the wine loses some of its sweetness and develops flavors reminiscent of apricots, orange rind, honey, and toffee. This time is the best to drink Sauternes. The better the vintage, the longer Sauternes takes to reach this stage, but once there, it stays at this plateau for many years — sometimes decades — and very gradually turns dark amber or light brown in color. Even in these final stages, Sauternes retains some of its complex flavors.

In good vintages, Sauternes can age for 50 to 60 years or more. Château d'Yquem and Château Climens are particularly long-lived. (We recently had a half-bottle of 1893 Château d'Yquem that was glorious!)

Sauternes is at its best when served cold, but not ice cold, at about 52 to 53°F (11°C). Mature Sauternes can be served a bit warmer. Because the wine is so rich, Sauternes is an ideal companion for *foie gras* although, ordinarily, the wine is far more satisfying after dinner than as an apéritif. As for desserts, Sauternes is excellent with ripe fruits, lemon-flavored cakes, or pound cake.

The years to buy

The 1980s were truly exceptional for Sauternes. Following are the best vintages of Sauternes since 1959:

- **1996:** Good
- **1990:** Great
- **1989:** Very good to great
- **1988:** Outstanding (best since 1959)
- **1986:** Great
- **1983:** Very good to great
- **1976:** Good (ready to drink)
- **1975:** Great
- **1971:** Good (ready to drink)
- **1967:** Very good to great
- **1962:** Very good (ready to drink)
- **1959:** Outstanding

Sauternes look-alikes

There are many sweet, botrytis-infected wines similar to Sauternes that sell for considerably less money than Sauternes or Barsacs. These wines are not as intense or as complex in flavor, but they are fine values (in the $12 to $20 price range).

Directly north and adjacent to Barsac is the often overlooked Cérons wine region. You can probably convince many of your friends that a Cérons, served blind, is a Sauternes or Barsac. In the Entre-Deux-Mers district of Bordeaux, look for the Cadillac, Loupiac, or Sainte-Croix-du-Mont appellations for less expensive versions of Sauternes.

Part IV
When You've Caught the Bug

The 5th Wave

By Rich Tennant

©RICHTENNANT

"No wonder the salesman said this was a dessert wine. I can hear the 'snickers' from my guests."

In this part . . .

The incubation period of the wine bug is unpredictable. Some people no sooner express interest in wine than they become engrossed in the subject. Other people exhibit mild symptoms for many years before succumbing to the passion. (Lots of people never get bitten by the bug at all.)

But once you've been smitten by the wine bug, you know it. You find yourself subscribing to magazines that your friends never heard of, making new friends with whom you have little in common other than an interest in wine, boycotting restaurants with sub-standard wine lists, and planning vacations to wine regions!

However quickly you got to this stage, the following five chapters will provide fuel for your fire.

Chapter 17
Insider's Guide to Wine Buying

- -

In This Chapter

▶ Playing hardball with hard-to-get-wines

▶ Building your own black book of wine retailers

▶ Joining wine-buying clubs

▶ Buying directly from the winery

▶ Purchasing the future

▶ Shopping virtually

- -

*Y*ou read about a wine that sounds terrific. Your curiosity is piqued; you want to try it. But your local wine shop doesn't have the wine. Neither does the store in the next town.

Or you decide to balance out your wine collection with several mature wines. The few older wines you can find in wine shops aren't really what you want, and besides, they're so expensive!

How do other wine lovers manage to get their hands on special bottles of wine when you can't?

Wines That Play Hard to Get

There's a Catch-22 for wine lovers who have really caught the bug: The more desirable a wine is, the harder it is to get. And the harder it is to get, the more desirable it is.

Several forces conspire to frustrate consumers who want to get their hands on special bottles. First, some of the best wines are made in ridiculously small quantities. We wouldn't say that quantity and quality are necessarily incompatible in winemaking, but at the very highest echelons of quality, there usually isn't much quantity to go around.

We once bought six bottles of a grand cru red Burgundy produced by a small grower/winemaker, Hubert Lignier. The importer told us that Lignier made only 150 cases of that wine, and 50 of those cases came to the U.S. We found it incredible that we could buy half a case of such a rare wine for ourselves, leaving only 49.5 cases to satisfy the whole rest of the country! Right time, right place.

This brings us to the second factor conspiring against equal opportunity in wine buying: Wine buying is a competitive sport. If you're there first, you get the wine, and the next guy doesn't. (We've been on the short end of that deal plenty of times, too.)

These days, buying highly rated wines is especially competitive. When a wine receives a very high score from critics, wine lovers have just got to get the wine. A feeding frenzy results, not leaving much for Johnny-come-latelies. (See Chapter 18 for information on wine critics and Chapters 19 and 23 for more on wine ratings.)

Finally, most wines are sold by the winery just once, when the wine is young. In the case of some fine wines, such as top Bordeaux wines, the wine isn't at its best yet. But most store owners can't afford to store the wine for selling years later. This means that properly aged wines are usually hard to get.

Playing Hardball

When the wine plays hard-to-get, you have to play hardball. You have to look beyond your normal sources of supply. Your allies in this game are wine auction houses, wine shops in other cities, and the wineries themselves.

Pros and cons of buying wines at auctions

The clear advantage of buying wine through auction houses is the availability of older and rarer wines. In fact, auction houses are the principal source of mature wines — their specialty. You can buy wines at auctions that are practically impossible to obtain in any other way. (Many of these wines have been off the market for years, sometimes decades!) In general, you can obtain younger wines at better prices elsewhere.

The main disadvantage of buying wine at auction houses is that you frequently don't know the storage history of the wine you are thinking about buying. The wine may have been stored in somebody's warm basement for years. And if the wine does come from some well-known wine collector's temperature-controlled cellar, and thus has impeccable credentials, it will sell for a very high price.

Also, at almost all auction houses, you have to pay a buyer's premium, a tacked-on charge that's 10 or 15 percent of your bid. In general, prices of wine at auctions range from fair (sometimes, but rarely, you even find bargains) to exorbitant.

If you're personally present at an auction, be careful not to catch auction fever. The desire to win can motivate you to pay more for the wine than it's worth. Carefully planned, judicious bidding is in order. To plan your attack, you can obtain a catalog for the auction ahead of time, usually for a small fee. The catalog lists wines for sale by lots (usually groupings of three, six, or twelve bottles) with a suggested minimum bid per lot.

(Phone numbers for many U.S. auction houses are listed in the "Selling Your Wine" section of Chapter 21.)

Tips for improving your odds of getting a "good, old bottle" of wine

Acquiring and drinking old wines requires you to be a bit of a gambler. But you *can* reduce the odds against coming up with a bottle well past its peak by following a few easy tips:

- Buy from reputable wine merchants and auction houses. They often know the history of their older wines, and most likely acquired the wines from sources that they trust.

- Trade with knowledgeable wine friends who know the storage history of their wines.

- Stick to well-known wines with a proven history of longevity.

- Inspect the wine if you can. Look at the ullage (the space between the wine and the cork). Ullage of an inch or more can be a danger sign indicating that evaporation has occurred, either from excessive heat or lack of humidity — both of which can spoil the wine. (On a very old wine, say 35 or more years old, an inch of ullage is quite acceptable, though.) Another sign of poor storage is leakage or stickiness at the top of the bottle, suggesting that wine has seeped out through the cork.

- Inspect the color. A white wine that is excessively darkened or dulled, or a red wine that has become quite brown, can be oxidized and too old. (Shine a penlight flashlight through the bottom of the bottle to check the color of red wines.) But colors for red wines and Sauternes can be tricky sometimes; the wines can show quite a bit of brown and still be very much alive. If you're not sure about the color, get advice from someone who knows about older wines before plunking down your money.

- If you buy by telephone or fax, ask your wine merchant to physically look at the bottle and describe its fill level and color.

- Be wary if the price of the bottle seems too low. Often, what appears to be a bargain is a damaged or over-the-hill wine.

- Ask wine-knowledgeable friends or merchants about the particular wines that you are considering buying. Frequently, someone will be familiar with them.

Say a prayer, take out your corkscrew, and plunge in. Live dangerously!

Pros and cons of buying wine by catalog

A real plus of perusing wine shop catalogs and ordering wine from your armchair is, of course, the convenience (not to mention the time savings). Most major wine retail stores issue a wine catalog two or more times a year to customers on their mailing lists; just give a call to obtain a free catalog.

Other advantages of buying wine long-distance include the availability of scarce wines and (sometimes) lower prices than you might pay in your home market.

Sometimes, the *only* way to buy certain wines is by catalog. The sought-after wines made in small quantities are definitely not available in every market. If a wine you want is available locally, but you don't live in a market where pricing is competitive, you might decide that you can save money by ordering the wine from a retailer in another city — even after the added shipping costs.

The penalty box

Many governments have laws that prohibit the delivery of wine directly to consumers from outside the consumer's state. By permitting consumers to buy wine only from retail stores or wineries that are licensed by their own state, the local government can be sure that it's getting all the tax revenue it's entitled to on each sale. The companies that sell wine at wholesale to the retailers have a vested interest in preserving this situation, because free trade in wine could erode their business.

Members of these protectionist forces have become real activists in the second half of the 1990s, suing out-of-state wineries and wine shops that dare to ship wine to consumers, and even setting up scam operations with underage buyers to prove that the laws are necessary to prevent underage drinking. To avoid the risk of prosecution, some national shipping companies in the U.S. have discontinued wine shipments.

Although most wine shops and wineries remain sympathetic to out-of-state customers, deliveries to another state are increasingly risky for those businesses, unless their state governments and the buyer's state happen to have a reciprocal shipping arrangement. And the risk is all theirs, not the buyer's; the winery or store can lose its license, while all the buyer loses is any wine that's confiscated by the authorities.

If you want to buy wine out of state, discuss the issue with the shop or winery from which you plan to purchase the wine. If the shipment isn't legal, you can sometimes find a solution, such as having the merchant hold the wine for you to pick up personally, or shipping to a friend or relative in a legal state.

One minor disadvantage of buying wine by catalog is that an adult usually must be available to receive the wine. Also, because wine is perishable, you have to make certain that it's not delivered to you during hot (above 75°F/24°C) or cold (below 28°F/-2°C) weather. Spring and autumn are usually the best times for wine deliveries.

A final, more important disadvantage is that wine is a legally controlled substance whose free commerce is not permitted everywhere. The transportation of wine from one state to the next or from one province to the next — not to mention across national borders — is not necessarily legal. (For example, as of this writing, only 12 states in the U.S. allow wines to be shipped directly to consumers from California — but the picture is constantly changing.) If you're not sure what's permissible where you live, ask the store or winery you intend to purchase from, or check with your local (state or provincial) liquor authorities.

Some U.S. wine stores worth knowing

We can't possibly list *all* the leading wine stores that sell wine by catalog or newsletter. But the following purveyors are some of the best. Most of them either specialize in catalog sales or in certain kinds of fine wine that can be very difficult to obtain elsewhere. The stores' main wine specialties are listed here:

- Applejack Liquors, Wheat Ridge, CO; 303-233-3331 — perhaps the largest store in the U.S. — Bordeaux, Italian, California, Burgundy

- Bel-Air Wine Merchant/Twenty-Twenty Wine Co., West Los Angeles, CA; 310-447-2020 — Bordeaux (especially rare, old), California, Burgundy

- Brookline Liquor Mart, Allston, MA; 617-734-7700 — Italian, Burgundy, Rhône

- Burgundy Wine Company, New York, NY; 212-691-9092 — Burgundy, Rhône

- The Chicago Wine Company, Niles, IL; 708-647-8789 — Bordeaux, Burgundy, California

- D & M Wines & Liquors, San Francisco, CA; 800-637-0292 — Champagne (great prices)

- John Hart Fine Wine, Chicago, IL; 312-944-5385 — Bordeaux, Burgundy

- Kermit Lynch Wine Merchant, Berkeley, CA; 510-524-1524 — French country wines, Burgundy, Loire, Rhône

- MacArthur Liquors, Washington, D.C.; 202-338-1433 — California, Burgundy, Bordeaux, Italian, Rhône, Alsace

- ✔ McCarthy & Schiering, Seattle, WA; 206-524-9500 or 206-282-8500 — Washington, Oregon, Burgundy, Italian

- ✔ Marin Wine Cellar, San Rafael, CA; 415-459-3823 — Bordeaux (especially fine, rare, old)

- ✔ Mills Wine & Spirit Mart, Annapolis, MD; 800-261-WINE — Bordeaux, German, Italian

- ✔ Morrell & Co., New York, NY; 212-688-9370 — California, Italian, French

- ✔ Pop's Wines & Spirits, Island Park, NY; 516-431-0025 — Italian, Bordeaux, German

- ✔ The Rare Wine Company, Sonoma, CA; 800-999-4342 — Italian, French, Port, Madeira

- ✔ Rosenthal Wine Merchant, New York, NY; 212-249-6650 — Burgundy, Rhône

- ✔ Royal Wine Merchants, New York, NY; 212-689-4855 — French (especially rare Bordeaux), Italian

- ✔ Carlo Russo's Wine and Spirit World, Fort Lee, NJ; 800-946-3276 — Italian, Rhône, California

- ✔ Sam's Wine + Spirits, Chicago, IL; 800-777-9137 — French, Italian, California

- ✔ Sherry-Lehmann, New York, NY; 212-838-7500 — Bordeaux, Burgundy, California, Italian

- ✔ Wally's, Los Angeles, CA; 888-9-WALLYS — Italian, California, French

- ✔ The Wine Club, Santa Ana, CA; 800-966-5432; San Francisco, CA (800-966-7835) — Burgundy, Bordeaux, California

- ✔ Zachy's, Scarsdale, NY; 800-723-0241; Bordeaux, California, Italian, Burgundy; also, lots of half-bottles

Wine-of-the-month clubs

A rather recent phenomenon is the proliferation of wine-buying clubs. (They're not really clubs in the true sense of the word; they're just people trying to sell you wine.) It seems that a week doesn't go by without our receiving a solicitation from one of these groups trying to sign us up.

Most wine-buying clubs work on the principle of "The Book of the Month" club, except that the merchandise is wine. Wine-buying clubs are worthwhile if you don't want to take the time and trouble to select your own wines. You know the old advertisement: "Let Greyhound do the driving!"

But there's one inherent problem with these companies — you have to like the wine that they select for you. But the wines are usually reasonably priced. It's your decision: convenience versus choice.

One of the largest and most successful mail-order "personal wine services" (as they like to call themselves) is the Massachusetts-based Geerlings & Wade, founded in 1987. For more information about them, call 1-800-782-WINE (9463). Two other wine clubs are Tri-Wine, c/o Shaefer's Liquors (847-673-5711) and Taste of California (773-235-9463).

Wine online

If the sticky legalities relating to shipping wines across state lines (see "The penalty box," earlier in this chapter) ever become resolved in favor of free trade (or if the issue fades back into the dormant state it occupied until a few years ago), the field of online wine sales will probably blow wide open. In the meantime, most Internet wine sites seem more geared toward talking about wine and promoting their brands than toward selling the stuff.

One glaring exception is Virtual Vineyards (www.virtualvin.com). Peter Granoff, a proprietor of this online wine shop, was a pioneer in the field of Internet wine sales, and the experience shows — making his site the best source of wine online that we know. The shop features wines from dozens of California wineries as well as imported wines, and it focuses on wines from smaller, high-quality producers — not the wines that flood the usual distribution channels. Granoff and his wine shop partner Tim Gaiser bring a refreshingly down-to-earth, snob-free personality to the site despite their expertise. And their wine prices are good.

You can also bid for wine online. The Chicago Wine Company, a wine retailer (listed under "Some U.S. stores worth knowing" earlier in this chapter) as well as a wine auction company, offers its auction catalogs at www.tcwc.com. Another company, Winebid.com (www.winebid.com), also conducts auctions at its Web site.

Directly from the source

You can buy directly from wineries in two ways:

- ✔ You can visit the winery in person and carry away the wine.
- ✔ You can call and ask the winery to ship wine to you (assuming that such a shipment is legal).

Many smaller wineries sell a fairly large percentage of their wine to visitors. In New York state, for instance, some wineries sell as much as half of their annual production at their doorsteps!

Buying time

Every so often you might notice ads in the newspaper or in wine store catalogs urging you to buy futures of certain wines (usually Bordeaux, but sometimes California wines). The ads suggest that, to ensure getting a particular wine at the lowest price, you should buy it now for future delivery. In other words, "Give us your money now; you'll get the wine in due course, probably some time next year when the winery releases it."

Generally, we recommend that you don't buy futures. Often the same wine will be the same price, or only slightly higher, when it hits the market. To save little or nothing, you will have tied your money up for a year or more, while the store has made interest on it or spent it. And stores have gone bankrupt. During the recessionary economy of eight or nine years ago, in fact, some people who bought wine futures actually paid more for their wine than they would have paid if they had waited for the wine to arrive before purchasing it.

The only time that it's worth your while to buy wine futures is when you want to guarantee getting a certain wine that's made in small quantities (say, 3,000 cases or less annually), and you're pretty sure that the wine will be sold out before it reaches the stores.

For example, there are many small châteaux in the Pomerol section of Bordeaux — plus a few wineries in California, Washington state, Piedmont, and Tuscany, Italy — whose wines normally sell out on preorders, especially in the good (hyped) vintage years. Also, if a wine receives an extraordinarily high rating in the wine press (for example, the highly rated 1990 Château Montrose, plus other '95 and '96 Bordeaux wines), its price could double and even triple by the time the wine reaches the market; in those situations, if you *must* have the wine, you have to act fast to be able to buy the wine — even on futures.

The 1982 Bordeaux vintage was one glaring exception to our rule of avoiding wine futures. Because of the early, almost universal hype over the vintage, those who bought 1982 Bordeaux futures purchased them at a considerable savings. The wines' prices were 30 to 50 percent higher than the early offerings when the wines arrived on the market in 1985. This scenario has unfortunately repeated itself with the remarkably high-priced 1995 and 1996 Bordeaux vintages. Here's the bottom line: Buy futures only when you must have a particular wine and buying futures might be the only way you can buy it. For most wines, though, keep your wallet in your pocket until the wine is actually available.

Lots of people think that you can save money by buying directly from the winery. But you usually don't. To avoid undercutting the wine shops who also sell their wines, most wineries charge visitors standard retail-store prices for their wine. But you get two bonuses: the excitement of buying the wine where it's made and the good feeling of supporting the people behind the wine, who are trying hard to please you.

Most wineries will also happily ship you their wine, if it is legal for them to do so. If you live too far away to visit a particular winery, or if the winery's production is small or in high demand, ordering wine from the winery may be the only way to get a certain wine.

A few small wineries in California and Washington state, for example, produce wines that have been so praised by wine critics that they are available only to those people on the winery's mailing list. (In some cases, the availability of the wines is so tight that there's a waiting list to get on the mailing list, or a lottery determines who actually gets the wines from all those on the mailing list.)

Some wineries whose mailing lists we suggest you join (and the wines to get) include the following:

- **DeLille Cellars, Woodinville, WA; 425-489-0544:** A small Washington state winery making sensational, Bordeaux-styled red and white wines called Chaleur Estate; difficult to find outside of the state; try their mailing list.

- **Grace Family Vineyards, St. Helena, CA; 707-963-0808:** Dick Grace's intensely flavored Cabernet Sauvignons are undoubtedly some of the hardest to get, most sought-after wines in North America (if not the world). After all, he only makes 200 cases a year! Put yourself on his mailing list . . . if you're patient. It may be a while before you get any wine!

- **Leonetti Cellar, 1321 School Avenue, Walla Walla, WA 99362:** Definitely Washington state's most sought-after Cabernet Sauvignons and Merlots. It is impossible to obtain these classic, well-balanced wines unless you're on the mailing list. (The winery requests that you write instead of telephoning.)

- **Quilceda Creek Vintners, Snohomish, WA; 206-568-2389:** Only about 1,000 cases are made of this rich Cabernet Sauvignon. Getting on the mailing list is definitely your best (if not your only) bet!

- **Rafanelli Winery, Healdsburg, CA; 707-433-1385:** Dave Rafanelli's Dry Creek Valley (Sonoma) red Zinfandels set the standard for this variety. Unfined, unfiltered — and just about unavailable unless you get on the mailing list — these naturally made wines are worth the effort.

- **Ravenswood, Sonoma, CA; 707-938-1960:** Winemaker/proprietor Joel Peterson's talent for making outstanding red Zinfandels from special single-vineyard sites is almost legendary; it's difficult to get them unless you're on the mailing list.

- **Ridge Vineyards, Cupertino, CA; 408-867-3233:** Located in the Santa Cruz Mountains, one hour south of San Francisco, Ridge Vineyards is one of Calfornia's veteran wineries. And winemaker/CEO Paul Draper, one of the nicest guys in the business, has been at the helm most of the way. Although you can sometimes find Ridge's Cabernets and Zinfandels in retail stores, they do sell out quickly. And the winery has a "limited-release program" of some wines available only by mail.

✔ **Rosenblum Cellars, Alameda, CA; 510-865-7007:** Veterinarian Kent Rosenblum makes some mighty fine single-vineyard red Zinfandels on the side, when he's not treating sick cats, dogs, and horses! Although some of his wines are available in stores, you can get Rosenblum's best Zins only via the mailing list or by visiting the winery.

✔ **Williams & Selyem Winery, Healdsburg, CA; 707-433-6425:** In the Russian River Valley (Sonoma), Burt Williams and Ed Selyem produce some of the finest Pinot Noirs in North America, plus a great Chardonnay — practically impossible to get without being on their mailing list; but there's a waiting list for the mailing list.

Chapter 18

You Never Graduate from Wine School

Learning about wine is like space travel: When you get going, there's no end in sight. Fortunately for those who choose to be educated wine drinkers, learning about wine is a fascinating experience, full of new flavors, new places, and new friends.

Although we teach others about wine, we are also avid students of wine. We can't imagine that we'll ever reach the point where we say, "Now we know enough about wine; we can stop here." So off we go to another vineyard, to another wine tasting, or deep into the pages of another wine magazine. Every step brings not only more knowledge but also more appreciation of this amazing beverage.

Back to the Classroom

The best way to learn more about wine and to improve wine-tasting skills is to take a wine course. Wine classes provide the ideal combination of authoritative instruction and immediate feedback on your tasting impressions.

If you live in a medium-sized or large city, you're sure to find several wine courses available — offered either by private individuals, by universities, by local school districts as adult-education extension programs, or by local wine shops or restaurants. If you live near a wine-producing district, you might find a wine course offered by a winery itself.

Most wine courses are referred to as *wine appreciation courses* because they don't teach you how to make wine, they don't usually provide you with professional credentials, and they're not accredited. (Courses offered at an actual university can be an exception.) The purpose of most wine courses is to provide both information about wine and practice in tasting wine. (For information on professional wine credentials, see "One wine school in action" and "What do the initials MW mean?" later in this chapter.)

Introductory classes deal with how to taste wine, while more advanced classes discuss in depth the various wine regions of the world or the wines of a particular district. The instructors in wine schools are usually experienced professionals who work in the wine trade or who write about wine.

Brand promotion and education sometimes enjoy too cozy a relationship in the wine field. Many wine instructors, such as distributor salespeople or winery reps, have a vested interest in the brands of wine that they offer as examples and tasting samples in class. As long as the instructor has expertise beyond his or her own brands, you can still benefit from the instruction. But you should request disclosure of any commercial affiliations at the first class. And when possible, consider taking classes from independent instructors instead.

One wine school in action

The following announcement is a shameless plug: We run a wine school in New York City called International Wine Center. Our courses are geared towards people in the wine trade, but are open to anyone who is serious about learning. Unlike courses geared toward general consumers — where entertainment is as much a goal as education — courses for wine professionals are more comprehensive, and the information covered is more technical. For example, our courses range from 7 to 31 sessions in length, come with a textbook and self-study materials, have an examination, and provide a certificate to students who pass the exam corresponding to their level of study.

But whether they target wine lovers or those in the wine trade, most wine classes have a lot in common. A typical class usually lasts about two hours; students listen to a lecture on a particular topic and taste six to eight wines related to the subject at hand. The instructor encourages questions. References to maps of wine regions or sketches on the blackboard punctuate the discussion.

At most wine classes, each student sits before a place-setting of wine glasses — ideally one glass per wine to be tasted. Water and crackers are available to help students clear their palates between tastes of wine. Next to each student should be a large plastic cup for dumping leftover wine. Each student should receive a printed list of the wines tasted that evening, and other material about the subject of that particular class session.

For the name of a wine school or an individual who offers wine programs in your area, contact the Society of Wine Educators, Savage, MD (301-776-8569), which has members throughout the U.S., Canada, and some other countries. The Society offers wine instructors the opportunity to become Certified Wine Educators, and those who pass that exam are entitled to identify themselves with the initials CWE — a credential to look for when choosing a wine course.

Wine tastings of all shapes and sizes

Wine tastings are events designed to give enthusiasts the opportunity to sample a range of wines. The events can be very much like classes (seated, seminar-like events), or they can be more like parties (tasters milling around informally). Compared to a wine class, the participants at a wine tasting are more likely to have various levels of knowledge. Tastings don't come in beginner, intermediate, and advanced levels — one size fits all.

Wine tastings are popular because they override the limitations of sampling wine alone, at home. How many wines can you taste on your own (unless you don't mind throwing away nine-tenths of every bottle)? How many wines are you willing to buy on your own? And how much can you learn tasting wine in isolation — or with a friend whose expertise is no greater than yours?

At wine tastings, you can learn from your fellow tasters, as well as make new friends who share your interest in wine. Most importantly, you can taste wine in the company of some individuals whose palates are more experienced than yours, which is a real boon in training your palate.

We have led or attended literally thousands of wine tastings in our lives — so far. And it is fair to say that we have learned something about wine at almost all of them.

To attend a wine-tasting in your area, contact your wine merchant. Your local wine shop might sponsor wine-tasting events occasionally (apart from the informal sampling opportunities in the store itself), and should also be aware of wine schools or other organizations that conduct wine-tastings in your area.

When in Rome . . .

If you've never been to a wine tasting, we should warn you that a few matters of etiquette apply at most tastings. Familiarizing yourself with this etiquette will help you feel more comfortable. Otherwise, you're likely to be appalled by what you see or hear. Why are those people behaving like that?!

To spit or not to spit?

Remember we mentioned a large, plastic cup that each student in a wine class has for dumping out his leftover wine? Well, we lied. (We wanted to ease you into what we realize might be a shocking concept.) The cup is really for students to *spit out the wine* after tasting it.

Professional wine tasters long ago discovered that if they swallowed every wine they tasted, they'd be far less thoughtful tasters by the time they reached wine nine or ten. So spitting became acceptable. In wineries, professional tasters sometimes spit right onto the gravel floor or into the drains. In more elegant surroundings, they spit into a *spittoon,* usually a simple container like a large plastic cup (one per taster) or an ice bucket that two or three tasters share.

At first, naturally, some tasters are loath to spit out wine. Not only have they been brought up to believe that spitting is uncouth, but they've also paid good money for the opportunity to taste the wines. Why waste them?

Well, you can drink all of your wine at a wine-tasting, if you wish — and some people do. But we don't advise that you do, for the following reasons:

- Evaluating the later wines clearly will be difficult if you swallow the earlier ones. The alcohol you consume will cloud your judgment.

- Swallowing is not really necessary in order to taste the wine fully. If you leave the wine in your mouth for eight to ten seconds (see Chapter 2), you'll be able to taste it thoroughly — without having to worry about the effects of the alcohol.

- If you are driving to the tasting, you're taking a risk in driving home afterwards if you drink instead of spit. The stakes are high — your life and health, others' lives, and your driver's license. Why gamble?

The simple solution: Spit out the wine. Just about all experienced wine tasters do. Believe it or not, spitting will seem to be a very normal thing to do at wine tastings after a while. (And, in the meantime, it's one sure way to appear more experienced than you are!)

If you know that you can't bring yourself to spit, be sure to have something substantial to eat before going to a wine tasting. You absorb alcohol more slowly on a full stomach — and the simple crackers or bread at most wine tastings are not sufficient to do the trick.

Horizontal or vertical?

Two of the goofiest expressions in the world of wine are applied to wine tastings. Depending on the nature of the wines featured, wine-tasting events can be categorized as vertical tastings or as horizontal tastings. These categories have nothing to do with the position of the tasters themselves — they are usually seated, and they're never lying down (that went out of fashion after the Romans).

A vertical tasting is a wine tasting featuring several vintages of the same wine — Château Latour in each vintage from 1985 to 1995, for example. A horizontal tasting examines wines of a single vintage from several different wineries; usually the wines are of a similar type, such as 1995 Napa Valley Cabernets.

There's no particular name for tastings with less disciplined themes, but we'd like to suggest paisley.

What's with the sound effects?

Do you have to make that loud, slurping or gurgling noise that you hear "serious" wine tasters make at tastings?

Of course you don't. But the drawing of air into your mouth does enhance your ability to taste the wine (as explained in Chapter 2). With a little practice, you can gurgle without making loud, attention-getting noises.

More fine points of wine etiquette

Because smell is such an important aspect of wine tasting, courteous tasters will try not to interfere with other tasters' ability to smell. This means

- ✔ Smoking (anything) is a complete no-no at any wine tasting.
- ✔ Using any scent (perfume, after-shave lotion, scented hair spray, and so on) is undesirable. These foreign odors can really interfere with your ability to detect the wine's aroma.

Courteous wine tasters also do not volunteer their opinion about a wine until other tasters have had a chance to taste the wine. Serious tasters like to form their opinions independently and are sure to throw dirty looks at anyone who interrupts their concentration prematurely.

Most of these guidelines regarding wine-tasting etiquette apply to wine classes as well — and are also relevant when you visit wineries around the world.

Blind man's bluff

One of the favorite diversions of wine tasters is tasting wines blind. Before you conjure up thoughts of darkened rooms, blindfolded tasters, or other forms of hanky-panky, let us explain that the tasters are not blind, the bottles are. Or anyway, the bottles are wearing blindfolds.

In *blind tastings,* the identities of the wines are not known to the tasters. The theory behind this exercise is that knowing the identities might prejudice the tasters to prefer (or dislike) a particular wine for its reputation rather than for "what's in the glass," as they say. Sometimes, extremely skilled tasters taste wines blind and try to identify them (if they can!), in an effort to sharpen their tasting skills even further.

If you don't know enough about wine to be prejudiced by the labels, there's little point in tasting blind. Nevertheless, there's something about blind tasting that really helps you focus your concentration on what you're tasting — and that's always good practice.

The People and Places behind the Labels

One of the best — and most fun-filled — ways to learn about wine is to actually go to the region where the wine is made, and, if possible, speak to the winemakers and producers about their wine.

You'll discover that there's something special about the people who devote their lives to making wine. Maybe it's their creativity or their commitment to bringing so much pleasure to the world through their labor. Whatever the reason, they are exceptional people. We have found some of our dearest friends in the wine regions throughout the world.

You'll benefit from multiple sensory impressions on visits to wine regions — experiencing the climate firsthand, seeing the soil and the hills, touching the grapes, and so on. You can walk through the vineyards if you wish, visit nearby villages, eat the local food, and drink the wine of the region.

Junior year abroad

While in wine regions, you often have the opportunity to combine a bit of formal learning with your travel by taking courses on wine and/or food.

Dining with the winemaker

A popular type of wine event is the winemaker dinner, a multicourse dinner at which a winemaker or winery owner is the guest of honor. Wine drinkers pay a set price for the meal and taste samples of the winery's wines that are matched to each course.

As far as learning goes, winemaker dinners rank below seminar-style wine-tastings, but above many informal, reception-style tastings.

These dinners offer the chance to taste wines under ideal circumstances — with food — but we find that very little information of any value is disseminated, and there's little opportunity to ask questions.

In their potential for fun, however, winemaker dinners are right up there at the top of the list — even if you don't get to sit next to the winemaker.

If wanderlust carries you to the Chianti Classico region in Tuscany, for example, you can take either a five-day wine course taught by Italian wine expert Nick Belfrage, MW, or a one-week food course given by the proprietress of the magnificent Badia a Coltibuono estate, Lorenza de' Medici (of the historic Medici family). Both are given at the Coltibuono estate, and include meals and accommodations. Contact either: The Villa Table, Badia a Coltibuono, 53013 Gaiole in Chianti (SI), Italy; Telephone: 577-749498, Fax: 577-749235; or Judy Terrell Ebrey, P.O. Box 25228, Dallas, TX 75225; Telephone: 214-373-1161, Fax: 214-373-1162; E-mail: villatable@aol.com.

Another excellent wine and food course in Tuscany takes place at the impressive Tenuta di Capezzana estate, located west of Florence in the Carmignano wine region. The Capezzana Wine & Culinary Center is situated in the old family villa of Count Ugo and Countess Lisa Contini Bonacossi, whose Carmignano wine and olive oil are both top-notch. Countess Bonacossi is a renowned home cook in Tuscany, and supervises the Center. Food author Faith Willinger and Jean-Louis Mori are the center's codirectors. One session takes place each spring and fall; each session is limited to 14 participants. Students stay in a wing of the Bonacossi villa; meals and wine tastings are included with the course. In the U.S., contact Marlene Levinson; Telephone: 415-928-7711; Fax: 415-928-7789. In Italy, contact Beatrice Contini Bonacossi; Telephone: 055-8706091; Fax: 055-8706673.

In Germany, the German Wine Academy offers either six-day courses or four-day weekend courses at various times throughout the year. The courses include travel to wine-growing regions, visits to private estates and castles, wine tastings, and a cruise along the Rhine River. The courses are centered in historic Kloster Eberbach, near the city of Frankfurt, and are conducted in English. Meals and accommodations are provided. For further information, get in touch with the German Trade Promotion Office wherever you live. In the U.S., contact the German Wine Information Bureau, 245 Fifth Avenue, Suite 2204, New York, NY 10016; Telephone: 212-896-3336, Fax: 212-896-3342.

Similar courses on wine and/or food are available in other wine regions. Just consult the local tourist office of the country you are planning to visit.

Helpful tourist agencies

Government tourist agencies, whose function is to promote tourism to their own countries, will be more or less helpful in the planning of your trip, depending on the season, and the extent to which each country's wine regions are organized for tourists. Contact them well in advance and ask for maps, brochures, and any material they have that is specifically related to wine districts you wish to visit. Most governments also have wine promotional bureaus, often as part of their trade promotion offices in foreign cities. (In the U.S., most of these wine bureaus are located in New York.)

Also, some private organizations conduct tours and arrange for lodging in wine regions; we've included a few of these groups in the following listings. In case you think you might just enjoy seeing Europe by bike, we've added a couple of bicycle touring agencies as well.

France

Bordeaux, arguably the world's most famous wine region, has several tourism offices that can provide you with maps and local information. Also, we include one private Burgundy tour group. Contact any (or all) of the following organizations:

- **Conseil Interprofessionnel du Vin de Bordeaux:** Maison du Vin, 3, cours du XXX Juillet, 33075 Bordeaux; Telephone: (33) 56 00 22 66; Fax: (33) 56 00 22 77.

- **Conseil des Vins du Médoc:** 1, cours du XXX Juillet, 33075 Bordeaux; Telephone: (33) 56 48 18 62; Fax: (33) 56 79 11 05.

- **Wine Tours of Burgundy:** Hixson & Lefils, 6, Rue de Tamnes, 21700 Nuits-St. George; Telephone: (33) 80 61 48 39.

Italy

Only recently has Italy begun encouraging tours of its plentiful, rich wine regions. The new tourism movement called *agritourismo* (farm tourism) helps visitors vacation at working farms and wineries. Much of the tourism effort has focused on the Chianti Classico region in Tuscany, but Piedmont, the Veneto, Trentino-Alto Adige, and Umbria are also involved in the program. Contact the following two organizations:

- **Movimento del Turismo del Vino:** c/o Fattoria dei Barbi, 53024 Montalcino (SI), Italy; Telephone: 39 577 849421; Fax: 39 577 849356. This organization is made up of more than 200 estate owners throughout Italy, with an emphasis on Tuscany. Programs include cultural heritage and nature, as well as wine.

- **Stagioni del Chianti:** Via di Campoli 142, 50024 Mercatali Val di Pesa (FI), Italy; Telephone: 39 55 821481; Fax: 39 55 821449. Contact Katharina Trauttmansdorff. This organization provides accommodations at any of the following five wine estates in Tuscany: Castello di Brolio, Castello di Cacchiano, Castello di Fonterutoli, Rocca delle Macie, and Villa Vistarenni.

Europe by bike

A fun — and healthful — way to visit wine regions, and make new friends, is to travel by bicycle through various countries in Europe. The following two agencies are recommended:

- **Blue Marble Travel:** 31 South Street, Suite 309, Morristown, NJ 07960; Telephone: 973 326-9533; Fax: 973 326-8939. Though wine is not its only agenda, this group arranges various biking tours throughout most of the countries in western Europe, such as France, Italy, Germany, Switzerland, Austria, Spain, and Portugal. Some tours, such as "Champagne and the Upper Mosel," "White wine roads," "Red wine roads," "Bordeaux," and "Burgundy" obviously emphasize wine. Send for a brochure.

✔ **Butterfield & Robinson:** 70 Bond Street, Toronto, Ontario, Canada M5B 1X3; Telephone: 800 618 1147; Fax: 416 864 0541. This organization specializes in luxury biking and walking holidays in a number of wine regions, with an emphasis on France and Italy.

Calling ahead

When you do plan to visit a winery, you usually need to call or write ahead of time for an appointment.

The major exceptions are the many large wineries in Napa, California, where regular tours are conducted, or self-guided tours are available. Many wineries in the U.S. do have tasting rooms that are open every day during the busy tourism months and on weekends during the winter. In these tasting rooms, you can sample wines (sometimes for a small fee), buy wine, and buy souvenirs such as T-shirts or sweatshirts with the logo of the winery imprinted on them.

If you visit wineries that are not so formally geared toward tourism — which is most of the rest of the wine world — you can simply sample the wines, talk to the winemaker or proprietor when he's available (you *have* made an appointment, right?), take an informal tour of the winery, and buy some wine if you wish (an especially nice idea if the wine is not available back home).

California, here I come

The essential guidebook to use if you are planning to make a wine trip to California is The Wine Spectator's annual guide, *Wine Country Guide to California*. (It's available for $6.95 plus postage and handling.) This guide has a directory of all California wineries with tasting and tour information, telephone numbers, each winery's hours, and an indication as to whether appointments are needed. There are also maps of each of California's wine regions. Call 1-800-752-7799 for order information.

The guide also includes a listing of restaurants in California's various wine regions along with reviews of the restaurants and a listing of lodging available — inns, bed and breakfasts, hotels, and motels. It also provides information on other activities and attractions in the California wine country.

Armchair Travel

It takes time and money to travel around the world. Alternatively, you can travel through the wine world from the comfort of your living room, letting the written word carry you to faraway wine regions.

Many retail wine stores sell wine magazines, newsletters, and books. Most major book stores have a separate section for food and wine books, also.

Recommended reading

The following books are some of *the* established tomes; they will take you into greater depth on particular aspects of wine. Two good sources for many of these books are the Wine Appreciation Guild (telephone 800-231-9463) and Kellgren Specialty Books (telephone 800-274-4816); both companies have extensive catalogs devoted to wine books.

General knowledge

Hugh Johnson, *World Atlas of Wine* (fourth edition), New York, Simon & Schuster, 1994. England's Hugh Johnson is probably the world's best known and most respected wine writer. This is his seminal book, complete with detailed maps of all of the world's wine regions. (*Modern Encyclopedia of Wine* and *Pocket Encyclopedia of Wine* are two additional worthwhile books by Hugh Johnson.)

Oz Clarke, *Oz Clarke's Wine Advisor* (formerly *Wine Handbook,* a new edition every year), New York, Simon & Schuster, 1994. Oz Clarke, another Brit, is undoubtedly the wine world's most prolific wine writer — the Stephen King of winedom. It's difficult to keep up with all of his work. We like his Advisor because it's an easy-to-use, A-to-Z reference on all the important wine places, wine terms, and so on, in one convenient pocketbook.

Jancis Robinson, MW, (editor), *The Oxford Companion to Wine,* Oxford, Oxford University Press, 1994. An encyclopedic reference book that sets the standard in the wine field. We would expect no less from England's Jancis Robinson, one of the truly brilliant wine writers in the world. This book is a "must" for any serious wine student. (Also check out Robinson's *Vines, Grapes, and Wines,* published by Alfred A. Knopf.)

Bordeaux

Hubrecht Duijker and Michael Broadbent, *The Bordeaux Atlas and Encyclopedia of Châteaux,* New York, St. Martin's Press, 1997. This is the latest great Bordeaux reference book, written primarily by the prolific Dutchman, Hubrecht Duijker. Duijker's several atlases on various wine regions have established him as one of the best and most authoritative wine writers of modern times.

Robert M. Parker, Jr., *Bordeaux* (second edition), New York, Simon & Schuster, 1991. Robert Parker is certainly America's — if not the world's — most famous wine writer. He established his reputation on his knowledge of Bordeaux; he was also the first writer to use the 100-point rating system of wines. His second edition covers all major Bordeaux wines from 1961 to 1990 — an essential book for any Bordeaux lover. (Other books by Parker worth having include *Parker's Wine Buyer's Guide,* Fourth Edition, *The Wines of the Rhône Valley and Provence,* and *Burgundy.*)

David Peppercorn, MW, *Bordeaux* (second edition), London, Faber and Faber, 1991. Peppercorn's and Parker's books on arguably the most important wine region in the world are so well done that we had to include them both. England's David Peppercorn is rightfully regarded as one of the great Bordeaux experts in the world. Peppercorn's Bordeaux goes into more detail than Parker's book, but without the ratings.

Burgundy

Clive Coates, MW, *Côte d'Or,* Berkeley, University of California Press, 1997. Perhaps the prolific Mr. Coates' best book yet on his favorite wine region. Coates, another one of the great corps of British wine writers, covers all the major districts of the Côte d'Or (which is the home of all the great red and white Burgundy wines; see Chapter 10), reviews all the producers and provides detailed information on vintages. An authentic Burgundian reference book. (Also worthwhile reading, Coates' book on Bordeaux, *Grands Vins,* and his *The Wines of France.*)

Matt Kramer, *Making Sense of Burgundy,* New York, William Morrow & Company, 1990. The Burgundy area and its wines are given a brilliant, understanding treatment by Oregon's Matt Kramer. Burgundy is so complex a region that any fan of this fabled region will cherish this insightful tome. (Another recommended book by Kramer is *Making Sense of California Wine.*)

Remington Norman, MW, *The Great Domaines of Burgundy*, New York, Henry Holt, 1992. Although Kramer's book is more opinionated, Britain's Remington Norman's is more factually oriented. Both are excellent works on this very complicated wine region.

Champagne

Serena Sutcliffe, MW, *Champagne,* New York, Simon & Schuster, 1988. For Champagne lovers, few books will be as enjoyable to read and to look at as this wonderfully well written book by the U.K.'s Serena Sutcliffe, one of the great ladies of the wine world.

Tom Stevenson, *Champagne,* London, Sotheby's Publications, 1986. England's Tom Stevenson knows more about Champagne than the Champenois themselves! A truly sage, authentic guide to this wonderful beverage and region. (A new edition of this book is scheduled to be published in December, 1998.)

The Rhône Valley, Alsace, and the Loire Valley

Remington Norman, MW, *Rhône Renaissance,* San Francisco, Wine Appreciation Guild, 1996. A much-needed new book on a region that has gone through major changes in recent years.

Tom Stevenson, *Alsace,* London, Faber and Faber, 1993. Tom Stevenson's comprehensive, detailed style, which we first discovered in his excellent book, *Champagne,* is given full rein in this long overdue, superb reference on Alsace, France's great, neglected wine region. A must for all Alsace wine lovers.

Jacqueline Friedrich, *A Wine and Food Guide to the Loire,* New York, Henry Holt, 1996. If there has been any great wine region of France more neglected by wine writers than Alsace, it has to be the Loire Valley. Jacqueline Friedrich provides a complete, yet warmly personal, view of all the wine zones in the Loire, plus a rating of the various producers. She also includes a section at the end of each chapter on the foods of each district.

Old and rare wines

Michael Broadbent, MW, *The New Great Vintage Wine Book,* New York, Alfred A. Knopf, 1991. No one has tasted more great wines, especially old and rare ones, than England's Michael Broadbent. His guide to vintage wines going back to the 19th century concentrates on Bordeaux, Sauternes, and Burgundy. This is a book for the advanced wine buff.

Italy

Burton Anderson, *The Wine Atlas of Italy,* New York, Simon & Schuster, 1990. Anderson, originally from Minnesota but now living in Tuscany, is probably the world's most highly regarded writer on Italian wines. This atlas does for Italy, in more detail, what Hugh Johnson's does for the world. Complete and thorough, this is an essential book for Italian wine lovers.

Germany

Stuart Pigott, *The Wine Atlas of Germany*, London, Mitchell Beazley, 1995. Although British, Stuart Pigott lives in Germany and is regarded as one of the leading experts writing about the intricacies of German wine. The series editor of this atlas is Hugh Johnson, another German wine lover, and a man who knows something about putting together wine atlases. An excellent reference for German wines.

California

James Halliday, *Wine Atlas of California*, New York, Viking (Penguin), 1993. The erudite and affable James Halliday, an Australian writer and winemaker, has written a brilliant atlas on California's wines. (Also recommended by Halliday is *Wine Atlas of Australia and New Zealand.*)

Bob Thompson, *The Wine Atlas of California and the Pacific Northwest,* New York, Simon & Schuster, 1993. California's own Bob Thompson has long been recognized as one of the true experts on the wines of his region. This atlas also covers the Oregon and Washington state wine regions.

Jim Laube, *California Wine,* New York, Wine Spectator Press, 1995. *The Wine Spectator* is a leading consumer wine magazine in the U.S., and Jim Laube is their California wine expert. This easy-to-use, encyclopedic book is an excellent reference source; Laube lists all of California's wine producers alphabetically, with a rating of their wines, plus some useful wine maps.

Wine Buying Guide

Ed McCarthy and Mary Ewing Mulligan, MW, *Wine Buying Companion For Dummies,* Foster City, CA, IDG Books Worldwide, Inc., 1997. What other wine buying guide would we recommend? About 540 wines from all over the world are described and rated by us. Approximately half of the recommended wines are under $15 retail, and the other half cost between $15 and $50.

Wine magazines

Wine magazines can provide more topical information about wine than books can. They keep you up-to-date on the current happenings in the wine world, give you timely tasting notes on newly released wines, profile the currently hot wines and winemakers, and so on. Also, the classified ads in the back of most wine magazines are a good way to hear about wine-related equipment for sale, wine tours, and other useful offers.

Some magazines that we recommend include:

- ✔ *Decanter* — One of the oldest and one of the best, this magazine covers the world, but is especially strong on French and Italian wines. *Decanter* also occasionally issues supplements on major wine regions (such as "Bordeaux" or "Champagne"), which are included as part of your subscription. It's published monthly in London. Telephone: 800-875-2997 (U.S.) or 0181-646-6672 (U.K.).

- ✔ *Wine* — England's other major wine magazine, this one provides good coverage of Europe's wine regions, without attitude. It's published monthly in the U.K. Telephone: 01483-776345 (U.K.) or 914-735-8083 in North America.

- ✔ *Wine Spectator* — A lot of current news happenings are in the *Spectator,* including rather extensive coverage of the world's major wine regions, with plenty of tasting notes. This magazine is published twice monthly. Telephone: 800-752-7799.

✔ *Wine Enthusiast* — An experienced staff of wine writers covers the wine world in an authentic fashion. The magazine, an offshoot of a large wine accessories company (glasses, wine storage units, and so on), includes an extensive wine-buying guide. It is published monthly in Pleasantville, New York. Telephone: 800-356-8466.

✔ *The Wine News* — This very attractive magazine covers the world's major wine regions and includes tasting notes in its Buyline section. It's published bimonthly in Coral Gables, Florida. Telephone: 305-444-7250.

✔ *Wine & Spirits* — This magazine offers comprehensive, thoughtful coverage of wine and spirits. Extensive tastings notes are always included. It's published eight times a year in San Francisco, California, but the business office is in New York, NY. Telephone: 609-921-1060.

✔ *Appellation* — This is one of the newer wine magazines in the U.S. Based in Napa, California, *Appellation*'s emphasis at first had been on California wines, but recent issues indicate that its scope is now broader. The new wine editor is the respected Alexis Bespaloff. Published bimonthly. Telephone: 800-799-2679.

✔ *The Wine Trader* — Jerry Mead, publisher and editor of this magazine, calls himself The Wine Curmudgeon, probably because he's never afraid to tell it like it is when he disagrees with public policy or legislation regulating wine. You won't find straighter straight talk anywhere. Published in Carson City, NV. Telephone 702-884-2648.

Wine newsletters

Wine newsletters are an important part of the information pipeline in the wine world. They usually express the personal opinion of one writer, who has established his authority. They contain mainly wine-tasting notes, as opposed to magazines, which contain feature-length articles as well as tasting notes.

One nice thing about newsletters is that they accept no advertising; thus, they can maintain (in theory, at least) more impartiality than magazines. Most wine newsletters are intended for the intermediate to advanced wine buff.

✔ *The Wine Advocate* — Robert M. Parker, Jr., is an attorney-turned-wine critic. His approach to wine is methodical and thorough, complete with ratings of wine on a 100-point scale. Clear and easy-to-read with lots of charts and wine-buying tips, *The Wine Advocate* is a must read for all serious wine lovers (not for the complete beginner); it covers the world's major wine regions, but is especially strong on French wines. Published bimonthly; P. O. Box 311, Monkton, Maryland 21111. Telephone: 410-329-6477.

- ✔ *International Wine Cellar* — Steve Tanzer combines thoughtful articles, interviews with major wine figures, and extensive tasting notes — an intelligent guide for the advanced wine buff. Published bimonthly in New York; Tanzer Business Communications, Incorporated, P.O. Box 20021, New York, NY 10021.

- ✔ *The Vine* — England's Clive Coates, MW, is an authority on the wines of Burgundy and Bordeaux. So, as you might expect, *The Vine* (more of a booklet than a newsletter in design) focuses mainly on these two major wine regions; in fact, many of his issues provide in-depth coverage devoted solely to several leading producers of one region — red wines from Burgundy, for example. This newsletter is for the advanced wine lover. Published monthly in London. Telephone: 081-995-8962.

- ✔ *The Underground Wine Journal* — This newsletter uses the work of several writers, although much of the work is done by editors Christine R. Graham and John Tilson. It offers a well-rounded approach to the world's major wine regions, especially Burgundy, Champagne, Germany, California, Oregon, and Washington state. Published bimonthly; P.O. Box 3567, South Pasadena, CA 91031. Telephone: 626-441-6617.

Wine on the Internet

Wine lovers who are thirsty for wine knowledge can spend hours learning about wine from Internet sites. Many wineries and some wine importers have their own home pages, as do several wine magazines. Other sites feature groups of wineries. Here are just a few of the places where you can read about wine while you're online. (If you subscribe to one of the major online services, by the way, be sure to check out the wine corner there.)

- ✔ **Tastings.com** (`www.tastings.com`): Formerly the Food and Drink Network, this site presents the results of the World Wine Championships, a series of wine judgings conducted by the respected Beverage Testing Institute, based in Chicago.

- ✔ **WineSpectator.com** (`www.winespectator.com`): Here you can look up descriptions and ratings of just about any wine that *The Wine Spectator* magazine has ever reviewed. Also featured: articles that have appeared in the magazine, menus pairing food and wine, and more.

- ✔ **WineEnthusiast.com** (`www.wineenthusiast.com`): In addition to a catalog of wine accessories available for purchase, this site features articles and reviews from *Wine Enthusiast Magazine*.

- ✔ **Wine on the Internet** (`www.wines.com`): Features articles from *The Wine Trader* magazine and commentary by critic Jerry Mead; the opportunity to purchase California wines; a searchable database of wine terms; and information about a few individual wineries in the U.S. as well as abroad.

- ✔ **2 Chics and a Bottle of Wine** (2chicsandabottleofwine.com): This relatively new site offers information on wine, travel suggestions, and recipes, all in a breezy style aimed at female wine lovers.

- ✔ **NapaValley.com** (www.NapaValley.com): This site provides information about traveling to Napa Valley, local restaurants, spas, lodging, and so on. Naturally, it also features wineries. This site provides links to about two dozen winery sites (all of them Napa Valley wineries, of course) from giants such as Robert Mondavi Winery, Beringer Wine Estates, and Sterling Vineyards, to smaller, highly prestigious wineries such as Araujo Estate and Staglin Family Vineyards.

- ✔ **Robin Garr's Wine Lovers' Page** (www.wine-lovers-page.com): Many publications outside the wine field have rated this site as one of the best places on the Internet to learn about wine.

- ✔ **Behind the Vine** (www.behindthevine.com): Offers online visits to wine regions of the world, wine tips, and profiles of wineries.

- ✔ **Wine Web** (www.wineweb.com/wine): Features information on a selection of wineries that changes each month, and offers those companies' wines for sale.

- ✔ **Wine.com** (www.wine.com): This site describes itself as "Your ultimate wine connection." Based in Napa Valley, it features information about wineries in California and many other states.

- ✔ **World Wine Web** (www.winevin.com): This bilingual (French and English) site includes a wine encyclopedia arranged by country of production and a listing of wine books for sale, among other features.

Chapter 19
Describing and Rating Wine

- -

In This Chapter

▶ Ways to be a more thoughtful taster

▶ Tips for writing tasting notes

▶ Numeric shorthand for wine quality

- -

*W*hen we first got excited about wine, we tried to share our enthusiasm with a relative who appeared to have some interest in the subject (well, he drank a glass now and then). Each time we served a wine, we'd talk about it, comparing it in great detail to the wine we tasted the week before. But he wasn't interested. "I don't want to talk about wine — I just want to drink it!" he proclaimed.

On some fundamental level where wine is just a generic beverage, it's certainly possible to drink wine without talking about it. But if you're the kind of person who likes to talk about food, or if you've been bitten by the wine bug, you know that it's difficult (if not impossible) to enjoy wine without talking about it at least a little. Wine is a social pleasure that's enhanced by sharing with others.

Ironically, the experience of a wine is highly personal. If you and three other people are tasting the same wine at the same time, each of you will have your own impression of that wine based on personal likes and dislikes, physiology, and experience. Maybe some day, if humans learn how to do a "Vulcan mind-meld," someone else will be able to experience your experience of a wine — but until then, your taste is singular. The only way you can share your impressions with others is through conversation — talking about it.

Words Cannot Describe . . .

Language is our main vehicle for communicating our entire experience of life. We use language to tell the doctor where it hurts, to describe how radiant the bride looked, and to inform the bozo who almost sideswiped us what we think of his driving ability. When we taste something, language — words — communicates to others what we tasted and what our impression is.

Our vocabulary of taste is undeveloped, however. When we were young, we were taught a visual vocabulary: what is green, yellow, gold, and orange — and for that matter, what is pine green, jungle green, olive green, forest green, and sea green (thanks, Crayola!). No one ever taught us precisely what *bitter, astringent,* and *tart* are. Yet to talk about wine taste, we use these words as if we all agree on what they mean.

Any discussion of wine's taste is particularly complicated, because wine is a complex beverage that gives us multiple taste sensations:

- ✔ Olfactory sensations (all those *flavors* we perceive by smelling them in our mouths — as we discuss in Chapter 2)

- ✔ Basic taste sensations (sweetness, sourness, and bitterness)

- ✔ Tactile sensations (the bite of astringency, for example, as well as the prickliness, roughness, smoothness, or other textural impressions of a wine in our mouths)

- ✔ Sensations on the holistic level, a synthesis of all the wine's characteristics taken together

For example, say we just tasted an oaked Sauvignon Blanc from California. We might perceive the wine as oaky and herbaceous, with melon-like fruit flavor (olfactory impressions), very slightly sweet, yet with firm acidity (basic taste impressions), smooth and rich (tactile impressions), a delicious, vibrant wine with personality to spare (holistic impression). What sounds like some insufferable wine snob showing off is actually just some poor slob of a wine lover trying his best to report the taste data the wine is sending him.

You've probably gotten many a laugh from wine descriptions you've read. At face value, they sound preposterous: Unctuous, with butter and vanilla flavors that coat the sides of your mouth. Fleshy, with rich and deep velvety texture, suppleness, and smoothness. Some fatness in the mouth, with a long finish. (Wait! They forgot to say wet and "liquidy.") Imperfect medium that language is, however, it's the only way we have of communicating the taste of wine.

SNOB ALERT

What the words are worth

Once, we engaged in a humbling yet fascinating exercise. Several wine writers were given a wine to taste, along with eight published tasting notes from other writers. (Only one tasting note corresponded to the wine that we were tasting — the others described similar wines.) We were asked to identify the tasting note that corresponded to the wine we were tasting as well as the note that seemed the most inappropriate for the wine. The description we all voted *least* appropriate for the wine turned out to be the description taken from the back label of the wine bottle! Not one of us had correctly matched the description's words to our taste experience. Again, with another wine, we each discovered that *our* taste and *their* words failed to correspond. Our only possible conclusions were either that we can't taste very well, the writers can't write very well (present company included), or that communicating taste is a hopeless exercise.

Reading wine descriptions (or *tasting notes,* as they're often called) in wine newsletters or magazines can be as difficult as writing them. We must admit that our eyes often glaze over when we try to read tasting notes. And we're not alone. Frank Prial, wine columnist of *The New York Times,* once wrote that ". . . a stranger's tasting notes, to me anyway, are about as meaningful as a Beijing bus schedule."

When It's Your Turn to Speak

Describing your experience or impression of a wine involves two steps: First, you have to form the impression; second, you have to communicate it. When you drink wine with friends purely for enjoyment and appreciation — over dinner, for example — simple impressions and silly comments are perfectly appropriate. If a wine strikes you as unusually full and voluptuous, why *not* say that it's like Marilyn Monroe? If a wine seems tight and unyielding, go ahead and call it Ebenezer Scrooge. Everyone will know exactly what you mean.

In other circumstances, though, such as when you're attending a wine-tasting event, you perhaps want to form more considered impressions of each wine so that you can participate in the discussion and gain the most from the event (unless you relish the role of class clown). To form a considered impression, you need to taste thoughtfully.

Organizing your thoughts

The language you use to describe a wine starts with your own thoughts as you taste the wine. Thus, the process of tasting a wine and the process of describing it are intertwined.

Although wine tasting involves examining wine visually and smelling it as well as tasting it, those first two steps are a breeze compared to the third. When the wine is in your mouth, the multiple taste sensations — flavors, texture, sweetness or dryness, acidity, tannin, balance, length, body — occur practically all at once. In order to make sense of the information you receive from the wine, you have to impose some order on the impressions. (Turn to Chapter 2 for information on the steps involved in examining, smelling, and tasting wine.)

One way of organizing the impressions a wine sends you is to classify the those impressions according to the nature of the "taste":

- The wine's *aromatics* (the olfactory data, all the flavors you smell in your mouth)

- The wine's *structure* (its alcohol/sweetness/acid/tannin makeup and its basic tastes — the wine's bricks and mortar, so to speak)

- The wine's *texture* (the tactile data, how the wine feels in your mouth; texture is a function of the wine's structural components — a high acid, dry, low-alcohol white wine may feel thin or sharp, whereas a high-alcohol red wine with low tannin may feel soft and silky)

Another way of organizing the impressions a wine sends you is by the sequence of your impressions, as we describe in Chapter 2. The words that tasters use to describe the sequence are

- **Attack:** The first impression of sweetness, dryness, or viscosity as the wine enters your mouth

- **Evolution:** The development of the wine in your mouth, a stage when the wine's acidity registers — and subsequently, its tannin

- The **finish** or **aftertaste:** Flavors or impressions that register after the wine has been spat or swallowed; both the duration of the aftertaste and the nature of the flavors are considered noteworthy (a long finish is commendable, for example, and a bitter one is not)

To taste, perchance to drink

In wine circles, tasting and drinking are two different activities. Tasting involves thoughtful evaluation of a wine's quality, flavors, texture, aging potential, and so on; if more than a couple of wines are being tasted comparatively, usually tasters spit the wine out (as we mention in Chapter 18) in order to keep their thinking clear. Drinking involves consumption and sheer appreciation, without any particular analysis of the wine other than the judgment that you like it. (If you don't like it, you don't drink it.)

Unless you're a professional in the wine business, you don't ever have to taste a wine seriously; you can just drink it. However, many wine drinkers have discovered that wine tasting can be a fun way to learn more about wine.

Writing tasting notes

Some people have a special ability to remember tastes. But other people need to take notes in order to remember *what* they tasted, let alone what they thought of it. If you have the slightest difficulty remembering the names of wines, jot down the names of wines you try and like so that you can enjoy them — or similar wines — again.

It's a good idea to write comments about wines that you taste, too. Even if you're one of those lucky few who can remember everything you taste, we recommend that you write tasting notes now and then because the exercise of taking notes helps discipline your tasting methods.

By all means, you should note the appearance and aroma of each wine. Then jot down your mouth impressions of the wine, according to the thoughts you formed as you tasted the wine. You can and should give the wine a score to indicate your impression of its quality (see the section "Rating Wine Quality" later in this chapter for details of scoring wines).

When we take notes on wines, we automatically write the letters

- ✔ *C* (for color and appearance in general)
- ✔ *N* (for nose), and
- ✔ *T* (for taste)

one below the other, under the name of each wine on our tasting sheet, leaving space to record our impressions.

When we taste, we take each wine as it comes: If a wine is very aromatic, we write lots of things next to *N*, but if the aroma is understated we could just write *subtle* or even *not much.* When we taste the wine, we approach it sequentially, noting its attack and evolution, but we hold the wine long enough to note its balance and texture, too. Then (having spat), we often taste the wine again to determine what else it might be saying. Sometimes at that point we arrive at a summary description of the wine, like *a huge wine packed with fruit that's ready to drink now,* or *a lean, austere wine that will taste better with food than alone.* Our tasting notes are a combination of fragmented observation — *high acid, very tart* — and summary description.

At first, your own notes will be brief. Just a few words, like *soft, fruity* or *tannic,* or *hard* are fine to remind you later what the wine was like. And as an evaluation of overall quality, there's absolutely nothing wrong with *yum!*

Describing wine: Purism versus poetry

Some people have the idea that there's a right way and a wrong way to describe wine. Many *enologists* (people who have earned a degree in the science of winemaking), for example, usually favor a scientific approach to describing wine. This approach relies on descriptors that are objective, quantifiable, and reproduceable — such as the level of acidity in a wine (which is measurable) or specific aroma and flavor descriptors (reproduceable in laboratory tests). They dislike fanciful or unspecific terms, such as *rich, generous,* or *smooth.*

Other people who aren't scientists (ourselves included) believe that strictly scientific descriptions usually fail to communicate the spirit of a wine. We're all for noting the relative acidity, tannin, and alcohol levels of a wine, but we won't stop there; we like to describe the overall personality of a wine, even if we have to use language that's more personal than universal.

Sometimes, if a wine is really a great wine, tasters stumble into the most criticized realm of wine description: poetry. We never *try* to come up with picturesque metaphorical descriptions for wines, but sometimes a wine just puts the words in our mouths. One memorable wine in our early days of tasting was a 1970 Brunello di Montalcino that we described as a rainbow in the mouth, its flavors so perfectly blended that each one is barely percep- tible individually. Recently a friend of ours described a glass of young Port as "like rubbing a cat in the right direction."

If a wine inspires you to such fanciful description, by all means go with it; only a cold-blooded scientist would resist. The experience of that wine will become memorable through the personal words you use to name it.

But beware of anyone who is moved to poetry over every wine. The vast majority of wines are prosaic, and their descriptions should be, too.

And when you do lapse into metaphor over a wine, don't necessarily expect others to understand what you mean or even to approve. Literal types will be all over you, demanding to know what a rainbow tastes like and how a wine can possibly resemble a cat.

In the end, the experience of wine is so personal that the best any of us can do is to *try* to describe the experience to others. Your descriptions will be meaningful to people who share your approach and your language, especially if they are tasting the wine along with you. But someone else picking up your notes will find them incomprehensible. Likewise, you'll find some wine descriptions you read incomprehensible. Such is the nature of the exercise.

Rating Wine Quality

When a wine critic writes a tasting note, he usually accompanies it with a point score, a judgment of the wine's quality on a scale of 20 or 100. You'll see these numbers plastered all over the shelves in your wine shop and in wine advertisements.

Because words are such a difficult medium for describing wine, the popularity of number ratings has spread like wildfire. Many wine lovers don't bother to read the descriptions in a critic's wine reviews — they just run out to buy the wines with the highest scores. (Hey, they're the best wines, right?) Wines that receive high scores from the best-known critics sell out almost overnight as the result of the demand generated by their scores.

We saw a customer storm out of a wine shop because the store had sold out of a particular 95-point Cabernet and he would accept no substitute. Thank heaven IQs and SAT scores aren't interpreted so literally!

Numbers do provide a convenient shorthand for communicating a critic's opinion of a wine's quality. But number ratings are problematic, too, for a number of reasons.

✔ The sheer precision of the scores — one wine receiving a score of 86, for example, while another earns 88 — suggests that they have been assigned objectively, when in fact they represent either the subjective opinion of an individual critic or the combined subjective opinions of a panel of critics.

✔ Different critics can apply the same scale differently. For example, some might assign 95 points only to wines that are truly great compared to all wines of all types, while others could assign the same score to a wine that is great in its own class.

✔ Number scores tell you absolutely nothing about what the wine tastes like.

This last point, for us, is the most important. You might hate a wine that's rated highly — and not only that, but you might end up feeling like a hopeless fool who can't recognize quality when it's staring him in the face. Save your money and your pride by deciding what kinds of wine you like and then trying to figure out from the words whether or not a particular wine is your style — regardless of the number rating.

Despite the pitfalls of number ratings, you might be inclined to score wines yourself when you taste — and we encourage you to do that. Numbers can be very meaningful to the person assigning them.

To start, decide which scale you'll use. We suggest a scale with 100 as the highest score, because it is more intuitive than a scale ending in 20. Most 100-point scales are actually only 50-point scales, however, with 50 points (not zero) representing the poorest conceivable quality.

After deciding your scale, create several groupings of points, and write down the quality level that each group represents. It could be something like this:

- ✔ 95 – 100   Absolutely outstanding; one of the finest wines ever
- ✔ 90 – 94   Exceptional quality; excellent wine
- ✔ 85 – 89   Very good quality
- ✔ 80 – 84   Above-average quality; good
- ✔ 75 – 79   Average commercial quality (a "C" student)
- ✔ 70 – 74   Below average quality
- ✔ Below 70   Poor quality

Until you get the hang of using this system, you might just want to give each wine a range rather than a precise score, such as 80 – 84 (good) or 85 – 89 (very good). As you gain experience in tasting wine and rating wine quality, you become more opinionated and your scores will naturally become more precise.

Just remember that like every other critic, you have your own taste preferences that inevitably influence your scores, no matter how objective you try to be. Don't fall into the trap of thinking that all your friends who like wine should agree with you.

Chapter 20

Marrying Wine with Food (And Other Entertaining Issues)

· ·

In This Chapter

▶ Predictable reactions between wines and foods

▶ Guiding principles for matchmakers

▶ Classic combos that still work

▶ How much wine to serve your guests

· ·

*E*very now and then, we encounter a wine that stops us dead in our tracks. It's so sensational that we lose all interest in anything but that wine. We drink it with intent appreciation, trying to memorize the taste. We wouldn't dream of diluting its perfection with a mouthful of food.

But 999 times out of 1,000, we drink our wine with food. Wine is meant to go with food. And good food is meant to go with wine.

Matchmaker, Matchmaker, Make Me a Match . . .

Good. We've settled that. Wine goes with food, and food goes with wine. Any questions?

Of course we're being facetious. There are thousands of wines in the world, and every one is different. And there are thousands of basic foods in the world, each different — not to mention the infinite combinations of foods in prepared dishes (what we really eat). In reality, food-with-wine is about as simple an issue as boy-meets-girl.

The dynamics of food and wine

Every dish is dynamic — it's made up of several ingredients and flavors that interact to create a (more or less) delicious whole. Every wine is dynamic in exactly the same way. When food and wine combine in your mouth, the dynamics of each change; the result is completely individual to each dish-and-wine combination. (Dare we also mention that we each use our individual palates to judge the success of each combination? No wonder there are no rules!)

When wine meets food, several things can happen:

- ✔ The food can exaggerate a characteristic of the wine. For example, if you eat walnuts (which are tannic) with a tannic red wine, such as a Bordeaux, the wine tastes so dry and astringent that most people would consider it undrinkable.

- ✔ The food can diminish a characteristic of the wine. Protein diminishes tannin, for example, and an overly-tannic red wine — unpleasant on its own — could be judged delightful when you drink it with a rare steak.

- ✔ The flavor intensity of the food can obliterate the wine's flavor or vice versa. If you've ever drunk a big, rich red wine with a delicate filet of sole, you've had this experience first-hand.

- ✔ The wine can contribute new flavors to the dish. For example, a red Zinfandel that's gushing with berry fruit can bring its berry flavors to the dish, as if another ingredient had been added.

- ✔ The combination of wine and food can create an unwelcome third-party flavor that wasn't in either the wine or the food originally; we get a metallic flavor when we eat plain white meat turkey with red Bordeaux.

- ✔ The food and wine can interact perfectly, creating a sensational taste experience that is greater than the food or the wine alone. (This scenario is what we hope will happen every time we eat and drink, but it's as rare as a show-stopping dish.)

Fortunately, what happens between food and wine is not haphazard. Certain elements of food react in predictable ways with certain elements of wine, giving us a fighting chance at making successful matches. The major components of wine (alcohol, sweetness, acid, and tannin) relate to the basic tastes of food (sweetness, sourness, bitterness, and saltiness) like the way that the principle of wine balance operates: Some of the elements exaggerate each other, and some of them compensate for each other (see the discussion of balance in Chapter 2).

Here are some ways that food and wine interact, based on the components of the wine. Remember, each wine and each dish has more than one component, and the simple relationships we describe can be complicated by other elements in the wine or the food. Whether a wine is considered tannic, sweet, acidic, or high in alcohol depends on its dominant component. (See "Describing Taste" in Chapter 2.)

The fifth wheel

We've always understood that humans can perceive four basic tastes: sweet, sour, salty, and bitter. But some people who study food have concluded that a fifth taste exists. This taste is called umami (pronounced *oo MAH me*), and experts say that it is associated with a savory character in foods. Shellfish, oily fish, meats, and cheeses are some foods high in umami taste.

Umami-rich foods can increase the sensation of bitterness in wines served with them. To counteract this effect, try adding something salty (such as salt itself) or sour (such as vinegar) to your dish. Although this suggestion defies the adage that vinegar and wine don't get along, the results are the proof of the pudding.

Tannic wines

Tannic wines include most wines based on the Cabernet Sauvignon grape, including red Bordeaux, northern Rhône reds, Barolo and Barbaresco, and any wine — white or red — that has become tannic from aging in new oak barrels. These wines

- ✔ Can diminish the perception of sweetness in a food
- ✔ Can taste softer and less tannic when served with protein-rich, fatty foods, such as steak or cheese
- ✔ Can taste less bitter when paired with salty foods
- ✔ Can taste astringent, or mouth-drying, when drunk with spicy-hot foods

Sweet wines

Some wines that often have some sweetness include most inexpensive California white wines, White Zinfandel, many Rieslings (unless they are labeled "dry" or "trocken"), and medium-dry Vouvray. Sweet wines also include dessert wines such as Porto, sweetened Sherries, and late-harvest wines. These wines

- ✔ Can taste less sweet, but fruitier, when matched with salty foods
- ✔ Can make salty foods more appealing
- ✔ Can go well with sweet foods

Acidic wines

Acidic wines include most Italian white wines; Sancerre, Pouilly-Fumé, and Chablis; many red wines from Rioja; most dry Rieslings; and wines based on Sauvignon Blanc that are fully dry. These wines

- ✔ Can taste less acidic when served with salty foods
- ✔ Can taste less acidic when served with slightly sweet foods
- ✔ Can make foods taste slightly saltier
- ✔ Can counterbalance oily or fatty heaviness in food

High-alcohol wines

High alcohol wines include many California wines, both white and red; southern Rhône whites and reds; Barolo and Barbaresco; fortified wines such as Porto and Sherry; and most wines produced from grapes grown in warm climates. These wines

- ✔ Can overwhelm lightly flavored or delicate dishes
- ✔ Can go well with slightly sweet foods

Birds of a feather, or opposites attract?

These days, wine and food people acknowledge that two principles can help in matching wine with food: the complementary principle and the contrast principle. The complementary principle involves choosing a wine that is similar in some way to the dish you are planing to serve, while the contrast principle (not surprisingly) involves combining foods with wines that are dissimilar to them in some way.

The characteristics of a wine that can either resemble or contrast with the characteristics of a dish are

- ✔ **The wine's flavors:** Earthy, herbal, fruity, vegetal, and so on
- ✔ **The intensity of flavor in the wine:** Weak flavor intensity, moderately flavorful, or very flavorful
- ✔ **The wine's texture:** Crisp and firm, or soft and supple
- ✔ **The weight of the wine:** Light-bodied, medium-bodied, or full-bodied

You probably use the complementary principle often without realizing it: You choose a light-bodied wine to go with a light dish, a medium-bodied wine to go with a fuller dish, and a full-bodied wine to go with a heavy dish. Some other examples of the complementary principle in action are

- ✔ Dishes with flavors that resemble those in the wine. Think about the flavors in a dish the same way you think about the flavors in wine — as families of flavors. If a dish has mushrooms, it has an earthy flavor; if it has citrus or other elements of fruit, it has a fruity flavor (and so on). Then consider which wines would offer their own earthy flavor, fruity flavor, herbal flavor, spicy flavor, or whatever. The earthy flavors of white Burgundy complement risotto with mushrooms, for example, and an herbal Sancerre complements chicken breast with fresh herbs.

✔ Foods with texture that's similar to that of the wine. A California Chardonnay with a creamy, rich texture could match the rich, soft texture of lobster, for example.

✔ Foods and wines whose intensity of flavor match. A hearty meat dish like a stew would be at home with a hearty, full-bodied wine, especially if the wine had earthy flavors like the root vegetables in the stew.

The contrast principle seeks to find flavors or texture in a wine that are not in a dish but that would enhance it. A dish of fish or chicken in a rich cream and butter sauce, for example, might be matched with a dry Vouvray, a white wine whose crispness (thanks to its uplifting, high acidity) would counterbalance the heaviness of the dish.

A dish with earthy flavors such as portobello mushrooms and fresh fava beans (or potatoes and black truffles) might contrast nicely with the pure fruit flavor of an Alsace Riesling. You also apply the contrast principle every time you decide to serve simple food, like unadorned lamb chops or hard cheese and bread, with a gloriously complex aged wine.

In order to apply either principle, of course, you have to have a good idea of what the food is going to taste like and what various wines taste like. That second part can be a real stumbling block for people who don't devote every ounce of their free energy to learning about wine. The solution is to ask your wine merchant. A retailer might not have the world's greatest knack in wine and food pairings (then again, he or she might), but at least he should know what his wines taste like.

The wisdom of the ages

No matter how much you value imagination and creativity, there's no sense in reinventing the wheel. In wine-and-food terms, it pays to know the classic pairings because they work, and they're a sure thing. They didn't become classics by being mediocre.

Here are some famous and reliable combinations. Every wine region of the world has its own magic pairing, no doubt; but now that you ask, we realize that when we travel to wine regions, we're usually so busy writing notes on the wines and just enjoying the food that we fail to record most of the local food wisdom. Anyway, what good would it do you to know that Chianti is just fabulous with Tuscan wild boar?

SNOB ALERT

Location, location, location

We once attended a lunch at which all the wines — three per dish — had been chosen just to complement the food. But the featured wines didn't work perfectly with one particular dish (they were fine, if you ask us). The expert who planned the lunch rose to apologize. It seems that the chef had altered the recipe: Instead of sprinkling cayenne pepper around the rim of the plate, for color, he (gasp!) sprinkled the pepper on the food! The pepper changed the entire food/wine interaction.

For those who feel comfortable with rules, there's a lesson here: Be supremely attentive not just to the ingredients of a dish, but also to where they're situated!

Oysters and Chablis
Port with walnuts and Stilton cheese
Amarone with Gorgonzola cheese
Foie gras with Sauternes or with late-harvest Gewürztraminer
Dry amontillado Sherry with soup
Toasted almonds or green olives with fino or manzanilla Sherry
Goat cheese with Sancerre or Pouilly-Fumé

Lamb and red Bordeaux (we like Chianti with lamb, too, when we can't get wild boar)
Salmon with Pinot Noir
Grilled fish with Vinho Verde
Braised beef with Barolo
Grilled chicken with Beaujolais
Beef bourguignonne with red Burgundy
Dark chocolate with California Cabernet Sauvignon

Look for various additional suggestions on wine and food pairings scattered throughout Chapters 10 through 14 of this book. For a comprehensive table of wine and food pairings, see Appendix B of our *Wine Buying Companion For Dummies* (published by IDG Books Worldwide, Inc.).

Entertaining with Wine

When you're hosting a dinner party, you'll probably serve more wines than you would in the course of a normal dinner. Instead of just one wine all through the meal, you might want to serve a different wine with every course. Many people serve two wines at the table, a white with the first course and a red with the entree (and if they love wine, they'll use a cheese course as an excuse to serve a second, knockout red).

"A châque son gout" — personal taste rules

We recently happened to discuss food pairings for red Bordeaux wine with the owner of one of the five first growths of Bordeaux (see Chapter 10 for an explanation of first growths). "I don't like Bordeaux with lamb," he proclaimed. We were surprised; "But Bordeaux and lamb is a classic combination," we said. "No, I don't agree," he answered, holding his ground. After a moment, he added, "Of course, I don't like lamb."

Because you want every wine to taste even better than the one before it — besides blending perfectly with the food you're serving — you should give some thought to the sequence in which the wines will be served. One set of rules that no one has abolished yet (at least no one ever told us) suggests the following sequence:

- ✔ White wine before red wine
- ✔ Light wine before heavy wine
- ✔ Dry wine before sweet wine
- ✔ Simple wine before complex, richly flavored wine

Each of these principles operates independently. You needn't go crazy trying to follow all of them together, or you'll be able to drink nothing but light, dry simple whites and heavy, complex, sweet reds! A very light red wine served before a rich, full-bodied white can work just fine. If the food you're serving calls for only white wine, there's really no reason that both wines couldn't be white: a simpler, lighter white first and a richer, fuller-bodied white second. Likewise, both wines could be red, or you could serve a dry rosé followed by a red.

First things first

Even if you don't plan to serve hors d'oeuvres, you'll probably want to offer your guests a drink when they arrive to set a relaxing tone for the evening.

We like to serve Champagne (notice the capital C) as the apéritif because opening the bottle of Champagne is a ceremony that brings together everyone in the group. Champagne honors your guests. And a glass of Champagne is compelling enough that to spend a thoughtful moment tasting it doesn't seem rude; even people who think it's absurd to talk about wine understand that Champagne is too special to be ignored. Unlike many white wines, Champagne stands alone just fine, without food.

How much is enough

The necessary quantity of each wine depends on all sorts of issues, including the number of wines you serve (if there are several, you need less of each), the pace of service (if you plan a long, leisurely meal, you'll need more of each wine), and the size of your wine glasses. If you're using oversized glasses, you need more of each wine, because it's easy to pour more than you realize into each glass.

Assuming a full-blown dinner that includes an apéritif wine, two wines with dinner, and another with cheese — and guests who all drink moderately — we recommend that you plan to have one bottle of each wine for every four people. That gives each person four ounces of each wine, with plenty left over in the 25-ounce bottle for refills.

✔ When serving two wines, plan one bottle of each wine per couple.

✔ When serving four wines, plan one bottle of each wine per every four people.

One simpler rule of thumb is to figure, in total, a full bottle of wine per guest (total consumption). That quantity might sound high, but if your dinner is spread over several hours and you're serving a lot of food, it really isn't immoderate. If you're concerned that your guests might overindulge, be sure that their water glasses are always full so that they have an alternative to automatically reaching for the wine.

If your dinner party is special enough to have several food courses and several wines, we recommend giving each guest a separate glass for each wine. The glasses can be different for each wine, or they can be alike. All those glasses really look festive on the table. And with a separate glass for each wine, no guest feels compelled to empty each glass before going on to the next wine. (You also can tell at a glance who is drinking the wine and who isn't really interested in it, and you can adjust your pouring accordingly.)

Wine from Venus, food from Mars

Sooner or later you're bound to experience food-and-wine disaster — when the two taste miserable together. We've had many opportunities to test our solution to food-and-wine disaster, and it works: As long as the wine is good and the food is good, eat one first and drink the other afterwards — or vice versa.

Chapter 21

To Have and To Hold — or To Sell

*W*hen we first started buying wine, we operated from the gut. Carried away with the excitement of a wine tasting, we'd decide to buy four or six — or even 12 — bottles of our favorite wine of the evening. Sometimes, browsing the shelves of retail stores, we'd buy 12 different Zinfandels (see Chapter 14) with the intention of setting up our own comparative tasting, but we didn't always get around to it.

Our wine consumption couldn't keep pace with our curiosity to try new wines and our passion to possess wines we had tried and liked. Before we knew it, we had become wine collectors.

Luckily for us, we didn't make *too* many mistakes along the way. Nonetheless, we came to appreciate the wisdom of having a plan for our wine purchases. Wine, we decided, has something in common with rabbits: The population of bottles can very easily get out of hand.

Wine Collecting Just Happens

Most wines are consumed very quickly after they have been purchased. If this is your custom, you have plenty of company.

But many people who enjoy wine operate a bit differently. Oh, sure, they buy wine because they intend to *drink* it; they're just not exactly sure *when* they'll drink it. And until they do drink it, they'll get pleasure out of knowing that the bottles are waiting for them. If you count yourself in this second group, you are probably a wine collector at heart. The chase, to you, is every bit as thrilling as the consummation.

If you are a closet wine collector, a little forethought will help steer you toward an organized inventory of wines that you are pleased to own. But even if you never intend to have a wine collection, it's worthwhile to put at least a little thought into your wine purchases. Developing a strategy of wine buying can prevent a haphazard collection of uninteresting or worthless bottles from happening to you.

Formulating a wine-buying strategy involves assessing

- ✔ How much wine you drink
- ✔ How much wine you want to own (and can store properly)
- ✔ How much money you are prepared to spend on wine
- ✔ The types of wine you enjoy drinking

Unless you strike a balance on these issues, you could end up either broke, bored, or frustrated, or in the salad dressing and vinegar business!

The avowed noncollector

You are enthusiastic about wine and you enjoy buying it. But you have no intention of becoming a wine collector — you don't have the space, or you have better things to spend your money on.

In your circumstances, the only way to prevent a wine collection from happening is strict personal discipline. Determine how many bottles of wine you consume in a month (be sure to take entertaining into account) and never have more than that number of bottles on hand. If you drink wine at home two nights a week, for example, and entertain once a month, the number could be somewhere around 12 bottles.

When you buy wine, avoid purchasing robust, red wines that improve with age, but need time to develop. Avoid buying more than two bottles of any one wine unless you don't mind drinking the same wine frequently. Don't buy any bottle of wine that is so extraordinary or expensive that you might be tempted to hold it for a special occasion.

Resist the urge to subscribe to wine magazines. Do not browse wine-related Web sites.

The small collector

Moderation in wine collecting is as challenging as it is commendable.

Say you decide that a six-month inventory of wine seems reasonable for you. (That's probably about 75 bottles, given the same scenario of entertaining once a month and drinking wine two nights a week at home.)

You've just given yourself license to collect, because with 75 bottles, you could surely manage to devote a *case* (12 bottles) or two to wines that require long-term aging. You could also rationalize a full-case purchase of a wine you particularly like, figuring that you'd drink it twice a month for six months (but will you really?).

Your challenge is to maintain the proper balance between maturing wines and drinkable wines and enough diversity among your drinkable wines that you are not bored with your choices. To accomplish these two goals, you probably have to keep records of your inventory. You also need to think about the storage conditions of your wine — especially those long-term keepers. (See the "Age-worthy wines" section about long-term keepers.)

The serious collector

Congratulations! Most wine collectors don't ever really *decide* to become wine collectors; they just keep buying and buying until they *are* wine collectors. By making a calculated decision to own a few hundred bottles of wine, you have the opportunity to develop a collection that truly suits your palate and your goals, and to avoid common pitfalls of wine collecting.

Your challenge is to define your goals clearly, diversify your collection appropriately, and exercise patience in your wine buying. You'll also want to make sure that your wine is stored under optimal conditions; otherwise, many of your purchases will never bring you the pleasure you anticipate.

Is the sky the limit?

There are some wine collectors who have extensive cellars of over 10,000 bottles! This might be called taking one's hobby to the extreme. We believe that a collection of 1,000 to 1,500 bottles is definitely sufficient to handle *anyone's* needs nicely. Then again, 100 bottles isn't so bad, either!

Likely Suspects for Collectors Great and Small

Unless your intention is to fill your cellar with wines that bring you the greatest return when you later sell them (in other words, unless you aren't interested in actually *drinking* the wines you own), you should *like* a wine before buying it. (We're not talking about all those bottles you buy while you're playing the field and experimenting with new wines — just those that you're thinking of making a commitment to by buying in quantity.) Liking a wine before you buy it sounds like the plainest common sense, but you'd be surprised at how many people buy a wine merely because somebody gave it a high rating!

We remember a story about a television star who stocked her new wine cellar only with wines that scored 95 to 100 points from the major critics. We wish we could be there on the day she realizes that she doesn't actually *like* many of the wines she owns!

Balance in your inventory

A well-planned wine inventory features a range of wines: It can be heavy in one or two types of wine that you particularly enjoy, but it has other types of wine, too. Your inventory should also strike a balance between

- Wines that are ready to drink and wines that require additional aging
- Inexpensive wines ($5 to $15 a bottle) that can be enjoyed young and on simple occasions and important wines that demand a special occasion

If you like California Chardonnays or Cabernet Sauvignons, for example, you may decide to make them your specialty. But consider that you might grow weary of them if you had nothing else to drink night after night. By purchasing other wines as well, you can have the fun of exploring different types of wine — a pleasant way to educate your palate.

Table wines, of course, constitute the bulk of most wine collections. But it's a good idea to build in a little diversity with apéritif wines — such as Champagne or dry Sherry — and dessert wines — such as Port or sweet white wines — so that you'll be prepared when the occasion arises. (If you're like us, you'll invent plenty of occasions to open a bottle of Champagne!)

In planning your own wine inventory, you'd be prudent to include some age-worthy wines that you buy in their youth when their prices are lowest. Many of the better red wines, such as Bordeaux, Barolo, and Brunello di Montalcino, often aren't at their best for at least ten years after the vintage —

and some of them are difficult to find once they are ready to drink. Aging is also the rule for some fine white Burgundies (such as Corton-Charlemagne), better white Bordeaux, Sauternes, German late-harvest wines, and vintage Port (the latter usually requires about 20 years of aging before it matures!).

But don't limit yourself to wines so important that you are discouraged from opening anything when you just feel like having a glass of wine.

Everyday wines

Our candidates for everyday white wines include

- Simple white Burgundies, such as Mâcon-Villages, St.Véran, or Chablis (White Burgundies are made from the Chardonnay grape; for further information, see "Burgundy: The Other Great French Wine" in Chapter 10.)
- Sauvignon Blancs (from California, France, New Zealand, and so on)
- Chardonnays (from California, Australia, and so on)
- Pinot Gris (or the Italian equivalent, Pinot Grigio)
- Alsace Pinot Blancs (or the Italian equivalent, Pinot Bianco)

For everyday red wines, we like

- Barbera and Dolcetto (from Italy)
- Simple Chianti wines, from Italy (under $15)
- Red Zinfandel from California (under $15)

These red wines are enjoyable young, versatile enough to go well with the foods many people eat on an everyday basis (simple, hearty, flavorful foods), and sturdy enough to age for a couple of years if you don't get around to them (that is, they won't deteriorate quickly).

Other everyday red wines we recommend include

- Beaujolais
- Côtes du Rhône
- Pinot Noir (under $20)
- Merlot (under $20)
- Simple, lighter-bodied Bordeaux (under $15)

Age-worthy wines

Here we suggest categories of white and red wines that are suitable for aging. For recommendations of specific producers, see the section, "The best bets for investing or keeping," later in this chapter.

Age-worthy white wines we recommend include

- Above all, Grand Cru and Premier Cru white Burgundies — such as Corton-Charlemagne, Bâtard- and Chevalier-Montrachets, Meursault, and Chablis Grand Crus
- Better (over $25) white Bordeaux
- Some great German Rieslings
- Alsace Rieslings or Gewurztraminers

See Chapters 10 and 12 for an explanation of these wines.

Among the many long-lived red wines, some likely candidates for keeping (or *cellaring* — the term for letting wines mature) are

- Fine Bordeaux
- Grand Cru and Premier Cru Burgundies
- Big Italian reds, such as Barolo, Barbaresco, Chianti Classico Riserva, Brunello di Montalcino, Taurasi, and Super-Tuscan Cabernet/ Sangiovese blends
- From Spain, Rioja wines and Vega Sicilia
- From California, better Cabernet Sauvignons (and Cabernet blends)
- From the Rhône, Syrah-based wines such as Hermitage, Côte Rôtie, and Cornas
- Portugal's Barca Velha
- Australia's Grange (Penfolds) and the Henschke Shiraz wines, such as Hill of Grace
- The finer Champagnes (usually vintage Champagnes and *prestige cuvées;* see Chapter 15) and oloroso Sherries (see Chapter 16) are very age-worthy. So are the finest dessert wines, such as late-harvest German Rieslings (see Chapter 12), French Sauternes, sweet Vouvrays from the Loire Valley, vintage Port, and Madeira. (See Chapter 16 for Sauternes, Port, and Madeira.)

The charm of an aged wine

Aged wines are a thing apart from young wines — and some wines don't really reach their full expression until they have aged. Try drinking a highly acclaimed young red Bordeaux, say a 1995 Château Mouton Rothschild. You taste a mouthful of tannin and acidity, and although the wine has concentration, you probably wonder what all the fuss is about. Try it in ten to fifteen years; the aggressive tannins will have softened, a wonderful bouquet of cedar and black currants will emerge from the glass, and a natural sweetness of flavor will have developed.

As a fine wine matures in the bottle, a series of chemical and physical changes occur. These changes are poorly understood, but their effects are evident in the style of a mature red wine:

✔ The wine becomes paler in color.

✔ Its aroma evolves from the fruit aromas (and often oakiness) it had when young to a complex leathery and earthy bouquet.

✔ Its tannic, harsh flavor diminishes.

✔ Its texture becomes silky.

Fine wines seem to be easier to digest when they are mature. Besides visceral pleasure, they offer a special emotional satisfaction, too. Tasting an aged wine can be like traveling back in time, sharing a connection with people who have gone before in the great chain of humanity.

Where to Draw the Line

One of the toughest decisions you'll have to make is *how much* of a particular wine you should buy. When you believe that a certain wine is really exceptional (you love it, it's just received a great rating, and/or the vintage year is reputedly terrific), you'll probably have a natural tendency to buy large quantities.

We know a fellow who refinanced his house in order to buy 60 cases of 1982 Château Mouton-Rothschild! Actually, that decision wasn't as crazy as it sounds because first growth Bordeaux (see Chapter 10) from the great 1982 vintage was a sound investment. Our friend will most likely make an incredible profit on that purchase (when he sells the wine), as the Mouton probably cost him no more than $600 a case in 1985, possibly less, and its value is now $7,000 to $8,000 a case!

If you are about to buy a large quantity of a particular wine — say, two or more cases — the first question that you should ask yourself is, "Will I be able to sell this wine in the future, if I decide to do so?" (Consult with a wine-knowledgeable acquaintance if you're not sure of a wine's resale potential; also, see "Selling Your Wine" later in this chapter.)

If the wine that you are planning to buy in a large quantity has no proven track record for resale, we advise restraint — for several reasons:

✔ You may grow tired of the wine and end up with a case or more of it (borrr-ing!).

✔ Your tastes may change, or (as you gain experience) you may find that the wine you thought was so great doesn't live up to your expectations.

✔ The wine could age more quickly than you expected (which happens often), leaving you with several bottles of a wine that is past its prime.

Except for investment purposes, we would suggest that you never buy more than one case of a particular wine, *at the most*. We save "buying by the case" for just a very few of our proven favorite wines; most of the time, we limit ourselves to three or six bottles of particular wines that we know we like and we know have potential for long life. If we haven't tasted a particular wine before (or we're uncertain whether to buy a wine) and are curious about its potential, we'll buy just one bottle first — and try it.

Except for sure-fire "investment" wines, such as the 1982 Château Mouton-Rothschild, be careful not to overbuy sought-after wines for fear that they will sell out. There is always more wine to buy! You might regret not buying more bottles of a few particular wines when you had the opportunity, but the truth is that more good wine is being made every year. You can manage to let a few big fish get away now and then.

Orderliness Is Next to Peace of Mind

Whether you ever intended to collect wine or not, there might come a time when you realize that you are not only a wine drinker, but also a wine collector. Maybe you'll realize that you are a wine collector when you've accumulated your first 90 or 100 bottles.

With this realization comes the awareness that you need to keep track of all your wine so that

✔ You can find a bottle quickly when you're looking for it.

✔ You know what you own (many a bottle has gone *over the hill* because the owner forgot that he had it!).

✔ You can show off your wine collection to your friends (something like showing your baby's pictures).

You can keep track of your wine in many different ways.

A wine inventory on paper should include a list of the specific wines in your collection, the number of each, and the location. Alternatively, you can maintain a computerized inventory.

Cataloging our wine collection by computer turned out to be a lot easier than we expected. We used a database program (Filemaker, specifically) on our Macintosh to create the file. We set up a field for each of the following items:

- Vintage
- Producer
- Wine name
- Appellation
- Vineyard name
- Region
- Country
- Type (red, white, rosé, sparkling, apéritif, or dessert)
- Quantity owned
- Price paid (per bottle)
- Value (the latest estimated worth, per bottle)
- Size of bottle (to indicate 1.5-liter magnums, half-bottles, and so on)

Two summary fields provide the total number of bottles in our inventory at any one moment (or the total of any *segment* of our inventory, such as our red Bordeaux) as well as the current value of our inventory.

One of these days, we intend to make the file even more useful by adding a few more fields, such as

- Best drinking period
- Where purchased
- When consumed

A Healthy Environment for Your Wines

If you are an avowed noncollector who never has more than a one- or two-month supply of wine on hand, you do not need to worry about how your wines are stored. You can keep your bottles lying down on a rack in the den or the dining room or any other room, as long as they are not right next to the radiator or in direct sunlight. Even if they're standing upright, they'll survive for a few months.

If you've decided to collect a few bottles, however — or if you discover that a wine collection is happening to you — please take heed. If your wines are stored poorly, disappointment after disappointment is the inevitable outcome of all your efforts.

If you plan to keep wines indefinitely, you really need a wine storage facility that offers controlled temperature and humidity. This is especially important if you live in an area where the temperature exceeds 70°F (21°C) for any length of time.

Good wine storage not only can protect your fine wines from early demise, but also can give you the courage to age wines that need to be aged. Without proper storage, fine wine is either consumed long before it reaches its best drinking period (known in wine circles as *infanticide*), or it dies an untimely death in some closet, garage, or warm cellar.

The passive wine cellar

You might be fortunate enough to have conditions suitable for what is called a *passive* wine cellar (if you've recently inherited a castle in Scotland, for example).

If the place where you intend to store your wine is very cool (below 60°F, 15.5°C) and very damp (75 percent humidity or higher) all year round, you can be the lucky owner of a passive cellar. (It's called *passive* because you don't have to do anything to it, such as cool it or humidify it.) Usually, only deep cellars completely below ground level with thick stones or comparable insulation can be completely passive in most temperate climates.

Passive cellars are certainly the ideal way to store wines. And you can save a lot of money on their upkeep, to boot.

If you don't have a space that's already ideal for a passive wine cellar, you might decide that you can dig one. For instructions on building your own passive wine cellar, see Richard M. Gold's authoritative book, *How and Why To Build a Passive Wine Cellar* (Sand Hill Publishing, 1983, Box 461, North Amherst, MA 01059).

If you can't be passive, be bullish on wine storage

Most of us are neither fortunate enough to have a passive wine cellar nor fortunate enough to be able to create one without extraordinary expense and trouble (bulldozers, wrecking crews, and so on). But second best — an artificially cooled and/or humidified room — is still far better than nothing.

The following are key features of a good wine storage area:

- ✔ A good storage area should be cool — ideally, in the 53° to 59°F range (12° to 16°C).

- ✔ The temperature should be fairly constant — wide swings in temperature are not good for the wine.

- ✔ The area should be damp or humid — with a minimum of 70 percent humidity and a maximum of 95 percent (mold sets in above 95 percent).

- ✔ The area should be free from vibrations, which can travel through the wine; heavy traffic and motors going on and off — such as refrigerators or washers/dryers — are all detrimental to your wine.

- ✔ The area should be free from light, especially direct sunlight; the ultraviolet rays of the sun are especially harmful to wine.

- ✔ The storage area should be free from chemical odors, such as paints, paint remover, and so on.

Buy a *hygrometer* (an instrument that measures atmospheric humidity) for your wine storage facility. Our hygrometer gives us both the percentage of humidity and a digital reading of the temperature — information so valuable that we check it almost daily. (Hygrometers are advertised in wine accessory catalogs, such as *The Wine Enthusiast,* Pleasantville, NY; Telephone: 1-800-356-8466.)

Avoid refrigerators for wine storage. Don't leave good wine or Champagne in the refrigerator for indefinite periods of time — say, more than a few days; not only is the refrigerator motor harmful, but the excessively cold temperature (as low as 35°F, 1.6°C) tends to numb and flatten the flavors of the wine.

We built a room in our cellar for our wine storage area. Whatever area you use, as long as it has a climate control unit and is properly insulated (see the following sections in this chapter), your wine will keep well. For some professional advice on building your (nonpassive) wine cellar, we recommend the Fine Wine Rack and Cellar Company (Paul Wyatt, 650-591-9463).

Keeping it cool and damp

Professional cooling units are available. (You'll find them advertised in wine accessory catalogs and wine magazines.) These are climate-control units that humidify the air of a room as well as cool it. These units come in various capacities to suit rooms of different dimensions. They require professional installation and cost from $750 to $2,200, depending on their capacity.

The issue of humidity

Some wine collectors are not particularly concerned with the humidity levels of their cellars. High humidity causes mold, they argue, and it disfigures the labels. But dry air can cause your wine to either evaporate or leech out through the cork, causing *ullage* (space between the wine and the cork). The greater the ullage, the greater the chance of your wine becoming oxidized.

Because we recommend humidity between 70 percent and 95 percent, we believe that air conditioners, which dehumidify the air to about 50 percent, should *not* be used to cool your wine storage area.

Depending on where you live, you might not need to run your cooling unit all year. We keep ours going from about late May to late September. The additional expense for electricity comes to about $15 to $20 a month (in our area, northeastern U.S.) for four months — well worth it when you consider the value of the wine you are protecting. During the winter months when the air usually gets dry, we run a humidifier in our wine room, which is a lot cheaper than running the cooling unit.

Wine racks

Racking systems vary from elaborate redwood racks to simple metal or plastic types. The choice of material and configuration really hinges on how much you want to spend.

Large, diamond-shaped wooden (or synthetic composition) racks are popular because they efficiently store up to eight bottles per section and make maximum use of space. Such racks also permit the easy removal of individual bottles (see Figure 21-1).

A configuration of racks that gives each wine its own cubbyhole is more expensive; if you're checking out such racks, consider whether any of your oversized bottles (such as bulbous sparkling wine bottles) might be too large to fit the racks (and your half-bottles might be too small!).

Some wine collectors prefer to store their wine in the original wooden crates in which the wine was sold. (Many classic wines, such as Bordeaux and Vintage Port, come in these crates; you can usually pick up empty wooden crates in most wine stores.) The wooden crates are beneficial for storing wine because the wine remains in a dark environment inside the case, and the temperature changes very slowly thanks to the mass of wine bottles packed together in the closed case. Retrieving a bottle from the bottom row of the case can really be inconvenient, though.

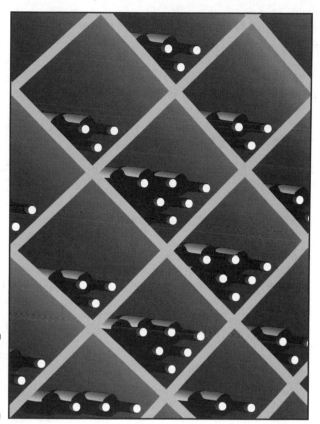

Figure 21-1:
Diamond-
shaped
wine rack.

Cardboard boxes are *not recommended* for wine storage. The chemicals used in the manufacture of the cardboard can eventually affect the wine. Also, the cardboard boxes become damaged, in time, from the moisture in the air, assuming that you are maintaining a proper humidity in your cellar.

Insulation

Far more important than your choice of racks is your choice of insulation.

We definitely *do not recommend* fiberglass insulation because it will absorb the moisture from your cooling unit. We've heard of cases in which the weight of the moisture inside the insulation actually caused parts of ceilings to come tumbling down, creating quite a mess.

The ideal insulation is a 3-inch thick, thermoplastic resin called *polyure-thane*. It is odorless, does not absorb moisture, and makes a fine seal. Even when a cooling unit is not running, temperatures will change extremely slowly in most wine rooms with this kind of insulation.

Wine caves: The apartment dweller's salvation

If you live in a house that has either a cellar or a separate area for your wine, consider yourself fortunate. What if you have no space — for instance, if you live in an apartment?

As an apartment dweller, you have three choices:

- ✔ Leave your wine in a friend's or relative's house (provided that *he* has adequate storage facilities — and that you trust him not to drink your wine!).
- ✔ Rent storage space in a refrigerated public warehouse.
- ✔ Buy a *wine cave* — also known as a wine vault — a self-contained, refrigerated unit that you plug into an electrical outlet.

We find the first two options barely acceptable because they don't give you immediate access to your wine. It's downright inconvenient to make a trip every time you want to get your hands on your own wine. And both of these options rob you of the pleasure of having your wines readily available in your home where you can look at them, fondle the bottles, or show them off to your friends.

If we lived in an apartment, we'd definitely own a wine cave. They come in all varieties — some are made of wood, some of metal, and some are a combination of both. Many of the nicer-looking wine caves resemble attractive pieces of furniture, either vertical or horizontal credenzas. Some have glass doors, and all of them can be locked.

Wine caves range in size and capacity from a tiny unit that holds only 24 bottles to the really large units that hold up to 2,800 bottles, with many sizes in between. Prices range from $400 to about $6,000. You'll find wine caves advertised extensively in wine accessory catalogs and in the back pages of wine magazines.

If you're planning to build a wine cellar or buy a wine cave, allow for expansion in your wine collection. Like most waistlines, wine cellars inevitably grow larger with the passing years.

Investment Wines

Some wines do become rarer and more valuable with age, and selling them for profit can be a temptation that's difficult for even the most dedicated wine lover to resist. In many places nowadays, individuals may legally sell their wines — either to a retail store or to an auction house. As a result, more and more people are selling wines that they no longer want or purchasing wines with the specific intention of reselling them. Check if it's legal to sell your wine in your locality.

It's definitely true that (a very small percentage of) wines are great investments. Certain wines are even safer to invest in than stocks or real estate because they only increase in value — they never decline in value. Even when the economy is shaky, some people always have enough money to buy fine wine.

Investment wines have certain attributes:

- They have been universally acknowledged by the wine press and the wine trade to be outstanding.
- They have potential for longevity.
- They are from very good to excellent vintages.
- They have been well stored so that they are in good condition.

Some investment wines also share a *rarity factor* — not many bottles were produced in the first place.

The best bets for investing or keeping

French wines certainly have the monopoly on the wine investment market worldwide. They have a well-established reputation, especially with the British, who more or less invented the wine investment market.

Fine red Bordeaux — with pedigree and reputation for longevity:

Château Pétrus
Château Lafite-Rothschild
Château Mouton-Rothschild
Château Latour
Château Margaux
Château Haut-Brion

Château Cheval-Blanc
Château Lafleur (Pomerol)
Château Trotanoy
Château Palmer
Château La Mission-Haut-Brion
Château Ausone

(The châteaux in the first column are *especially* good investments.)

Fine dry white Bordeaux — with pedigree and reputation for longevity:

Château Haut-Brion (Blanc)
Château Laville Haut Brion
Domaine de Chevalier

Fine red Burgundy — the most highly respected:

Domaine de la Romanée-Conti wines (especially Romanée-Conti, La Tache, Richebourg)
Domaine Leroy wines (especially Grand Crus, such as Musigny and Chambertin)

Fine white Burgundy — the most highly sought after:

Montrachet (Domaine de la Romanée-Conti; Ramonet)
Ramonet (his other GrandCru White Burgundies)
Domaine des Comtes Lafon (Premier Cru Meursaults)
Coche-Dury (Grand and Premier Crus)
Raveneau (Grand and Premier Cru Chablis)

Sauternes — the crème de la crème:

Château d'Yquem (clearly the *big gun,* investment-wise)
Château Climens
Château Coutet (Cuvée Madame, only)
Château de Fargues

Italian super-Tuscans and Brunello di Montalcino:

Sassicaia   Solaia
Tignanello   Ornellaia
Masseto   Biondi-Santi Brunello di Montalcino

Vintage Port — the Big Four of Portugal:

Taylor-Fladgate
Graham
Fonseca
Quinta do Noval (Nacional, only)

Spain's most prized wine:

Vega Sicilia Unico

Certain California Cabernet Sauvignons — the rarity factor:

Grace Family Vineyards Cabernet Sauvignon (any vintage)
Beaulieu Vineyards Private Reserve Cabernets (1970 vintage and older)
Heitz Martha's Vineyard Cabernet Sauvignon (1974 vintage and older)

The Big Two from Down Under:

Penfolds Grange (especially older vintages)
Henschke "Hill of Grace" Shiraz

The mortality factor

The inevitable question of your life expectancy, of course, must enter into the equation when you are considering how much wine to buy — unless you don't mind leaving your wine to your heirs.

Our hero is the late, great wine writer, André Simon. When he died at the age of 94, André reputedly had only *two* magnums of wine left in his once extensive cellar. Now *that's* good planning!

Selling Your Wine

Because wine is a regulated beverage, you can't necessarily sell your wine without complications. But it is getting easier all the time.

Selling your privately owned wine is now completely legal in many states of the U.S. — California, New York, and Illinois included. In other places, you might be permitted to sell it to a store only, or through a charity auction only. Check with your local beverage control authorities to learn what rules apply in your area.

New York is currently one of the hottest wine auction markets around, thanks to the relatively recent legalization of wine auctions. (You can either sell or buy wines at these auctions.) The crusade is led by four large retail stores, Morrell & Company (212-688-9370); Sherry-Lehmann, in conjunction with Sotheby's Auction House (212-606-7207); Zachy's, together with Christie's Auction House (914-723-0241); and Acker, Merrall & Condit (212-787-1700).

In Illinois, The Chicago Wine Company (708-647-8789), John Hart Fine Wine Limited (312-944-5385), and Davis & Company (312-587-9500) are three leading buyers of privately owned wine.

In California, Butterfield & Butterfield Auction House (415-861-7500, extension 307) and The Rare Wine Company (800-999-4342) will happily buy your well-stored fine wines.

Most large retail wine stores (in places where it is legal to do so) will also buy wine from you. Usually quite a few classified advertisements are listed in the back of wine magazines from stores and wine companies looking to buy wine.

When selling your wine, bear in mind a few factors about most auction houses, wine companies, and retail stores:

- ✔ They are interested mainly in valuable, prestigious, or rare wines; they're not looking to buy some bomb you might be trying to unload.

- ✔ Wines in good condition are what they really want; some places won't buy wines that aren't at their best — but some will.

- ✔ All, of course, charge a premium for their services, ranging from 10 to 25 percent of the sale price. Some auction houses pass most of the premium on to the buyer rather than to the seller.

- ✔ Some outlets pay you only after they sell your wine; others will pay you upfront. Shop around for the best deal.

Insuring your precious investment

If your wine collection increases in size to the point that it becomes one of your most valuable assets, you should definitely think about insurance coverage. Normal homeowners' policies do not cover wine in case of fire, theft, breakage, and so on (some policies might cover up to a few thousand dollars' worth). You can purchase a rider on your homeowner's policy covering such items as wine or crystal, however.

Figure the annual cost of wine insurance to be about 40 to 50 cents per $100 of wine insured. For instance, if your wine inventory is worth $75,000, your annual premium might be about $315.

You can appraise your own collection — especially for older wines — simply by looking at auction prices in the catalogues of the various auction houses listed earlier in this chapter; prices for younger wines are readily available in newspaper and magazine advertisements. Or, if you prefer, check the wine magazine classifieds for wine appraisers, who will do the job for you when you mail them a copy of your inventory. You should update your appraised wine inventory list every three years.

Most insurance companies will issue riders to your homeowner's policy covering wine and other precious items. The Chubb Group of Insurance Companies and Sedgwick James are two such insurance firms that are familiar with wine insurance coverage.

Part V
The Part of Tens

The 5th Wave   By Rich Tennant

"We're not what you'd call a 'prestige vineyard'. This year most of our grapes will be used to make a very nice Windex."

In this part . . .

This is the place to turn for quick answers and easy solutions. The next time a friend tells you that expensive wines are always better, the next time you're wondering when to drink that special wine, the next time someone tells you that Champagnes don't age — check out the advice in this part.

Chapter 22

Answers to Ten Common Questions about Wine

. . . .

*I*n our years of teaching about wine and helping customers in wine shops, we've noticed that the same questions about wine pop up again and again. Here are our answers. (By the way, if you're counting, you'll note that we actually have 11 questions and answers; we couldn't resist throwing in another question, about older wines, at the end of this chapter.)

What's a good wine?

This is probably the question most frequently asked by customers in wine shops. When they ask this question, they usually mean, "Please recommend a good wine to me," to which the retailer will usually respond with a barrage of questions, such as:

- ✔ "Do you prefer red wines or white wines?"
- ✔ "How much do you want to spend for a bottle?"
- ✔ "Are you planning to serve the wine with any particular dish?"

Hundreds of good wines are in every wine shop. Twenty or thirty years ago, there were far fewer — but winemaking and grape growing know-how has progressed dramatically to the point that there are few poor wines now. But you won't necessarily like every one of those good wines. There is simply no getting around the fact that taste is personal. If you want to drink a good wine that's right for you, you have to decide what the characteristics of that wine could be. And then get advice from a knowledgeable retailer.

When should I drink this wine?

Wine retailers frequently hear this question from customers, too. The answer, for most wines, is "Any time now."

The great majority of wines are ready to drink when you buy them. Some of them might improve marginally if you hold them for a year or so (and many of them will maintain their drinkability), but they won't improve enough for you to notice, unless you're a particularly thoughtful and experienced taster.

Some fine wines are an exception: They not only benefit from aging but they *need* to age, in order to achieve their potential quality. For example, assuming that the wines are well stored (turn to Chapter 21 for specifics of wine storage):

- You can usually count on 20 to 30 years of life from top quality red Bordeaux wines in good years such as 1982, 1986, 1989, 1990, 1995, or 1996.

- The best Barolos, Barbarescos, and Brunello di Montalcinos can age for 20 to 25 years in good vintages.

- The best white Burgundies and white Bordeaux will mature — and improve — with 10 to 15 years of aging or more, in good vintage years.

- Most of today's red Burgundies, with the *possible* exception of the 1990 and 1995 vintages, should be consumed within 10 to 15 years (the less expensive ones even earlier).

For a listing of good vintage years, refer to Appendix C. For the names of some specific producers in each category whose wines we recommend, refer to Chapters 10 and 11.

Is wine fattening?

A glass of dry wine contains about 85 percent water, 12 percent ethyl alcohol, and small quantities of tartaric acid and various other components. Wine contains no fat.

A four-ounce serving of dry white wine has about 104 calories, and four ounces of red wine has about 110 calories. Sweeter wines contain about 10 percent more calories depending on how sweet they are; fortified wines that are higher in alcohol than table wines also contain additional calories because of the higher alcohol.

What grape variety is this wine made from?

Many wines today tell you what grape variety they're made from right on the front label — it's often the very name of the wine — or on the back label. Traditional European wines blended from several grape varieties usually don't give you that information: a) because the winemakers consider the name of the place more important than the grapes anyway, and b) because often the grapes they use are local varieties whose names few people would recognize.

If you really want to know what grape varieties make a Soave, Valpolicella, Châteauneuf-du-Pape, Rioja, Côtes du Rhône, or other blended European wines, you'll have to look it up. (See our charts in Chapters 10, 11, and 12.)

Which vintage should I buy?

This question assumes that you have a choice among several vintages of the same wine. Most of the time, however, you don't. Nearly every wine that you find in your wine shop is available in only one vintage, which is referred to as the *current* vintage.

For white wines, the current vintage represents grapes that were harvested as recently as nine months ago or as long as three years ago, depending on the style of the wine; for red wines, the current vintage is a date one to four years ago.

Classified-growth red Bordeaux wines (see Chapter 10) are the notable exception to the preceding rule: Most wine shops feature several vintages of these wines simultaneously. A few other fine wines — such as Burgundies, Barolos, or Rhône wines — might also be available in multiple vintages, but often they're not because the quantities produced are small and the wines sell out.

A red Rioja or a Chianti Classico might appear to be available in multiple vintages, but if you read the label carefully, you'll see that one vintage of the Rioja could be a *crianza* (aged two years before release), another might be a *reserva* (aged three years), and another might be a *gran reserva* (aged five years) — so they are each actually different wines, not multiple vintages of the same wine. Likewise, a Chianti might be available in an aged *riserva* version as well as a *non-riserva* style.

Most of the time, for most wines, the vintage to buy is the vintage you *can* buy, the current vintage. For the exceptional cases, consult our Vintage Chart in Appendix C.

Are there any wines without sulfites?

Sulfur dioxide exists naturally in wine as a result of fermentation. It also exists naturally in other fermented foods, such as bread, cookies, and beer. (Various sulfur derivatives are used regularly as preservatives in packaged foods.)

Winemakers use sulfur dioxide at various stages of the winemaking process because it stabilizes the wine (preventing it from turning to vinegar or deteriorating from oxygen exposure), and it safeguards the flavor of the wine. Sulfur has been an important winemaking tool since Roman times.

Very few winemakers refrain from using sulfur dioxide; most use it out of concern that their wine will change after it is bottled or that its shelf life will be shortened. Depending on where you live, your wine shop might carry two or three wines whose sulfite content is so low that their labels do not have to carry the phrase *Contains Sulfites* (which the U.S. government requires on the label of any wine that contains more than 10 parts per million of sulfites).

If you wish to limit your consumption of sulfites, dry red wines should be your first choice, followed by dry white wines. Sweet wines contain the most sulfur dioxide. For more information, turn to "Contains sulfites" in Chapter 1.

Are there any organic wines?

Yes, there are — depending on what you mean by organic.

If you mean wines that are made from organically grown grapes, dozens of brands qualify now. And many more winemakers are in the course of making their vineyards organic (it's a gradual process that can't happen overnight), switching from chemical fertilizers, herbicides, and pesticides to compost and natural pest prevention and seeking to restore the soil's microbial activity. Many vineyards that practice organic farming are not officially certified as organic for their wines, however.

Organic winemaking has traditionally meant the production of wine from organically grown grapes without the use of chemical additives in the winemaking. Use of the term *organic wine* has therefore been limited to those producers who do not use sulfur dioxide — a very limited group. (See "Contains sulfites" in Chapter 1 and "Are there any wines without sulfites?" in this chapter.)

The U.S. Department of Agriculture is in the process of establishing a National Organic Program. Depending on the standards set by that program, wines that are made from organic grapes and contain as much as 100 parts per million of sulfur dioxide could be considered organic (lots of wineries could qualify under those conditions) — or the permissable level of sulfur dioxide could be a much more restrictive 10 parts per million. Time will tell.

What is the bottom line? Depending on what you mean by organic wine, you can probably find it, but not without doing a little digging. Try asking your wine merchant.

What's new oak?

You don't have to read very many wine columns before realizing that many winemakers use *new oak* for their wines and are proud of it. The term refers to 60-gallon oak barrels (usually French oak but sometimes American oak) that winemakers use to either ferment or age their better white wines and to age their better red wines.

The amount of oaky aroma and flavor that a barrel is able to give to a wine — and the amount of tannin — is a function of how often the barrel has been used. After a few years, the insides of the casks or barrels become encrusted with crystalline acid deposits from the wine so that the wood itself might not even come in contact with each new wine that's put into it.

Most winemakers who use new oak barrels replace them after just three to five vintages. To avoid being hit with a big expense all at once, winemakers might replace 20 percent of their barrels each year. Their *new oak* is therefore 20 percent brand new, 20 percent one year old, 20 percent two years-old, and so on. When a winemaker replaces 20 percent of his oak barrels every year, he might say that he practices a *five-year rotation* for his oak. If he replaces one-third of his barrels every year, he uses a *three-year rotation*.

What is a wine expert?

A wine expert is someone with a high level of knowledge about wine in general (including grape growing and winemaking) and the various wines of the world. A wine expert also has a high degree of skill in tasting wine.

More often than not, wine experts gain their expertise through informal study, work experience, or experience gained as *amateurs* (lovers) of wine. The only official, state-accredited programs in wine are *enology* (winemaking) and *viticulture* (grape growing) programs offered by universities. These programs are valuable for people who plan to become winemakers or grape growers, but they represent scientific overkill for people whose goal is breadth of knowledge about wine.

Because wine experts gain their expertise through informal study and experience, it can be difficult to know whether someone is really a wine expert. In fact, if someone *claims* to be a wine expert and knows more about wine than you do, the only way you can determine that he's *not* a wine expert is by becoming more of an expert yourself.

How do I know when to drink the special older wines I've been keeping?

Unfortunately, no precise answer to this question exists because all wines age at a different pace. Even two bottles that appear to be exactly the same (name, vintage, and so on) and are stored under the same conditions can age differently.

When you have a specific wine in mind, you can get advice in several different ways:

- ✔ Consult the comments of critics like Robert Parker, Michael Broadbent, or Clive Coates, who almost always list a suggested drinking period for wines they review in their newsletters and books (listed in Chapter 18); their educated guesses are usually quite reliable.

- ✔ If you're not in a hurry for an answer, send a letter to a wine magazine (also listed in Chapter 18). These magazines consult their staff experts and answer reader questions in the "Letters to the Editor" section. For a speedier reply, turn to a chat room in one of the major wine Web sites, such as www.winespectator.com, www.wineenthusiastmag.com, or www.tastings.com.

✔ Call or write to the winery; in the case of fine, older vintages, the winemaker and his staff are usually happy to give you their opinion on the best time to drink their wine — and they typically have more experience with the wine than anyone else.

✔ If you have several bottles of the same wine, try one from time to time to see how it is developing. Your own palate is really the best guide — you might enjoy the wine younger, or older, than any of the experts who are writing about it.

Do old wines require special handling?

Like people, wine can become somewhat fragile as it advances into its later stages. For one thing, it doesn't like to travel. If you must move old wine, give it several days' rest afterwards, before opening the bottle. (Red Burgundies and other Pinot Noirs are especially disturbed by journeys.)

Older wine, with its delicate bouquet and flavors, can be easily overwhelmed by strongly flavored foods and sauces. Simple cuts of meat or just hard cheeses and good, crusty bread are usually fine companions for mature wine.

If you're going to drink an older wine, don't over-chill it (whether it's white or red). Older wines show their best at moderate temperatures. Temperatures below 60°F (15.5°C) inhibit development in the glass.

Decant red wines or vintage Ports to separate the clear wine from any sediment that formed in the bottle. (For tips on decanting, see Chapter 8.) Stand the bottle up two or three days before you plan to open it so that the sediment can drift to the bottom. An important concern in decanting an old wine is giving the wine *too* much aeration: A wine in its last stages will deteriorate rapidly upon exposure to air, often within a half hour — sometimes in ten or fifteen minutes.

When you decant an old wine, taste it immediately and be prepared to drink it rapidly if it shows signs of fading.

Chapter 23
Ten Wine Myths Demystified

● ●

*A*s you leaf through the pages of this chapter, you will probably recognize several of the myths mentioned here. They all represent common thinking — and common misinformation — about wine. We set the record straight.

Wine is for experts

True, wine is for experts. Wine involves so much detailed information — vintages, winemakers, winemaking techniques, history, tradition, new trends — that there's plenty of stuff for experts to sink their teeth into. Wine is definitely for them.

But wine isn't *only* for experts. Wine is for anyone who likes the taste of wine.

Wine is a beverage, one of the oldest beverages in history. Millions of people all over the world drink wine without knowing anything about the wine they're drinking other than the fact that it's the local wine of their region, it's the wine their brother-in-law recommended, or it tastes good.

Wine is a beverage, plain and simple. It is fermented grape juice, the product of a simple, natural process. The next time you worry that maybe you don't know enough to be a wine lover, consider this: If people in the wine business had to rely on experts alone to drink their wines, they'd have been out of business long ago!

Wine has to be expensive to be good

For wine, as for any other product, the more you pay for a bottle, the better the quality generally is. But the best quality doesn't always mean the best wine for the following reasons:

- ✔ Your taste is personal, and you might not like a wine that everyone else says is great.
- ✔ All wines are not suitable for all situations.

You certainly can enjoy even a $5 wine under many circumstances. At large family gatherings, on picnics, at the beach, and so on, an expensive, top-quality wine would be out-of-place — too serious and important.

Likewise, expensive wines are seldom the best choice in restaurants — considering typical restaurant prices. Instead, we either look for the best value on the wine list (keeping in mind what we are eating) or experiment with some moderately priced wine that we haven't tried before. (There will *always* be some wines that you haven't tried.)

Quality isn't the only consideration in choosing a wine. Often, the very best wine of all — for your taste, or for a certain situation — will be inexpensive.

Imported wines are better

First of all, imported from where? If you live in Europe, California wine is imported wine; if you live in the U.S., European wine is imported wine. How can they both be better than each other?

We have a friend in the U.S. who only drinks French wine. He insists that all California wine is inferior. We love to serve him a good California wine *blind* (that is, with the label covered), and watch his reaction when he discovers it's from California — after he has praised the wine!

Nowadays, every principal winemaking country is making some excellent wine. The "Imported wines are better" myth is just a bit of snobbery, let's face it.

Here's a daring suggestion that flies in the face of the imported wine myth: Discover your own local wines. If you live in southern Pennsylvania, New England, Ohio, Texas, Idaho, Vancouver, or Toronto, for example (not to mention Sydney, Melbourne, and Santiago), people are making wine practically in your own backyard. Try them. How do you think the Burgundians discovered that Burgundy is worth drinking?

White wine with fish, red with meat

As guidelines go, this isn't a bad one. But we said guideline, not rule. Anyone who slavishly adheres to this generalization as if it were a rule deserves the boredom of eating and drinking exactly the same thing every day of his life!

Do you want a glass of white wine with your burger? Go ahead, order it. You're the one who's doing the eating and drinking, not your friend and not the server who's taking your order.

Even if you're a perfectionist who's always looking for the perfect food and wine combination, you'll find yourself wandering from the guideline. The best wine for a grilled salmon steak is probably red — like a Pinot Noir or a Bardolino — and not white at all. Veal and pork do equally well with red or white wines, depending on how the dish is prepared. And what could be better with hot dogs on the barbecue than a cold glass of rosé?

No one is going to arrest you if you have white wine with everything, or red wine with everything, or even Champagne with everything! There are no rules. (We offer a few additional suggestions for possible wine-food pairings in Chapter 20.)

Numbers don't lie

It's natural to turn to critics for advice. We do it all the time, when we're trying to decide which movie to see, when we're choosing a new restaurant to try, or when we want to know what someone else thinks of a particular book.

In most cases, we weigh the critics' opinions against our own experience and tastes. Say a steak house just got three stars and a fabulous review from the dining critic. Do we rush to the telephone to make a reservation? Not if we don't like red meat! When the movie critics give two thumbs up, do we automatically assume that we'll like the movie — or do we listen to their commentary and decide whether the movie might be too violent, silly, or serious for us? You know the answer to that.

Yet many wine drinkers, when they hear that a wine just got more than 90 points, go out of their way to get that wine. The curiosity to try a wine that scores well is understandable. But the rigid belief that such a wine a) is necessarily a great wine, and b) is a wine you will like, is simply misguided.

The critics' scores are nothing more than the critics' professional opinion — and opinion, like taste, is always personal. (Chapter 19 tells you more about scoring wine.)

Vintages always matter/vintages don't matter

The difference between one vintage and the next of the same wine is the difference between the weather in the vineyards from one year to the next (barring extenuating circumstances such as new ownership of the winery, or the hiring of a new winemaker). The degree of vintage variation is thus equivalent to the degree of weather variation.

In some parts of the world the weather varies a lot from year to year, and *for wines from those regions*, vintages certainly do matter. In Bordeaux, Burgundy, Germany, and most of Italy, for example, problems (frost, hail, ill-timed rain, or insufficient heat) can affect one vintage for the worse, while the next year there may be no such problems. Where there is a lot of weather variation, the quality of the wine can swing from mediocre to outstanding from one year to the next.

In places where the weather is more predictable year after year (like much of California, Australia, and South Africa), vintages can still vary, but the swing is narrower. Serious wine lovers who care about the intimate details of the wines they drink will find the differences meaningful, but most people won't.

Another exception to the "Vintages always matter" myth is inexpensive wine. Top-selling wines that are produced in large volume are usually blended from many vineyards in a fairly large area. Swings in quality from year to year are not important.

Wine authorities are experts

Wine is an incredibly vast subject. It involves biochemistry, botany, geology, chemistry, climatology, history, culture, politics, laws, and business. How can anyone be an expert in all of that?

To compound the problem, some people in authoritative positions within the wine field — such as some wine writers — might have had little, if any, education, training, or background in wine before they were given jobs by some wine company or columns by some magazine or newspaper publisher and "ordained" a wine authority overnight.

Also, different aspects of wine appeal to different people. Depending on what they particularly like about wine, people tend to specialize in some of wine's disciplines at the expense of others. (Now you know why it takes two of us to write this book.)

Don't expect any one person to be able to answer all your questions about wine in the most accurate and up-to-date manner. Just like doctors and lawyers, wine professionals specialize. They have to.

Old wines are good wines

The idea of rare old bottles of wine being auctioned off for tens of thousands of dollars apiece, like fine art, is fascinating enough to capture anyone's imagination. But valuable old bottles of wine are even rarer than valuable old coins because, unlike coins, wine is perishable.

The great majority of the world's wines don't have what it takes to age for decades. Most wines are meant to be enjoyed in the first one to five years of their lives.

Even those wines that have the potential to develop slowly over many years will achieve their potential only if they are properly stored. (See Chapter 21 for information on storing wines.)

The purpose of wine is to be enjoyed — usually, sooner rather than later.

Great wines are supposed to taste bad when they're young

If this myth were true, wouldn't that be convenient for anyone who made poor wine! "It's a great wine," the winery owner could argue. "It's *supposed* to taste bad when it's young."

In the past, some of the great wines of the world, like red Bordeaux, were so tough and tannic that you really couldn't drink them until they had a few decades under their belts. As recently as the 1975 vintage of Bordeaux, some collectors believed that the undrinkability of the young wines was proof positive of their age-worthiness.

Winemakers today believe that a great wine must be in balance when it's young in order to be a balanced wine when it's old. (Refer to Chapter 2 for a discussion of balance.) Although the tannins in old wines usually soften and/ or drop out in the form of sediment, most wines today that are extraordinarily tannic when young don't have enough fruit to last until their tannins fade.

Of course, for a wine to be in balance doesn't mean that it's ready to drink. A great wine can have enormous tannin when it's young, along with its enormous fruit. It might be balanced, even if it's still embryonic. You may be able to appreciate the wine's balance when it's young; you may even enjoy the wine to some degree, but its true greatness is years away.

Champagnes don't age

We don't know who started the myth to the contrary, but Champagne *does* age well! Depending on the particular year, vintage Champagne can age especially well. We have enjoyed two outstanding 1928 vintage Champagnes, Krug and Moët & Chandon's Dom Pérignon, neither of which showed any sign of decline. The oldest Champagne that we've ever tasted, a 1914 Pol Roger, was also in fine shape.

But Champagne demands excellent storage. If kept in a cool, dark, humid place, many Champagnes can age for decades, especially in the great vintages. They lose some effervescence with the years, but take on a complexity of flavor somewhat similar to a fine white Burgundy. Champagnes in magnum bottles (1.5 l) do generally age better than those in regular size (750 ml) bottles.

 If you want to try some very fine, reliable, older bottles of vintage Champagne, look for either Krug or Salon in the 1964, 1969, 1973, or 1976 vintage. If stored well, they will be magnificent. Dom Pérignon is also reliable — the 1961 and 1969 DPs are legendary.

The following houses produce Champagnes known to age well:

- ✔ **Krug:** All their Champagnes are remarkably long lived
- ✔ **Pol Roger:** Especially Cuvée Sir Winston Churchill
- ✔ **Moët & Chandon:** Cuvée Dom Pérignon, ageless when well stored
- ✔ **Louis Roederer:** Cristal, Cristal Rosé, and Vintage Brut all age well
- ✔ **Jacquesson:** Signature and Vintage Blanc de Blancs

- **Bollinger:** All their Champagnes, especially the Grande Année
- **Gosset:** Grand Millésime and Celebris
- **Salon:** Remarkable Blanc de Blancs; needs at least 15 years of aging
- **Veuve Clicquot:** La Grande Dame and the Vintage Brut
- **Taittinger:** The Blanc de Blancs, Comtes de Champagne
- **Billecart-Salmon:** The Blanc de Blancs
- **Pommery:** Especially Cuvée Louise
- **Laurent-Perrier:** Cuvée Grand Siècle
- **Philipponnat:** Clos des Goisses

Recent great vintages for Champagne are 1996, 1990, 1988, 1985, and 1982.

Part VI
Appendixes

The 5th Wave   By Rich Tennant

"I want something that will go well
with a retired admiral and his wife,
a best-selling author from the Hamptons,
and a media wonk."

In this part . . .

Here we give you some useful tools of the trade, like a vintage chart, an extensive pronunciation guide to wine terms and names, and a glossary of wine terms. We were going to include a listing of every winery in the world that makes Chardonnay, but we ran out of space.

Appendix A

Pronunciation Guide to Wine Terms

• •

*N*othing will set a wine snob on your case more quickly than a mispronounced name of a famous wine or wine region. In order not to give snobs their smug satisfaction, we provide pronunciations of dozens of words here, for easy reference. This list is not exhaustive, however; the pronunciation of other, less common names and terms appears throughout the book. Accented syllables, if any, are indicated with capital letters.

Name or term = Pronunciation

Aglianico del Vulture = *ah lee AHN ee coh del VUL toor ay*

Albariño = *ahl bah REE nyoh*

Aligoté = *ah lee go tay*

Aloxe-Corton = *ah luss cor tohn*

Alsace = *al zass*

Alto-Adige = *AH dee jhay*

amontillado = *ah mon tee YAH doh*

Anjou = *ahn jhew*

Arneis = *ahr NASE*

Au Bon Climat = *oh bone klee maht*

Auslese = *OUSE lay seh*

Auxerrois = *aus ser whah*

Auxey-Duresses = *awk say deh ress*

Barbaresco = *bar bah RES co*

Barbera = *bar BEAR ah*

Name or term = Pronunciation

Bardolino = *bar doe LEE noh*

Barolo = *bah RO lo*

Batard-Montrachet = *bah tar mon rah shay*

Beaujolais = *boh jhoe lay*

Beaulieu Vineyards = *bo l'yuh*

Bianco di Custoza = *bee AHN coh dee cus TOEZ ah*

Blanchot = *blahn shoh*

botrytis = *boh TRY tis*

Bougros = *boo groh*

Bourgogne = *boor guh nyuh*

Bourgueil = *bor goye*

Brouilly = *broo yee*

Brunello di Montalcino = *brew NEL lo dee mon tahl CHEE no*

brut = *brute*

Name or term = Pronunciation	*Name or term = Pronunciation*
Burgenland = *BURR ghen land*	Côte Chalonnaise = *coat shal oh naze*
Cabernet Sauvignon = *cab er nay saw vee nyon*	Côte d'Or = *coat dor*
Canaiolo = *cahn eye OH loh*	Côte de Nuits = *coat deh nwee*
Carmignano = *car mee NYAH no*	Côte de Nuits-Villages = *coat deh nwee vey lahj*
Chablis = *shah blee*	Côte Rôtie = *coat roe tee*
Chardonnay = *shar doh nay*	Côtes du Ventoux = *coat due vahn too*
Chassagne-Montrachet = *shah san yuh mon rah shay*	cuvée = *coo vay*
Château de Fieuzal = *fee oo zahl*	Dolcetto = *dohl CHET oh*
Château Grillet = *gree yay*	Domaine Leroy = *lay wah*
Château Haut-Brion = *oh bree ohn*	Eisele Vineyard = *EYE seh lee*
Château Lafite-Rothschild = *lah feet roth sheeld*	Entre-Deux-Mers = *ahn truh duh mair*
Château Margaux = *mahr go*	Eyrie Vineyards = *EYE ree*
Château Mouton-Rothschild = *moo tohn roth sheeld*	Fleurie = *fluh ree*
Château Petrus = *peh troos*	Fourchaume = *for chahm*
Château Trotanoy = *trot ahn wah*	Friuli-Venezia Giulia = *free OO lee-veh NETZ ee ah JOO lee ah*
Châteauneuf-du-Pape = *shah toe nuf dew pahp*	Galicia = *gah LEETH ee ah*
Chénas = *shay nahs*	Garrafeira = *gar ah FAIR ah*
Chenin Blanc = *shen in blahnk*	Gattinara = *gah tee NAH rah*
Chevalier-Montrachet = *sheh vah lyay mon rah shay*	Gavi = *GAH vee*
Chianti = *key AHN tee*	Genevrières = *jen ev ree aire*
Chianti Rufina = *ROO fee nah*	Gewürztraminer = *geh VAIRTZ trah mee ner*
Chinon = *she nohn*	Gigondas = *jhee gohn dahs*
Chiroubles = *sheh roob leh*	Givry = *jee vree*
Clos du Val = *clo dew val*	grands crus classés = *grahn crew clas say*
Colheita = *col YAI tah*	Graves = *grahv*
Colli Orientali = *CO lee or ee en TAH lee*	Grenouilles = *greh n'wee*
Collio = *CO lee oh*	Grgich = *GHER gitch*
Condrieu = *cohn dree uh*	Grüner Veltliner = *GREW ner VELT lee ner*
Corton-Charlemagne = *cor tawn shahr luh mahn*	halbtrocken = *HAHLB tro ken*
Côte de Beaune = *coat deh bone*	Haut-Médoc = *oh may doc*
	Hermitage = *er mee tahj*
	Julian Chivite = *HOO lee ahn chi VEE tay*

Name or term = Pronunciation

Juliénas = *jool yay nahs*

Kabinett = *KAB ee net*

La Jota Vineyard = *lah HO tah*

La Moutonne = *lah moo tohn*

Languedoc-Roussillon = *lahn gweh doc roo see yawn*

Les Clos = *lay cloh*

Les Forêts = *lay for ay*

Les Preuses = *lay preuhz*

Liebfraumilch = *LEEB frow milsh*

Listrac = *lee strahk*

Loire = *lwahr*

Lugana = *loo GAH nah*

Mâcon = *mah cawn*

Mâcon-Villages = *mac cawn vee lahj*

Malvasia = *mal va SEE ah*

Margaux = *mahr go*

Médoc = *meh doc*

Melon de Bourgogne = *meh lohn deh boor guh nyuh*

Menetou-Salon = *meh neh too sah lohn*

Mercurey = *mer cure ay*

Meritage = *MER eh tej*

Merlot = *mer loh*

Meursault = *muhr so*

Moët = *moh ett*

Mont de Milieu = *mon deh meh lyew*

Montagny = *mon tah nyee*

Montée de Tonnerre = *mon tay deh tun nair*

Montepulciano d'Abruzzo = *mon tay pul chee AH noh dah BRUTE so*

Monthélie = *mohn teh lee*

Montlouis = *mon loo wee*

Montmains = *mon man*

Name or term = Pronunciation

Montrachet = *mon rah shay*

Morgon = *mor gohn*

Mosel-Saar-Ruwer = *MOH zel-zar-ROO ver*

Moulin-á-Vent = *moo lahn ah vahn*

Moulis = *moo lees*

Müller-Thurgau = *MULE lair TOOR gow*

Muscadet = *moos cah day*

Muscat = *moos caht*

Nahe = *NAH heh*

Nantais = *nahn tay*

Nebbiolo = *neb bee OH lo*

Neuchatel = *NOI sha tel*

Niebaum-Coppola = *NEE baum COPE poh lah*

Niederosterreich = *nee der OZ ter ryke*

Nuits-St.-Georges = *nwee san jorg*

Orvieto = *or vee AE toh*

Pauillac = *poy yac*

Pays d'Oc = *pay ee doc*

Penedés = *pen eh DAIS*

Pernand-Vergelesses = *pair nahn vair juh less*

Perrier-Jouët = *per ree yay joo ett*

Pessac-Léognan = *pay sac lay oh nyahn*

Pfalz = *FALLZ*

Pinot Bianco = *pee noh bee AHN coh*

Pinot Blanc = *pee noh blahnk*

Pinot Grigio = *pee noh GREE joe*

Pinot Gris = *pee noh gree*

Pinot Noir = *pee noh nwahr*

Pinotage = *pee noh TAHJ*

Pouilly-Fuissé = *pwee fwee say*

Pouilly-Fumé = *pwee foo may*

premier cru = *prem yay crew*

(continued)

Name or term = Pronunciation
Priorato = *pree oh RAH to*
Puligny-Montrachet = *poo lee nyee mon rah shay*
Qualitätswein = *KAL ee tates vine*
Quincy = *can see*
Quinta = *KEEN ta*
Regaleali = *ray gah lay AH lee*
Regnie = *ray nyay*
Reuilly = *ruh yee*
Rheingau = *RYNE gow*
Rheinhessen = *RYNE hess ehn*
Rías Baixas = *REE ahse BYCE ahse*
Ribera del Duero = *ree BEAR ah del doo AIR oh*
Ribolla Gialla = *ree BOHL lah JAHL lah*
Riesling = *REESE ling*
Rioja = *ree OH hah*
Rueda = *roo AE dah*
Rully = *rue yee*
Saint-Amour = *sant ah more*
Saint-Aubin = *sant oh ban*
Saint-Nicolas-de-Bourgueil = *san nih coh lahs deh bor goye*
Saint-Romain = *san ro man*
Saint-Véran = *san veh rahn*
Sancerre = *sahn sair*
Sangiovese = *san joe VAY say*
Saumur = *soh muhr*
Sauvignon Blanc = *saw vee nyon blahnk*
Savennieres = *sah ven nyair*
Savigny-lès-Beaune = *sah vee nyee lay bone*
Scheurebe = *SHOY reb beh*
Semillon = *SEM eh lon*
Sémillon = *seh mee yohn*

Name or term = Pronunciation
Sèvre-et-Maine = *sev'r et mehn*
Soave = *so AH vay*
Spanna = *SPAH nah*
Spätlese = *SHPATE lay seh*
spumante = *spoo MAHN tay*
St-Estèphe = *sant eh steff*
St-Julien = *sant jhoo lee ehn*
St.-Emilion = *sant ay meal yon*
Steiermark = *STY er mark*
Tempranillo = *tem prah NEE yoh*
Tinto = *TEEN toe*
Tocai Friulano = *toe KYE free ou LAH noh*
Torgiano = *tor gee AH no*
Tre Venezie = *tray veh NETZ ee ay*
Trebbiano = *treb bee AH noh*
Trentino-Alto Adige = *tren TEE noh-AHL toh AH dee jhay*
trocken = *TRO ken*
Vacqueyras = *vah keh rahs*
Vaillons = *vye yon*
Valais = *vah lay*
Valmur = *vahl moor*
Valpolicella = *val po lee CHEL lah*
Vaudésir = *voh deh zeer*
Vega Sicilia = *VAY gah see SEAL yah*
Vendange Tardive = *vahn dahnj tahr deev*
Veneto = *VEN eh toh*
Verdejo = *ver DAY ho*
Verdicchio = *ver DEE key oh*
Vernaccia di San Gimignano = *ver NOTCH cha dee san jee mee NYAH noh*
Vinho = *VEEN yo*
Vinho Verde = *VEEN yo VAIRD*

Name or term = Pronunciation

Vino Nobile di Montepulciano = *NO be lay dee mon tay pul chee AH no*

Viognier = *vee oh nyay*

Vosne-Romanée = *vone roh mah nay*

Vouvray = *voo vray*

Wachau = *va COW*

Weissburgunder = *VICE boor gun der*

Wien = *vee EN*

Willamette Valley = *wil LAM ette*

Appendix B
Glossary of Wine Terms

● ●

*H*ere, for handy reference, are definitions of dozens of the most common wine terms and wine-tasting terms.

acidity: A component of wine, generally consisting of tartaric acid (a natural acid in grapes) and comprising approximately 0.5 to 0.7 percent of the wine by volume.

aerate: To expose wine to air in preparation for drinking it, usually with the intention of allowing off-odors to escape from an older wine, or softening the harshness of a younger wine.

alcohol level: The percentage of alcohol by volume that a wine has; most white wines have an alcohol level between 9 and 14 percent, and most red wines have an alcohol level between 11 and 14 percent.

American oak: Oak wood from a U.S. forest; the barrels made from such wood; some winemakers in certain wine regions (such as Spain and Australia) favor American oak for aging their wines.

ample: A descriptor for wines that gives the impression of being full and expansive in your mouth.

AOC: abbreviation for *Appellation d'Origine Contrôlée,* sometimes shortened to *Appellation Contrôlée* and abbreviated as AC; translates to *protected place name*; France's official category for its highest-ranking types of wine, whose name, origin, grape varieties and other defining factors are regulated by law.

appellation: Name; often used to mean the official geographic origin of a wine, which is part of a wine's official name.

aroma: The smell of a wine. Some purists use the term *aroma* only for the straightforward, youthful smells of a wine, and use the term *bouquet* for the more complex smells of an aged wine. But we use *aroma* as a general term for all wine smells.

aromatic: A descriptor for a wine that has a pronounced smell, used particularly in reference to fruity and floral smells. Some white grape varieties are also dubbed *aromatic* because the wines made from them tend to be extremely strong in aroma.

aromatic compounds: Those substances in wine, derived from the grapes, from winemaking or from aging, that are responsible for a wine's aromas and flavors.

astringent: A descriptor for the mouth-drying, mouth-roughening tactile character of some wines, caused by tannin, acid, or the combination of both.

attack: The first impression a wine gives you when you taste it. A wine's attack is usually related to sensations gathered in the front of your mouth, especially the tip of your tongue, which is usually the first place the wine touches.

balance: The interrelationship of a wine's alcohol, residual sugar, acid and tannin; when no one component stands out obtrusively on the palate, a wine is said to be well-balanced; a prized characterisitic in wines.

barrel: A relatively small wooden container for aging red wine, generally 60 gallons in size and generally made of oak.

barrel-aged: A term that applies to wines that are fermented in containers of inert material, such as stainless steel, and subsequently placed into wooden barrels for a period of maturation; the term also applies to the maturation period of wines that also fermented in the barrel.

barrel-fermented: A term that applies to white wines that are fermented in oak barrels rather than in containers of inert material, such as stainless steel; the oaky character of such wines is generally more subtle than that of wines that have been merely barrel-aged.

big: A general descriptor for wines that are either very full or very intense.

black fruits: A general term for wine aromas and flavors that suggest blackberries, blueberries, black cherries, black currants, or other black fruits.

black grapes: Wine grapes that have a reddish or blue pigmentation in their skins; used to make red wine.

blend: To mix together two or more individual lots of wine, usually wines from different grape varieties (but also applies to wines from different vineyards, different regions, or different vintages); a wine derived from the juice of different grape varieties is called a blend.

bodega: A winery in Spain; also the Spanish word for a building where wine is stored.

body: The impression of a wine's weight in your mouth. A wine's body is generally described as light, medium, or full.

bottle-age: Maturation of a wine after it has been bottled; most wines undergo a short period of bottle age at the winery before release, while fine wines require additional bottle age from the consumer.

bouquet: Evolved, mature aromas.

bright: Indicates a wine whose characteristics are perceived vividly by the senses. A wine can be visually bright, or it can have bright aromas and flavors; in both cases, the opposite is dull.

cask: A relatively large wooden container for making or storing wine.

castello: Italian for *castle;* refers to a winery estate.

cedary: Having aromas or flavors that resemble the smell of cedar wood.

character: An anthropomorphic attribute of wines that give the impression of being solid and having substance and integrity.

charry: Having aromas or flavors that suggest burnt wood or charred wood.

château: A French name for a grand winery estate, commonly used in the Bordeaux region as well as other regions.

classico: An Italian term applicable to certain DOC or DOCG wines whose vineyards are situated in the original, classic part of the territory from which that particular type of DOC/DOCG wine can be made.

clone: A subvariety of a grape variety, exhibiting characteristics that are specific to it as compared to other manifestations of that grape variety.

colheita: Vintage, in Portuguese.

commune: A village.

compact: A descriptor for wines that give the impression of being intense but not full.

complex: Not simple. A complex wine has many different aromas and flavors, and "has a lot going on."

concentrated: A descriptor for aromas and flavors that are dense rather than dilute.

concentration: A characteristic of wines whose flavors or fruit character are tightly knit as opposed to being dilute or watery.

cosecha: Vintage, in Spanish.

crisp: A wine that feels clean and slightly brittle in your mouth. It's the opposite of "soft." Crispness is usually the result of high acidity, and crisp wines therefore are usually relatively light in body and go well with food.

decant: To transfer wine from the bottle to another container, either for the purpose of aerating the wine or to pour a red wine off its sediment.

depth: A characteristic of fine wines that give the impression of having underground layers of taste, rather than being flat and one-dimensional.

dilute: A descriptor for wines whose aromas and flavors are thin and watery, as opposed to concentrated.

district: A geographic entity more specific than a region and less specific than a commune.

DO: Abbreviation for *Denominación de Origen,* which translates to *place name;* Spain's official category for wines whose name, origin, grape varieties and other defining factors are regulated by law.

DOC: Abbreviation for *Denominazione di Origine Controllata,* which translates to *controlled place name;* Italy's official category for wines whose name, origin, grape varieties and other defining factors are regulated by law; also an abbreviation for Portugal's highest official wine category, *Denominação de Origem Controlada,* translated similarly and having the same meaning.

DOCG: Abbreviation for *Denominazione di Origine Controllata e Garantita,* which translates to *controlled and guaranteed place name;* Italy's official category for its highest-ranking wines.

domaine: A French term for wine estate, commonly used in the Burgundy region.

dry: A wine that is not sweet. The word *dry* can also describe the texture of a wine that feels rough in your mouth, as in *dry texture* or dry *mouthfeel.* But when it is used alone, it refers specifically to lack of sweetness.

dull: A wine whose expression is muddled and unclear. This term can apply to a wine's appearance, to its aromas and flavors, or to its general style.

earthy: Having aromas and flavors that suggest earth, such as wet soil, dry earth, certain minerally aromas and so forth. This term is sometimes used as a general descriptor for wines that are rustic and lack refinement.

elegance: An attribute of wines that express themselves in a fine or delicate manner as opposed to an intense or forceful way.

estate: A property that grows grapes and produces wines from its own vineyards; wines labelled *estate* are made from vineyards owned by (or in some cases, under the direct control of) the same entity that owns the winery and makes the wine; use of the term is regulated by law in most areas.

fermentation: The natural process by which the sugar in grape juice is transformed into alcohol (and the juice is thus transformed into wine) through the action of yeasts.

finish: The final impressions a wine gives after you have swallowed it or spat it out.

firm: A descriptor for wines that are not soft, but are not harsh and tough; generally relates to the tannic content of a red wine or the acidity of a white wine.

flabby: A term used to describe wines that are too soft.

flavor compounds: Organic substances in grapes responsible for many of the aromas and flavors of wines.

flavor intensity: The degree to which a wine's flavors are pronounced and easily observable.

flavors: Aromatic constituents of a wine that are perceived in the mouth.

fleshy: A descriptor for a rich textural or tactile impression of some wines.

fortified wine: A wine which has had alcohol added to it.

French oak: Oak wood from the forests of France, considered the finest type of oak for aging most white wines; the barrels made from such wood.

fruit character: Those characteristics of a wine that derive from the grapes, such as a wine's aromas and flavors, its grape tannin, natural acidity, and extract.

fruity: Having aromas and flavors suggestive of fruit. This is a broad descriptor; in some cases the fruity aroma or flavor of a wine can be described more precisely as suggestive of fresh fruit, dried fruit, or cooked fruit, or

even more precisely as a specific fresh, dried, or cooked fruit, such as fresh apples, dried figs, or strawberry jam.

full: A descriptor for wines that give the impression of being large in your mouth. A wine's fullness can derive from high alcohol or from other aspects of the wine.

garrafeira: A Portuguese term for a reserva wine with specific aging requirements — for red wines, at least three years of aging in oak and bottle before release.

generous: A descriptor for wines whose characterisitcs are expressive and easy to perceive.

gran reserva: On Spanish red wines, a wine that has aged at least five years in oak and in bottle before release from the winery.

grape tannin: Those tannins in a red wine that are attributable to the grapes from which the wine was made.

grape variety: A type of grape within a species.

harmonious: A descriptor of wines that are not only well balanced but also express themselves in a particularly graceful manner.

herbal: Having aromas and flavors that suggest herbs, such as fresh herbs, dried herbs, or specific herbs (rosemary, thyme, tarragon, and so forth).

intense: A descriptor for wines that express themselves strongly. When used in reference to a wine's aromas and flavors, this word describes the volume of those aromas or flavors — how strong the smell of lemon is in the wine, for example. When used in refernce to a wine's total expression, this word describes an impression of general forcefulness that the wine gives.

lees: Grape solids and dead yeast cells which precipitate to the bottom of a white wine following fermentation.

length: A characteristic of fine wines that gives a sustained sensory impression across the tongue.

maceration: The process of soaking the skins of red grapes in their grape juice to dissolve the skins' color, tannin, and other substances in the juice; the term is often used for the entire period during which the skins and juice are in contact, including the period of fermentation.

malolactic fermentation: A natural conversion of malic acid into lactic acid, which softens the total acidity of a wine; an optional process in white wine production.

maturation: The aging period at the winery during which a wine evolves to a state of readiness for bottling; the process of development and evolution which fine wines undergo after they are bottled.

medium sweet: A term to indicate the perceived level of wines that are sweeter than medium-dry, but not fully sweet.

medium-dry: A term to indicate the perceived sweetness of wines that are very slightly sweet.

minerally: Having aromas or flavors that suggest minerals (as opposed to organic substances such as plants or animals). This is a broad descriptor; in some cases the minerally aroma or flavor of a wine can be described more precisely as suggestive of chalk, iron, steel, and so forth.

New World: Collective term for those winemaking countries of the world that are situated outside of Europe.

new oak: An imprecise term to indicate both oak barrels that are brand new (also called "first year oak") and barrels that have been used approximately one to four times previously.

nutty: Having aromas or flavors that suggest nuts. This is a broad descriptor; in some cases the nutty aroma or flavor of a wine can be described more precisely as suggestive of roasted nuts, toasted nuts, nut butter, or cashews, almonds, hazelnuts, and so forth.

oaky: A wine that has characteristics deriving from oak, such as toastiness, smokiness, a charry smell or taste, vanilla aroma, or a higher tannin level than the wine might ordinarily have. Usually these oaky characteristics occur as the wine ages in oak barrels, but in very inexpensive wines they might have been added as an actual flavoring.

off-dry: A generalized term for wines that are neither fully dry nor very sweet.

Old World: Collective term for the winemaking countries of Europe.

old oak: Oak barrels or casks that are old enough to have lost most of their oaky character, generally five years old and older.

old vines: An unregulated term for grape vines whose fruit quality presumably is quite good due to the fact the vines are old — generally forty years old or older — and therefore produce very little crop.

palate: A term used by wine tasters as a synonym for "mouth," or to refer to the characteristics of a wine that become manifest in the taster's mouth.

petrol: Having aromas or flavors that suggest diesel fuel.

phylloxera: A parasite louse that feeds on the roots of vitis vinifera grape vines, resulting in the vines' premature death.

plummy: Having aromas or flavors that suggest ripe plums.

plush: A textural or tactile descriptor for wines that feel luxurious in your mouth.

powerful: An anthropomorphic descriptor for wines that convey an impression of strength and intensity.

pretty: An anthropomorphic descriptor for wines that are attractive for their delicacy and finesse.

primary aromas: Fresh aromas in a wine that derive from the grapes used to make that wine.

red grapes: Wine grapes that have a reddish or blue pigmentation in their skins; also called black grapes.

region: A geographical entity less specific than a district, but more specific than a country; when speaking of Italian wines, the term "region" applies to the political entity as well as to the wine zones within that area.

reserva: On a Spanish wine, a wine that has aged longer at the winery (usually in some specified combination of oak aging and bottle aging) than a non-reserva version of the same type of wine; red reserva wines must age at least three years before release; on a Portuguese wine, a wine of superior quality from one vintage.

reserve: A designation for wines that are presumably finer than the non-reserve, or normal version of the same wine; use of the term is unregulated in the U.S. and in France.

residual sugar: Sugar remaining in the wine after fermentation.

rich: A descriptor of wines that offer an abundance of flavor, texture, or other sensory perceptions.

riserva: Italian word for "reserve," indicating a wine that has aged longer before release from the winery than a non-reserve version of the same type of wine, and suggesting higher quality; the period of time a wine must age before it is entitled to use the term "riserva" (and sometimes the conditions of that aging) is defined by individual DOC regulations for each wine.

round: A descriptor for wines that are perceived to be neither flat nor angular. Roundness relates to the wine's structure, that is, its particular make-up of acid, tannin, sweetness and alcohol.

second-label wine: A less expensive, second wine or a second brand of wine made by a winery from grapes or wine not considered worthy of the wine's primary label.

sediment: The solid residue in a bottle of red wine which forms as the wine matures.

serious: A metaphorical descriptor for a wine that is of high quality.

silky: Having a supple, smooth texture.

single-vineyard wine: A wine that is made from the grapes of a single (presumably exceptionally good) plot of land and bottled without being blended with wine from other vineyards, and that usually carries the name of the vineyard on its label; the term is unregulated in that the term "vineyard" is not defined as to size or ownership.

skin contact: The process during which the juice of grapes rest in contact with the grape skins; in red wine, the process by which the wines absorb color, tannin, and other substances; not normally used in white wine production, but occasionally used to enhance the aromatic character of the wine.

smoky: Having aromas or flavors that suggest smoke or smoked wood.

smooth: Descriptor for a wine whose texture is not rough or harsh.

soft: Textural descriptor for a wine whose alcohol and sugar (if any) dominate its acidity and tannin, resulting in a lack of hardness or roughness.

stemmy: Descriptor for red wines that give the impression of having dry, raspy, woody tannins.

stems: The woody part of a grape bunch, which are high in tannin; usually the stems are removed and discarded prior to fermentation.

stony: Having aromas or flavors that suggest stones. In some cases the stony aroma or flavor of a wine can be described more precisely as suggestive of wet stones.

structural components: Principally, a wine's alcohol, acid, tannin, and sugar (if any).

structure: That part of the impression a wine conveys that derives from perception of the wine's structural elements (in white wine, mainly alcohol, acid, and sugar).

style: The set of characteristics through which a wine manifests itself.

supple: A descriptor for wines that seem fluid in texture in the mouth, without roughness or sharpness.

süssreserve: German for *sweet reserve;* unfermented grape juice that is added to a white wine to increase the wine's residual sugar and sweetness.

sweetness: The impression of sugary taste in a wine, which can be due to the presence of residual sugar or to other sweet-tasting substances in the wine, such as alcohol.

tannic: A word used to describe wines that seem to be high in tannin.

tannin: A substance in the skins, stems, and seeds of grapes; a principal component of red wines, which — unlike white wines — are made using the grape skins. Tannin also is a component of oak barrels.

tarry: Having aromas or flavors that suggest fresh tar.

tart: A descriptor for aromas or flavors of under-ripe fruit. This term can also apply to a wine that is too high in acid.

taste: A general term for the totality of impressions a wine gives in the mouth; more specifically, the primary tastes found in wine: sweetness, sourness, and bitterness.

terroir: French word that is the collective term for the growing conditions in a vineyard, such as climate, soil, drainage, slope, altitude, topography, and so on.

texture: A wine's consistency or feel in the mouth.

thin: A word used to describe wines that are lacking in substance.

tight: A descriptor for wines that seem to be inexpressive. This term can apply to a wine's aromas and flavors, or to its structure.

underbrush: Aromas or flavors that suggest wet leaves, dampness, and slight decay.

varietal character: The characteristics of a specific grape variety; the characteristics of a wine that are attributable to the grape variety from which it was made.

varietal: A wine named for the sole or the principal grape variety from which it was made.

vegetal: Having aromas or flavors that suggest vegetation or vegetables.

vin de pays: French phrase for *country wine;* legally, a category of French wine that holds lower status than AOC wines.

vinification: The activity of making grape juice into wine.

vintage: The year in which a wine's grapes grew and were harvested; sometimes used as a synonym for the grape harvest.

viticulture: The activity of growing grapes.

vitis vinifera: The species to which most of the world's wine grapes belong.

weight: The impression of a wine's volume in the mouth.

well-balanced: A term used to describe wines whose acid, alcohol, tannin (if any), and residual sugar (if any) relate to each other in such a way that none of the four components seems too dominant.

wood tannin: Those tannins in a wine that are attributable to the barrels in which the wine aged, as opposed to the grapes.

yeasts: One-cell microorganisms responsible for transforming grape juice into wine.

Vintage Wine Chart: 1977 – 1996

. . . .

*A*ny vintage wine chart must be regarded as a rough guide — a general, average rating of the vintage year in a particular wine region. Remember that many wines will always be exceptions to the vintage's rating. For example, some wine producers will manage to find a way to make a decent — even fine — wine in a so-called poor vintage.

WINE REGION	1977	1978	1979	1980	1981	1982	1983	1984	1985
Bordeaux									
Médoc, Graves	70d	85c	80c	75d	80c	95b	85b	70d	90c
Pomerol, St-Emil	65d	80c	80c	70d	80c	95b	85b	65d	85c
Burgundy									
Côte de Nuits-Red	60d	90c	80c	85c	65d	75c	85c	75c	85c
Côte Beaune-Red	55d	85c	80d	80c	70d	75d	80d	70d	85c
Burgundy, White	75d	90c	85c	75d	80d	80d	80d	75d	85c
Rhône Valley									
Northern Rhône	70c	100b	85c	80c	75d	85c	90b	75c	90c
Southern Rhône	65d	95b	85c	75d	85c	70d	85c	70d	80c
Alsace	70d	75d	80c	75d	85c	75d	95c	70d	90b
Champagne	NV	70d	85c	NV	85c	90c	80c	NV	90b
Sauternes	55d	70c	75c	80c	80c	70c	90a	70c	80c
Germany	60d	60d	80c	65d	80c	75d	90c	65d	85c
Rioja (Spain)	70d	85c	75c	75c	85c	90c	80c	70c	80c
Vintage Port	90b	NV	NV	80b	NV	80b	85b	NV	90a
Italy									
Piedmont	65d	90b	80c	75c	70c	90b	75c	65d	95b
Tuscany	85c	75d	80c	70d	80d	80c	85c	60d	95c
California North Coast									
Cabernet Sauvignon	85c	85b	80c	80c	75c	75c	70d	85c	90b
Chardonnay	80d	85d	80d	85d	85d	75d	80d	80d	85c

WINE REGION	1986	1987	1988	1989	1990	1991	1992	1993	1994	1995	1996
Bordeaux											
Médoc, Graves	90a	75c	85a	90b	95a	75b	75b	80a	85a	90a	90a
Pomerol, St-Emil	85a	75d	85a	90b	95a	65c	75b	80a	85a	90a	85a
Burgundy											
Côte de Nuits-Red	75d	85c	85b	85b	95b	85b	75b	85a	80b	90a	90a
Côte Beaune-Red	70d	80d	85b	85c	90b	70c	80b	85a	80b	90a	90a
Burgundy, White	90c	80c	80c	90b	85c	70d	85b	75c	85c	90a	90a
Rhône Valley											
Northern Rhône	80b	80c	90c	95b	90a	90b	75c	65c	85a	90a	85a
Southern Rhône	75c	60d	85c	95a	95b	70c	75c	80b	85a	90a	80b
Alsace	80c	75c	85c	95b	95b	75c	85b	80b	90b	85b	85b
Champagne	80b	NV	85b	85c	95b	NV	NV	85b	NV	90a	95a
Sauternes	90a	70c	95a	90b	95a	70c	70c	65c	75b	85a	85a
Germany	75c	70c	85c	90b	95b	80c	85c	85c	90b	85b	95a
Rioja (Spain)	80c	80c	85b	90b	85b	75c	85b	85b	90b	90b	85a
Vintage Port	NV	NV	NV	NV	NV	90a	95a	NV	95a	NV	NV
Italy											
Piedmont	85c	80c	90a	95a	95b	80c	70c	85b	80b	85a	95a
Tuscany	85c	75c	90a	70c	90b	75c	70c	75c	85b	90a	75b
California North Coast											
Cabernet Sauvignon	80c	85c	75c	80b	95b	95a	90b	85b	95a	90a	90a
Chardonnay	90d	75d	85c	75d	90c	85c	90c	90c	85c	90b	85b

Key:

100	=	Outstanding
95	=	Excellent
90	=	Very Good
85	=	Good
80	=	Fairly Good
75	=	Average

70	=	Below Average
65	=	Poor
50-60	=	Very Poor

a = Too young to drink
b = Can be consumed now, but will improve with time
c = Ready to drink
d = May be too old
NV = Non-vintage year

WINE REGION	Recent Past Great Vintages
Bordeaux	
Médoc, Graves	1959, 1961, 1970
Pomerol, St-Emil	1961, 1964, 1970, 1975
Burgundy	
Côte de Nuits-Red	1959, 1964, 1969
Côte Beaune-Red	1959, 1969
Burgundy, White	1962, 1966, 1969, 1973
Rhône Valley	
Northern Rhône	1959, 1961, 1966, 1969, 1970, 1972 (Hermitage)
Southern Rhône	1961, 1967
Alsace	1959, 1961, 1967, 1976
Champagne	1961, 1964, 1969, 1971, 1975
Sauternes	1959, 1962, 1967, 1975
Germany	1959, 1971, 1976
Rioja (Spain)	1964, 1970
Vintage Port	1963, 1966, 1970
Italy	
Piedmont	1964, 1971
Tuscany	1967, 1970 (Brunello di Montalcino), 1971
California North Coast	
Cabernet Sauvignon	1951, 1958, 1968, 1970, 1974

Index

(continued)

• R •

IDG BOOKS WORLDWIDE BOOK REGISTRATION

Register This Book and Win!

We want to hear from you!

Visit **http://my2cents.dummies.com** to register this book and tell us how you liked it!

- ✔ Get entered in our monthly prize giveaway.

- ✔ Give us feedback about this book — tell us what you like best, what you like least, or maybe what you'd like to ask the author and us to change!

- ✔ Let us know any other ...*For Dummies*® topics that interest you.

Your feedback helps us determine what books to publish, tells us what coverage to add as we revise our books, and lets us know whether we're meeting your needs as a ...*For Dummies* reader. You're our most valuable resource, and what you have to say is important to us!

Not on the Web yet? It's easy to get started with *Dummies 101*®: *The Internet For Windows*® *98* or *The Internet For Dummies*®, 5th Edition, at local retailers everywhere.

Or let us know what you think by sending us a letter at the following address:

...*For Dummies* Book Registration
Dummies Press
7260 Shadeland Station, Suite 100
Indianapolis, IN 46256-3945
Fax 317-596-5498

...FOR DUMMIES™

BESTSELLING BOOK SERIES FROM IDG